Medical Coding Success

By Lewis Morris

www.insiderswords.com/MedicalCoding

ISBN-13: 978-1728801544

Table of Contents

What is "Insider Language"?

Recent research has confirmed what we have known for decades: The strongest students and leaders in industry have a mastered an Insider Language in their subject and field. This Insider language is made up of the technical terms and vocabulary necessary to communicate effectively in classes or the workplace. For those who master it, learning is easier, faster, and much more enjoyable.

Most students who are surveyed report that the greatest challenge to any course of study is learning the vocabulary. When we examine typical college courses, we discover that there is, on average, 250 Insider Terms a student must learn over the course of a semester. Further, most exams rely heavily on this set of words for assessment purposes. The structure of multiple choice exams lends itself perfectly to the testing of this Insider Language. Students who can differentiate between Insider Language terms can handle challenging exam questions with ease and confidence.

From recent research on learning and vocabulary we have learned:

- Your knowledge of any subject is contained in the content-specific words you know. The more of these terms that you know, the easier it is to understand and recall important information; the easier it will be to communicate your ideas to peers, professors, supervisors, and co-workers. The stronger your content-area vocabulary is, the higher your scores will be on your exams and written assignments.

- Students who develop a strong Insider Language perform better on tests, learn faster, retain more information, and express greater satisfaction in learning.

- Familiarizing yourself with subject-area vocabulary before formal study (pre-learning) is the most effective way to learn this language and reap the most benefit.

- The vocabulary on standardized exams come directly from the stated objectives of the test-makers. This means that the vocabulary found on standardized exams is predictable. Our books focus on this vocabulary.

- Most multiple-choice exams are glorified vocabulary quizzes. Think about the format of a multiple-choice question. The question stem is a definition of a term and the choices (known as distractors) are 4 or 5 similar words. Your task is to differentiate between the meanings of those terms and choose the correct word.

- It takes a person several exposures to a new word to be able to use it with confidence in conversation or in writing. You need to process these words several different ways to make them part of your long-term memory.

The goals of this book are:

- To give you an "Insider Language" for your subject.
- Pre-teach the most important words before you set out on a traditional course of review or study.
- Teach you the most important words in your subject area.
- Teach you strategies for learning subject-area words on your own.
- Boost your confidence in your ability to master this language and support you in your study.
- Reduce the stress of studying and provide you with fun activities that work.

How it works:

The secret to mastering Insider Language is through repetition and exposure. We have eleven steps for you to follow:

1. Read the word and definition in the glossary out loud. "See it, Say it"
2. Identify the part of speech the word belongs to such as noun, verb, adverb, or adjective. This will help you group the word and identify similar words.
3. Place the word in context by using it in a sentence. Write this sentence down and read it aloud.
4. Use "Chunking" to group the words. Make a diagram or word cloud using these groups.
5. Make connections to the words by creating analogies.
6. Create mnemonics that help you recognize patterns and orders of words by substituting the words for more memorable items or actions.
7. Examine the morphology of the word, that is, identify the root, prefix, and suffix that make up the word. Identify similar and related words.
8. Complete word games and puzzles such as crosswords and word searches.
9. Complete matching questions that require you to differentiate between related words.
10. Complete Multiple-choice questions containing the words.
11. Create a visual metaphor or "memory cartoon" to make a mental picture of the word and related processes.

By completing this word study process, you will be exposed to the terminology in various ways that will activate your memory and create a lasting understanding of this language.

The strategies in this book are designed to make you an independent expert at learning insider language. These strategies include:

- Verbalizing the word by reading it and its definition aloud ("See It, Say It"). This allows you to make visual, auditory, and speech connections with its meaning.

- Identifying the type of word (Noun, verb, adverb, and adjective). Making this distinction helps you understand how to visualize the word. It helps you "chunk" the words into groups, and gives you clues on how to use the word.

- Place the word in context by using it in a sentence. Write this sentence down and read it aloud. This will give you an example of how the word is used.

- "Chunking". By breaking down the word list into groups of closely related words, you will learn them better and be able to remember them faster. Once you have group the terms, you can then make word clouds using a free online service. These word clouds provide visual cues to remembering the words and their meanings.

- Analogies. By creating analogies for essential words, you will be making connections that you can see on paper. These connections can trigger your memory and activate your ability to use the word in your writing as you begin to use them. Many of these analogies also use visual cues. In a sense, you can make a mental picture from the analogy.

- Mnemonics. A device such as a pattern of letters, ideas, or associations that assists in remembering something. A mnemonic is especially useful for remembering the order of a set of words or the order of a process.

- Morphology. The study of word roots, prefixes, and suffixes. By examining the structure of the words, you will gain insight into other words that are closely related, and learn how to best use the word.

- Visual metaphors. This is the most sophisticated and entertaining strategy for learning vocabulary. Create a "memory cartoon" using one or more of the vocabulary terms. This activity triggers the visual part of your memory and makes fast, permanent, imprints of the word on your memory. By combining the terms in your visual metaphor, you can "chunk" the entire set of vocabulary terms into several visual metaphors and benefit from the brain's tendency to group these terms.

The activities in this book are designed to imprint the words and their meanings in your memory in different ways. By completing each activity, you will gain the necessary exposures to the word to make it a permanent part of your vocabulary. Each activity uses a different part of your memory. The result is that you will be comfortable using these words and be able to tell the difference between closely related words. The activities include:

A. Crossword Puzzles and Word Searches- These are proven to increase test scores and improve comprehension. Students frequently report that they are fun and engaging, while requiring them to analyze the structure and meaning of the words.

B. Matching- This activity is effective because it forces you to differentiate between many closely related terms.

C. Multiple Choice- This classic question format lends itself to vocabulary study perfectly. Most exams are in this format because they are simple to make, easy to score, and are a reliable type of assessment. (Perfect for the Vocabulary Master!) One strategy to use with multiple choice questions that enhance their effectiveness is to cover the answer choices while you read the question. After reading the question, see if you can answer it before looking at the choices. Then look at the choices to see if you match one of them.

Conducting a thorough "word study" of your insider language will take time and effort, but the rewards will be well worth it. By following this guide and completing the exercises thoughtfully, you will become a stronger, more effective, and satisfied student. Best of luck on your mastery of this Insider Language!

Insider Language Strategies

“See It, Say It!” Reading your Insider Language set aloud

"IT IS BETTER TO FAIL IN ORIGINALITY THAN TO SUCCEED IN IMITATION."
-HERMAN MELVILLE

Reading aloud is the foundation for the development of an Insider Language. It is the single most important thing you can do for vocabulary acquisition. Done correctly, it engages the visual, auditory, and speech centers of the brain and hastens its storage in your long-term memory.

Reading aloud demonstrates the relationship between the printed word and its meaning.

You can read aloud on a higher level than you can initially understand, so reading aloud makes complex ideas more accessible and exposes you to vocabulary and patterns that are not part of your typical speech. Reading aloud helps you understand the complicated text better and makes more challenging text easier to grasp and understand. Reading aloud helps you to develop the "habits of mind" the strongest students use.

Reading aloud will make connections to concepts in the reading that requires you to relate the new vocabulary to things you already know. Go to the glossary at the end of this book and for each word complete the five steps outlined below:

1. Read the word and its definition aloud. Focus on the sound of the word and how it looks on the paper.
2. Read the word aloud again try to say three or four similar words; this will help you build connections to closely related words.
3. Read the word aloud a third time. Try to make a connection to something you have read or heard.
4. Visualize the concept described in the term. Paint a mental picture of the word in use.
5. Try to think of the opposite of the word. Discovering a close antonym will help you place this word in context.

Create a sentence using the word in its proper context

"OPPORTUNITIES DON'T HAPPEN. YOU CREATE THEM." -CHRIS GROSSER

Context means the circumstances that form the setting for an event, statement, or idea, and which it can be fully understood and assessed. Synonyms for context include conditions, factors, situation, background, and setting.
Place the word in context by using it in a sentence. Write this sentence down and read it aloud. By creating sentences, you are practicing using the word correctly. If you strive to make these sentences interesting and creative, they will become more memorable and effective in activating your long-term memory.

Identify the Parts of Speech

"SUCCESS IS NOT FINAL; FAILURE IS NOT FATAL: IT IS THE COURAGE TO CONTINUE THAT COUNTS." -WINSTON S. CHURCHILL

Read through each term in the glossary and make a note of what part of speech each term is. Studying and identifying parts of speech shows us how the words relate to each other. It also helps you create a visualization of each term. Below are brief descriptions of the parts of speech for you to use as a guide.

VERB: A word denoting action, occurrence, or existence. Examples: walk, hop, whisper, sweat, dribbles, feels, sleeps, drink, smile, are, is, was, has.

NOUN: A word that names a person, place, thing, idea, animal, quality, or action. Nouns are the subject of the sentence. Examples: dog, Tom, Florida, CD, pasta, hate, tiger.

ADJECTIVE: A word that modifies, qualifies, or describes nouns and pronouns. Generally, adjectives appear immediately before the words they modify. Examples: smart girl, gifted teacher, old car, red door.

ADVERB: A word that modifies verbs, adjectives and other adverbs. An "ly" ending almost always changes an adjective to an adverb. Examples: ran swiftly, worked slowly, and drifted aimlessly. Many adverbs do not end in "ly." However, all adverbs identify when, where, how, how far, how much, etc. Examples: run hot, lived hard, moved right, study smart.

Chunking

"YOUR POSITIVE ACTION COMBINED WITH POSITIVE THINKING RESULTS IN SUCCESS." SHIV KHERA

Chunking is when you take a set of words and break it down into groups based on a common relationship. Research has shown that our brains learn by chunking information. By grouping your terms, you will be able to recall large sets of these words easily. To help make your chunking go easily use an online word cloud generator to make a set of word clouds representing your chunks.

1. Study the glossary and decide how you want to chunk the set of words. You can group by part of speech, topic, letter of the alphabet, word length, etc. Try to find an easy way to group each term.
2. Once you have your different groups, visit www.wordclouds.com to create a custom word cloud for each group. Print each one of these clouds and post it in a prominent place to serve as constant visual aids for your learning.

Analogies

"CHOOSE THE POSITIVE. YOU HAVE CHOICE, YOU ARE MASTER OF YOUR ATTITUDE, CHOOSE THE POSITIVE, THE CONSTRUCTIVE. OPTIMISM IS A FAITH THAT LEADS TO SUCCESS."– BRUCE LEE

An analogy is a comparison in which an idea or a thing is compared to another thing that is quite different from it. Analogies aim at explaining an idea by comparing it to something that is familiar. Metaphors and similes are tools used to create analogies.

Analogies are useful for learning vocabulary because they require you to analyze a word (or words), and then transfer that analysis to another word. This transfer reinforces the understanding of all the words.

As you analyze the relationships between the analogies you are creating, you will begin to understand the complex relationships between the seemingly unrelated words.

_A__ is to __B_ as __C_ is to __D_

This can be written using colons in place of the terms "is to" and "as."

A:B::C:D

The two items on the left (items A & B) describe a relationship and are separated by a single colon. The two items on the right (items C & D) are shown on the right and are also separated by a colon. Together, both sides are then separated by two colons in the middle, as shown here: Tall: Short :: Skinny: Fat. The relationship used in this analogy is the antonym.

How to create an analogy

Start with the basic formula for an analogy:

____ : ____ :: ____ : ____

Next, we will examine a simple synonym analogy:

automobile : car :: box : crate

The key to figuring out a set of word analogies is determining the relationship between the paired set of words.

Here is a list of the most common types of Analogies and examples

Synonym	Scream : Yell :: Push : Shove
Antonym	Rich : Poor :: Empty : Full
Cause is to Effect	Prosperity : Happiness :: Success : Joy
A Part is to its Whole	Toe : Foot :: Piece : Set
An Object to its Function	Car : Travel :: Read : Learn
A Item is to its Category	Tabby : House Cat :: Doberman : Dog
Word is a symptom of the other	Pain : Fracture :: Wheezing : Allergy
An object and it's description	Glass : Brittle :: Lead : Dense
The word is lacking the second word	Amputee : Limb :: Deaf : Hearing
The first word Hinders the second word	Shackles : Movement :: Stagger : Walk
The first word helps the action of the second	Knife : Bread :: Screwdriver : Screw
This word is made up of the second word	Sweater : Wool :: Jeans : Denim
A word and it's definition	Cede: Break Away :: Abolish : To get rid of

Using words from the glossary, make a set of analogies using each one. As a bonus, use more than one glossary term in a single analogy.

__________________ : ________________ :: ______________________ : __________________

Name the relationship between the words in your analogy:______________________________

__________________ : ________________ :: ___________________ : ______________________

Name the relationship between the words in your analogy:______________________________

__________________ : ________________ :: ______________________ : __________________

Name the relationship between the words in your analogy:______________________________

Mnemonics

"IT ISN'T THE MOUNTAINS AHEAD TO CLIMB THAT WEAR YOU OUT; IT'S THE PEBBLE IN YOUR SHOE." -MUHAMMAD ALI

A mnemonic is a learning technique that helps you retain and remember information. Mnemonics are one of the best learning methods for remembering lists or processes in order. Mnemonics make the material more meaningful by adding associations and creating patterns. Interestingly, mnemonics may work better when they utilize absurd, startling, or shocking examples and references. Mnemonics help organize the information so that you can easily retrieve it later. By giving you associations and cues, mnemonics allow you to form a mental structure ordering a list or process to help you remember it better. This mental structure allows you to create a structure of association between items that may not appear to have any relationship. Mnemonics typically use references that are easy to visualize and thus easier to remember. Through visualization of vivid images and references, the information is much easier to imprint into long-term memory. The power of making mnemonics lies in converting dull, inert and uninspiring information into something vibrant and memorable.

How to make simple and effective mnemonics

Some of the best mnemonics help us remember simple rules or lists in order.

Step 1. Take a list of terms you are trying to remember in order. For example, we will use the scientific method:

observation, question, hypothesis, methods, results, and conclusion.

Next, we will replace each word on the list with a new word that starts with the same letter. These new words will together form a vivid sentence that is easy to remember:

Objectionable Queens Haunted Macho Rednecks Creatively.

As silly as the above sentence seems, it is easy to remember, and now we can call on this sentence to remind us of the order of the scientific method.

Visit http://www.mnemonicgenerator.com/ and try typing in a list of words. It is fun to see the mnemonics that it makes and shows how easy it is to make great mnemonics to help your studying.

Using vivid words in your mnemonics allows you to see the sentence you are making. Words that are gross, scary, or name interesting animals are helpful. Profanity is also useful because the shock value can trigger memory. The following are lists of vivid words to use in your mnemonics:

Gross words

Moist, Gurgle, Phlegm, Fetus, Curd, Smear, Squirt, Chunky, Orifice, Maggots, Viscous, Queasy, Bulbous, Pustule, Putrid, Fester, Secrete, Munch, Vomit, Ooze, Dripping, Roaches, Mucus, Stink, Stank, Stunk, Slurp, Pus, Lick, Salty, Tongue, Fart, Flatulence, Hemorrhoid.

Interesting Animals

Aardvark, Baboon, Chicken, Chinchilla, Duck, Dragonfly, Emu, Electric Eel, Frog, Flamingo, Gecko, Hedgehog, Hyena, Iguana, Jackal, Jaguar, Leopard, Lynx, Minnow, Manatee, Mongoose, Neanderthal, Newt, Octopus, Oyster, Pelican, Penguin, Platypus, Quail, Racoon, Rattlesnake, Rhinoceros, Scorpion, Seahorse, Toucan, Turkey, Vulture, Weasel, Woodpecker, Yak, Zebra.

Superhero Words

Diabolical, Activate, Boom, Clutch, Dastardly, Dynamic, Dynamite, Shazam, Kaboom, Zip, Zap, Zoom, Zany, Crushing, Smashing, Exploding, Ripping, Tearing.

Scary Words

Apparition, Bat, Chill, Demon, Eerie, Fangs, Genie, Hell, Lantern, Macabre, Nightmare, Owl, Ogre, Phantasm, Repulsive, Scarecrow, Tarantula, Undead, Vampire, Wraith, Zombie.

There are several types of mnemonics that can help your memory.

1. Images

Visual mnemonics are a type of mnemonic that works by associating an image with characters or objects whose name sounds like the item that must be memorized. This is one of the easiest ways to create effective mnemonics. An example would be to use the shape of numbers to help memorize a long list of them. Numbers can be memorized by their shapes, so that: 0 -looks like an egg; 1 -a pencil, or a candle; 2 -a snake; 3 -an ear; 4 -a sailboat; 5 -a key; 6 -a comet; 7 -a knee; 8 -a snowman; 9 -a comma.

Another type of visual mnemonic is the word-length mnemonic in which the number of letters in each word corresponds to a digit. This simple mnemonic gives pi to seven decimal places:

3.141582 becomes "How I wish I could calculate pi."

Of course, you could use this type of mnemonic to create a longer sentence showing the digits of an important number. Some people have used this type of mnemonic to memorize thousands of digits.

Using the hands is also an important tool for creating visual objects. Making the hands into specific shapes can help us remember the pattern of things or the order of a list of things.

2. Rhyming
Rhyming mnemonics are quick ways to make things memorable. A classic example is a mnemonic for the number of days in each month:
"30 days hath September, April, June, and November.
All the rest have 31
Except February, my dear son.
It has 28, and that is fine
But in Leap Year it has 29."

Another example of a rhyming mnemonic is a common spelling rule:
"I before e except after c
or when sounding like a
in neighbor and weigh."

Use **rhymer.com** to get large lists of rhyming words.

3. Homonym
A homonym is one of a group of words that share the same pronunciation but have different meanings, whether spelled the same or not.

Try saying what you're attempting to remember out loud or very quickly, and see if anything leaps out. If you know other languages, using similar-sounding words from those can be effective.

You could also browse this list of homonyms
at http://www.cooper.com/alan/homonym_list.html.

4. Onomatopoeia
An Onomatopeia is a word that phonetically imitates, resembles or suggests the source of the sound that it describes. Are there any noises made by the thing you're trying to memorize? Is it often associated with some other sound? Failing that, just make up a noise that seems to fit.

Achoo, ahem, baa, bam, bark, beep, beep beep, belch, bleat, boo, boo hoo, boom, burp, buzz, chirp, click clack, crash, croak, crunch, cuckoo, dash, drip, ding dong, eek, fizz, flit, flutter, gasp, grrr, ha ha, hee hee, hiccup, hiss, hissing, honk, icky, itchy, jiggly, jangle, knock knock, lush, la la la, mash, meow, moan, murmur, neigh, oink, ouch, plop, pow, quack, quick, rapping, rattle, ribbit, roar, rumble, rustle, scratch, sizzle, skittering, snap crackle pop, splash, splish splash, spurt, swish, swoosh, tap, tapping, tick tock, tinkle, tweet, ugh, vroom, wham, whinny, whip, whooping, woof.

5. Acronyms
An acronym is a word or name formed as an abbreviation from the initial components of a word, such as NATO, which stands for North Atlantic Treaty Organization. If you're trying to memorize something involving letters, this is often a good bet. A lot of famous mnemonics are acronyms, such as ROYGBIV which stands for the order of colors in the light spectrum (Red, Orange, Yellow, Green, Blue, Indigo, and Violet).
A great acronym generator to try is: www.all-acronyms.com.

A different spin on an acronym is a backronym. A **backronym** is a specially constructed phrase that is supposed to be the source of a word that is an acronym. A backronym is constructed by creating a new phrase to fit an already existing word, name, or acronym.

The word is a combination of *backward* and *acronym*, and has been defined as a "reverse acronym." For example, the United States Department of Justice assigns to their Amber Alert program the meaning "**A**merica's **M**issing: **B**roadcast **E**mergency **R**esponse." The process can go either way to make good mnemonics.

Visit: https://arthurdick.com/projects/backronym/ to try out a simple backronym generator.

6. Anagrams
An anagram is a direct word switch or word play, the result of rearranging the letters of a word or phrase to produce a new word or phrase, using all the original letters exactly once; for example, the word anagram can be rearranged into nag-a-ram.

Try re-arranging letters or components and see if anything memorable emerges. Visit http://www.nameacronym.net/ to use a simple anagram generator.

One particularly memorable form of anagram is the spoonerism, where you swap the initial syllables or letters of words to make new phrases. These are usually humorous, and this makes them easier to remember. Here are some examples:

"Is it kisstomary to cuss the bride?" (as opposed to "customary to kiss")
"The Lord is a shoving leopard." (instead of "a loving shepherd")
"A blushing crow." ("crushing blow")
"A well-boiled icicle" ("well-oiled bicycle")
"You were fighting a liar in the quadrangle." ("lighting a fire")
"Is the bean dizzy?" (as opposed to "is the dean busy?")

7. Stories
Make up quick stories or incidents involving the material you want to memorize. For larger chunks of information, the stories can get more elaborate. Structured stories are particularly good for remembering lists or other sequenced information. Have a look at https://en.wikipedia.org/wiki/Method_of_loci for a more advanced memory sequencing technique.

Visual Metaphors

"Limits, like fear, is often an illusion." -Michael Jordan

What is a Metaphor?

A metaphor is a figure of speech that refers to one thing by mentioning another thing. Metaphors provide clarity and identify hidden similarities between two seemingly unrelated ideas. A visual metaphor is an image that creates a link between different ideas.

Visual metaphors help us use our understanding of the world to learn new concepts, skills, and ideas. Visual metaphors help us relate new material to what we already know. Visual metaphors must be clear and simple enough to spark a connection and understanding. Visual metaphors should use familiar things to help you be less fearful of new, complex, or challenging topics. Metaphors trigger a sense of familiarity so that you are more accepting of the new idea. Metaphors work best when you associate a familiar, easy to understand idea with a challenging, obscure, or abstract concept.

How to make a visual metaphor

1. Brainstorm using the words of the concept. Use different fonts, colors, or shapes to represent parts of the concept.

2. Merge these images together

3. Show the process using arrows, accents, etc.

4. Think about the story line your metaphor projects.

Examples of visual metaphors:

A skeleton used to show a framework of something.

A cloud showing an outline.

A bodybuilder whose muscles represent supporting ideas and details.

A sandwich where the meat, tomato, and lettuce represent supporting ideas.

A recipe card to show a process.

Your metaphor should be accurate. It should be complex enough to convey meaning, but simple and clear enough to be easily understood.

Morphology

"SCIENCE IS THE CAPTAIN, AND PRACTICE THE SOLDIERS." LEONARDO DA VINCI

Morphology is the study of the origin, roots, suffixes, and prefixes of the words. Understanding the meaning of prefixes, suffixes, and roots make it easier to decode the meaning of new vocabulary. Having the ability to decode using morphology increases text comprehension when initially reading as well.
The capability of identifying meaningful parts of words (morphemes), including prefixes, suffixes, and roots can be helpful. Identifying morphemes improves decoding accuracy and fluency. Reading speed improves when you can decode larger chunks of text quickly. When you can recognize morphemes in words, you will be better able to make sense of new words in context. Below are charts containing the most common prefixes, suffixes, and root words. Use them to help you decode your vocabulary terms.

Prefixes

Prefix	Meaning	Example words and meanings	
a, ab, abs	away from	absent abdicate	not to be present, to give up an office or throne.
ad, a, ac, af, ag, an, ar, at, as	to, toward	Advance advantage	To move forward To have the upper hand
anti	against	Antidote antisocial antibiotic	To repair poisoning refers to someone who's not social
bi, bis	two	bicycle binary biweekly	two-wheeled cycle two number system every two weeks
circum, cir	around	circumnavigate circle	Travel around the world a figure that goes all around
com, con, co, col	with, together	Complete Complement	To finish To go along with
de	away from, down, the opposite of	depart detour	to go away from to go out of your way
dis, dif, di	apart	dislike dishonest distant	not to like not honest away
En-, em-	Cause to	Entrance	the way in.
epi	upon, on top of	epitaph epilogue epidemic	writing upon a tombstone speech at the end, on top of the rest
equ, equi	equal	equalize equitable	to make equal fair, equal
ex, e, ef	out, from	exit eject exhale	to go out to throw out to breathe out
Fore-	Before	Forewarned	To have prior warning

Prefix	Meaning	Example Words and Meanings	
in, il, ir, im, en	in, into	Infield Imbibe	The inner playing field to take part in
in, il, ig, ir, im	not	inactive ignorant irreversible irritate	not active not knowing not reversible to put into discomfort
inter	between, among	international interact	among nations to mix with
mal, male	bad, ill, wrong	malpractice malfunction	bad practice fail to function, bad function
Mid	Middle	Amidships	In the middle of a ship
mis	wrong, badly	misnomer	The wrong name
mono	one, alone, single	monocle	one lensed glasses
non	not, the reverse of	nonprofit	not making a profit
ob	in front, against, in front of, in the way of	Obsolete	No longer needed
omni	everywhere, all	omnipresent omnipotent	always present, everywhere all powerful
Over	On top	Overdose	Take too much medication
Pre	Before	Preview	Happens before a show.
per	through	Permeable pervasive	to pass through, all encompassing
poly	many	Polygamy polygon	many spouses figure with many sides
post	after	postpone postmortem	to do after after death
pre	before, earlier than	Predict Preview	To know before To view before release
pro	forward, going ahead of, supporting	proceed pro-war promote	to go forward supporting the war to raise or move forward
re	again, back	retell recall reverse	to tell again to call back to go back
se	apart	secede seclude	to withdraw, become apart to stay apart from others
Semi	Half	Semipermeable	Half-permeable

Prefix	Meaning	Example Words and Meanings	
Sub	under, less than	Submarine	under water
super	over, above, greater	superstar superimpose	a start greater than her stars to put over something else
trans	across	transcontinental transverse	across the continent to lie or go across
un, uni	one	unidirectional unanimous unilateral	having one direction sharing one view having one side
un	not	uninterested unhelpful unethical	not interested not helpful not ethical

Roots

Root	Meaning	Example words & meanings	
act, ag	to do, to act	Agent Activity	One who acts as a representative Action
Aqua	Water	Aquamarine	The color of water
Aud	To hear	Auditorium	A place to hear music
apert	open	Aperture	An opening
bas	low	Basement Basement	Something that is low, at the bottom A room that is low
Bio	Living thing	Biological	Living matter
cap, capt, cip, cept, ceive	to take, to hold, to seize	Captive Receive Capable Recipient	One who is held To take Able to take hold of things One who takes hold or receives
ced, cede, ceed, cess	to go, to give in	Precede Access Proceed	To go before Means of going to To go forward
Cogn	Know	Cognitive	Ability to think
cred, credit	to believe	Credible Incredible Credit	Believable Not believable Belief, trust
curr, curs, cours	to run	Current Precursory Recourse	Now in progress, running Running (going) before To run for aid
Cycle	Circle	Lifecycle	The circle of life
dic, dict	to say	Dictionary Indict	A book explaining words (sayings)

Root	Meaning	Examples and meanings	
duc, duct	to lead	Induce Conduct Aqueduct	To lead to action To lead or guide Pipe that leads water somewhere
equ	equal, even	Equality Equanimity	Equal in social, political rights Evenness of mind, tranquility
fac, fact, fic, fect, fy	to make, to do	Facile Fiction Factory Affect	Easy to do Something that is made up Place that makes things To make a change in
fer, ferr	to carry, bring	Defer Referral	To carry away Bring a source for help/information
Gen	Birth	Generate	To create something
graph	write	Monograph Graphite	A writing on a particular subject A form of carbon used for writing
Loc	Place	Location	A place
Mater	Mother	Maternity	Expecting birth
Mem	Recall	Memory	The recall experiences
mit, mis	to send	Admit Missile	To send in Something sent through the air
Nat	Born	Native	Born in a place
par	equal	Parity Disparate	Equality No equal, not alike
Ped	Foot	Podiatrist	Foot doctor
Photo	Light	Photograph	A picture
plic	to fold, to bend, to turn	Complicate Implicate	To fold (mix) together To fold in, to involve
pon, pos, posit, pose	to place	Component Transpose Compose Deposit	A part placed together with others A place across To put many parts into place To place for safekeeping
scrib, script	to write	Describe Transcript Subscription	To write about or tell about A written copy A written signature or document
sequ, secu	to follow	Sequence	In following order

Root	Meaning	Examples and Meanings	
Sign	Mark	Signal	to alert somebody
spec, spect, spic	to appear, to look, to see	Specimen Aspect	An example to look at One way to see something
sta, stat, sist,	to stand, or make stand	Constant	Standing with
stit, sisto	Stable, steady	Status Stable Desist	Social standing Steady (standing) To stand away from
Struct	To build	Construction	To build a thing
tact	to touch	Contact Tactile	To touch together To be able to be touched
ten, tent, tain	to hold	Tenable Retentive Maintain	Able to be held, holding Holding To keep or hold up
tend, tens, tent	to stretch	Extend Tension	To stretch or draw out Stretched
Therm	Temperature	Thermometer	Detects temperature
tract	to draw	Attract Contract	To draw together An agreement drawn up
ven, vent	to come	Convene Advent	To come together A coming
Vis	See	Invisible	Cannot be seen
ver, vert, vers	to turn	Avert Revert Reverse	To turn away To turn back To turn around

Crossword Puzzles

1. Using the Across and Down clues, write the correct words in the numbered grid below.

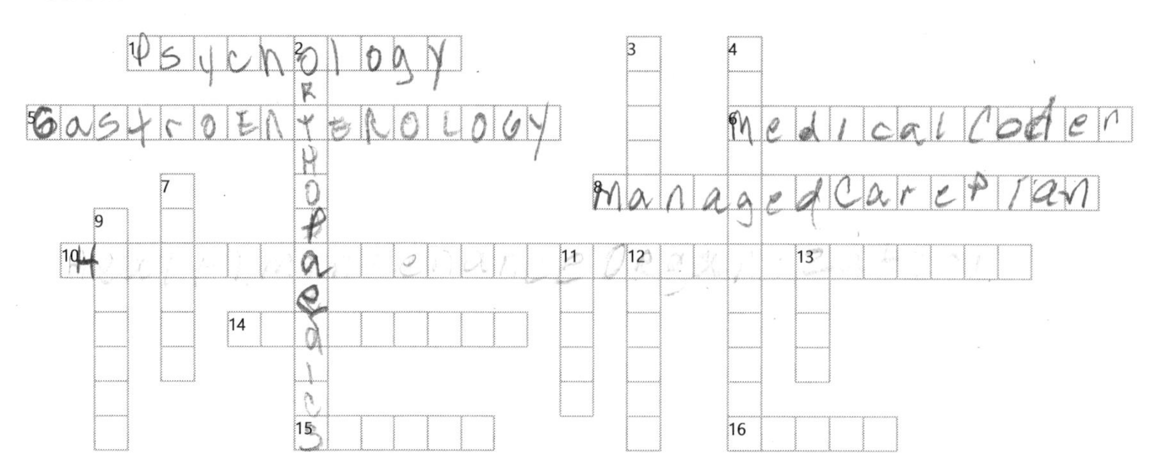

ACROSS

1. The science of dealing with mental processes and their effects on behavior
5. the diagnosis and treatment of diseases and disorders of the digestive system, including the liver, stomach and intestines, and medical conditions such as ulcers, tumors and colitis
6. Responsible for assigning various medical codes to services and healthcare plans described by a physician on a patient's super-bill.
8. A health insurance plan whereby patients can only receive coverage if they see providers who operate in the insurance company's network.
10. Networks of healthcare providers that offer healthcare plans to people for medical services exclusively in their network.
14. The use of radiation, ultrasound, X-rays, computerized tomography, magnetic resonance imaging, mammography, and other imaging technologies to diagnose diseases and internal disorders
15. A disease caused by a lack of vitamin c, characterized by weakness, bleeding and pain in joints and muscles, bleeding gums, and abnormal bone and tooth growth
16. The bones that form the framework of the head and enclose and protect the brain and other sensory organs

DOWN

2. the diagnosis and treatment, including surgery, of diseases and disorders of the musculoskeletal system, including bones, joints, tendons, ligaments, muscles and nerves
3. Tiny, hairlike structures on the outside of some cells, providing mobility
4. The patient's information required for filing a claim, such as age, sex, address, and family information. An insurance company may deny a claim if it contains inaccurate demographics.
7. An organ located in the upper left abdomen behind the ribs that removes and destroys old red blood cells and helps fight infection
9. A term used to describe something related to a fever, such as febrile seizures
11. A federal program that allows a person terminated from their employer to retain health insurance they had with that employer.
12. Involuntary contraction of genital muscles experienced at the peak of sexual excitement
13. The colored part of the eye

A. Gastroenterology
C. Spleen
E. Scurvy
G. Medical Coder
I. Psychology
K. Cilia
M. Demographics
O. Skull

B. Health Maintenance Organization
D. Managed Care Plan
F. Iris
H. Orthopaedics
J. Radiology
L. Orgasm
N. COBRA
P. Febrile

2. Using the Across and Down clues, write the correct words in the numbered grid below.

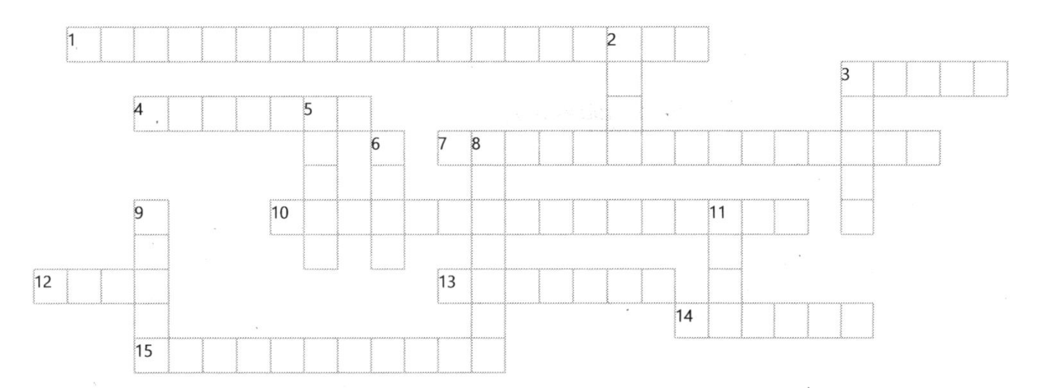

ACROSS

1. A unique number ascribed to a person's medical record so it can be differentiated from other medical records.
3. A federal program that allows a person terminated from their employer to retain health insurance they had with that employer.
4. The sum a person pays to an insurance company on a regular (usually monthly or yearly) basis to receive health insurance.
7. A health insurance plan whereby patients can only receive coverage if they see providers who operate in the insurance company's network.
10. An employee in the healthcare system such as a physician's assistant or a nurse practitioner who perform duties in administration, nursing, and other ancillary care.
12. Another term for an egg cell
13. The diagnosis and management, including surgery, of disorders of the urinary tract in both males and females, as well as the male reproductive system
14. A salt solution or any substance that contains salt
15. the specialized care and treatment of a newborn up to six weeks of age

DOWN

2. A yellow-green liquid produced in the liver whose function is to remove waste from the liver and break down fats as food is digested
3. Tiny, hairlike structures on the outside of some cells, providing mobility
5. An open sore that occurs on the skin or on a mucous membrane because of the destruction of surface tissue
6. An inflamed, raised area of skin that is pus-filled
8. Immunology
9. A thin fold of membrane partly closing the opening of the vagina
11. A "warning" signal that comes before a migraine headache or an epileptic seizure, which might include emotions or sensations of movement or discomfort

A. Urology
B. Ovum
C. Allergy
D. Medical Record Number
E. Ulcer
F. Managed Care Plan
G. Saline
H. Cilia
I. Premium
J. Aura
K. Medical Assistant
L. Neonatology
M. Boil
N. COBRA
O. Hymen
P. Bile

3. Using the Across and Down clues, write the correct words in the numbered grid below.

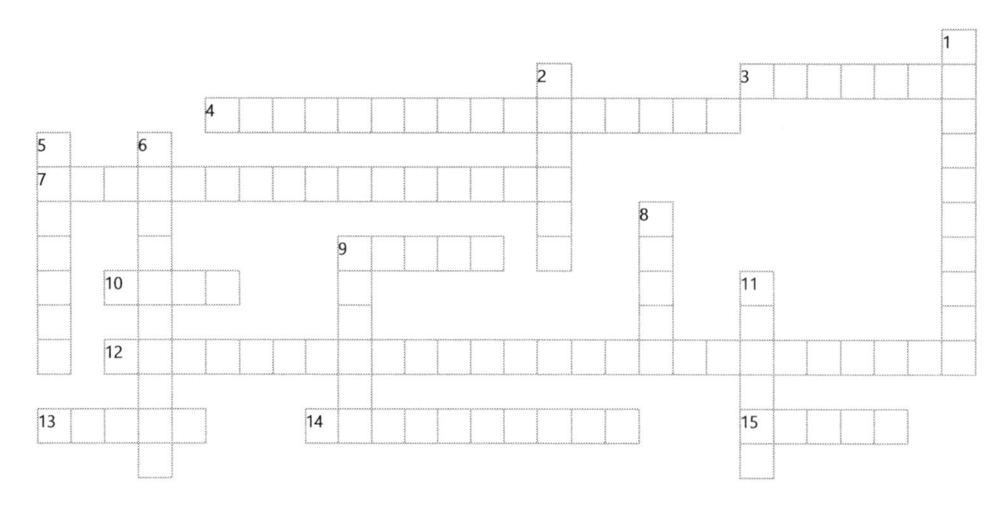

ACROSS

3. A chemical produced by a gland or tissue that is released into the bloodstream
4. This is when a provider refuses to accept Medicare payments as a sufficient amount for the services rendered to a patient.
7. the diagnosis and non-surgical treatment of adult health problems
9. The main part of the large intestine, between the cecum and the rectum
10. A pus- filled abscess in the follicle of an eyelash
12. The digital version of EOB, which specifies the details of payments made on a claim either by an insurance company or required by the patient.
13. Two organs in the chest that take in oxygen from the air and release carbon dioxide
14. A fixed payment that a patient makes to a health insurance company or provider to recoup costs incurred from various healthcare services.
15. The lowest section of the small intestine, which attaches to the large intestine

DOWN

1. The amount a patient must pay before an insurance carrier starts their healthcare coverage.
2. Occurs when a patient or a provider tries to convince an insurance company to pay for healthcare after it has decided not to cover costs for someone on a claim.
5. An abnormal passageway from one organ to another or from an organ to the body surface
6. Oncology
8. The two pairs of skinfolds that protect the opening of the vagina
9. The clear, dome-shaped front portion of the eye's outer covering
11. A condition in which the blood does not contain enough hemoglobin, the compound that carries oxygen from the lungs to other parts of the body

A. Cornea
B. Anemia
C. Lungs
D. Fistula
E. Stye
F. Colon
G. Appeal
H. Deductible
I. Non participation
J. Ileum
K. Hematology
L. Capitation
M. Internal Medicine
N. Labia
O. Electronic Remittance Advice
P. Hormone

4. Using the Across and Down clues, write the correct words in the numbered grid below.

ACROSS

2. The name for Medicare representatives who process Medicare claims.
4. The fraudulent practice of ascribing a higher ICD-9 code to a healthcare procedure in an attempt to get more money than necessary from the insurance company or patient.
6. A bundle of fibers that transmit electrical messages between the brain and areas of the body
7. The soft tissue inside of a tooth that contains blood vessels and nerves
9. A parasitic flatworm that can infest humans
10. The two pairs of skinfolds that protect the opening of the vagina
12. An investigation or audit performed to optimize the number of inpatient and outpatient services a provider performs.
13. Facilities that review and correct medical claims as necessary before sending them to insurance companies for final processing.
14. Referring to 61st through 90th days of inpatient treatment, the law requires that patients pay for a portion of their healthcare during Medicare coinsurance days.

DOWN

1. A codeset under ICD-9-CM used to organize healthcare services rendered for reasons other than illness or injury.
3. A colorless, odorless, tasteless radioactive gas that is produced by materials in soil, rocks, and building materials
5. Not obstructed; open
6. Another term for a nerve cell
8. Loss of sensation or ability to move
10. A noncancerous tumor of fatty tissue
11. The hollow female reproductive organ in which a fertilized egg is implanted and a fetus develops

A. Lipoma
B. Clearinghouse
C. Radon
D. Patent
E. Fiscal Intermediary
F. Upcoding
G. V Codes
H. Uterus
I. Palsy
J. Neuron
K. Pulp
L. Utilization Review
M. Labia
N. Nerve
O. Fluke
P. Medicare Coinsurance Days

5. Using the Across and Down clues, write the correct words in the numbered grid below.

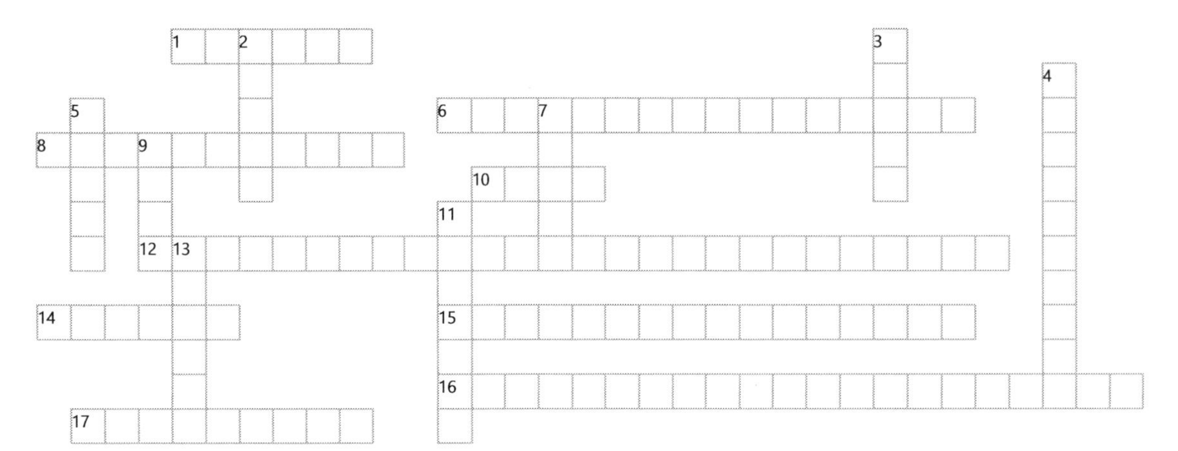

ACROSS

1. An egg cell that has not developed completely
6. The person who pays for a patient's medical expenses, also known as the guarantor.
8. A number given to a patient by their insurance carrier that identifies the group or plan under which they are covered.
10. A brown to dark-brown spot on the skin that can be flat or raised
12. A digital network that allows healthcare providers to access quality medical billing software and technologies without needing to purchase and maintain it themselves.
14. A group of diseases in which cells grow unrestrained in an organ or tissue in the body
15. A maximum sum as explained in a healthcare plan an insurance company will pay for certain services or treatments.
16. Refers to a binding agree between a provider, patient, and insurance company wherein the provider agrees to charges that it will write off on behalf of the patient.
17. Occurs when a person has a stay at a healthcare facility for more than 24 hours.

DOWN

2. The beginning of the large intestine, which is connected to the appendix at its lower end
3. The clear, watery fluid that separates from clotted blood
4. The amount a patient must pay before an insurance carrier starts their healthcare coverage.
5. An agent that is believed to cause several degenerative brain diseases
7. The expansion and contraction of a blood vessel due to the blood pumped through it
9. A waste product of the metabolism of proteins that is formed by the liver and secreted by the kidneys
11. A hospital or an area of a hospital dedicated to treating people who are dying, often of a specific cause
13. The double- layered membrane that lines the lungs and chest cavity and allows for lung movement during breathing

A. Pleura
B. Serum
C. Responsible Party
D. Group Number
E. Deductible
F. Oocyte
G. Hospice
H. Inpatient
I. Mole
J. Cecum
K. Contractual Adjustment
L. Application Service Provider
M. Urea
N. Prion
O. Pre determination
P. Pulse
Q. Cancer

6. Using the Across and Down clues, write the correct words in the numbered grid below.

ACROSS

1. This is when a provider refuses to accept Medicare payments as a sufficient amount for the services rendered to a patient.
6. An area of buildup of fat deposits in an artery, causing narrowing of the artery and possibly heart disease
8. The liquid part of the blood, containing substances such as nutrients, salts, and proteins
11. Facilities that review and correct medical claims as necessary before sending them to insurance companies for final processing.
12. The patient's information required for filing a claim, such as age, sex, address, and family information. An insurance company may deny a claim if it contains inaccurate demographics.
13. A cavity within bone or a channel that contains blood
14. An artificial feeding technique in which liquids are passed into the stomach by way of a tube inserted through the nose
15. A fluid-filled sac that cushions and reduces friction in certain parts of the body
16. A term used to describe a child in the womb from fertilization to 8 weeks following fertilization

DOWN

2. A group of diseases caused by the microorganism rickettsia, spread by the bites of fleas, mites, or ticks
3. This type of care is administered at reduced or zero cost to patients who cannot afford healthcare.
4. An organ located in the pelvis whose function is to collect and store urine until it is expelled
5. Abnormal crackling or bubbling sounds heard in the lungs during breathing
7. The hollow female reproductive organ in which a fertilized egg is implanted and a fetus develops
9. Density lipoprotein- a type of lipoprotein that is the major carrier of cholesterol in the blood, with high levels associated with narrowing of the arteries and heart disease
10. A small, rounded tissue mass
13. A sample of cells spread across a glass slide to be examined through a microscope

A. Sinus
B. Plasma
C. Typhus
D. Clearinghouse
E. Smear
F. Plaque
G. Rales
H. Non participation
I. Bladder
J. Charity Care
K. Bursa
L. Low
M. Gavage
N. Demographics
O. Uterus
P. Embryo
Q. Node

7. Using the Across and Down clues, write the correct words in the numbered grid below.

ACROSS

4. Whoever owes the healthcare provider money has financial responsibility for the services rendered.
7. Healthy tissue that is used to replace diseased or defective tissue
8. A document attached to a processed medical claim wherein the insurance company explains the services they will cover for a patient's healthcare treatments.
12. An optional health insurance payments plan whereby a person apportions part of their untaxed earnings to an account reserved for healthcare expenses.
13. A document that summarizes the services, treatments, payments, and charges that a patient received on a given day.
15. A group of diseases in which cells grow unrestrained in an organ or tissue in the body
16. Immunology

DOWN

1. This term refers to the discrepancy between the limits of healthcare insurance coverage and the Medicare Part D coverage limits for prescription drugs.
2. This act established guidelines and requirements for health and life insurance policies including appeals and disclosure of grievances.
3. A salt solution or any substance that contains salt
5. The opening at the center of the iris in the eye that constricts (contracts) and dilates (widens) in response to light
6. Loss of sensation or ability to move
7. A number given to a patient by their insurance carrier that identifies the group or plan under which they are covered.
9. Sexual intercourse
10. Providers, patients, or insurance companies may be found fraudulent if they are deliberately achieving their ends through misrepresentation, dishonesty, and general illegal activity.
11. The expansion and contraction of a blood vessel due to the blood pumped through it
14. A surgically formed opening on a body surface

A. Graft	B. ERISA	C. Medical Savings Account
D. Allergy	E. Fraud	F. Saline
G. Explanation of Benefits	H. Cancer	I. Donut Hole
J. Day Sheet	K. Pulse	L. Stoma
M. Financial Responsibility	N. Pupil	O. Group Number
P. Palsy	Q. Coitus	

8. Using the Across and Down clues, write the correct words in the numbered grid below.

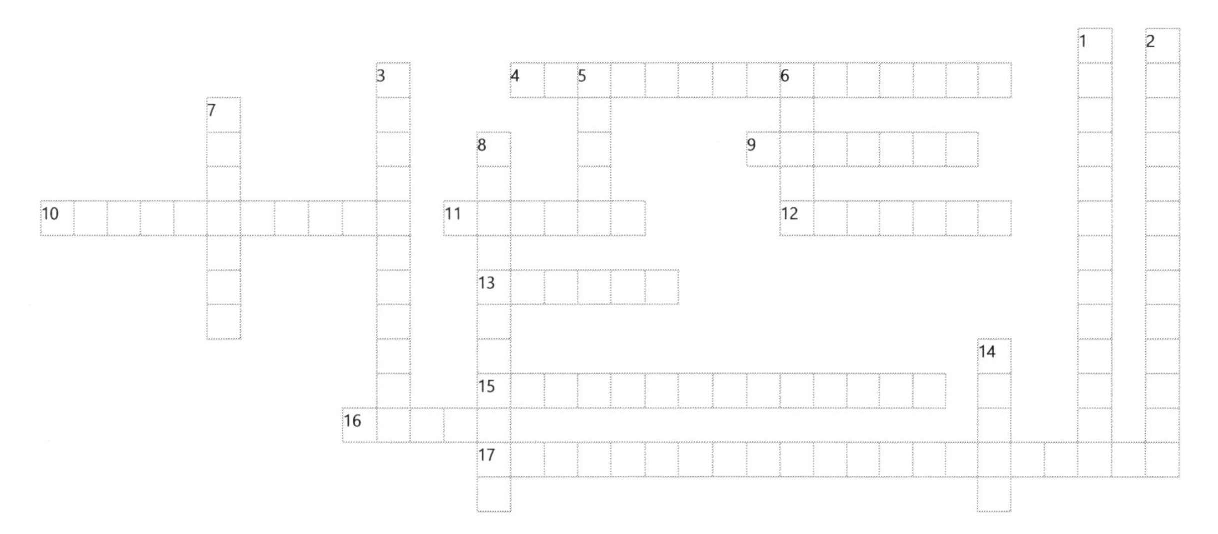

ACROSS

4. The diagnosis and treatment of circulatory problems of the extremities, especially the legs
9. An additional dose of a vaccine taken after the first dose to maintain or renew the first one
10. A MAC based in Columbia, South Carolina that is also a subsidiary of Blue Cross Blue Shield.
11. One of two organs that are part of the urinary tract
12. A drug that neutralizes stomach acids
13. A surgical stitch that helps close an incision or wound so that it can heal properly
15. the administration of medications as a means to block pain or diminish consciousness for surgery, usually by injection or inhalation
16. An enzyme that plays a role in increasing a low blood pressure
17. Refers to a binding agree between a provider, patient, and insurance company wherein the provider agrees to charges that it will write off on behalf of the patient.

DOWN

1. The unit of a hospital reserved for patients that need immediate treatment and close monitoring by healthcare professionals for serious illnesses, conditions, and injuries.
2. The sum an insurance company will reimburse to cover a healthcare service or procedure.
3. Standards for privacy regarding a patient's medical history and all related events, treatments, and data as outlined by HIPAA.
5. A digestive disorder in which nutrients cannot be properly absorbed from food, causing weakness and loss of weight
6. A surgically formed opening on a body surface
7. An abnormal passageway from one organ to another or from an organ to the body surface
8. The percentage of coverage that a patient is responsible for paying after an insurance company pays the portion agreed upon in a health plan.
14. The expansion and contraction of a blood vessel due to the blood pumped through it

A. Palmetto GBA
B. Fistula
C. Intensive Care
D. Vascular Surgery
E. Pulse
F. Stoma
G. Antacid
H. Booster
I. Contractual Adjustment
J. Sprue
K. Kidney
L. Privacy Rule
M. Renin
N. Allowed Amount
O. Suture
P. Anesthesiology
Q. Co Insurance

9. Using the Across and Down clues, write the correct words in the numbered grid below.

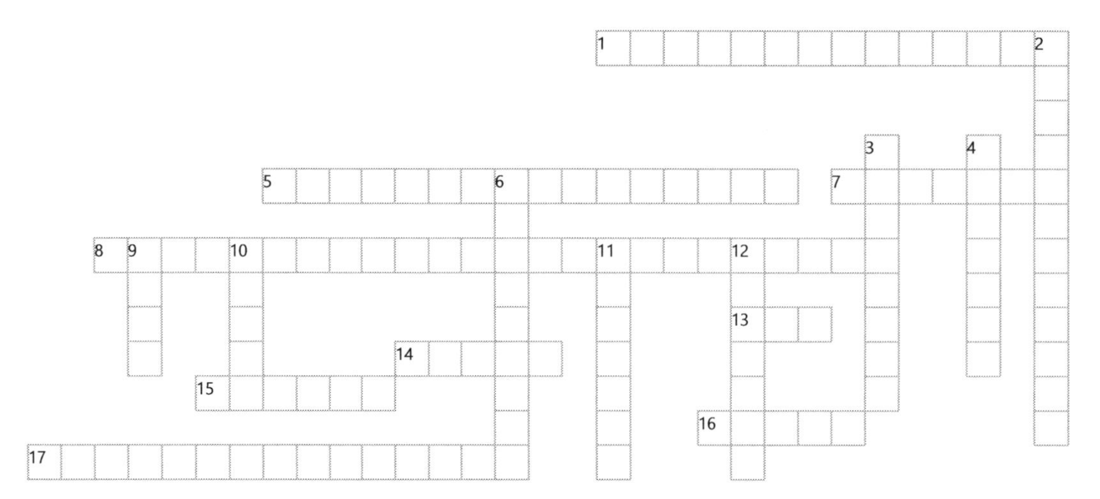

ACROSS

1. the control of pain or discomfort through medication, stress reduction, relaxation, exercise, massage, heat, cold, or providing a comfortable environment
5. The person who pays for a patient's medical expenses, also known as the guarantor.
7. A hormone that stimulates the release of gastric acid in the stomach
8. Digitized medical record for a patient managed by a provider onsite.
13. Density lipoprotein- a type of lipoprotein that is the major carrier of cholesterol in the blood, with high levels associated with narrowing of the arteries and heart disease
14. A device used to hold tissues in place, such as to support a skin graft
15. A chemical, originating in a cell, that regulates reactions in the body
16. Providers, patients, or insurance companies may be found fraudulent if they are deliberately achieving their ends through misrepresentation, dishonesty, and general illegal activity.
17. The diagnosis and treatment of circulatory problems of the extremities, especially the legs

DOWN

2. Medical billing specialists utilize this unique codeset for identifying a healthcare provider's specialty field.
3. A document that summarizes the services, treatments, payments, and charges that a patient received on a given day.
4. An unaware clenching or grinding of the teeth, usually during sleep
6. A type of health insurance plan whereby a patient can receive care with any provider in exchange for higher deductibles and co-pays. Indemnity is also known as fee -for-service insurance.
9. A well-defined, separate part of an organ
10. A poisonous substance
11. The passageways that air moves through while traveling in and out of the lungs during breathing
12. The artificial growth of cells, tissue, or microorganisms such as bacteria in a laboratory

A. Day Sheet
B. Lobe
C. Bruxism
D. Responsible Party
E. Pain Management
F. Gastrin
G. Culture
H. Indemnity
I. Fraud
J. Electronic Medical Records
K. Taxonomy Code
L. Low
M. Enzyme
N. Airways
O. Vascular Surgery
P. Toxin
Q. Stent

10. Using the Across and Down clues, write the correct words in the numbered grid below.

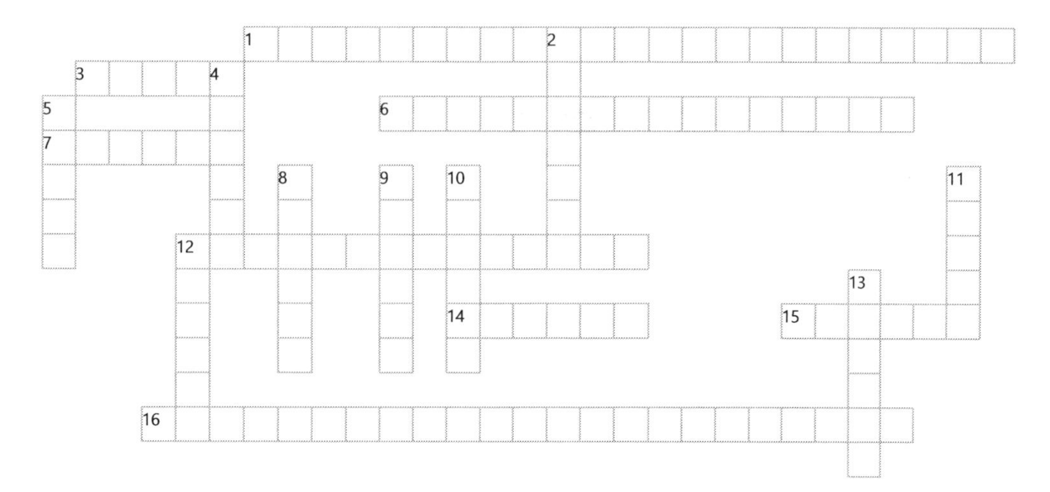

ACROSS

1. A method of transferring money electronically from a patient's bank account to a provider or an insurance carrier.
3. A usually mild and temporary condition common in children in which the walls of the airways become inflamed and narrow, resulting in wheezing and coughing
6. An employee in the healthcare system such as a physician's assistant or a nurse practitioner who perform duties in administration, nursing, and other ancillary care.
7. A disorder characterized by inflamed airways and difficulty breathing
12. the control of pain or discomfort through medication, stress reduction, relaxation, exercise, massage, heat, cold, or providing a comfortable environment
14. A group of diseases caused by the microorganism rickettsia, spread by the bites of fleas, mites, or ticks
15. A codeset under ICD-9-CM used to organize healthcare services rendered for reasons other than illness or injury.
16. A unique number a patient or a company may have to produce for billing purposes in order to receive healthcare from a provider.

DOWN

2. A painless sore that has a thick, rubbery base and a defined edge
4. The liquid part of the blood, containing substances such as nutrients, salts, and proteins
5. A tunnel-like passage
8. The complete set of an organism's genes
9. A group of diseases in which cells grow unrestrained in an organ or tissue in the body
10. The cell that results when an egg is fertilized by a sperm
11. Small, eight- legged animals that can attach to humans and animals and feed on blood
12. A persisting fear of and desire to avoid something
13. Enlargement of the thyroid gland, which produces a swelling on the neck

A. Genome	B. Ticks	C. Pain Management
D. Plasma	E. V Codes	F. Cancer
G. Phobia	H. Tax Identification Number	I. Chancre
J. Zygote	K. Electronic Funds Transfer	L. Croup
M. Canal	N. Goiter	O. Typhus
P. Medical Assistant	Q. Asthma	

11. Using the Across and Down clues, write the correct words in the numbered grid below.

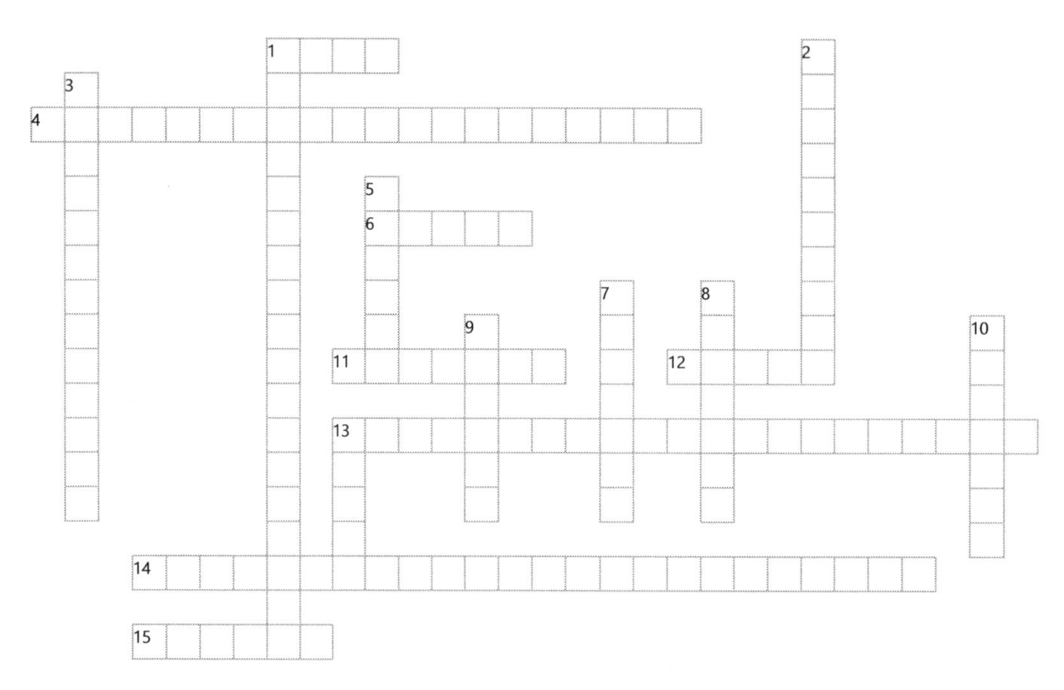

ACROSS

1. A structure consisting of the colored area of the eye and the middle layer of the eye that contains blood vessels
4. A medical condition a patient had before receiving coverage from an insurance company.
6. A bundle of fibers that transmit electrical messages between the brain and areas of the body
11. A term used to describe something that is related to the liver
12. The amount that must be paid to a provider before they receive any treatment or services.
13. A document attached to a processed medical claim wherein the insurance company explains the services they will cover for a patient's healthcare treatments.
14. A formal request typically submitted by an insurance carrier to determine if other health coverage exists for a patient.
15. A device that is used to immobilize a part of the body

DOWN

1. Claims have a specific timeframe in which they can be sent off to an insurance company for processing.
2. The diagnosis and treatment of mental, emotional and behavioral disorders
3. The application process for a provider to coordinate with an insurance company.
5. A chemical, originating in a cell, that regulates reactions in the body
7. A plentiful mineral in the body and the basic component of teeth and bones
8. The diagnosis and management, including surgery, of disorders of the urinary tract in both males and females, as well as the male reproductive system
9. Muscle damage resulting from excessive stretching or forceful contraction
10. The structure of bodies; commonly refers to the study of body structure
13. This act established guidelines and requirements for health and life insurance policies including appeals and disclosure of grievances.

A. Calcium
B. Duplicate Coverage Inquiry
C. Pre existing Condition
D. Splint
E. Hepatic
F. Untimely Submission
G. Psychiatry
H. Anatomy
I. Credentialing
J. Co Pay
K. Explanation of Benefits
L. Strain
M. Nerve
N. ERISA
O. Urology
P. Enzyme
Q. Uvea

12. Using the Across and Down clues, write the correct words in the numbered grid below.

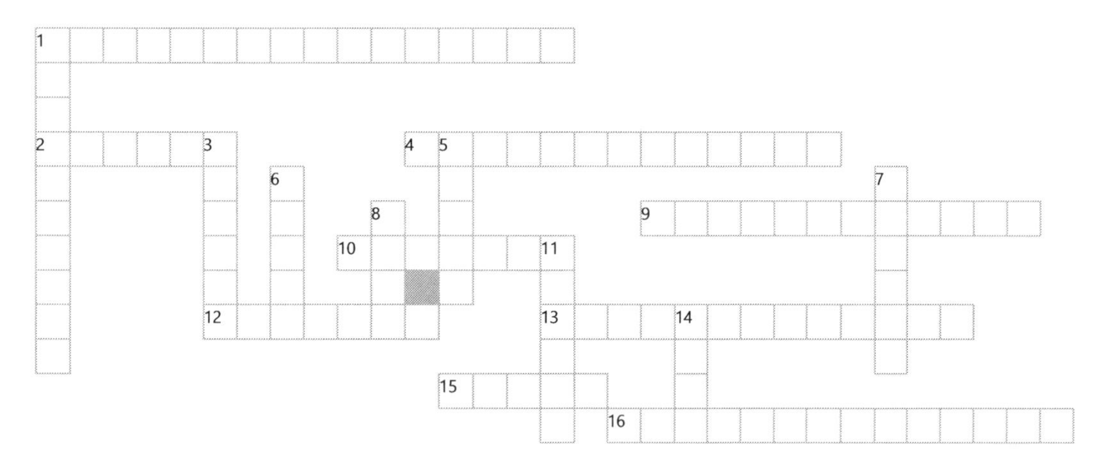

ACROSS

1. A process similar to preauthorization whereby patients must check with insurance companies to see if a desired healthcare treatment or service is deemed medically necessary
2. The process of translating a physician's documentation about a patient's medical condition and health services rendered into medical codes that are then plugged into a claim for processing.
4. the diagnosis and treatment, including surgery, of diseases and disorders of the eye, such as cataracts and glaucoma
9. the diagnosis and treatment, including surgery, of diseases and disorders of the musculoskeletal system, including bones, joints, tendons, ligaments, muscles and nerves
10. An additional dose of a vaccine taken after the first dose to maintain or renew the first one
12. Excess fluid in the abdominal cavity, which leads to swelling
13. A field on a claim for describing what kind of healthcare services or procedures a provider administered.
15. An exact copy of a gene, cell, or organism
16. the specialty that provides comprehensive and ongoing medical care to all members of the family unit

DOWN

1. The science of dealing with mental processes and their effects on behavior
3. A brain tumor arising from cells that support nerve cells
5. Loss of sensation or ability to move
6. Waves of pain in the abdomen that increase in strength, disappear, and return
7. A raised, firm, thick scar that forms as a result of a defect in the natural healing process
8. A small, rounded tissue mass
11. A membrane lining the inside of the back of the eye that contains light-sensitive nerve cells that convert focused light into nerve impulses, making vision possible
14. Another term for an egg cell

A. Psychology
B. Ovum
C. Type of Service
D. Colic
E. Ascites
F. Pre Certification
G. Retina
H. Node
I. Orthopaedics
J. Clone
K. Coding
L. Family Practice
M. Glioma
N. Ophthalmology
O. Palsy
P. Booster
Q. Keloid

13. Using the Across and Down clues, write the correct words in the numbered grid below.

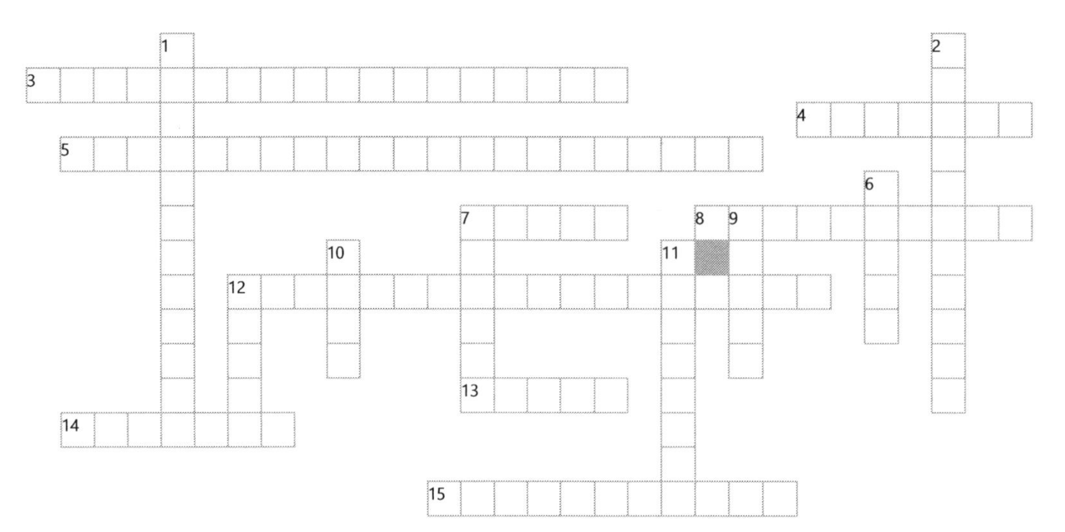

ACROSS

3. A two-digit code used on claims to explain what type of provider performed healthcare services on a patient.
4. A noncancerous tumor of the uterus made up of smooth muscle and connective tissue
5. This refers to the amount a patient owes a provider after an insurance company pays for their portion of the medical expenses.
7. Small, eight- legged animals that can attach to humans and animals and feed on blood
8. The diagnosis and treatment of mental, emotional and behavioral disorders
12. This is when provider performs another procedure on a patient covered by a CPT code after first performing a different CPT procedure on them.
13. The common term for urticaria, an itchy, inflamed rash that results from an allergic reaction
14. A noncancerous tumor of connective tissue
15. A document that outlines the costs associated for each medical service designated by a CPT code.

DOWN

1. Responsible for assigning various medical codes to services and healthcare plans described by a physician on a patient's super-bill.
2. the specialized care and treatment of a newborn up to six weeks of age
6. A constituent of plants that cannot be digested, which helps maintain healthy functioning of the bowels
7. A candidiasis infection
9. An artificially constructed or an abnormal passage connecting two usually separate structures in the body
10. An inflamed, raised area of skin that is pus-filled
11. A joint federal and state assistance program started in 1965 to provide health insurance to lower-income persons.
12. An involuntary muscle contraction

A. Place of Service Code
B. Fiber
C. Fee Schedule
D. Boil
E. Psychiatry
F. Fibroid
G. Ticks
H. Shunt
I. Medicaid
J. Thrush
K. Medical Coder
L. Spasm
M. Neonatology
N. Secondary Procedure
O. Hives
P. Patient Responsibility
Q. Fibroma

14. Using the Across and Down clues, write the correct words in the numbered grid below.

ACROSS

3. Sexual intercourse
4. A reduced flow of blood throughout the body, usually caused by severe bleeding or a weak heart
7. The basic unit of dna, which is responsible for passing genetic information
8. A health insurance plan whereby patients can only receive coverage if they see providers who operate in the insurance company's network.
10. A membrane lining the inside of the back of the eye that contains light-sensitive nerve cells that convert focused light into nerve impulses, making vision possible
12. The technique of creating pictures of structures inside of the body using x-rays, ultrasound waves, or magnetic fields
15. A small lump of tissue that is usually abnormal
17. These are the entities that offer healthcare services to patients, including hospitals, physicians, and private clinics, hospices, nursing homes, and other healthcare facilities.

DOWN

1. A type of health insurance plan whereby a patient can receive care with any provider in exchange for higher deductibles and co-pays. Indemnity is also known as fee -for-service insurance.
2. The individual covered under a group policy. For instance, an employee of a company with a group health policy would be one of many subscribers on that policy.
5. A reduced level of oxygen in tissues
6. The amount a patient must pay before an insurance carrier starts their healthcare coverage.
9. An exact copy of a gene, cell, or organism
11. Additions to CPT codes that explain alterations and modifications to an otherwise routine treatment, exam, or service.
13. Healthy tissue that is used to replace diseased or defective tissue
14. A noncancerous tumor of connective tissue
16. A hard plaster or fiberglass shell that molds to a body part such as an arm and holds it in place for proper healing

A. Retina
B. Modifier
C. Fibroma
D. Subscriber
E. Hypoxia
F. Healthcare Provider
G. Graft
H. Clone
I. Shock
J. Coitus
K. Imaging
L. Gene
M. Deductible
N. Nodule
O. Cast
P. Managed Care Plan
Q. Indemnity

15. Using the Across and Down clues, write the correct words in the numbered grid below.

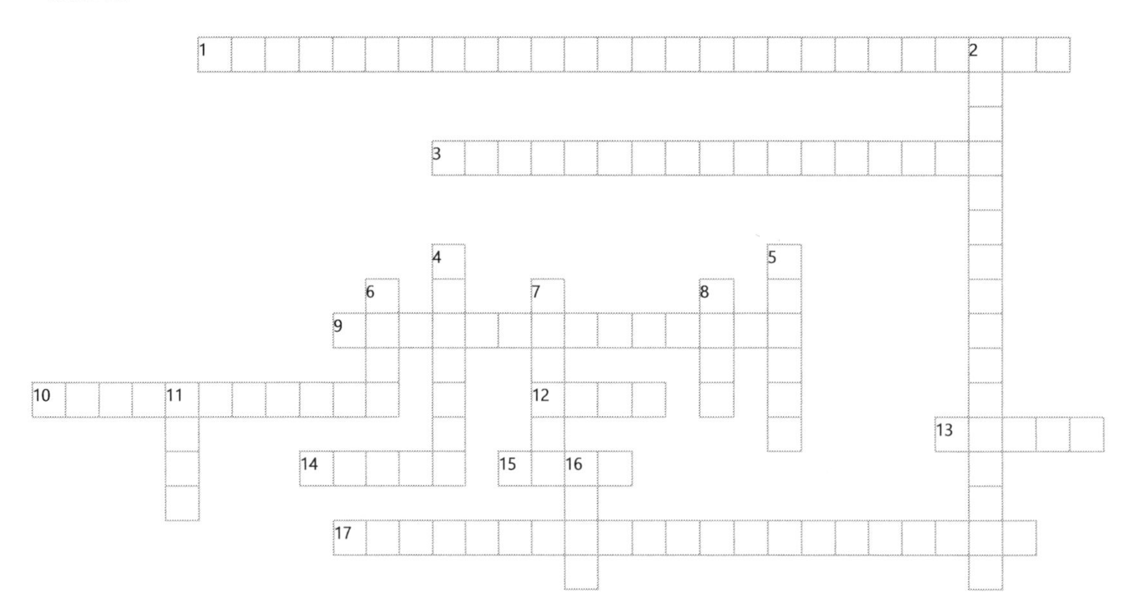

ACROSS

1. The digital version of EOB, which specifies the details of payments made on a claim either by an insurance company or required by the patient.
3. The diagnosis and treatment of acute and chronic diseases and conditions of the respiratory system, such as bronchitis, asthma, emphysema and occupational lung disease
9. the medical and surgical care for diseases of the ears, nose and throat (ENT)
10. A document that outlines the costs associated for each medical service designated by a CPT code.
12. A form of phototherapy that combines the use of psoralens and ultraviolet light to treat skin disorders
13. A term describing something related to or caused by a virus
14. Abnormal buildup of fluid in the body, which may cause visible swelling
15. A contagious, harmless growth caused by a virus that occurs on the skin or a mucous membrane
17. An optional health insurance payments plan whereby a person apportions part of their untaxed earnings to an account reserved for healthcare expenses.

DOWN

2. the diagnosis and non-surgical treatment of adult health problems
4. A disorder in which a person eats large amounts of food then forces vomiting or uses laxatives to prevent weight gain (called binging and purging)
5. A gas that is colorless, odorless, and tasteless
6. A pus- filled abscess in the follicle of an eyelash
7. The medical term for nearsightedness
8. An inflamed, raised area of skin that is pus-filled
11. A lump filled with either fluid or soft material, occurring in any organ or tissue
16. An area of inflammation or a group of spots on the skin

A. Myopia
B. Otolaryngology
C. Cyst
D. Pulmonary Medicine
E. Wart
F. Oxygen
G. Boil
H. Edema
I. Stye
J. Bulimia
K. PUVA
L. Viral
M. Internal Medicine
N. Medical Savings Account
O. Rash
P. Fee Schedule
Q. Electronic Remittance Advice

16. Using the Across and Down clues, write the correct words in the numbered grid below.

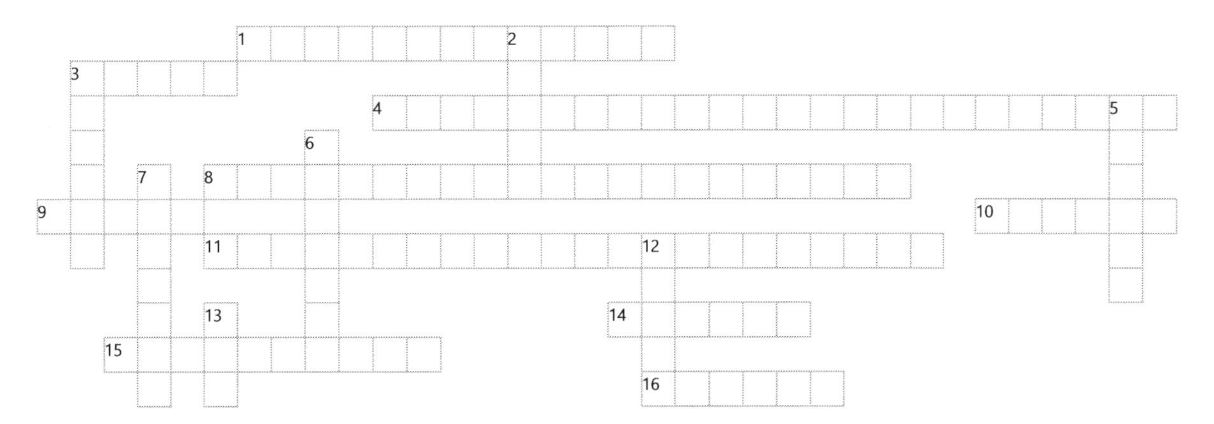

ACROSS

1. The sum an insurance company will reimburse to cover a healthcare service or procedure.
3. A digestive disorder in which nutrients cannot be properly absorbed from food, causing weakness and loss of weight
4. Responsible for using information regarding services and treatments performed by a healthcare provider to complete a claim for filing with an insurance company.
8. This refers to the amount a patient owes a provider after an insurance company pays for their portion of the medical expenses.
9. Tiny, hairlike structures on the outside of some cells, providing mobility
10. An automatic, involuntary response of the nervous system to a stimulus
11. Occurs when a patient is covered by more than one insurance plan.
14. A hard, fluid-filled pad along the inside joint of the big toe
15. The diagnosis and treatment of mental, emotional and behavioral disorders
16. A substance that causes vomiting

DOWN

2. A slippery fluid produced by mucous membranes that lubricates and protects the internal surfaces of the body
3. The infection of a wound or tissue with bacteria, causing the spread of the bacteria into the bloodstream
5. An organ located in the upper left abdomen behind the ribs that removes and destroys old red blood cells and helps fight infection
6. A noncancerous tumor of connective tissue
7. A measure of a person's physical strength, flexibility, and endurance
12. A parasitic flatworm that can infest humans
13. An electrocardiogram, which is a record of the electrical impulses that trigger the heartbeat

A. Patient Responsibility
B. Cilia
C. Fitness
D. ECG
E. Psychiatry
F. Mucus
G. Reflex
H. Coordination of Benefits
I. Spleen
J. Medical Billing Specialist
K. Sprue
L. Allowed Amount
M. Sepsis
N. Fibroma
O. Fluke
P. Emetic
Q. Bunion

17. Using the Across and Down clues, write the correct words in the numbered grid below.

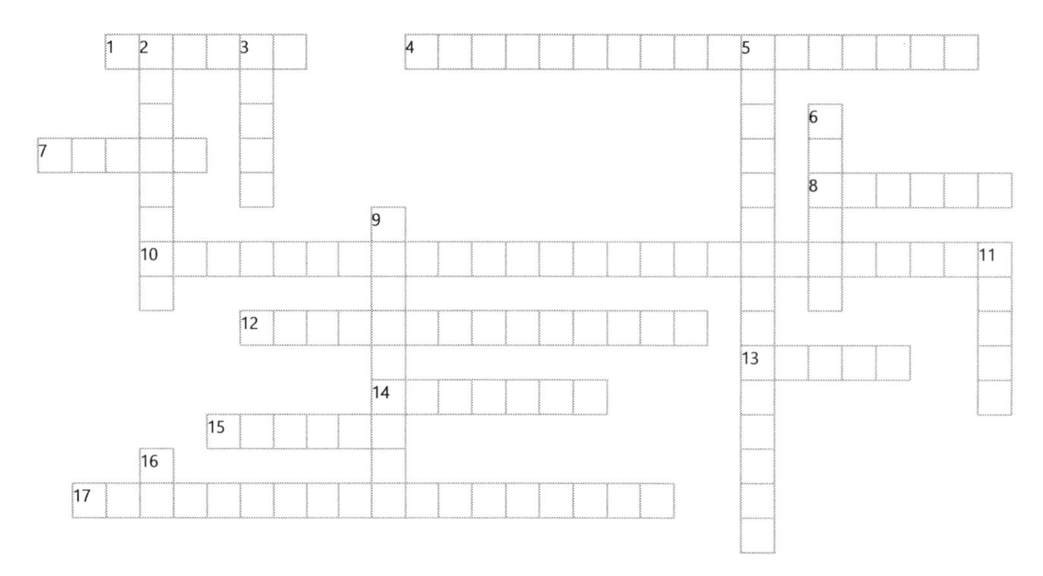

ACROSS

1. Involuntary contraction of genital muscles experienced at the peak of sexual excitement
4. The diagnosis and treatment of acute and chronic diseases and conditions of the respiratory system, such as bronchitis, asthma, emphysema and occupational lung disease
7. A group of common infections occurring on the skin, hair, and nails that are caused by a fungus
8. A persisting fear of and desire to avoid something
10. The largest organization of physicians in the U.S. dedicated to improving the quality of healthcare administered by providers across the country.
12. the medical and surgical care for diseases of the ears, nose and throat (ENT)
13. The main part of the large intestine, between the cecum and the rectum
14. An organ, tissue, or device surgically inserted and left in the body
15. A surgical stitch that helps close an incision or wound so that it can heal properly
17. The amount a patient is required to pay.

DOWN

2. This is when a provider recommends another provider to a patient to receive specialized treatment.
3. An artificially constructed or an abnormal passage connecting two usually separate structures in the body
5. A claim sent electronically to an insurance carrier from a provider's billing software.
6. The infection of a wound or tissue with bacteria, causing the spread of the bacteria into the bloodstream
9. Occurs when a person has a stay at a healthcare facility for more than 24 hours.
11. A bundle of fibers that transmit electrical messages between the brain and areas of the body
16. The abbreviation for diagnosis codes, also known as ICD -9 codes.

A. American Medical Association
B. Tinea
C. Referral
D. Colon
E. Maximum Out of Pocket
F. Electronic Claim
G. Otolaryngology
H. Pulmonary Medicine
I. Sepsis
J. Orgasm
K. Inpatient
L. Implant
M. Shunt
N. Nerve
O. Dx
P. Suture
Q. Phobia

18. Using the Across and Down clues, write the correct words in the numbered grid below.

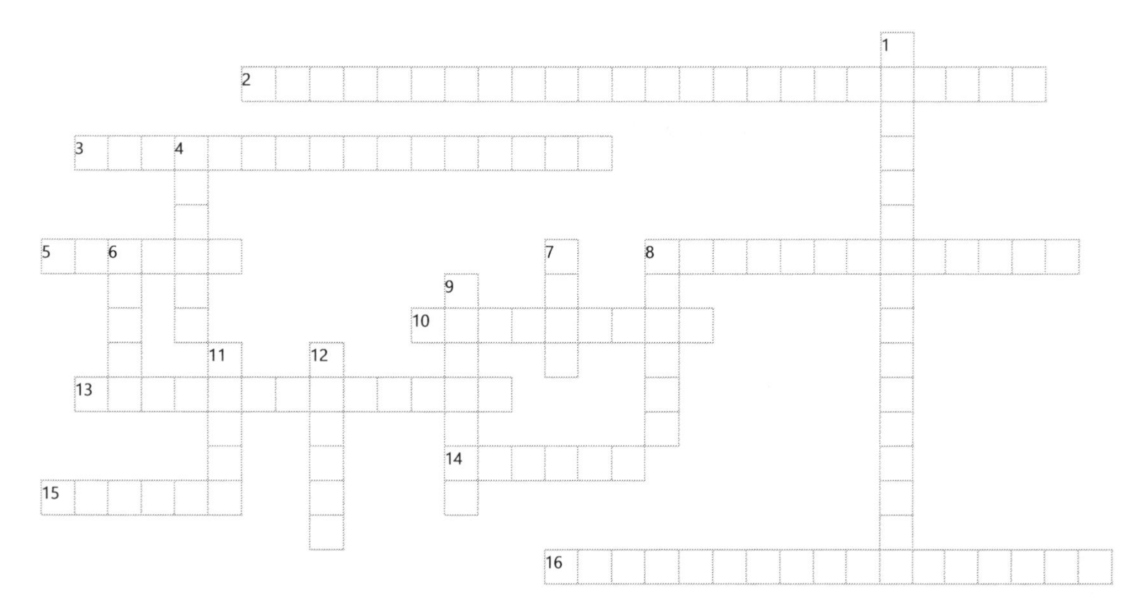

ACROSS

2. The organization responsible for establishing guidelines and investigating fraud and misinformation within the healthcare industry.
3. The document attached to a processed claim that explains the information regarding coverage and payments on a claim.
5. The medical term for nearsightedness
8. The sum an insurance company will reimburse to cover a healthcare service or procedure.
10. A type of health insurance plan whereby a patient can receive care with any provider in exchange for higher deductibles and co-pays. Indemnity is also known as fee -for-service insurance.
13. A claim filed by a provider after they have filed claims for primary and secondary health insurance coverage on behalf of a patient.
14. The area of the retina that allows fine details to be observed at the center of vision
15. An involuntary, rhythmic, shaking movement caused by alternating contraction and relaxation of muscles
16. the specialty that includes treatment of any symptom, illness or injury requiring urgent evaluation and

DOWN

1. the diagnosis and non-surgical treatment of adult health problems
4. An element for the formation of thyroid hormones
6. A poisonous form of oxygen that is present in the earth's upper atmosphere, where it helps to screen the earth from damaging ultraviolet rays
7. A condition in which the area of the brain involved in maintaining consciousness is somehow affected, resulting in a state of unconsciousness in which the patient does not respond to stimulation
8. A mental disorder characterized by an inability to relate to other people and extreme withdrawal
9. A tumor made of blood vessels or lymph vessels that is not cancerous
11. A constituent of plants that cannot be digested, which helps maintain healthy functioning of the bowels
12. A surgical technique in which the flow of blood or another body fluid is redirected around a blockage

A. Autism
B. Allowed Amount
C. Myopia
D. Ozone
E. Macula
F. Office of Inspector General
G. Indemnity
H. Internal Medicine
I. Emergency Medicine
J. Iodine
K. Tremor
L. Bypass
M. Tertiary Claim
N. Coma
O. Angioma
P. Fiber
Q. Remittance Advice

19. Using the Across and Down clues, write the correct words in the numbered grid below.

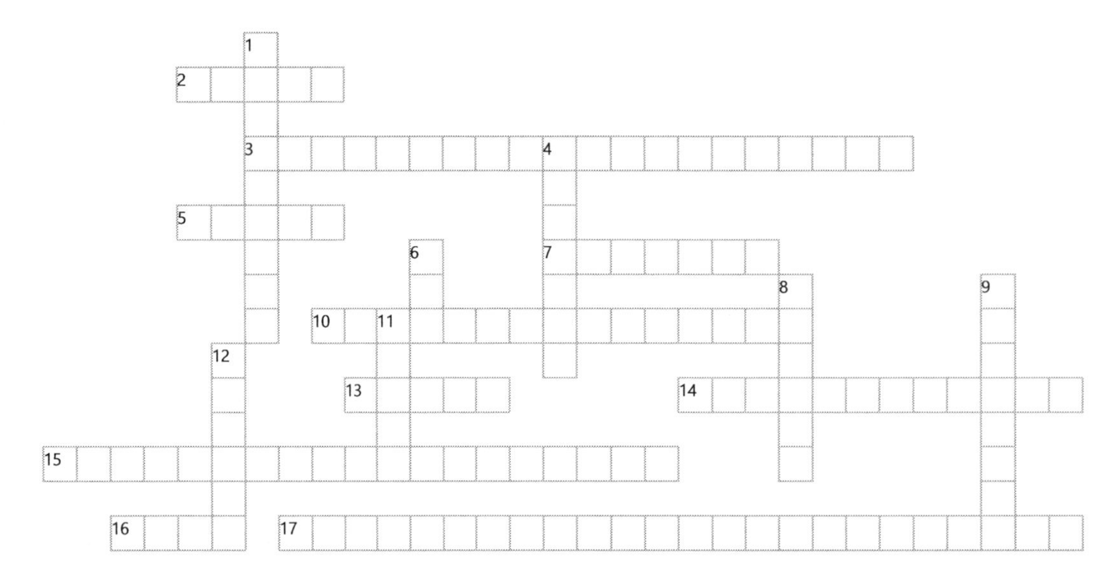

ACROSS

2. A tunnel-like passage
3. Refers to insurance payments made directly to a healthcare provider for medical services received by the patient.
5. This act established guidelines and requirements for health and life insurance policies including appeals and disclosure of grievances.
7. A plentiful mineral in the body and the basic component of teeth and bones
10. The diagnosis and treatment of circulatory problems of the extremities, especially the legs
13. A group of common infections occurring on the skin, hair, and nails that are caused by a fungus
14. the diagnosis and treatment, including surgery, of diseases and disorders of the musculoskeletal system, including bones, joints, tendons, ligaments, muscles and nerves
15. This term refers to the amount of money a patient owes a provider that goes to paying their yearly deductible.
16. Another term for an egg cell
17. Digitized medical record for a patient managed by a provider onsite.

DOWN

1. Occurs when a person has a stay at a healthcare facility for more than 24 hours.
4. The federal health insurance program for active and retired service members, their families, and the survivors of service members.
6. An involuntary, repetitive movement such as a twitch
8. A group of diseases caused by the microorganism rickettsia, spread by the bites of fleas, mites, or ticks
9. Additions to CPT codes that explain alterations and modifications to an otherwise routine treatment, exam, or service.
11. The column of bones and cartilage running along the midline of the back that surrounds and protects the spinal cord and supports the head
12. Mucus and other material produced by the lining of the respiratory tract; also called sputum

A. Electronic Medical Records
B. Spine
C. Applied to Deductible
D. Orthopaedics
E. Typhus
F. Tinea
G. Inpatient
H. ERISA
I. Canal
J. Vascular Surgery
K. Tic
L. Calcium
M. Modifier
N. TRICARE
O. Phlegm
P. Ovum
Q. Assignment of Benefits

20. Using the Across and Down clues, write the correct words in the numbered grid below.

ACROSS

1. An artificial feeding technique in which liquids are passed into the stomach by way of a tube inserted through the nose
4. The amount a patient is required to pay.
6. One of the two bones that form the hip on either side of the body
8. A unit that is used to measure the energy content in food
11. A claim filed by a provider after they have filed claims for primary and secondary health insurance coverage on behalf of a patient.
14. A thin, oval-shaped membrane that separates the inner ear from the outer ear and is responsible for transmitting sound waves
15. Immunology
16. Tiny, hairlike structures on the outside of some cells, providing mobility
17. An area of buildup of fat deposits in an artery, causing narrowing of the artery and possibly heart disease

DOWN

2. A drug that neutralizes stomach acids
3. the diagnosis and medical treatment of the nervous system and brain, including conditions such as strokes and seizures
5. The examination of a body following death, possibly to determine the cause of death or for research
7. A surgically formed opening on a body surface
9. A group of diseases in which cells grow unrestrained in an organ or tissue in the body
10. A mental disorder characterized by an inability to relate to other people and extreme withdrawal
12. A large blood vessel that carries blood from the heart to tissues and organs in the body
13. A structure that allows fluid flow in only one direction

A. Plaque
B. Tertiary Claim
C. Autism
D. Artery
E. Valve
F. Cancer
G. Neurology
H. Cilia
I. Ilium
J. Eardrum
K. Allergy
L. Autopsy
M. Calorie
N. Gavage
O. Maximum Out of Pocket
P. Antacid
Q. Stoma

21. Using the Across and Down clues, write the correct words in the numbered grid below.

ACROSS

1. A candidiasis infection
6. The federal health insurance program for active and retired service members, their families, and the survivors of service members.
7. Fluid released during ejaculation that contains sperm along with fluids produced by the prostate gland and the seminal vesicles
12. The limit per year for coverage under certain available healthcare services for Medicare enrollees.
13. A government insurance program started in 1965 to provide healthcare coverage for persons over 65 and eligible people with disabilities.
14. A poisonous form of oxygen that is present in the earth's upper atmosphere, where it helps to screen the earth from damaging ultraviolet rays
15. A surgical technique in which the flow of blood or another body fluid is redirected around a blockage
16. A hormone that stimulates the release of gastric acid in the stomach
17. the specialty that provides comprehensive and ongoing medical care to all members of the family unit

DOWN

2. This refers to medical care and treatment for persons who are terminally ill.
3. This term refers to a provider's relationship with a health insurance company.
4. the diagnosis and treatment of disorders of the heart and major blood vessels
5. Abnormal buildup of fluid in the body, which may cause visible swelling
8. This act established guidelines and requirements for health and life insurance policies including appeals and disclosure of grievances.
9. The soft tissue inside of a tooth that contains blood vessels and nerves
10. A salt solution or any substance that contains salt
11. An unaware clenching or grinding of the teeth, usually during sleep

A. Cardiology
B. Bruxism
C. Saline
D. Bypass
E. ERISA
F. TRICARE
G. Ozone
H. Family Practice
I. Edema
J. Gastrin
K. Pulp
L. Hospice
M. Semen
N. Utilization Limit
O. In Network
P. Thrush
Q. Medicare

22. Using the Across and Down clues, write the correct words in the numbered grid below.

ACROSS

1. The roof of the mouth
4. Occurs when an insurance company finds there is insufficient evidence on a claim to prove that a provider performed coded medical services and so they reduce or remove those codes.
6. Any service administered in a hospital or other healthcare facility other than room and board.
9. The colored part of the eye
11. This term refers to the discrepancy between the limits of healthcare insurance coverage and the Medicare Part D coverage limits for prescription drugs.
13. A provider within a health insurance company's network that has contracted with the company to provide discounted services to a patient covered under the company's plan.
15. This refers to the amount a patient owes a provider after an insurance company pays for their portion of the medical expenses.

DOWN

1. A persisting fear of and desire to avoid something
2. A term describing something related to or caused by a virus
3. The area of the retina that allows fine details to be observed at the center of vision
4. A document that summarizes the services, treatments, payments, and charges that a patient received on a given day.
5. A lump filled with either fluid or soft material, occurring in any organ or tissue
7. A drug that causes the pupil to constrict
8. A measure of the acidic or basic character of a substance
10. The smallest known disease- causing microorganism
12. A small lump of tissue that is usually abnormal
14. The opening at the center of the iris in the eye that constricts (contracts) and dilates (widens) in response to light

A. Viral
B. Pupil
C. Macula
D. Donut Hole
E. Miotic
F. Nodule
G. pH
H. Day Sheet
I. Ancillary Services
J. Patient Responsibility
K. Phobia
L. Virus
M. Downcoding
N. Palate
O. Network Provider
P. Iris
Q. Cyst

23. Using the Across and Down clues, write the correct words in the numbered grid below.

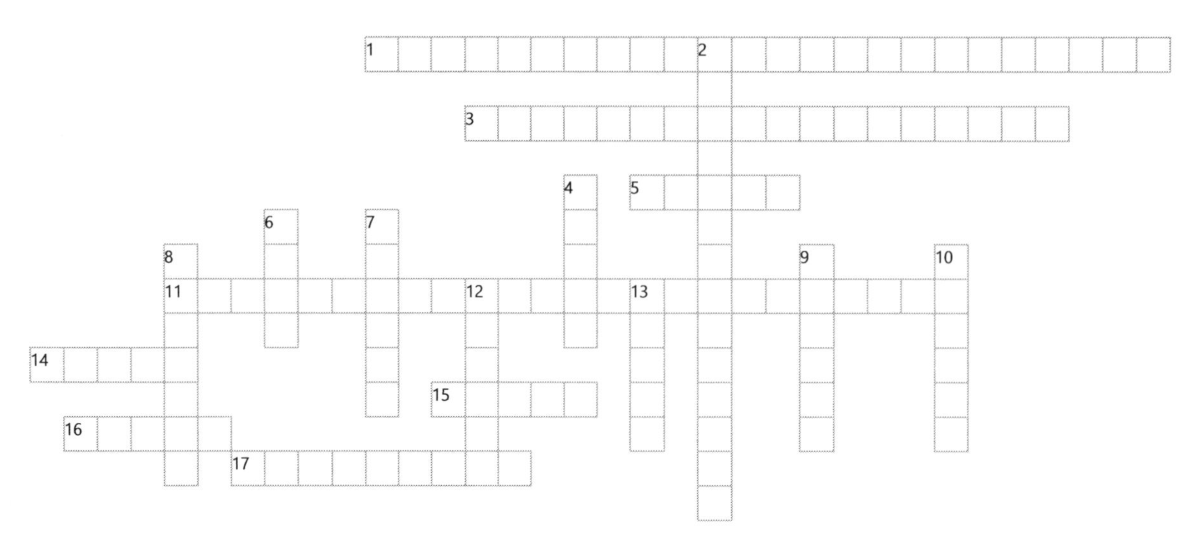

ACROSS

1. A formal request typically submitted by an insurance carrier to determine if other health coverage exists for a patient.
3. The amount a patient is required to pay.
5. Healthy tissue that is used to replace diseased or defective tissue
11. A fee for nursing services a patient is charged during the course of receiving healthcare.
14. The bone located between the hip and the knee
15. The beginning of the large intestine, which is connected to the appendix at its lower end
16. Tiny, hairlike structures on the outside of some cells, providing mobility
17. A document used by healthcare staff and physicians to write down information about a patient receiving care.

DOWN

2. the medical and surgical care for diseases of the ears, nose and throat (ENT)
4. The term used to refer to an unborn child from 8 weeks after fertilization to birth
6. A contagious, harmless growth caused by a virus that occurs on the skin or a mucous membrane
7. The double- layered membrane that lines the lungs and chest cavity and allows for lung movement during breathing
8. A noncancerous tumor of the uterus made up of smooth muscle and connective tissue
9. Mucus and other material produced by the lining of the respiratory tract; also called sputum
10. The bulging of an organ or tissue through a weakened area in the muscle wall
12. Occurs when a patient or a provider tries to convince an insurance company to pay for healthcare after it has decided not to cover costs for someone on a claim.
13. A surgically formed opening on a body surface

A. Graft
B. Wart
C. Maximum Out of Pocket
D. Femur
E. Stoma
F. Fibroid
G. Appeal
H. Superbill
I. Phlegm
J. Incremental Nursing Charge
K. Fetus
L. Pleura
M. Cecum
N. Otolaryngology
O. Cilia
P. Hernia
Q. Duplicate Coverage Inquiry

24. Using the Across and Down clues, write the correct words in the numbered grid below.

ACROSS

1. The person who pays for a patient's medical expenses, also known as the guarantor.
5. A medical condition a patient had before receiving coverage from an insurance company.
8. Abnormal buildup of fluid in the body, which may cause visible swelling
9. Refers to the ratio of payments received relative to the total amount owed to providers.
11. The millions of fingerlike projections on the lining of the small intestine that aid in the absorption of food
12. The infection of a wound or tissue with bacteria, causing the spread of the bacteria into the bloodstream
14. The lowest section of the small intestine, which attaches to the large intestine
15. The abbreviation for diagnosis codes, also known as ICD -9 codes.
16. Providers, patients, or insurance companies may be found fraudulent if they are deliberately achieving their ends through misrepresentation, dishonesty, and general illegal activity.
17. The diagnosis and treatment of acute and chronic diseases and conditions of the respiratory system, such as bronchitis, asthma, emphysema and occupational lung disease

DOWN

2. The column of bones and cartilage running along the midline of the back that surrounds and protects the spinal cord and supports the head
3. An unaware clenching or grinding of the teeth, usually during sleep
4. The sum an insurance company will reimburse to cover a healthcare service or procedure.
6. A coiled organ in the inner ear that plays a large role in hearing by picking up sound vibrations and transmitting them as electrical signals
7. Occurring at an abnormal position or time
10. The technique of creating pictures of structures inside of the body using x-rays, ultrasound waves, or magnetic fields
13. The enzyme found in gastric juice that helps digest protein

A. Ectopic
B. Ileum
C. Allowed Amount
D. Pre existing Condition
E. Pulmonary Medicine
F. Pepsin
G. Spine
H. Villi
I. Imaging
J. Fraud
K. Sepsis
L. Edema
M. Dx
N. Cochlea
O. Responsible Party
P. Collection Ratio
Q. Bruxism

25. Using the Across and Down clues, write the correct words in the numbered grid below.

ACROSS

1. An organ, tissue, or device surgically inserted and left in the body
6. The organization responsible for establishing guidelines and investigating fraud and misinformation within the healthcare industry.
11. A disorder characterized by inflamed airways and difficulty breathing
12. The millions of fingerlike projections on the lining of the small intestine that aid in the absorption of food
14. An agent that is believed to cause several degenerative brain diseases
15. Instruments resembling tweezers that are used to handle objects or tissue during surgery
16. A characteristic sound of blood flowing irregularly through the heart
17. The group of bones in the lower part of the trunk that support the upper body and protect the abdominal organs
18. The largest organization of physicians in the U.S. dedicated to improving the quality of healthcare administered by providers across the country.

DOWN

2. the administration of medications as a means to block pain or diminish consciousness for surgery, usually by injection or inhalation
3. A document used by healthcare staff and physicians to write down information about a patient receiving care.
4. This is when a provider refuses to accept Medicare payments as a sufficient amount for the services rendered to a patient.
5. the diagnosis and treatment of diseases and disorders of the digestive system, including the liver, stomach and intestines, and medical conditions such as ulcers, tumors and colitis
7. Involuntary contraction of genital muscles experienced at the peak of sexual excitement
8. The basic unit of dna, which is responsible for passing genetic information
9. the specialized care and treatment of a newborn up to six weeks of age
10. The medical term for nearsightedness
13. A birth defect in which a normal body opening or canal is absent

A. Implant
B. Prion
C. Superbill
D. Forceps
E. Office of Inspector General
F. American Medical Association
G. Asthma
H. Murmur
I. Anesthesiology
J. Orgasm
K. Villi
L. Myopia
M. Pelvis
N. Non participation
O. Gene
P. Atresia
Q. Neonatology
R. Gastroenterology

26. Using the Across and Down clues, write the correct words in the numbered grid below.

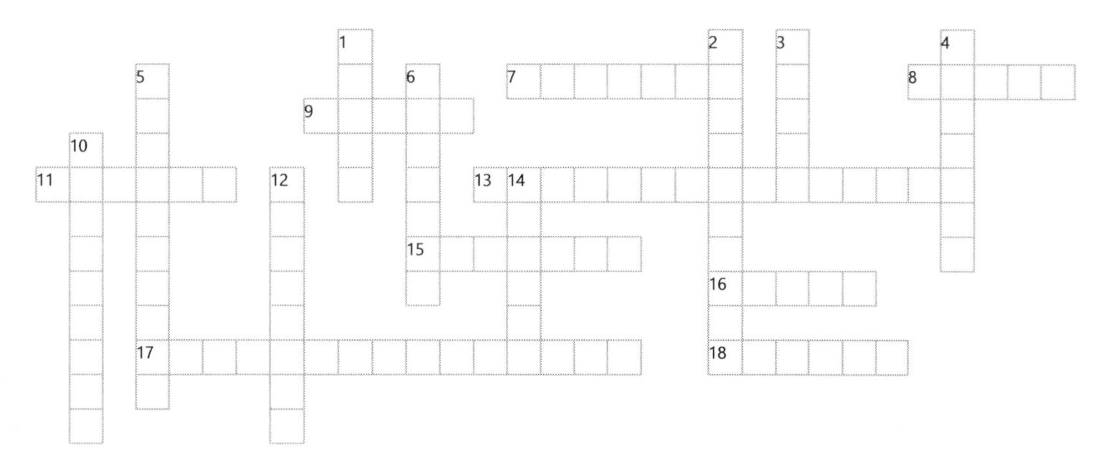

ACROSS

7. A groove or slit on the body or in an organ
8. A milky fluid containing white blood cells, proteins, and fats
9. An open sore that occurs on the skin or on a mucous membrane because of the destruction of surface tissue
11. An infectious viral disease primarily affecting animals; can be transmitted to humans through an infected animal's bite
13. A plan provided by an employer to provide healthcare options to a large group of employees.
15. The structure of bodies; commonly refers to the study of body structure
16. One of the two bones that form the hip on either side of the body
17. Refers to the ratio of payments received relative to the total amount owed to providers.
18. The infection of a wound or tissue with bacteria, causing the spread of the bacteria into the bloodstream

DOWN

1. The outer, visible portion of the female genitals
2. The care and treatment of infants, children, and adolescents
3. An artificially constructed or an abnormal passage connecting two usually separate structures in the body
4. Difficulty breathing
5. the treatment of diseases and internal disorders of the elderly
6. Supplemental health insurance under Medicaid for eligible persons who need help covering co-pays, deductibles, and other large fees.
10. The use of radiation, ultrasound, X-rays, computerized tomography, magnetic resonance imaging, mammography, and other imaging technologies to diagnose diseases and internal disorders
12. A document that summarizes the services, treatments, payments, and charges that a patient received on a given day.
14. A membrane lining the inside of the back of the eye that contains light-sensitive nerve cells that convert focused light into nerve impulses, making vision possible

A. Ulcer
B. Vulva
C. Geriatrics
D. Lymph
E. Fissure
F. Retina
G. Ilium
H. Anatomy
I. Radiology
J. Rabies
K. Pediatrics
L. Dyspnea
M. Collection Ratio
N. Shunt
O. Sepsis
P. Day Sheet
Q. Medigap
R. Group Health Plan

27. Using the Across and Down clues, write the correct words in the numbered grid below.

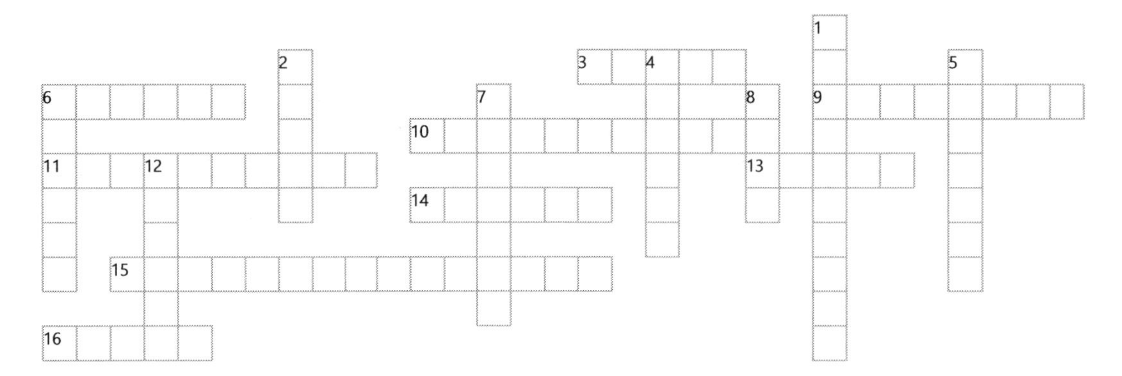

ACROSS

3. A colorless, odorless, tasteless radioactive gas that is produced by materials in soil, rocks, and building materials
6. Abnormally pale skin
9. This is when a provider recommends another provider to a patient to receive specialized treatment.
10. Standards for privacy regarding a patient's medical history and all related events, treatments, and data as outlined by HIPAA.
11. This term refers to healthcare treatment that doesn't require an overnight hospital stay, including a routine visit to a primary care doctor or a non-invasive surgery.
13. One of the two bones that form the hip on either side of the body
14. The tearing or stretching of the ligaments in a joint, characterized by pain, swelling, and an inability to move the joint
15. A provider within a health insurance company's network that has contracted with the company to provide discounted services to a patient covered under the company's plan.
16. A surgically formed opening on a body surface

DOWN

1. the diagnosis and treatment of disorders of the heart and major blood vessels
2. A group of common infections occurring on the skin, hair, and nails that are caused by a fungus
4. The inner skin layer
5. An unaware clenching or grinding of the teeth, usually during sleep
6. A persisting fear of and desire to avoid something
7. A noncancerous tumor of the uterus made up of smooth muscle and connective tissue
8. A blood vessel that carries blood toward the heart
12. Mucus and other material produced by the lining of the respiratory tract; also called sputum

A. Phobia
B. Dermis
C. Sprain
D. Tinea
E. Ilium
F. Fibroid
G. Pallor
H. Privacy Rule
I. Referral
J. Radon
K. Phlegm
L. Stoma
M. Bruxism
N. Outpatient
O. Cardiology
P. Network Provider
Q. Vein

28. Using the Across and Down clues, write the correct words in the numbered grid below.

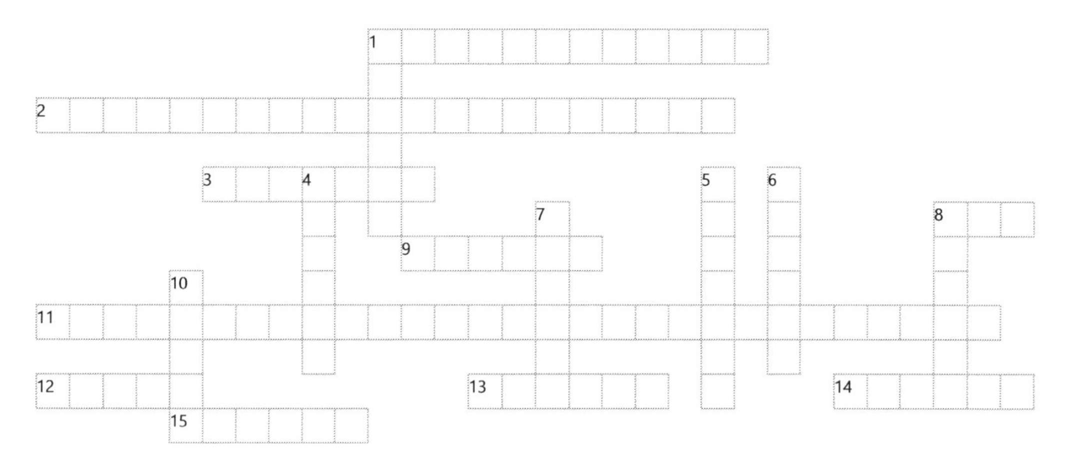

ACROSS

1. When a patient does their own research to find a provider and acts outside of their primary care physician's referral.
2. Refers to a binding agree between a provider, patient, and insurance company wherein the provider agrees to charges that it will write off on behalf of the patient.
3. An organ located in the pelvis whose function is to collect and store urine until it is expelled
8. Density lipoprotein- a type of lipoprotein that is the major carrier of cholesterol in the blood, with high levels associated with narrowing of the arteries and heart disease
9. A substance that causes vomiting
11. Networks of healthcare providers that offer healthcare plans to people for medical services exclusively in their network.
12. A colorless, odorless, tasteless radioactive gas that is produced by materials in soil, rocks, and building materials
13. The infection of a wound or tissue with bacteria, causing the spread of the bacteria into the bloodstream
14. A surgical technique in which the flow of blood or another body fluid is redirected around a blockage
15. The chest

DOWN

1. An organ located in the upper left abdomen behind the ribs that removes and destroys old red blood cells and helps fight infection
4. The inner skin layer
5. An organ, tissue, or device surgically inserted and left in the body
6. The bulging of an organ or tissue through a weakened area in the muscle wall
7. Involuntary sudden contraction of the diaphragm along with the closing of the vocal cords, producing a "hiccup" sound
8. A noncancerous tumor of fatty tissue
10. A device used to hold tissues in place, such as to support a skin graft

A. Contractual Adjustment
B. Spleen
C. Low
D. Bladder
E. Hernia
F. Dermis
G. Emetic
H. Thorax
I. Radon
J. Bypass
K. Sepsis
L. Stent
M. Hiccup
N. Health Maintenance Organization
O. Self Referral
P. Implant
Q. Lipoma

29. Using the Across and Down clues, write the correct words in the numbered grid below.

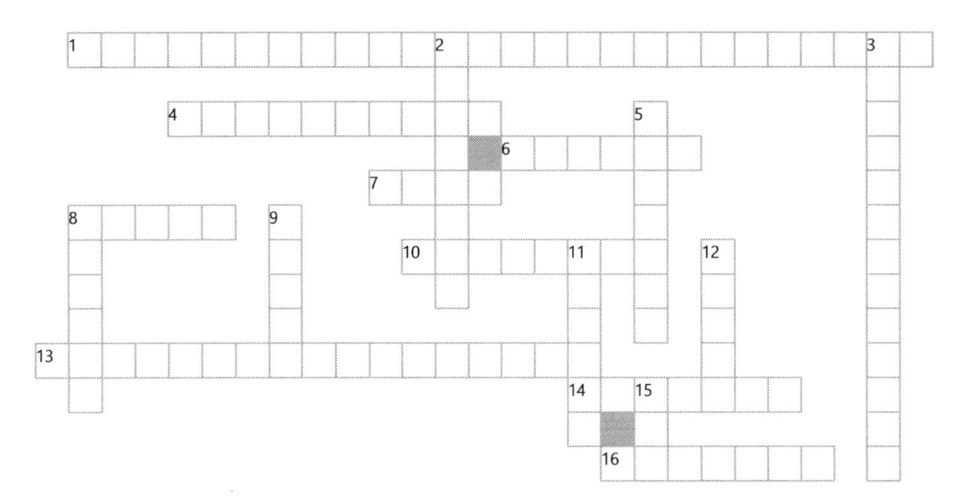

ACROSS

1. The digital version of EOB, which specifies the details of payments made on a claim either by an insurance company or required by the patient.
4. The diagnosis and treatment of mental, emotional and behavioral disorders
6. A small, round organ making up the neck of the uterus and separating it from the vagina
7. A yellow-green liquid produced in the liver whose function is to remove waste from the liver and break down fats as food is digested
8. A group of cells or an organ that produces substances (such as hormones and enzyme) that are used by the body
10. The end date for an insurance policy contract, or the date after which a person no longer receives or is no longer eligible for health insurance with company.
13. the specialty that includes treatment of any symptom, illness or injury requiring urgent evaluation and
14. The passageways that air moves through while traveling in and out of the lungs during breathing
16. A hormone that stimulates the release of gastric acid in the stomach

DOWN

2. A person covered by a health insurance plan.
3. Facilities that review and correct medical claims as necessary before sending them to insurance companies for final processing.
5. A measure of a person's physical strength, flexibility, and endurance
8. A brain tumor arising from cells that support nerve cells
9. Waves of pain in the abdomen that increase in strength, disappear, and return
11. Occurs when a patient or a provider tries to convince an insurance company to pay for healthcare after it has decided not to cover costs for someone on a claim.
12. A mental disorder characterized by extreme excitement, happiness, overactivity, and agitation
15. Ribonucleic acid, which helps to decode and process the information contained in dna

A. RNA
B. Enrollee
C. Airways
D. Bile
E. Gland
F. Mania
G. Glioma
H. Fitness
I. Term Date
J. Gastrin
K. Colic
L. Emergency Medicine
M. Psychiatry
N. Appeal
O. Electronic Remittance Advice
P. Cervix
Q. Clearinghouse

30. Using the Across and Down clues, write the correct words in the numbered grid below.

ACROSS

3. A method of transferring money electronically from a patient's bank account to a provider or an insurance carrier.
6. A unique number a patient or a company may have to produce for billing purposes in order to receive healthcare from a provider.
8. A measure of the acidic or basic character of a substance
9. The sum an insurance company will reimburse to cover a healthcare service or procedure.
10. Can be a secondary policy or another insurance company that covers a patient's healthcare costs after receiving coverage from their primary insurance.
13. The organization responsible for establishing guidelines and investigating fraud and misinformation within the healthcare industry.
15. The clear, dome-shaped front portion of the eye's outer covering
16. A hard plaster or fiberglass shell that molds to a body part such as an arm and holds it in place for proper healing
17. Procedures and services not covered by a person's health insurance plan.

DOWN

1. Payment made by the patient for healthcare at the time they receive it at a provider's facilities.
2. A tumor made of blood vessels or lymph vessels that is not cancerous
4. A process by which insurance claims are checked for errors before being sent to an insurance company for final processing.
5. The unit of a hospital reserved for patients that need immediate treatment and close monitoring by healthcare professionals for serious illnesses, conditions, and injuries.
7. A hard, fluid-filled pad along the inside joint of the big toe
11. A membrane lining the inside of the back of the eye that contains light-sensitive nerve cells that convert focused light into nerve impulses, making vision possible
12. A drug that causes the pupil to constrict
14. Tiny, hairlike structures on the outside of some cells, providing mobility

A. Self Pay	B. Allowed Amount	C. Tax Identification Number
D. Scrubbing	E. Electronic Funds Transfer	F. pH
G. Retina	H. Office of Inspector General	I. Miotic
J. Cast	K. Cornea	L. Bunion
M. Angioma	N. Cilia	O. Intensive Care
P. Non Covered Charge	Q. Supplemental Insurance	

31. Using the Across and Down clues, write the correct words in the numbered grid below.

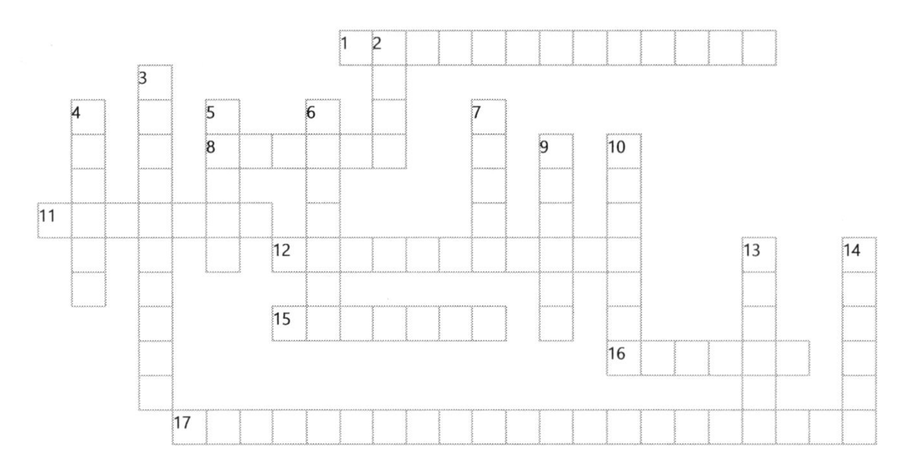

ACROSS

1. The sum an insurance company will reimburse to cover a healthcare service or procedure.
8. An egg cell that has not developed completely
11. A hormone that stimulates the release of gastric acid in the stomach
12. A document that outlines the costs associated for each medical service designated by a CPT code.
15. Payment made by the patient for healthcare at the time they receive it at a provider's facilities.
16. A thickened area of skin due to consistent pressure or friction, or the area around a bone break where new bone is formed
17. Can be a secondary policy or another insurance company that covers a patient's healthcare costs after receiving coverage from their primary insurance.

DOWN

2. A well-defined, separate part of an organ
3. A fixed payment that a patient makes to a health insurance company or provider to recoup costs incurred from various healthcare services.
4. A surgical technique in which the flow of blood or another body fluid is redirected around a blockage
5. A poisonous substance
6. The practice, maintenance, and study of health
7. A poisonous form of oxygen that is present in the earth's upper atmosphere, where it helps to screen the earth from damaging ultraviolet rays
9. Physical injury or emotional shock
10. Describes a disease that is always present in a certain population of people
13. The double- layered membrane that lines the lungs and chest cavity and allows for lung movement during breathing
14. An element for the formation of thyroid hormones

A. Capitation
B. Fee Schedule
C. Self Pay
D. Lobe
E. Callus
F. Allowed Amount
G. Ozone
H. Endemic
I. Toxin
J. Trauma
K. Oocyte
L. Bypass
M. Gastrin
N. Supplemental Insurance
O. Hygiene
P. Pleura
Q. Iodine

32. Using the Across and Down clues, write the correct words in the numbered grid below.

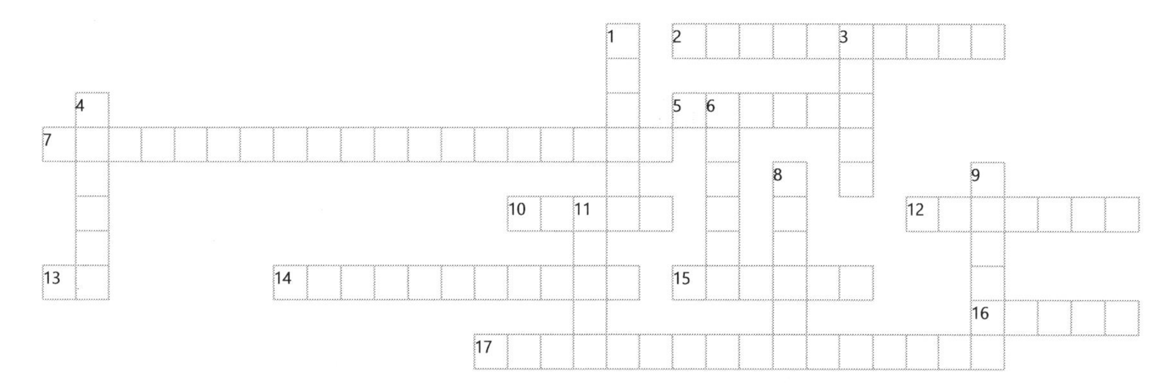

ACROSS

2. The care and treatment of infants, children, and adolescents
5. Mucus and other material produced by the lining of the respiratory tract; also called phlegm
7. The median amount Medicare will repay a provider for certain services and treatments.
10. The amount that must be paid to a provider before they receive any treatment or services.
12. The diagnosis and management, including surgery, of disorders of the urinary tract in both males and females, as well as the male reproductive system
13. The abbreviation for diagnosis codes, also known as ICD -9 codes.
14. Standards for privacy regarding a patient's medical history and all related events, treatments, and data as outlined by HIPAA.
15. A system used to classify sick or injured people according to the severity of their conditions
16. The interval from onset of contractions to birth of a baby
17. the diagnosis and non-surgical treatment of adult health problems

DOWN

1. The clear, dome-shaped front portion of the eye's outer covering
3. An abnormal mass that occurs when cells in a certain area reproduce unchecked
4. A small, round organ making up the neck of the uterus and separating it from the vagina
6. Abnormally pale skin
8. The roof of the mouth
9. A small lump of tissue that is usually abnormal
11. The expansion and contraction of a blood vessel due to the blood pumped through it

A. Triage
B. Pediatrics
C. Cornea
D. Palate
E. Tumor
F. Privacy Rule
G. Co Pay
H. Pulse
I. Dx
J. Pallor
K. Cervix
L. Sputum
M. Internal Medicine
N. Nodule
O. Urology
P. Labor
Q. Relative Value Amount

33. Using the Across and Down clues, write the correct words in the numbered grid below.

ACROSS

1. This is when provider performs another procedure on a patient covered by a CPT code after first performing a different CPT procedure on them.
4. A disorder characterized by inflamed airways and difficulty breathing
5. A maximum sum as explained in a healthcare plan an insurance company will pay for certain services or treatments.
7. An investigation or audit performed to optimize the number of inpatient and outpatient services a provider performs.
12. A small lump of tissue that is usually abnormal
13. An electrocardiogram, which is a record of the electrical impulses that trigger the heartbeat
14. A large blood vessel that carries blood from the heart to tissues and organs in the body
15. the specialty that provides comprehensive and ongoing medical care to all members of the family unit
16. The sum a person pays to an insurance company on a regular (usually monthly or yearly) basis to receive health insurance.
17. A process similar to preauthorization whereby patients must check with insurance companies to see if a desired healthcare treatment or service is deemed medically necessary

DOWN

2. This term refers to the discrepancy between the limits of healthcare insurance coverage and the Medicare Part D coverage limits for prescription drugs.
3. The roof of the mouth
6. Small eight-legged animals, many of which burrow and feed on blood
8. An involuntary, rhythmic, shaking movement caused by alternating contraction and relaxation of muscles
9. The smallest known disease- causing microorganism
10. A contagious, harmless growth caused by a virus that occurs on the skin or a mucous membrane
11. A substance that causes vomiting

A. Virus
B. Wart
C. Palate
D. Asthma
E. Tremor
F. Emetic
G. Artery
H. Pre Certification
I. Pre determination
J. Secondary Procedure
K. ECG
L. Nodule
M. Family Practice
N. Premium
O. Utilization Review
P. Donut Hole
Q. Mites

34. Using the Across and Down clues, write the correct words in the numbered grid below.

ACROSS

3. Damage to part of the brain because of a lack of blood supply or the rupturing of a blood vessel
4. The diagnosis and treatment of circulatory problems of the extremities, especially the legs
10. An organ located in the pelvis whose function is to collect and store urine until it is expelled
11. Oncology
14. Standards for privacy regarding a patient's medical history and all related events, treatments, and data as outlined by HIPAA.
16. When a patient does their own research to find a provider and acts outside of their primary care physician's referral.
17. A term describing something related to or caused by a virus
18. Occurring at an abnormal position or time

DOWN

1. The diagnosis and management, including surgery, of disorders of the urinary tract in both males and females, as well as the male reproductive system
2. The muscular passage connecting the uterus with the outside genitals
5. A possibly life-threatening condition in which breathing stops, for either a short or long period of time
6. A term used to describe something related to a fever, such as febrile seizures
7. A measure of the acidic or basic character of a substance
8. A pus- filled abscess in the follicle of an eyelash
9. The clear, dome-shaped front portion of the eye's outer covering
12. A high- pitched sound produced during breathing because of narrowing of the airways
13. The main part of the large intestine, between the cecum and the rectum
15. Density lipoprotein- a type of lipoprotein that is the major carrier of cholesterol in the blood, with high levels associated with narrowing of the arteries and heart disease

A. Urology
B. Viral
C. Cornea
D. Stroke
E. Ectopic
F. Colon
G. Hematology
H. Wheeze
I. Privacy Rule
J. Vascular Surgery
K. Vagina
L. Bladder
M. Low
N. pH
O. Febrile
P. Stye
Q. Apnea
R. Self Referral

35. Using the Across and Down clues, write the correct words in the numbered grid below.

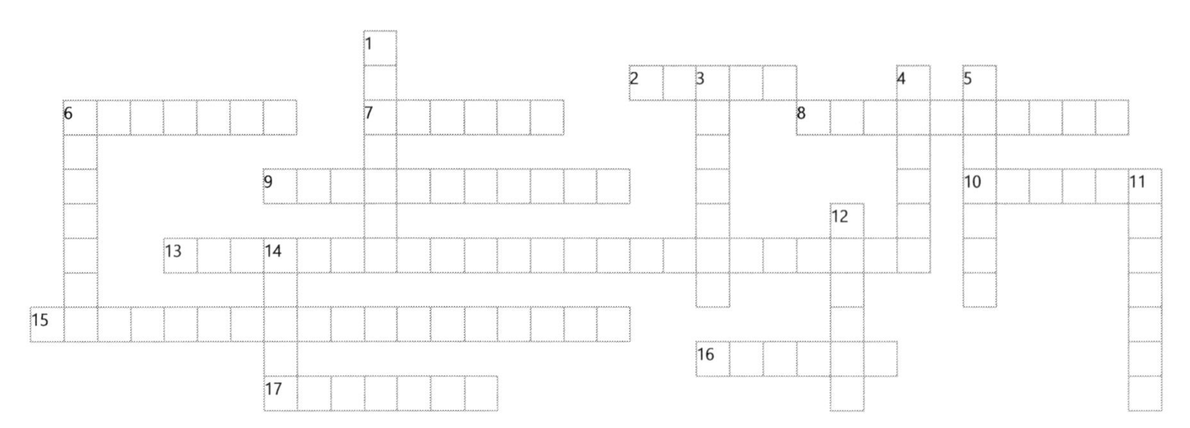

ACROSS

2. The beginning of the large intestine, which is connected to the appendix at its lower end
6. A painless sore that has a thick, rubbery base and a defined edge
7. A salt solution or any substance that contains salt
8. Oncology
9. A number given to a patient by their insurance carrier that identifies the group or plan under which they are covered.
10. A noncancerous tumor made of mucous material and fibrous connective tissue
13. This refers to medical implements that can be reused such as stretchers, wheelchairs, canes, crutches, and bedpans.
15. This is when provider performs another procedure on a patient covered by a CPT code after first performing a different CPT procedure on them.
16. A persisting fear of and desire to avoid something
17. The passageways that air moves through while traveling in and out of the lungs during breathing

DOWN

1. A groove or slit on the body or in an organ
3. A plentiful mineral in the body and the basic component of teeth and bones
4. Not obstructed; open
5. A chemical produced by a gland or tissue that is released into the bloodstream
6. A unit that is used to measure the energy content in food
11. The examination of a body following death, possibly to determine the cause of death or for research
12. The thick, greasy substance that covers the skin of a newborn baby
14. The two upper chambers of the heart

A. Group Number
B. Hematology
C. Autopsy
D. Phobia
E. Durable Medical Equipment
F. Airways
G. Calcium
H. Calorie
I. Myxoma
J. Hormone
K. Patent
L. Chancre
M. Vernix
N. Secondary Procedure
O. Saline
P. Cecum
Q. Atria
R. Fissure

36. Using the Across and Down clues, write the correct words in the numbered grid below.

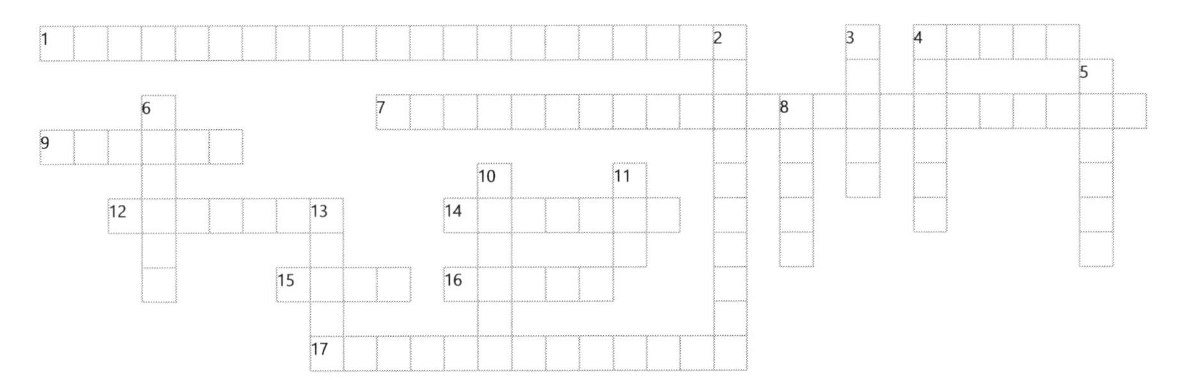

ACROSS

1. A document attached to a processed medical claim wherein the insurance company explains the services they will cover for a patient's healthcare treatments.
4. The thicker of the two long bones in the lower leg; commonly called the shin
7. Whoever owes the healthcare provider money has financial responsibility for the services rendered.
9. An egg cell that has not developed completely
12. A coiled organ in the inner ear that plays a large role in hearing by picking up sound vibrations and transmitting them as electrical signals
14. A chemical produced by a gland or tissue that is released into the bloodstream
15. A waste product of the metabolism of proteins that is formed by the liver and secreted by the kidneys
16. The largest organ in the body, producing many essential chemicals and regulating the levels of most vital substances in the blood
17. The sum an insurance company will reimburse to cover a healthcare service or procedure.

DOWN

2. A physician or medical assistant with expertise in a specific area of medicine.
3. A poisonous substance produced by certain animals
4. A system used to classify sick or injured people according to the severity of their conditions
5. The hollow female reproductive organ in which a fertilized egg is implanted and a fetus develops
6. The cell that results when an egg is fertilized by a sperm
8. The opening at the center of the iris in the eye that constricts (contracts) and dilates (widens) in response to light
10. An element for the formation of thyroid hormones
11. Deoxyribonucleic acid; responsible for passing genetic information in nearly all organisms
13. The two upper chambers of the heart

A. DNA
B. Explanation of Benefits
C. Iodine
D. Venom
E. Liver
F. Uterus
G. Cochlea
H. Urea
I. Triage
J. Hormone
K. Oocyte
L. Financial Responsibility
M. Zygote
N. Pupil
O. Tibia
P. Atria
Q. Specialist
R. Allowed Amount

37. Using the Across and Down clues, write the correct words in the numbered grid below.

ACROSS

1. Refers to the discrepancy between a provider's fee for healthcare services and the amount that an insurance company is willing to pay for those services that a patient is not responsible for.
3. The diagnosis and treatment of acute and chronic diseases and conditions of the respiratory system, such as bronchitis, asthma, emphysema and occupational lung disease
9. An abnormal passageway from one organ to another or from an organ to the body surface
11. A disorder marked by high levels of uric acid in the blood
12. A sample of cells spread across a glass slide to be examined through a microscope
14. The double- layered membrane that lines the lungs and chest cavity and allows for lung movement during breathing
15. Occurs when a patient or a provider tries to convince an insurance company to pay for healthcare after it has decided not to cover costs for someone on a claim.
16. The individual covered under a group policy. For instance, an employee of a company with a group health policy would be one of many subscribers on that policy.
17. The application process for a provider to coordinate with an insurance company.

DOWN

2. A vibration felt when the hand is placed flat on the chest; caused by abnormal blood flow through the heart as a result of disease
4. A term used to describe something situated on or near the midline of the body or a body structure
5. Another term for a nerve cell
6. This refers to medical care and treatment for persons who are terminally ill.
7. A hard plaster or fiberglass shell that molds to a body part such as an arm and holds it in place for proper healing
8. A thick, yellowish or greenish fluid that contains dead white blood cells, tissues, and bacteria; occurs at the site of a bacterial infection
10. A bundle of fibers that transmit electrical messages between the brain and areas of the body
11. An artificial feeding technique in which liquids are passed into the stomach by way of a tube inserted through the nose
13. A form of phototherapy that combines the use of psoralens and ultraviolet light to treat skin disorders

A. Subscriber	B. Cast	C. Thrill	D. Fistula
E. Medial	F. Pus	G. Nerve	H. PUVA
I. Pleura	J. Credentialing	K. Gout	L. Write Off
M. Smear	N. Neuron	O. Gavage	P. Hospice
Q. Pulmonary Medicine	R. Appeal		

38. Using the Across and Down clues, write the correct words in the numbered grid below.

ACROSS

1. Payment made by the patient for healthcare at the time they receive it at a provider's facilities.
8. Muscle damage resulting from excessive stretching or forceful contraction
9. A term used to describe a child in the womb from fertilization to 8 weeks following fertilization
10. A group of cells or an organ that produces substances (such as hormones and enzyme) that are used by the body
12. This term is used in ICD-9 codes to describe conditions with unspecified diagnoses.
14. A chemical, originating in a cell, that regulates reactions in the body
15. A term describing something related to or caused by a virus
16. Abnormal crackling or bubbling sounds heard in the lungs during breathing
17. The sum an insurance company will reimburse to cover a healthcare service or procedure.

DOWN

2. An area of buildup of fat deposits in an artery, causing narrowing of the artery and possibly heart disease
3. A noncancerous tumor of the uterus made up of smooth muscle and connective tissue
4. A painless sore that has a thick, rubbery base and a defined edge
5. The diagnosis and management, including surgery, of disorders of the urinary tract in both males and females, as well as the male reproductive system
6. A structure that allows fluid flow in only one direction
7. A brown to dark-brown spot on the skin that can be flat or raised
11. The bone located between the hip and the knee
13. One of the two bones that form the hip on either side of the body

A. Embryo
B. Enzyme
C. Fibroid
D. Viral
E. Strain
F. Allowed Amount
G. Valve
H. Ilium
I. Gland
J. Chancre
K. Plaque
L. Rales
M. Mole
N. Urology
O. Not Otherwise Specified
P. Self Pay
Q. Femur

39. Using the Across and Down clues, write the correct words in the numbered grid below.

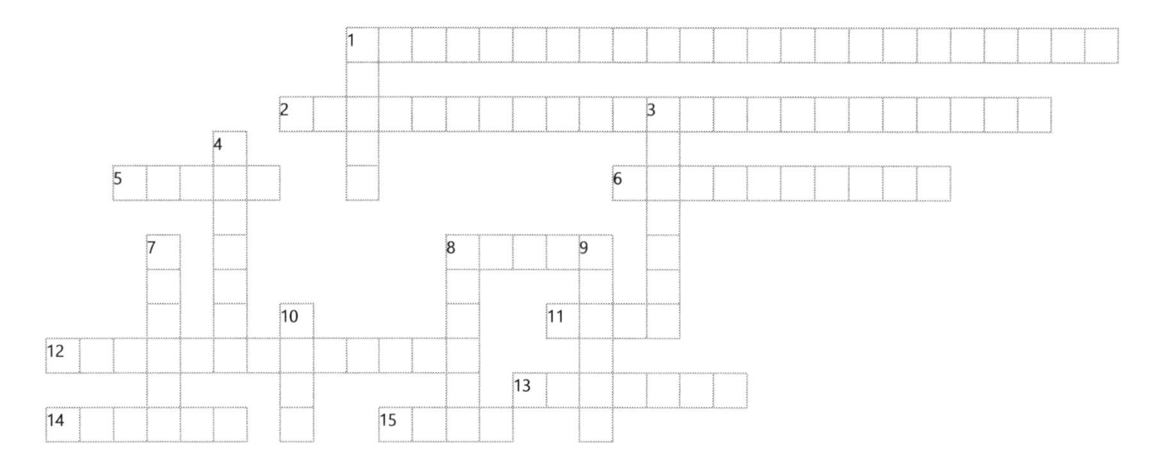

ACROSS

1. The name for the organization or individual that manages healthcare group benefits, claims, and administrative duties on behalf of a group plan or a company with a group plan.
2. A unique number a patient or a company may have to produce for billing purposes in order to receive healthcare from a provider.
5. Law passed in 1996 with an aim to improve the scope of healthcare services and establish regulations for securing healthcare records from unwanted parties.
6. Occurs when an insurance company finds there is insufficient evidence on a claim to prove that a provider performed coded medical services and so they reduce or remove those codes.
8. Tiny, hairlike structures on the outside of some cells, providing mobility
11. A desire to eat materials that are not food
12. The sum an insurance company will reimburse to cover a healthcare service or procedure.
13. A disorder in which a person eats large amounts of food then forces vomiting or uses laxatives to prevent weight gain (called binging and purging)
14. A large blood vessel that carries blood from the heart to tissues and organs in the body
15. A hard plaster or fiberglass shell that molds to a body part such as an arm and holds it in place for proper healing

DOWN

1. A poisonous substance
3. A bacterial infection of the small intestine that causes severe watery diarrhea, dehydration, and possibly death
4. A unit that is used to measure the energy content in food
7. Damage to part of the brain because of a lack of blood supply or the rupturing of a blood vessel
8. Sexual intercourse
9. Medical term for the armpit
10. A contagious, harmless growth caused by a virus that occurs on the skin or a mucous membrane

A. Cilia
B. Cast
C. HIPAA
D. Toxin
E. Artery
F. Bulimia
G. Downcoding
H. Cholera
I. Tax Identification Number
J. Coitus
K. Allowed Amount
L. Wart
M. Pica
N. Stroke
O. Calorie
P. Axilla
Q. Third Party Administrator

40. Using the Across and Down clues, write the correct words in the numbered grid below.

ACROSS

3. These are the entities that offer healthcare services to patients, including hospitals, physicians, and private clinics, hospices, nursing homes, and other healthcare facilities.
7. The amount that must be paid to a provider before they receive any treatment or services.
8. The organization responsible for establishing guidelines and investigating fraud and misinformation within the healthcare industry.
11. A mental disorder characterized by extreme excitement, happiness, overactivity, and agitation
12. A device used to hold tissues in place, such as to support a skin graft
13. A tumor made of blood vessels or lymph vessels that is not cancerous
14. Sexual intercourse
15. The document attached to a processed claim that explains the information regarding coverage and payments on a claim.
16. Whoever owes the healthcare provider money has financial responsibility for the services rendered.

DOWN

1. A process by which insurance claims are checked for errors before being sent to an insurance company for final processing.
2. Refers to healthcare services or treatments that a patient requires to treat a serious medical condition or illness.
4. A term describing something related to or caused by a virus
5. A formal medical billing term that refers to insurance claims that haven't been paid or balances owed by patients overdue by more than 30 days.
6. A contagious, harmless growth caused by a virus that occurs on the skin or a mucous membrane
9. The bone located between the hip and the knee
10. The clear, watery fluid that separates from clotted blood
12. Fluid released during ejaculation that contains sperm along with fluids produced by the prostate gland and the seminal vesicles

A. Viral
B. Femur
C. Remittance Advice
D. Office of Inspector General
E. Serum
F. Coitus
G. Wart
H. Angioma
I. Financial Responsibility
J. Co Pay
K. Aging
L. Semen
M. Medical Necessity
N. Healthcare Provider
O. Mania
P. Scrubbing
Q. Stent

1. Using the Across and Down clues, write the correct words in the numbered grid below.

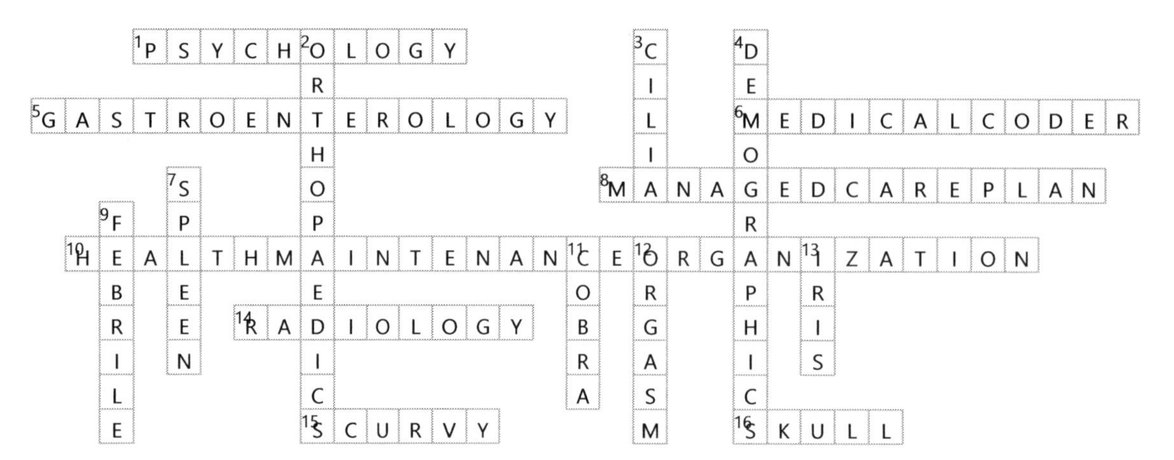

ACROSS

1. The science of dealing with mental processes and their effects on behavior
5. the diagnosis and treatment of diseases and disorders of the digestive system, including the liver, stomach and intestines, and medical conditions such as ulcers, tumors and colitis
6. Responsible for assigning various medical codes to services and healthcare plans described by a physician on a patient's super-bill.
8. A health insurance plan whereby patients can only receive coverage if they see providers who operate in the insurance company's network.
10. Networks of healthcare providers that offer healthcare plans to people for medical services exclusively in their network.
14. The use of radiation, ultrasound, X-rays, computerized tomography, magnetic resonance imaging, mammography, and other imaging technologies to diagnose diseases and internal disorders
15. A disease caused by a lack of vitamin c, characterized by weakness, bleeding and pain in joints and muscles, bleeding gums, and abnormal bone and tooth growth
16. The bones that form the framework of the head and enclose and protect the brain and other sensory organs

DOWN

2. the diagnosis and treatment, including surgery, of diseases and disorders of the musculoskeletal system, including bones, joints, tendons, ligaments, muscles and nerves
3. Tiny, hairlike structures on the outside of some cells, providing mobility
4. The patient's information required for filing a claim, such as age, sex, address, and family information. An insurance company may deny a claim if it contains inaccurate demographics.
7. An organ located in the upper left abdomen behind the ribs that removes and destroys old red blood cells and helps fight infection
9. A term used to describe something related to a fever, such as febrile seizures
11. A federal program that allows a person terminated from their employer to retain health insurance they had with that employer.
12. Involuntary contraction of genital muscles experienced at the peak of sexual excitement
13. The colored part of the eye

A. Gastroenterology
B. Health Maintenance Organization
C. Spleen
D. Managed Care Plan
E. Scurvy
F. Iris
G. Medical Coder
H. Orthopaedics
I. Psychology
J. Radiology
K. Cilia
L. Orgasm
M. Demographics
N. COBRA
O. Skull
P. Febrile

2. Using the Across and Down clues, write the correct words in the numbered grid below.

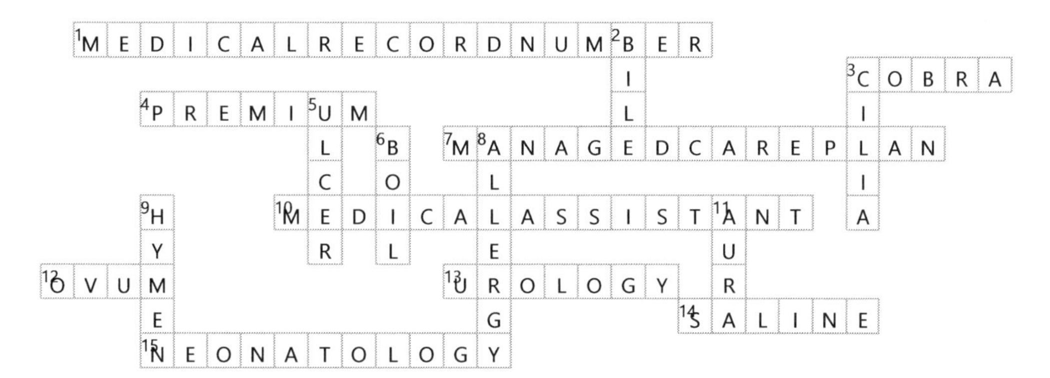

ACROSS

1. A unique number ascribed to a person's medical record so it can be differentiated from other medical records.
3. A federal program that allows a person terminated from their employer to retain health insurance they had with that employer.
4. The sum a person pays to an insurance company on a regular (usually monthly or yearly) basis to receive health insurance.
7. A health insurance plan whereby patients can only receive coverage if they see providers who operate in the insurance company's network.
10. An employee in the healthcare system such as a physician's assistant or a nurse practitioner who perform duties in administration, nursing, and other ancillary care.
12. Another term for an egg cell
13. The diagnosis and management, including surgery, of disorders of the urinary tract in both males and females, as well as the male reproductive system
14. A salt solution or any substance that contains salt
15. the specialized care and treatment of a newborn up to six weeks of age

DOWN

2. A yellow-green liquid produced in the liver whose function is to remove waste from the liver and break down fats as food is digested
3. Tiny, hairlike structures on the outside of some cells, providing mobility
5. An open sore that occurs on the skin or on a mucous membrane because of the destruction of surface tissue
6. An inflamed, raised area of skin that is pus-filled
8. Immunology
9. A thin fold of membrane partly closing the opening of the vagina
11. A "warning" signal that comes before a migraine headache or an epileptic seizure, which might include emotions or sensations of movement or discomfort

A. Urology
B. Ovum
C. Allergy
D. Medical Record Number
E. Ulcer
F. Managed Care Plan
G. Saline
H. Cilia
I. Premium
J. Aura
K. Medical Assistant
L. Neonatology
M. Boil
N. COBRA
O. Hymen
P. Bile

3. Using the Across and Down clues, write the correct words in the numbered grid below.

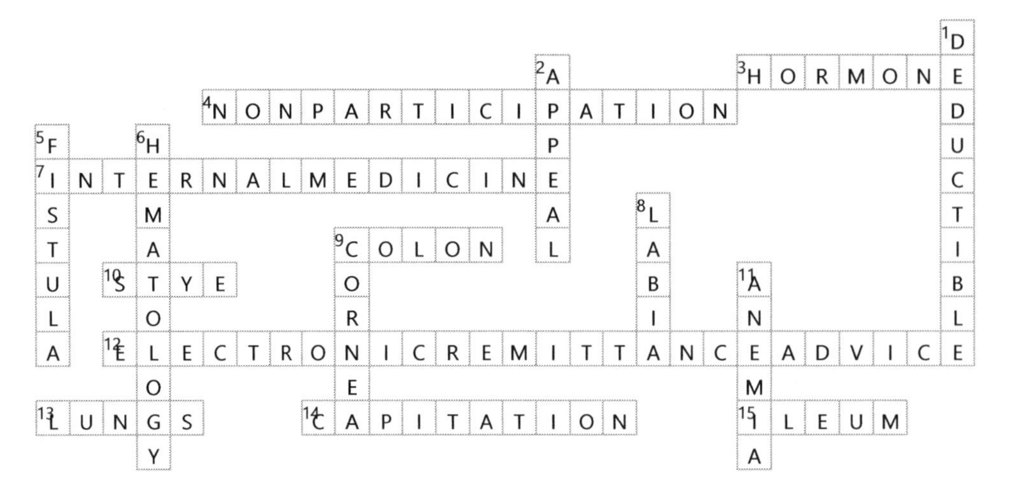

ACROSS

3. A chemical produced by a gland or tissue that is released into the bloodstream
4. This is when a provider refuses to accept Medicare payments as a sufficient amount for the services rendered to a patient.
7. the diagnosis and non-surgical treatment of adult health problems
9. The main part of the large intestine, between the cecum and the rectum
10. A pus- filled abscess in the follicle of an eyelash
12. The digital version of EOB, which specifies the details of payments made on a claim either by an insurance company or required by the patient.
13. Two organs in the chest that take in oxygen from the air and release carbon dioxide
14. A fixed payment that a patient makes to a health insurance company or provider to recoup costs incurred from various healthcare services.
15. The lowest section of the small intestine, which attaches to the large intestine

DOWN

1. The amount a patient must pay before an insurance carrier starts their healthcare coverage.
2. Occurs when a patient or a provider tries to convince an insurance company to pay for healthcare after it has decided not to cover costs for someone on a claim.
5. An abnormal passageway from one organ to another or from an organ to the body surface
6. Oncology
8. The two pairs of skinfolds that protect the opening of the vagina
9. The clear, dome-shaped front portion of the eye's outer covering
11. A condition in which the blood does not contain enough hemoglobin, the compound that carries oxygen from the lungs to other parts of the body

A. Cornea
B. Anemia
C. Lungs
D. Fistula
E. Stye
F. Colon
G. Appeal
H. Deductible
I. Non participation
J. Ileum
K. Hematology
L. Capitation
M. Internal Medicine
N. Labia
O. Electronic Remittance Advice
P. Hormone

4. Using the Across and Down clues, write the correct words in the numbered grid below.

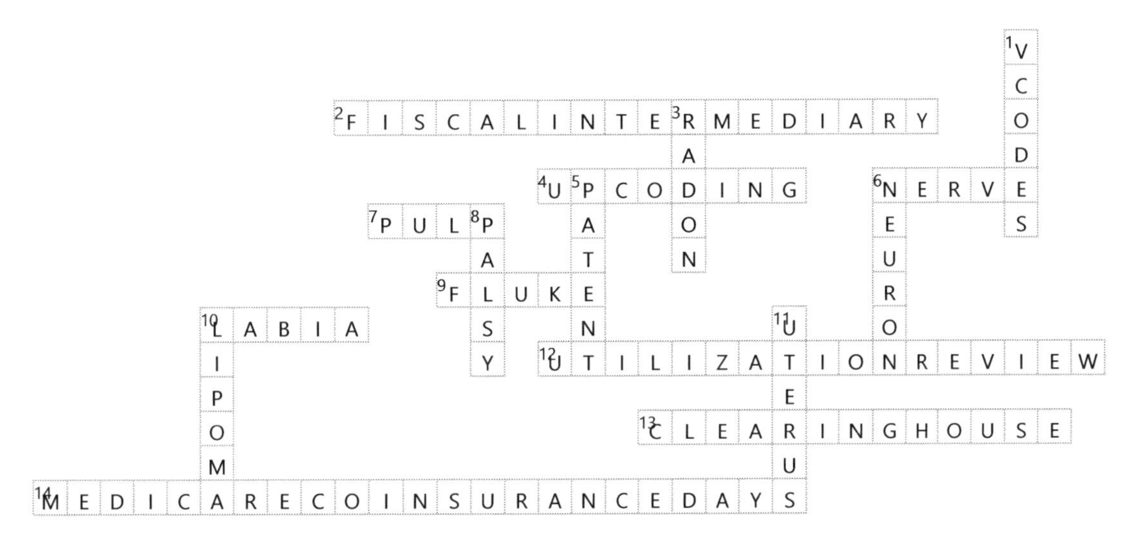

ACROSS

2. The name for Medicare representatives who process Medicare claims.
4. The fraudulent practice of ascribing a higher ICD-9 code to a healthcare procedure in an attempt to get more money than necessary from the insurance company or patient.
6. A bundle of fibers that transmit electrical messages between the brain and areas of the body
7. The soft tissue inside of a tooth that contains blood vessels and nerves
9. A parasitic flatworm that can infest humans
10. The two pairs of skinfolds that protect the opening of the vagina
12. An investigation or audit performed to optimize the number of inpatient and outpatient services a provider performs.
13. Facilities that review and correct medical claims as necessary before sending them to insurance companies for final processing.
14. Referring to 61st through 90th days of inpatient treatment, the law requires that patients pay for a portion of their healthcare during Medicare coinsurance days.

DOWN

1. A codeset under ICD-9-CM used to organize healthcare services rendered for reasons other than illness or injury.
3. A colorless, odorless, tasteless radioactive gas that is produced by materials in soil, rocks, and building materials
5. Not obstructed; open
6. Another term for a nerve cell
8. Loss of sensation or ability to move
10. A noncancerous tumor of fatty tissue
11. The hollow female reproductive organ in which a fertilized egg is implanted and a fetus develops

A. Lipoma
B. Clearinghouse
C. Radon
D. Patent
E. Fiscal Intermediary
F. Upcoding
G. V Codes
H. Uterus
I. Palsy
J. Neuron
K. Pulp
L. Utilization Review
M. Labia
N. Nerve
O. Fluke
P. Medicare Coinsurance Days

5. Using the Across and Down clues, write the correct words in the numbered grid below.

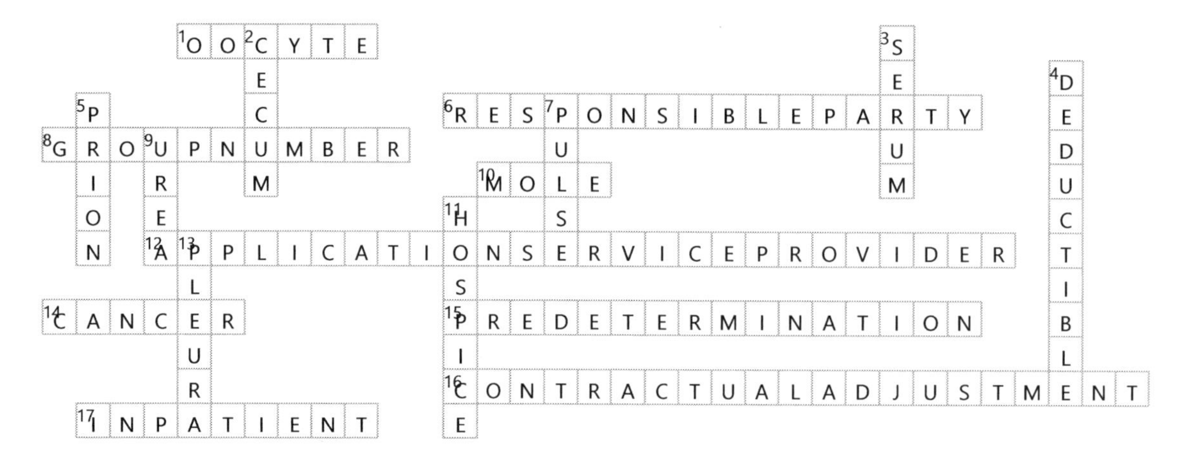

ACROSS

1. An egg cell that has not developed completely
6. The person who pays for a patient's medical expenses, also known as the guarantor.
8. A number given to a patient by their insurance carrier that identifies the group or plan under which they are covered.
10. A brown to dark-brown spot on the skin that can be flat or raised
12. A digital network that allows healthcare providers to access quality medical billing software and technologies without needing to purchase and maintain it themselves.
14. A group of diseases in which cells grow unrestrained in an organ or tissue in the body
15. A maximum sum as explained in a healthcare plan an insurance company will pay for certain services or treatments.
16. Refers to a binding agree between a provider, patient, and insurance company wherein the provider agrees to charges that it will write off on behalf of the patient.
17. Occurs when a person has a stay at a healthcare facility for more than 24 hours.

DOWN

2. The beginning of the large intestine, which is connected to the appendix at its lower end
3. The clear, watery fluid that separates from clotted blood
4. The amount a patient must pay before an insurance carrier starts their healthcare coverage.
5. An agent that is believed to cause several degenerative brain diseases
7. The expansion and contraction of a blood vessel due to the blood pumped through it
9. A waste product of the metabolism of proteins that is formed by the liver and secreted by the kidneys
11. A hospital or an area of a hospital dedicated to treating people who are dying, often of a specific cause
13. The double- layered membrane that lines the lungs and chest cavity and allows for lung movement during breathing

A. Pleura
B. Serum
C. Responsible Party
D. Group Number
E. Deductible
F. Oocyte
G. Hospice
H. Inpatient
I. Mole
J. Cecum
K. Contractual Adjustment
L. Application Service Provider
M. Urea
N. Prion
O. Pre determination
P. Pulse
Q. Cancer

6. Using the Across and Down clues, write the correct words in the numbered grid below.

ACROSS

1. This is when a provider refuses to accept Medicare payments as a sufficient amount for the services rendered to a patient.
6. An area of buildup of fat deposits in an artery, causing narrowing of the artery and possibly heart disease
8. The liquid part of the blood, containing substances such as nutrients, salts, and proteins
11. Facilities that review and correct medical claims as necessary before sending them to insurance companies for final processing.
12. The patient's information required for filing a claim, such as age, sex, address, and family information. An insurance company may deny a claim if it contains inaccurate demographics.
13. A cavity within bone or a channel that contains blood
14. An artificial feeding technique in which liquids are passed into the stomach by way of a tube inserted through the nose
15. A fluid-filled sac that cushions and reduces friction in certain parts of the body
16. A term used to describe a child in the womb from fertilization to 8 weeks following fertilization

DOWN

2. A group of diseases caused by the microorganism rickettsia, spread by the bites of fleas, mites, or ticks
3. This type of care is administered at reduced or zero cost to patients who cannot afford healthcare.
4. An organ located in the pelvis whose function is to collect and store urine until it is expelled
5. Abnormal crackling or bubbling sounds heard in the lungs during breathing
7. The hollow female reproductive organ in which a fertilized egg is implanted and a fetus develops
9. Density lipoprotein- a type of lipoprotein that is the major carrier of cholesterol in the blood, with high levels associated with narrowing of the arteries and heart disease
10. A small, rounded tissue mass
13. A sample of cells spread across a glass slide to be examined through a microscope

A. Sinus
B. Plasma
C. Typhus
D. Clearinghouse
E. Smear
F. Plaque
G. Rales
H. Non participation
I. Bladder
J. Charity Care
K. Bursa
L. Low
M. Gavage
N. Demographics
O. Uterus
P. Embryo
Q. Node

7. Using the Across and Down clues, write the correct words in the numbered grid below.

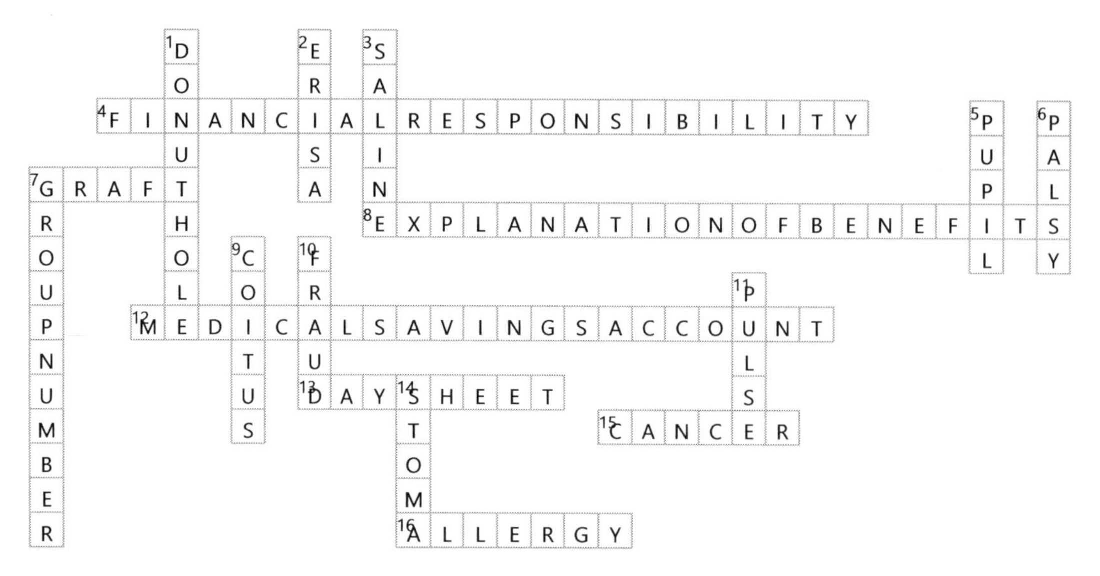

ACROSS

4. Whoever owes the healthcare provider money has financial responsibility for the services rendered.
7. Healthy tissue that is used to replace diseased or defective tissue
8. A document attached to a processed medical claim wherein the insurance company explains the services they will cover for a patient's healthcare treatments.
12. An optional health insurance payments plan whereby a person apportions part of their untaxed earnings to an account reserved for healthcare expenses.
13. A document that summarizes the services, treatments, payments, and charges that a patient received on a given day.
15. A group of diseases in which cells grow unrestrained in an organ or tissue in the body
16. Immunology

DOWN

1. This term refers to the discrepancy between the limits of healthcare insurance coverage and the Medicare Part D coverage limits for prescription drugs.
2. This act established guidelines and requirements for health and life insurance policies including appeals and disclosure of grievances.
3. A salt solution or any substance that contains salt
5. The opening at the center of the iris in the eye that constricts (contracts) and dilates (widens) in response to light
6. Loss of sensation or ability to move
7. A number given to a patient by their insurance carrier that identifies the group or plan under which they are covered.
9. Sexual intercourse
10. Providers, patients, or insurance companies may be found fraudulent if they are deliberately achieving their ends through misrepresentation, dishonesty, and general illegal activity.
11. The expansion and contraction of a blood vessel due to the blood pumped through it
14. A surgically formed opening on a body surface

A. Graft	B. ERISA	C. Medical Savings Account
D. Allergy	E. Fraud	F. Saline
G. Explanation of Benefits	H. Cancer	I. Donut Hole
J. Day Sheet	K. Pulse	L. Stoma
M. Financial Responsibility	N. Pupil	O. Group Number
P. Palsy	Q. Coitus	

8. Using the Across and Down clues, write the correct words in the numbered grid below.

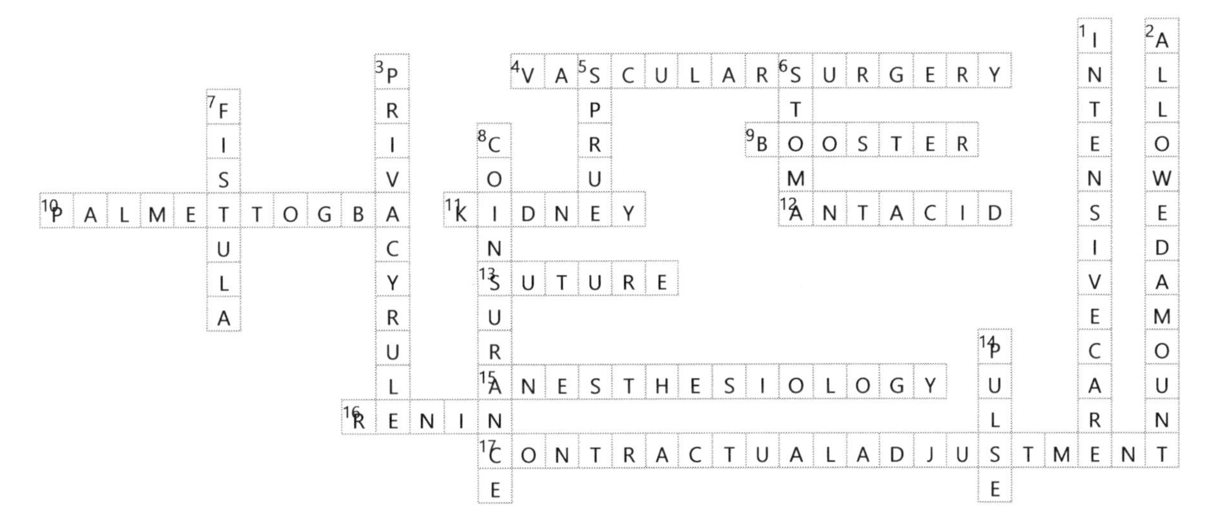

ACROSS

4. The diagnosis and treatment of circulatory problems of the extremities, especially the legs
9. An additional dose of a vaccine taken after the first dose to maintain or renew the first one
10. A MAC based in Columbia, South Carolina that is also a subsidiary of Blue Cross Blue Shield.
11. One of two organs that are part of the urinary tract
12. A drug that neutralizes stomach acids
13. A surgical stitch that helps close an incision or wound so that it can heal properly
15. the administration of medications as a means to block pain or diminish consciousness for surgery, usually by injection or inhalation
16. An enzyme that plays a role in increasing a low blood pressure
17. Refers to a binding agree between a provider, patient, and insurance company wherein the provider agrees to charges that it will write off on behalf of the patient.

DOWN

1. The unit of a hospital reserved for patients that need immediate treatment and close monitoring by healthcare professionals for serious illnesses, conditions, and injuries.
2. The sum an insurance company will reimburse to cover a healthcare service or procedure.
3. Standards for privacy regarding a patient's medical history and all related events, treatments, and data as outlined by HIPAA.
5. A digestive disorder in which nutrients cannot be properly absorbed from food, causing weakness and loss of weight
6. A surgically formed opening on a body surface
7. An abnormal passageway from one organ to another or from an organ to the body surface
8. The percentage of coverage that a patient is responsible for paying after an insurance company pays the portion agreed upon in a health plan.
14. The expansion and contraction of a blood vessel due to the blood pumped through it

A. Palmetto GBA
B. Fistula
C. Intensive Care
D. Vascular Surgery
E. Pulse
F. Stoma
G. Antacid
H. Booster
I. Contractual Adjustment
J. Sprue
K. Kidney
L. Privacy Rule
M. Renin
N. Allowed Amount
O. Suture
P. Anesthesiology
Q. Co Insurance

9. Using the Across and Down clues, write the correct words in the numbered grid below.

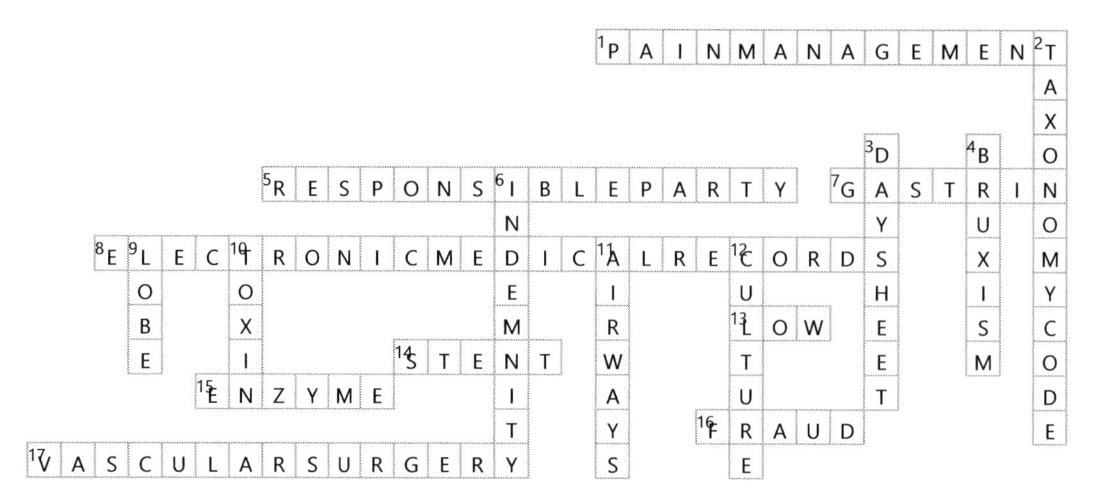

ACROSS

1. the control of pain or discomfort through medication, stress reduction, relaxation, exercise, massage, heat, cold, or providing a comfortable environment
5. The person who pays for a patient's medical expenses, also known as the guarantor.
7. A hormone that stimulates the release of gastric acid in the stomach
8. Digitized medical record for a patient managed by a provider onsite.
13. Density lipoprotein- a type of lipoprotein that is the major carrier of cholesterol in the blood, with high levels associated with narrowing of the arteries and heart disease
14. A device used to hold tissues in place, such as to support a skin graft
15. A chemical, originating in a cell, that regulates reactions in the body
16. Providers, patients, or insurance companies may be found fraudulent if they are deliberately achieving their ends through misrepresentation, dishonesty, and general illegal activity.
17. The diagnosis and treatment of circulatory problems of the extremities, especially the legs

DOWN

2. Medical billing specialists utilize this unique codeset for identifying a healthcare provider's specialty field.
3. A document that summarizes the services, treatments, payments, and charges that a patient received on a given day.
4. An unaware clenching or grinding of the teeth, usually during sleep
6. A type of health insurance plan whereby a patient can receive care with any provider in exchange for higher deductibles and co-pays. Indemnity is also known as fee -for-service insurance.
9. A well-defined, separate part of an organ
10. A poisonous substance
11. The passageways that air moves through while traveling in and out of the lungs during breathing
12. The artificial growth of cells, tissue, or microorganisms such as bacteria in a laboratory

A. Day Sheet	B. Lobe	C. Bruxism
D. Responsible Party	E. Pain Management	F. Gastrin
G. Culture	H. Indemnity	I. Fraud
J. Electronic Medical Records	K. Taxonomy Code	L. Low
M. Enzyme	N. Airways	O. Vascular Surgery
P. Toxin	Q. Stent	

10. Using the Across and Down clues, write the correct words in the numbered grid below.

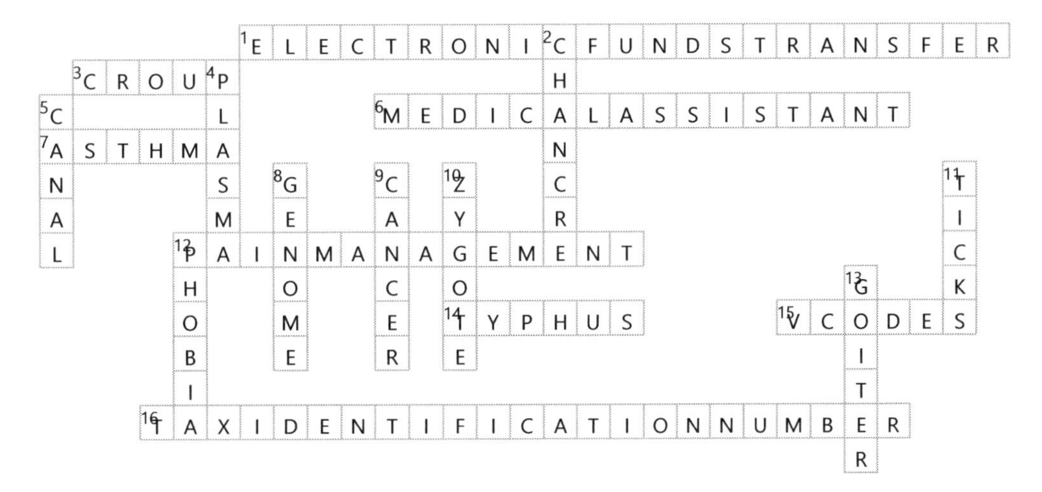

ACROSS

1. A method of transferring money electronically from a patient's bank account to a provider or an insurance carrier.
3. A usually mild and temporary condition common in children in which the walls of the airways become inflamed and narrow, resulting in wheezing and coughing
6. An employee in the healthcare system such as a physician's assistant or a nurse practitioner who perform duties in administration, nursing, and other ancillary care.
7. A disorder characterized by inflamed airways and difficulty breathing
12. the control of pain or discomfort through medication, stress reduction, relaxation, exercise, massage, heat, cold, or providing a comfortable environment
14. A group of diseases caused by the microorganism rickettsia, spread by the bites of fleas, mites, or ticks
15. A codeset under ICD-9-CM used to organize healthcare services rendered for reasons other than illness or injury.
16. A unique number a patient or a company may have to produce for billing purposes in order to receive healthcare from a provider.

DOWN

2. A painless sore that has a thick, rubbery base and a defined edge
4. The liquid part of the blood, containing substances such as nutrients, salts, and proteins
5. A tunnel-like passage
8. The complete set of an organism's genes
9. A group of diseases in which cells grow unrestrained in an organ or tissue in the body
10. The cell that results when an egg is fertilized by a sperm
11. Small, eight- legged animals that can attach to humans and animals and feed on blood
12. A persisting fear of and desire to avoid something
13. Enlargement of the thyroid gland, which produces a swelling on the neck

A. Genome
B. Ticks
C. Pain Management
D. Plasma
E. V Codes
F. Cancer
G. Phobia
H. Tax Identification Number
I. Chancre
J. Zygote
K. Electronic Funds Transfer
L. Croup
M. Canal
N. Goiter
O. Typhus
P. Medical Assistant
Q. Asthma

11. Using the Across and Down clues, write the correct words in the numbered grid below.

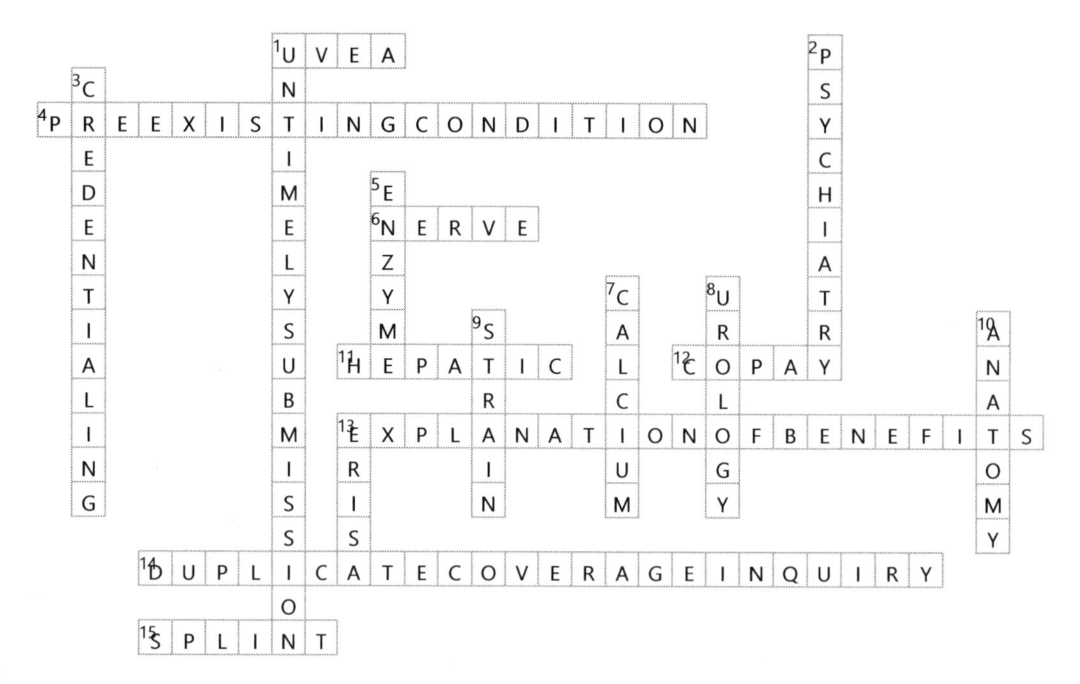

ACROSS

1. A structure consisting of the colored area of the eye and the middle layer of the eye that contains blood vessels
4. A medical condition a patient had before receiving coverage from an insurance company.
6. A bundle of fibers that transmit electrical messages between the brain and areas of the body
11. A term used to describe something that is related to the liver
12. The amount that must be paid to a provider before they receive any treatment or services.
13. A document attached to a processed medical claim wherein the insurance company explains the services they will cover for a patient's healthcare treatments.
14. A formal request typically submitted by an insurance carrier to determine if other health coverage exists for a patient.
15. A device that is used to immobilize a part of the body

DOWN

1. Claims have a specific timeframe in which they can be sent off to an insurance company for processing.
2. The diagnosis and treatment of mental, emotional and behavioral disorders
3. The application process for a provider to coordinate with an insurance company.
5. A chemical, originating in a cell, that regulates reactions in the body
7. A plentiful mineral in the body and the basic component of teeth and bones
8. The diagnosis and management, including surgery, of disorders of the urinary tract in both males and females, as well as the male reproductive system
9. Muscle damage resulting from excessive stretching or forceful contraction
10. The structure of bodies; commonly refers to the study of body structure
13. This act established guidelines and requirements for health and life insurance policies including appeals and disclosure of grievances.

A. Calcium
B. Duplicate Coverage Inquiry
C. Pre existing Condition
D. Splint
E. Hepatic
F. Untimely Submission
G. Psychiatry
H. Anatomy
I. Credentialing
J. Co Pay
K. Explanation of Benefits
L. Strain
M. Nerve
N. ERISA
O. Urology
P. Enzyme
Q. Uvea

12. Using the Across and Down clues, write the correct words in the numbered grid below.

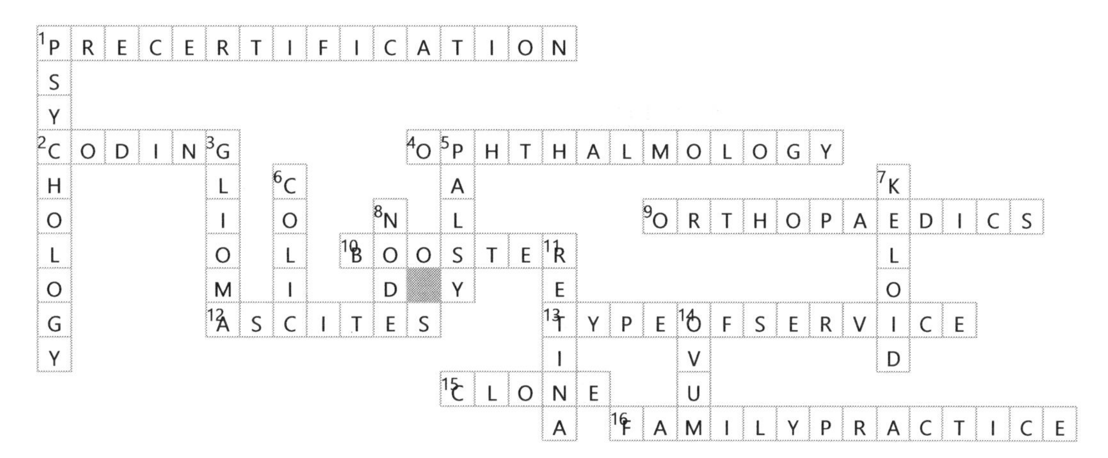

ACROSS

1. A process similar to preauthorization whereby patients must check with insurance companies to see if a desired healthcare treatment or service is deemed medically necessary
2. The process of translating a physician's documentation about a patient's medical condition and health services rendered into medical codes that are then plugged into a claim for processing.
4. the diagnosis and treatment, including surgery, of diseases and disorders of the eye, such as cataracts and glaucoma
9. the diagnosis and treatment, including surgery, of diseases and disorders of the musculoskeletal system, including bones, joints, tendons, ligaments, muscles and nerves
10. An additional dose of a vaccine taken after the first dose to maintain or renew the first one
12. Excess fluid in the abdominal cavity, which leads to swelling
13. A field on a claim for describing what kind of healthcare services or procedures a provider administered.
15. An exact copy of a gene, cell, or organism
16. the specialty that provides comprehensive and ongoing medical care to all members of the family unit

DOWN

1. The science of dealing with mental processes and their effects on behavior
3. A brain tumor arising from cells that support nerve cells
5. Loss of sensation or ability to move
6. Waves of pain in the abdomen that increase in strength, disappear, and return
7. A raised, firm, thick scar that forms as a result of a defect in the natural healing process
8. A small, rounded tissue mass
11. A membrane lining the inside of the back of the eye that contains light-sensitive nerve cells that convert focused light into nerve impulses, making vision possible
14. Another term for an egg cell

A. Psychology
B. Ovum
C. Type of Service
D. Colic
E. Ascites
F. Pre Certification
G. Retina
H. Node
I. Orthopaedics
J. Clone
K. Coding
L. Family Practice
M. Glioma
N. Ophthalmology
O. Palsy
P. Booster
Q. Keloid

13. Using the Across and Down clues, write the correct words in the numbered grid below.

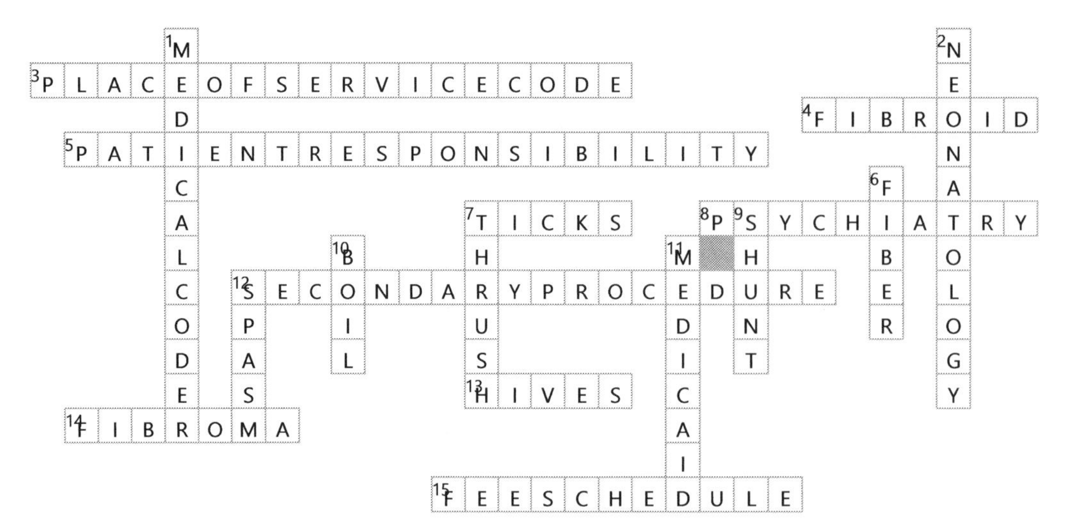

ACROSS

3. A two-digit code used on claims to explain what type of provider performed healthcare services on a patient.
4. A noncancerous tumor of the uterus made up of smooth muscle and connective tissue
5. This refers to the amount a patient owes a provider after an insurance company pays for their portion of the medical expenses.
7. Small, eight- legged animals that can attach to humans and animals and feed on blood
8. The diagnosis and treatment of mental, emotional and behavioral disorders
12. This is when provider performs another procedure on a patient covered by a CPT code after first performing a different CPT procedure on them.
13. The common term for urticaria, an itchy, inflamed rash that results from an allergic reaction
14. A noncancerous tumor of connective tissue
15. A document that outlines the costs associated for each medical service designated by a CPT code.

DOWN

1. Responsible for assigning various medical codes to services and healthcare plans described by a physician on a patient's super-bill.
2. the specialized care and treatment of a newborn up to six weeks of age
6. A constituent of plants that cannot be digested, which helps maintain healthy functioning of the bowels
7. A candidiasis infection
9. An artificially constructed or an abnormal passage connecting two usually separate structures in the body
10. An inflamed, raised area of skin that is pus-filled
11. A joint federal and state assistance program started in 1965 to provide health insurance to lower-income persons.
12. An involuntary muscle contraction

A. Place of Service Code	B. Fiber	C. Fee Schedule
D. Boil	E. Psychiatry	F. Fibroid
G. Ticks	H. Shunt	I. Medicaid
J. Thrush	K. Medical Coder	L. Spasm
M. Neonatology	N. Secondary Procedure	O. Hives
P. Patient Responsibility	Q. Fibroma	

14. Using the Across and Down clues, write the correct words in the numbered grid below.

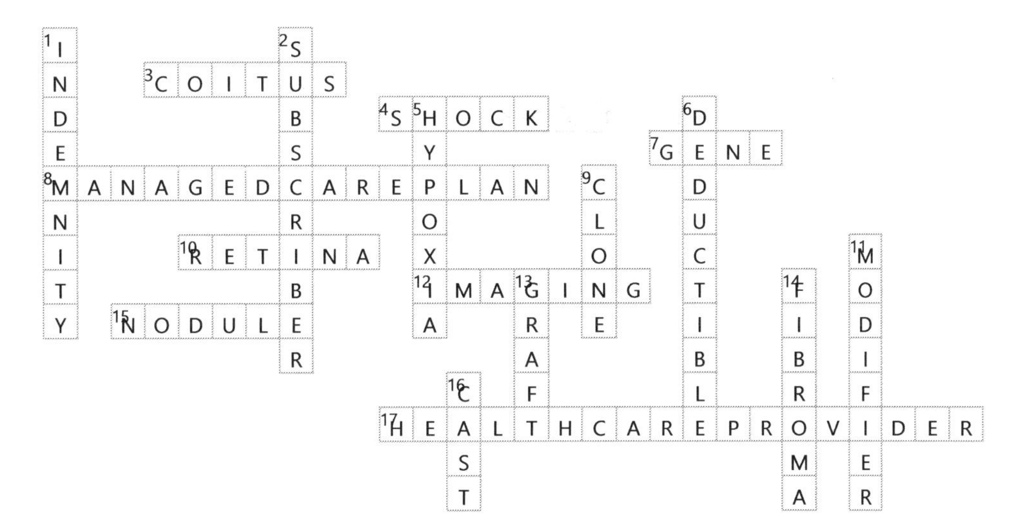

ACROSS

3. Sexual intercourse
4. A reduced flow of blood throughout the body, usually caused by severe bleeding or a weak heart
7. The basic unit of dna, which is responsible for passing genetic information
8. A health insurance plan whereby patients can only receive coverage if they see providers who operate in the insurance company's network.
10. A membrane lining the inside of the back of the eye that contains light-sensitive nerve cells that convert focused light into nerve impulses, making vision possible
12. The technique of creating pictures of structures inside of the body using x-rays, ultrasound waves, or magnetic fields
15. A small lump of tissue that is usually abnormal
17. These are the entities that offer healthcare services to patients, including hospitals, physicians, and private clinics, hospices, nursing homes, and other healthcare facilities.

DOWN

1. A type of health insurance plan whereby a patient can receive care with any provider in exchange for higher deductibles and co-pays. Indemnity is also known as fee -for-service insurance.
2. The individual covered under a group policy. For instance, an employee of a company with a group health policy would be one of many subscribers on that policy.
5. A reduced level of oxygen in tissues
6. The amount a patient must pay before an insurance carrier starts their healthcare coverage.
9. An exact copy of a gene, cell, or organism
11. Additions to CPT codes that explain alterations and modifications to an otherwise routine treatment, exam, or service.
13. Healthy tissue that is used to replace diseased or defective tissue
14. A noncancerous tumor of connective tissue
16. A hard plaster or fiberglass shell that molds to a body part such as an arm and holds it in place for proper healing

A. Retina
B. Modifier
C. Fibroma
D. Subscriber
E. Hypoxia
F. Healthcare Provider
G. Graft
H. Clone
I. Shock
J. Coitus
K. Imaging
L. Gene
M. Deductible
N. Nodule
O. Cast
P. Managed Care Plan
Q. Indemnity

15. Using the Across and Down clues, write the correct words in the numbered grid below.

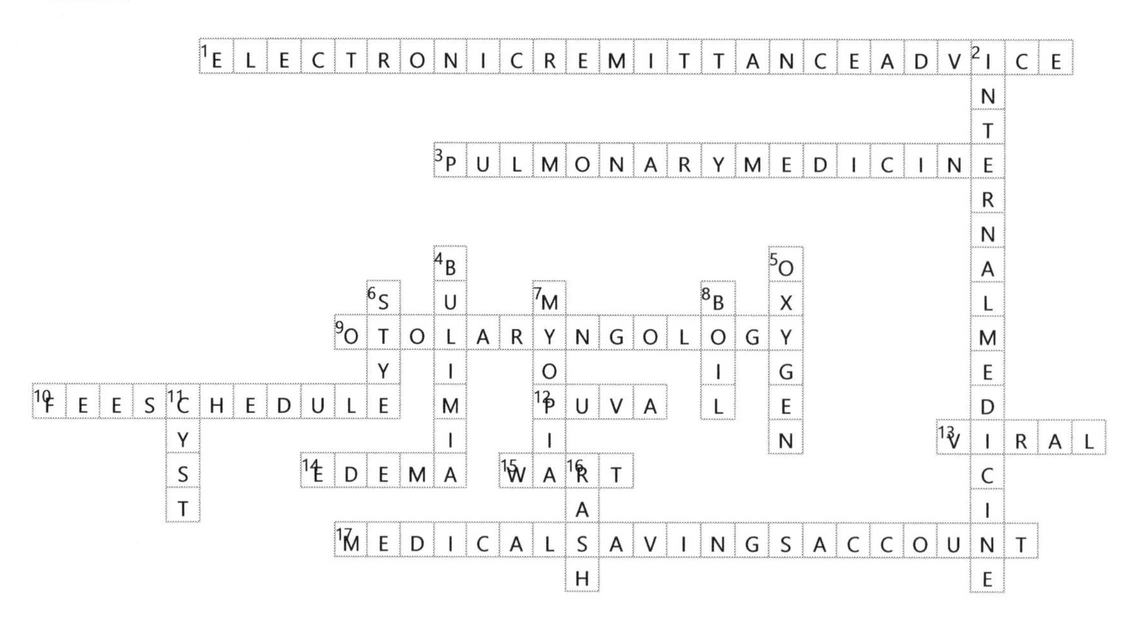

ACROSS

1. The digital version of EOB, which specifies the details of payments made on a claim either by an insurance company or required by the patient.
3. The diagnosis and treatment of acute and chronic diseases and conditions of the respiratory system, such as bronchitis, asthma, emphysema and occupational lung disease
9. the medical and surgical care for diseases of the ears, nose and throat (ENT)
10. A document that outlines the costs associated for each medical service designated by a CPT code.
12. A form of phototherapy that combines the use of psoralens and ultraviolet light to treat skin disorders
13. A term describing something related to or caused by a virus
14. Abnormal buildup of fluid in the body, which may cause visible swelling
15. A contagious, harmless growth caused by a virus that occurs on the skin or a mucous membrane
17. An optional health insurance payments plan whereby a person apportions part of their untaxed earnings to an account reserved for healthcare expenses.

DOWN

2. the diagnosis and non-surgical treatment of adult health problems
4. A disorder in which a person eats large amounts of food then forces vomiting or uses laxatives to prevent weight gain (called binging and purging)
5. A gas that is colorless, odorless, and tasteless
6. A pus- filled abscess in the follicle of an eyelash
7. The medical term for nearsightedness
8. An inflamed, raised area of skin that is pus-filled
11. A lump filled with either fluid or soft material, occurring in any organ or tissue
16. An area of inflammation or a group of spots on the skin

A. Myopia	B. Otolaryngology	C. Cyst
D. Pulmonary Medicine	E. Wart	F. Oxygen
G. Boil	H. Edema	I. Stye
J. Bulimia	K. PUVA	L. Viral
M. Internal Medicine	N. Medical Savings Account	O. Rash
P. Fee Schedule	Q. Electronic Remittance Advice	

16. Using the Across and Down clues, write the correct words in the numbered grid below.

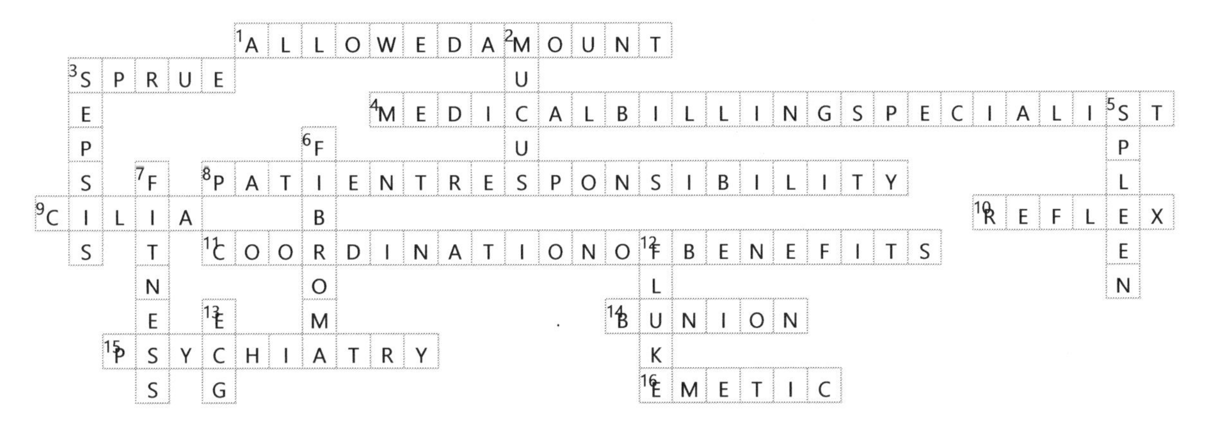

ACROSS

1. The sum an insurance company will reimburse to cover a healthcare service or procedure.
3. A digestive disorder in which nutrients cannot be properly absorbed from food, causing weakness and loss of weight
4. Responsible for using information regarding services and treatments performed by a healthcare provider to complete a claim for filing with an insurance company.
8. This refers to the amount a patient owes a provider after an insurance company pays for their portion of the medical expenses.
9. Tiny, hairlike structures on the outside of some cells, providing mobility
10. An automatic, involuntary response of the nervous system to a stimulus
11. Occurs when a patient is covered by more than one insurance plan.
14. A hard, fluid-filled pad along the inside joint of the big toe
15. The diagnosis and treatment of mental, emotional and behavioral disorders
16. A substance that causes vomiting

DOWN

2. A slippery fluid produced by mucous membranes that lubricates and protects the internal surfaces of the body
3. The infection of a wound or tissue with bacteria, causing the spread of the bacteria into the bloodstream
5. An organ located in the upper left abdomen behind the ribs that removes and destroys old red blood cells and helps fight infection
6. A noncancerous tumor of connective tissue
7. A measure of a person's physical strength, flexibility, and endurance
12. A parasitic flatworm that can infest humans
13. An electrocardiogram, which is a record of the electrical impulses that trigger the heartbeat

A. Patient Responsibility
B. Cilia
C. Fitness
D. ECG
E. Psychiatry
F. Mucus
G. Reflex
H. Coordination of Benefits
I. Spleen
J. Medical Billing Specialist
K. Sprue
L. Allowed Amount
M. Sepsis
N. Fibroma
O. Fluke
P. Emetic
Q. Bunion

17. Using the Across and Down clues, write the correct words in the numbered grid below.

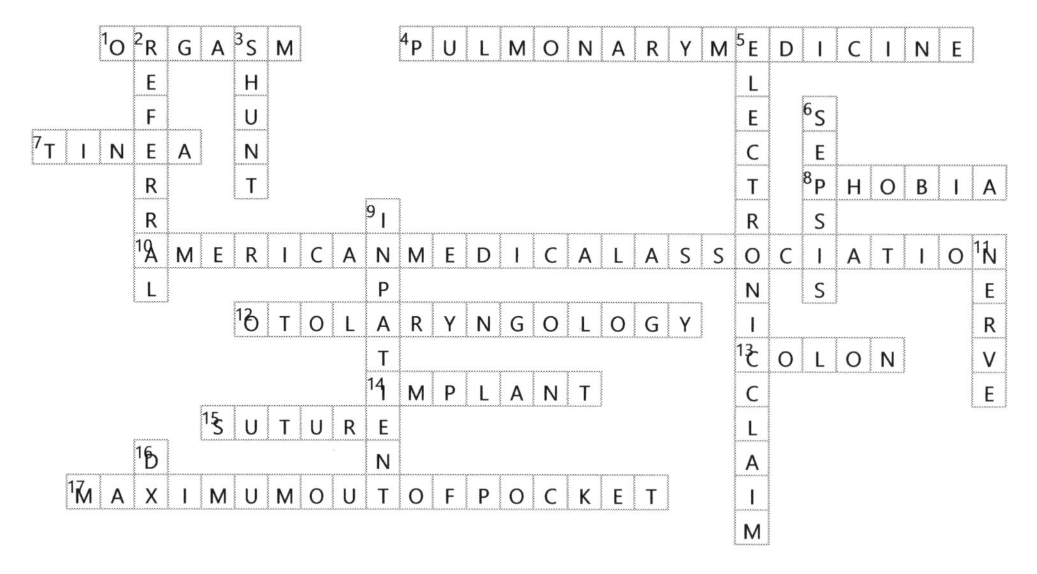

ACROSS

1. Involuntary contraction of genital muscles experienced at the peak of sexual excitement
4. The diagnosis and treatment of acute and chronic diseases and conditions of the respiratory system, such as bronchitis, asthma, emphysema and occupational lung disease
7. A group of common infections occurring on the skin, hair, and nails that are caused by a fungus
8. A persisting fear of and desire to avoid something
10. The largest organization of physicians in the U.S. dedicated to improving the quality of healthcare administered by providers across the country.
12. the medical and surgical care for diseases of the ears, nose and throat (ENT)
13. The main part of the large intestine, between the cecum and the rectum
14. An organ, tissue, or device surgically inserted and left in the body
15. A surgical stitch that helps close an incision or wound so that it can heal properly
17. The amount a patient is required to pay.

DOWN

2. This is when a provider recommends another provider to a patient to receive specialized treatment.
3. An artificially constructed or an abnormal passage connecting two usually separate structures in the body
5. A claim sent electronically to an insurance carrier from a provider's billing software.
6. The infection of a wound or tissue with bacteria, causing the spread of the bacteria into the bloodstream
9. Occurs when a person has a stay at a healthcare facility for more than 24 hours.
11. A bundle of fibers that transmit electrical messages between the brain and areas of the body
16. The abbreviation for diagnosis codes, also known as ICD -9 codes.

A. American Medical Association
B. Tinea
C. Referral
D. Colon
E. Maximum Out of Pocket
F. Electronic Claim
G. Otolaryngology
H. Pulmonary Medicine
I. Sepsis
J. Orgasm
K. Inpatient
L. Implant
M. Shunt
N. Nerve
O. Dx
P. Suture
Q. Phobia

18. Using the Across and Down clues, write the correct words in the numbered grid below.

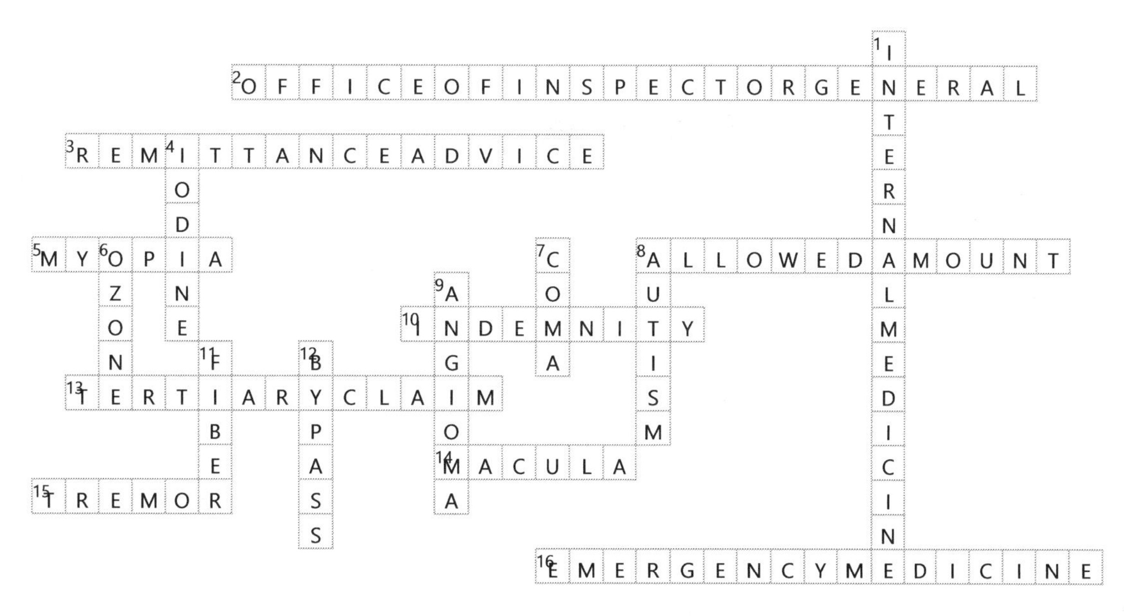

ACROSS

2. The organization responsible for establishing guidelines and investigating fraud and misinformation within the healthcare industry.
3. The document attached to a processed claim that explains the information regarding coverage and payments on a claim.
5. The medical term for nearsightedness
8. The sum an insurance company will reimburse to cover a healthcare service or procedure.
10. A type of health insurance plan whereby a patient can receive care with any provider in exchange for higher deductibles and co-pays. Indemnity is also known as fee -for-service insurance.
13. A claim filed by a provider after they have filed claims for primary and secondary health insurance coverage on behalf of a patient.
14. The area of the retina that allows fine details to be observed at the center of vision
15. An involuntary, rhythmic, shaking movement caused by alternating contraction and relaxation of muscles
16. the specialty that includes treatment of any symptom, illness or injury requiring urgent evaluation and

DOWN

1. the diagnosis and non-surgical treatment of adult health problems
4. An element for the formation of thyroid hormones
6. A poisonous form of oxygen that is present in the earth's upper atmosphere, where it helps to screen the earth from damaging ultraviolet rays
7. A condition in which the area of the brain involved in maintaining consciousness is somehow affected, resulting in a state of unconsciousness in which the patient does not respond to stimulation
8. A mental disorder characterized by an inability to relate to other people and extreme withdrawal
9. A tumor made of blood vessels or lymph vessels that is not cancerous
11. A constituent of plants that cannot be digested, which helps maintain healthy functioning of the bowels
12. A surgical technique in which the flow of blood or another body fluid is redirected around a blockage

A. Autism
B. Allowed Amount
C. Myopia
D. Ozone
E. Macula
F. Office of Inspector General
G. Indemnity
H. Internal Medicine
I. Emergency Medicine
J. Iodine
K. Tremor
L. Bypass
M. Tertiary Claim
N. Coma
O. Angioma
P. Fiber
Q. Remittance Advice

19. Using the Across and Down clues, write the correct words in the numbered grid below.

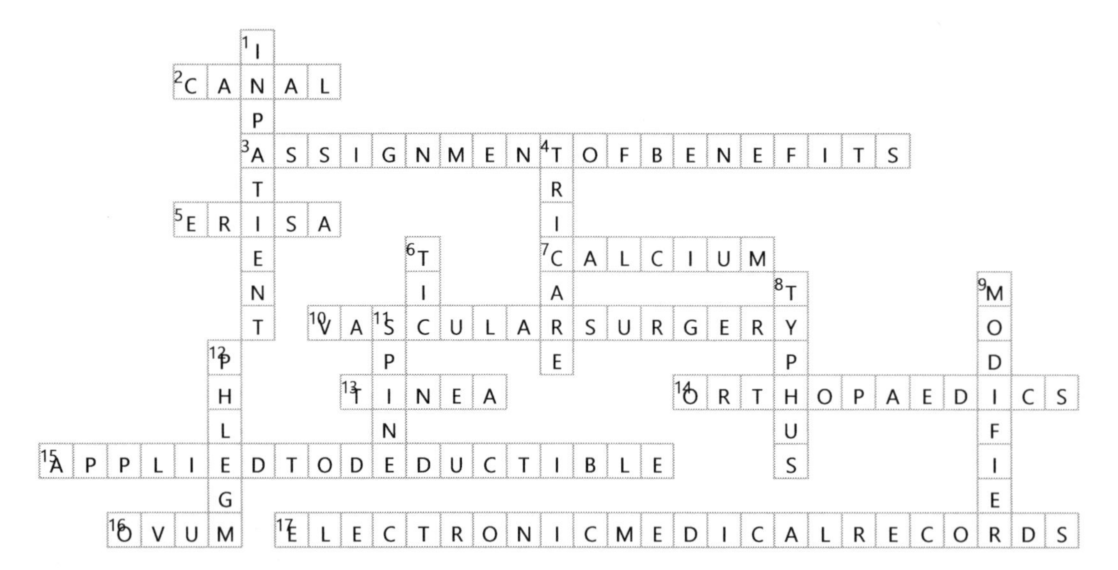

ACROSS

2. A tunnel-like passage
3. Refers to insurance payments made directly to a healthcare provider for medical services received by the patient.
5. This act established guidelines and requirements for health and life insurance policies including appeals and disclosure of grievances.
7. A plentiful mineral in the body and the basic component of teeth and bones
10. The diagnosis and treatment of circulatory problems of the extremities, especially the legs
13. A group of common infections occurring on the skin, hair, and nails that are caused by a fungus
14. the diagnosis and treatment, including surgery, of diseases and disorders of the musculoskeletal system, including bones, joints, tendons, ligaments, muscles and nerves
15. This term refers to the amount of money a patient owes a provider that goes to paying their yearly deductible.
16. Another term for an egg cell
17. Digitized medical record for a patient managed by a provider onsite.

DOWN

1. Occurs when a person has a stay at a healthcare facility for more than 24 hours.
4. The federal health insurance program for active and retired service members, their families, and the survivors of service members.
6. An involuntary, repetitive movement such as a twitch
8. A group of diseases caused by the microorganism rickettsia, spread by the bites of fleas, mites, or ticks
9. Additions to CPT codes that explain alterations and modifications to an otherwise routine treatment, exam, or service.
11. The column of bones and cartilage running along the midline of the back that surrounds and protects the spinal cord and supports the head
12. Mucus and other material produced by the lining of the respiratory tract; also called sputum

A. Electronic Medical Records
B. Spine
C. Applied to Deductible
D. Orthopaedics
E. Typhus
F. Tinea
G. Inpatient
H. ERISA
I. Canal
J. Vascular Surgery
K. Tic
L. Calcium
M. Modifier
N. TRICARE
O. Phlegm
P. Ovum
Q. Assignment of Benefits

20. Using the Across and Down clues, write the correct words in the numbered grid below.

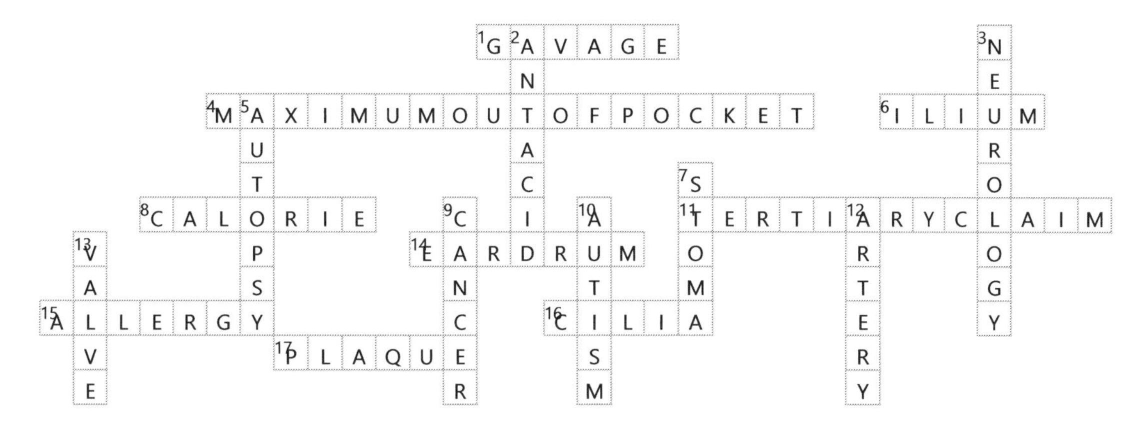

ACROSS

1. An artificial feeding technique in which liquids are passed into the stomach by way of a tube inserted through the nose
4. The amount a patient is required to pay.
6. One of the two bones that form the hip on either side of the body
8. A unit that is used to measure the energy content in food
11. A claim filed by a provider after they have filed claims for primary and secondary health insurance coverage on behalf of a patient.
14. A thin, oval-shaped membrane that separates the inner ear from the outer ear and is responsible for transmitting sound waves
15. Immunology
16. Tiny, hairlike structures on the outside of some cells, providing mobility
17. An area of buildup of fat deposits in an artery, causing narrowing of the artery and possibly heart disease

DOWN

2. A drug that neutralizes stomach acids
3. the diagnosis and medical treatment of the nervous system and brain, including conditions such as strokes and seizures
5. The examination of a body following death, possibly to determine the cause of death or for research
7. A surgically formed opening on a body surface
9. A group of diseases in which cells grow unrestrained in an organ or tissue in the body
10. A mental disorder characterized by an inability to relate to other people and extreme withdrawal
12. A large blood vessel that carries blood from the heart to tissues and organs in the body
13. A structure that allows fluid flow in only one direction

A. Plaque
B. Tertiary Claim
C. Autism
D. Artery
E. Valve
F. Cancer
G. Neurology
H. Cilia
I. Ilium
J. Eardrum
K. Allergy
L. Autopsy
M. Calorie
N. Gavage
O. Maximum Out of Pocket
P. Antacid
Q. Stoma

21. Using the Across and Down clues, write the correct words in the numbered grid below.

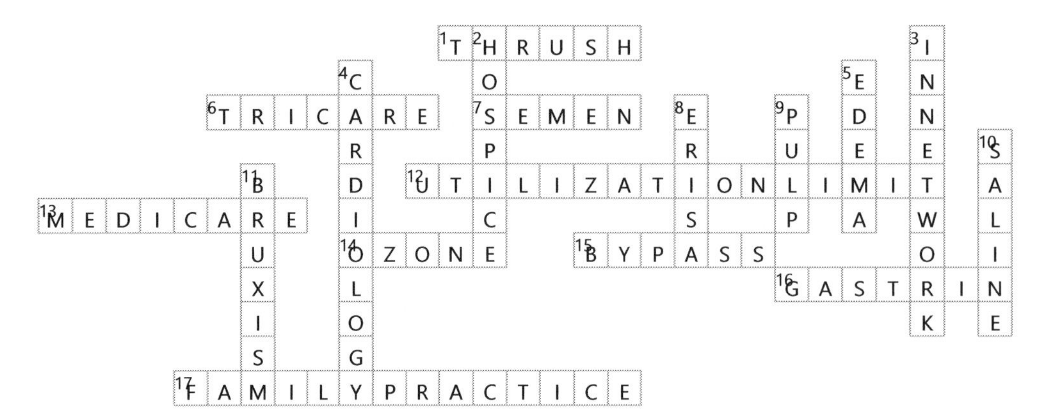

ACROSS

1. A candidiasis infection
6. The federal health insurance program for active and retired service members, their families, and the survivors of service members.
7. Fluid released during ejaculation that contains sperm along with fluids produced by the prostate gland and the seminal vesicles
12. The limit per year for coverage under certain available healthcare services for Medicare enrollees.
13. A government insurance program started in 1965 to provide healthcare coverage for persons over 65 and eligible people with disabilities.
14. A poisonous form of oxygen that is present in the earth's upper atmosphere, where it helps to screen the earth from damaging ultraviolet rays
15. A surgical technique in which the flow of blood or another body fluid is redirected around a blockage
16. A hormone that stimulates the release of gastric acid in the stomach
17. the specialty that provides comprehensive and ongoing medical care to all members of the family unit

DOWN

2. This refers to medical care and treatment for persons who are terminally ill.
3. This term refers to a provider's relationship with a health insurance company.
4. the diagnosis and treatment of disorders of the heart and major blood vessels
5. Abnormal buildup of fluid in the body, which may cause visible swelling
8. This act established guidelines and requirements for health and life insurance policies including appeals and disclosure of grievances.
9. The soft tissue inside of a tooth that contains blood vessels and nerves
10. A salt solution or any substance that contains salt
11. An unaware clenching or grinding of the teeth, usually during sleep

A. Cardiology
B. Bruxism
C. Saline
D. Bypass
E. ERISA
F. TRICARE
G. Ozone
H. Family Practice
I. Edema
J. Gastrin
K. Pulp
L. Hospice
M. Semen
N. Utilization Limit
O. In Network
P. Thrush
Q. Medicare

22. Using the Across and Down clues, write the correct words in the numbered grid below.

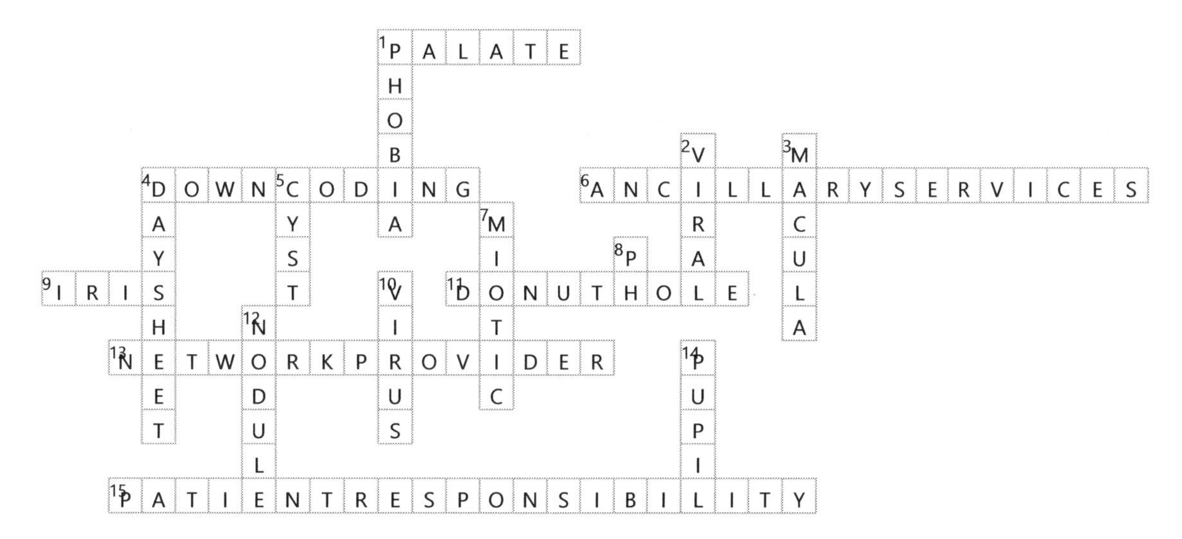

ACROSS

1. The roof of the mouth
4. Occurs when an insurance company finds there is insufficient evidence on a claim to prove that a provider performed coded medical services and so they reduce or remove those codes.
6. Any service administered in a hospital or other healthcare facility other than room and board.
9. The colored part of the eye
11. This term refers to the discrepancy between the limits of healthcare insurance coverage and the Medicare Part D coverage limits for prescription drugs.
13. A provider within a health insurance company's network that has contracted with the company to provide discounted services to a patient covered under the company's plan.
15. This refers to the amount a patient owes a provider after an insurance company pays for their portion of the medical expenses.

DOWN

1. A persisting fear of and desire to avoid something
2. A term describing something related to or caused by a virus
3. The area of the retina that allows fine details to be observed at the center of vision
4. A document that summarizes the services, treatments, payments, and charges that a patient received on a given day.
5. A lump filled with either fluid or soft material, occurring in any organ or tissue
7. A drug that causes the pupil to constrict
8. A measure of the acidic or basic character of a substance
10. The smallest known disease- causing microorganism
12. A small lump of tissue that is usually abnormal
14. The opening at the center of the iris in the eye that constricts (contracts) and dilates (widens) in response to light

A. Viral
B. Pupil
C. Macula
D. Donut Hole
E. Miotic
F. Nodule
G. pH
H. Day Sheet
I. Ancillary Services
J. Patient Responsibility
K. Phobia
L. Virus
M. Downcoding
N. Palate
O. Network Provider
P. Iris
Q. Cyst

23. Using the Across and Down clues, write the correct words in the numbered grid below.

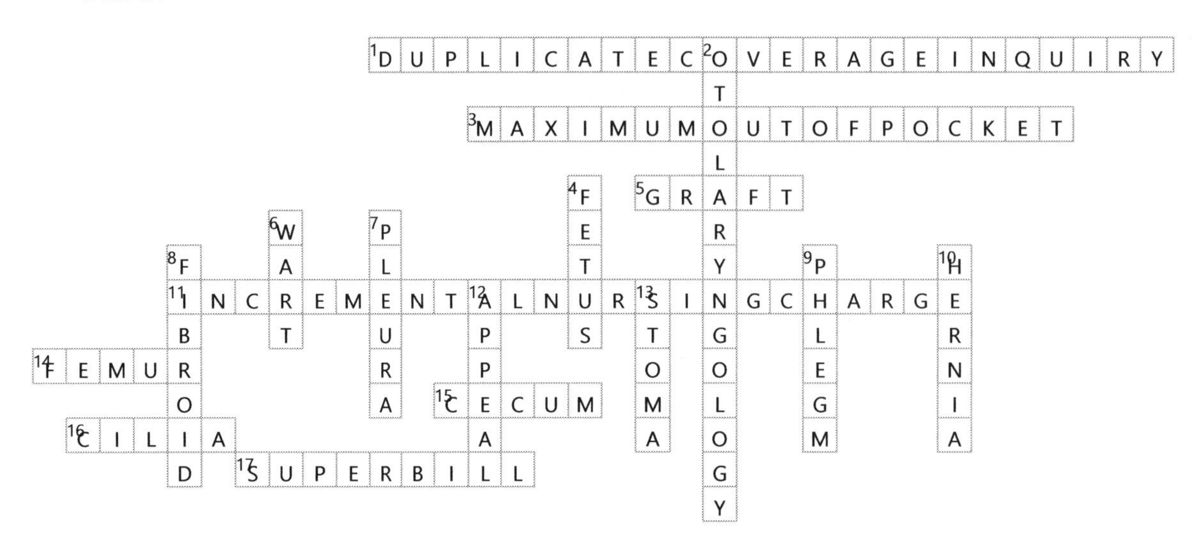

ACROSS

1. A formal request typically submitted by an insurance carrier to determine if other health coverage exists for a patient.
3. The amount a patient is required to pay.
5. Healthy tissue that is used to replace diseased or defective tissue
11. A fee for nursing services a patient is charged during the course of receiving healthcare.
14. The bone located between the hip and the knee
15. The beginning of the large intestine, which is connected to the appendix at its lower end
16. Tiny, hairlike structures on the outside of some cells, providing mobility
17. A document used by healthcare staff and physicians to write down information about a patient receiving care.

DOWN

2. the medical and surgical care for diseases of the ears, nose and throat (ENT)
4. The term used to refer to an unborn child from 8 weeks after fertilization to birth
6. A contagious, harmless growth caused by a virus that occurs on the skin or a mucous membrane
7. The double- layered membrane that lines the lungs and chest cavity and allows for lung movement during breathing
8. A noncancerous tumor of the uterus made up of smooth muscle and connective tissue
9. Mucus and other material produced by the lining of the respiratory tract; also called sputum
10. The bulging of an organ or tissue through a weakened area in the muscle wall
12. Occurs when a patient or a provider tries to convince an insurance company to pay for healthcare after it has decided not to cover costs for someone on a claim.
13. A surgically formed opening on a body surface

A. Graft
B. Wart
C. Maximum Out of Pocket
D. Femur
E. Stoma
F. Fibroid
G. Appeal
H. Superbill
I. Phlegm
J. Incremental Nursing Charge
K. Fetus
L. Pleura
M. Cecum
N. Otolaryngology
O. Cilia
P. Hernia
Q. Duplicate Coverage Inquiry

24. Using the Across and Down clues, write the correct words in the numbered grid below.

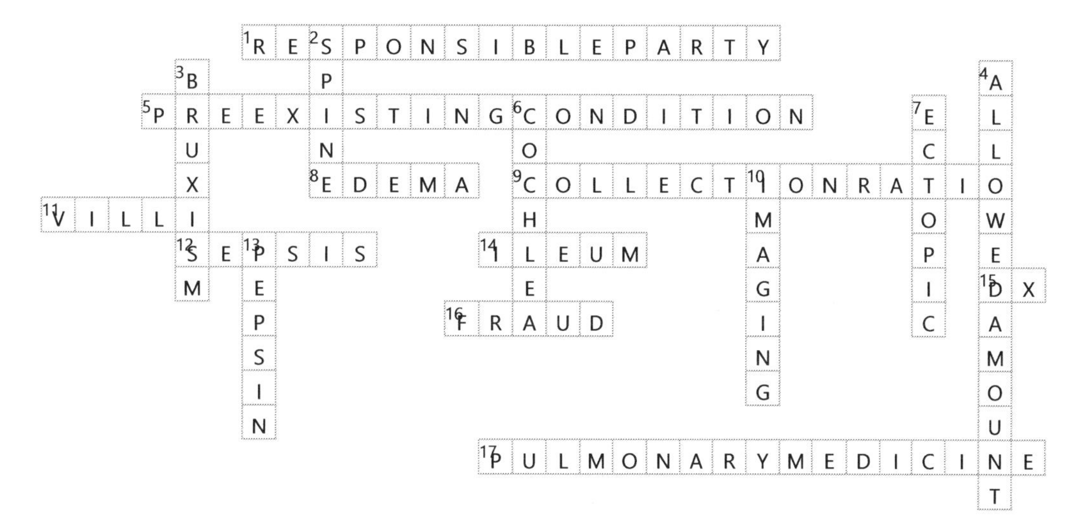

ACROSS

1. The person who pays for a patient's medical expenses, also known as the guarantor.
5. A medical condition a patient had before receiving coverage from an insurance company.
8. Abnormal buildup of fluid in the body, which may cause visible swelling
9. Refers to the ratio of payments received relative to the total amount owed to providers.
11. The millions of fingerlike projections on the lining of the small intestine that aid in the absorption of food
12. The infection of a wound or tissue with bacteria, causing the spread of the bacteria into the bloodstream
14. The lowest section of the small intestine, which attaches to the large intestine
15. The abbreviation for diagnosis codes, also known as ICD -9 codes.
16. Providers, patients, or insurance companies may be found fraudulent if they are deliberately achieving their ends through misrepresentation, dishonesty, and general illegal activity.
17. The diagnosis and treatment of acute and chronic diseases and conditions of the respiratory system, such as bronchitis, asthma, emphysema and occupational lung disease

DOWN

2. The column of bones and cartilage running along the midline of the back that surrounds and protects the spinal cord and supports the head
3. An unaware clenching or grinding of the teeth, usually during sleep
4. The sum an insurance company will reimburse to cover a healthcare service or procedure.
6. A coiled organ in the inner ear that plays a large role in hearing by picking up sound vibrations and transmitting them as electrical signals
7. Occurring at an abnormal position or time
10. The technique of creating pictures of structures inside of the body using x-rays, ultrasound waves, or magnetic fields
13. The enzyme found in gastric juice that helps digest protein

A. Ectopic	B. Ileum	C. Allowed Amount
D. Pre existing Condition	E. Pulmonary Medicine	F. Pepsin
G. Spine	H. Villi	I. Imaging
J. Fraud	K. Sepsis	L. Edema
M. Dx	N. Cochlea	O. Responsible Party
P. Collection Ratio	Q. Bruxism	

25. Using the Across and Down clues, write the correct words in the numbered grid below.

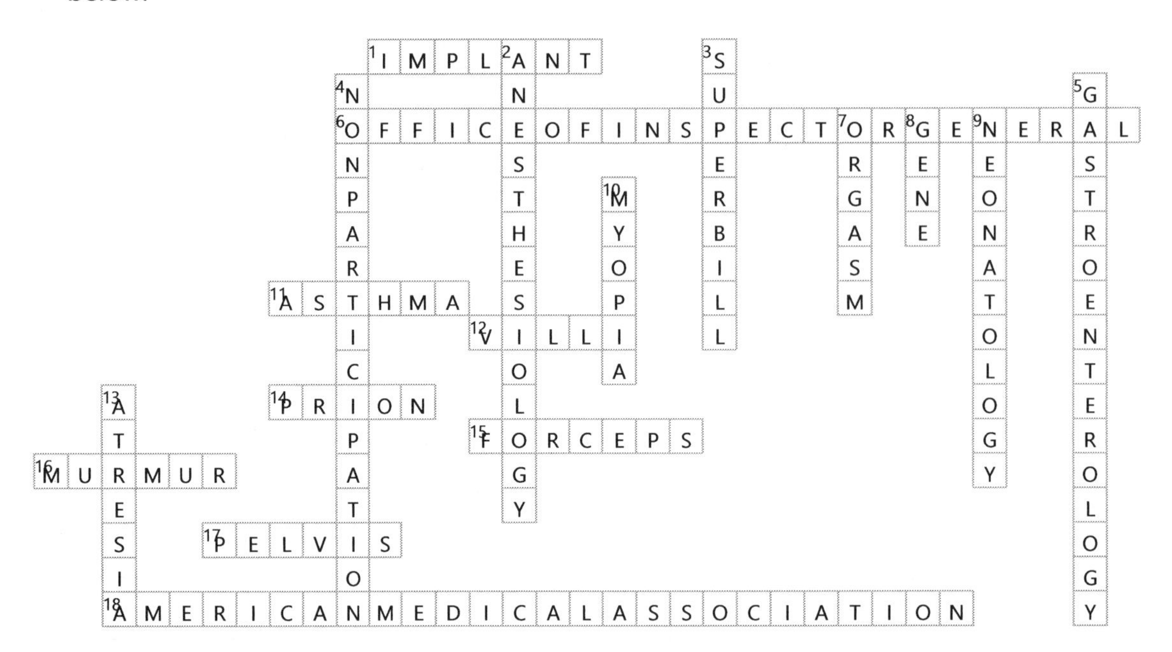

ACROSS

1. An organ, tissue, or device surgically inserted and left in the body
6. The organization responsible for establishing guidelines and investigating fraud and misinformation within the healthcare industry.
11. A disorder characterized by inflamed airways and difficulty breathing
12. The millions of fingerlike projections on the lining of the small intestine that aid in the absorption of food
14. An agent that is believed to cause several degenerative brain diseases
15. Instruments resembling tweezers that are used to handle objects or tissue during surgery
16. A characteristic sound of blood flowing irregularly through the heart
17. The group of bones in the lower part of the trunk that support the upper body and protect the abdominal organs
18. The largest organization of physicians in the U.S. dedicated to improving the quality of healthcare administered by providers across the country.

DOWN

2. the administration of medications as a means to block pain or diminish consciousness for surgery, usually by injection or inhalation
3. A document used by healthcare staff and physicians to write down information about a patient receiving care.
4. This is when a provider refuses to accept Medicare payments as a sufficient amount for the services rendered to a patient.
5. the diagnosis and treatment of diseases and disorders of the digestive system, including the liver, stomach and intestines, and medical conditions such as ulcers, tumors and colitis
7. Involuntary contraction of genital muscles experienced at the peak of sexual excitement
8. The basic unit of dna, which is responsible for passing genetic information
9. the specialized care and treatment of a newborn up to six weeks of age
10. The medical term for nearsightedness
13. A birth defect in which a normal body opening or canal is absent

A. Implant	B. Prion	C. Superbill
D. Forceps	E. Office of Inspector General	F. American Medical Association
G. Asthma	H. Murmur	I. Anesthesiology
J. Orgasm	K. Villi	L. Myopia
M. Pelvis	N. Non participation	O. Gene
P. Atresia	Q. Neonatology	R. Gastroenterology

26. Using the Across and Down clues, write the correct words in the numbered grid below.

```
         V          P S    D
   G     U M  FISSURE H   LYMPH
   E    ULCER       D U    S
 R R     V D        I N    P
RABIES D A I GROUPHEALTHPLAN
 D A   A   G  E     T      E
 I T   Y   ANATOMY  R      A
 O R   S   P  I     ILIUM
 L I   H      N     C
 O COLLECTIONRATIO  SEPSIS
 G S   E
 Y     T
```

ACROSS

7. A groove or slit on the body or in an organ
8. A milky fluid containing white blood cells, proteins, and fats
9. An open sore that occurs on the skin or on a mucous membrane because of the destruction of surface tissue
11. An infectious viral disease primarily affecting animals; can be transmitted to humans through an infected animal's bite
13. A plan provided by an employer to provide healthcare options to a large group of employees.
15. The structure of bodies; commonly refers to the study of body structure
16. One of the two bones that form the hip on either side of the body
17. Refers to the ratio of payments received relative to the total amount owed to providers.
18. The infection of a wound or tissue with bacteria, causing the spread of the bacteria into the bloodstream

DOWN

1. The outer, visible portion of the female genitals
2. The care and treatment of infants, children, and adolescents
3. An artificially constructed or an abnormal passage connecting two usually separate structures in the body
4. Difficulty breathing
5. the treatment of diseases and internal disorders of the elderly
6. Supplemental health insurance under Medicaid for eligible persons who need help covering co-pays, deductibles, and other large fees.
10. The use of radiation, ultrasound, X-rays, computerized tomography, magnetic resonance imaging, mammography, and other imaging technologies to diagnose diseases and internal disorders
12. A document that summarizes the services, treatments, payments, and charges that a patient received on a given day.
14. A membrane lining the inside of the back of the eye that contains light-sensitive nerve cells that convert focused light into nerve impulses, making vision possible

A. Ulcer	B. Vulva	C. Geriatrics	D. Lymph
E. Fissure	F. Retina	G. Ilium	H. Anatomy
I. Radiology	J. Rabies	K. Pediatrics	L. Dyspnea
M. Collection Ratio	N. Shunt	O. Sepsis	P. Day Sheet
Q. Medigap	R. Group Health Plan		

27. Using the Across and Down clues, write the correct words in the numbered grid below.

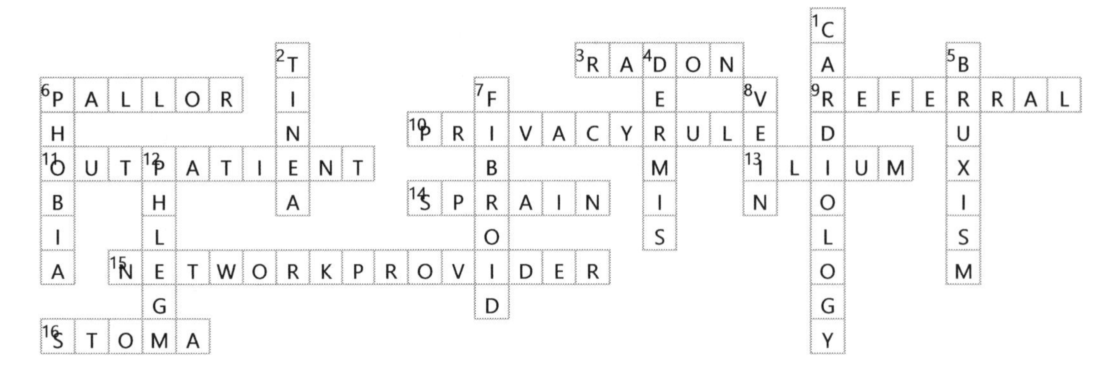

ACROSS

3. A colorless, odorless, tasteless radioactive gas that is produced by materials in soil, rocks, and building materials
6. Abnormally pale skin
9. This is when a provider recommends another provider to a patient to receive specialized treatment.
10. Standards for privacy regarding a patient's medical history and all related events, treatments, and data as outlined by HIPAA.
11. This term refers to healthcare treatment that doesn't require an overnight hospital stay, including a routine visit to a primary care doctor or a non-invasive surgery.
13. One of the two bones that form the hip on either side of the body
14. The tearing or stretching of the ligaments in a joint, characterized by pain, swelling, and an inability to move the joint
15. A provider within a health insurance company's network that has contracted with the company to provide discounted services to a patient covered under the company's plan.
16. A surgically formed opening on a body surface

DOWN

1. the diagnosis and treatment of disorders of the heart and major blood vessels
2. A group of common infections occurring on the skin, hair, and nails that are caused by a fungus
4. The inner skin layer
5. An unaware clenching or grinding of the teeth, usually during sleep
6. A persisting fear of and desire to avoid something
7. A noncancerous tumor of the uterus made up of smooth muscle and connective tissue
8. A blood vessel that carries blood toward the heart
12. Mucus and other material produced by the lining of the respiratory tract; also called sputum

A. Phobia
B. Dermis
C. Sprain
D. Tinea
E. Ilium
F. Fibroid
G. Pallor
H. Privacy Rule
I. Referral
J. Radon
K. Phlegm
L. Stoma
M. Bruxism
N. Outpatient
O. Cardiology
P. Network Provider
Q. Vein

28. Using the Across and Down clues, write the correct words in the numbered grid below.

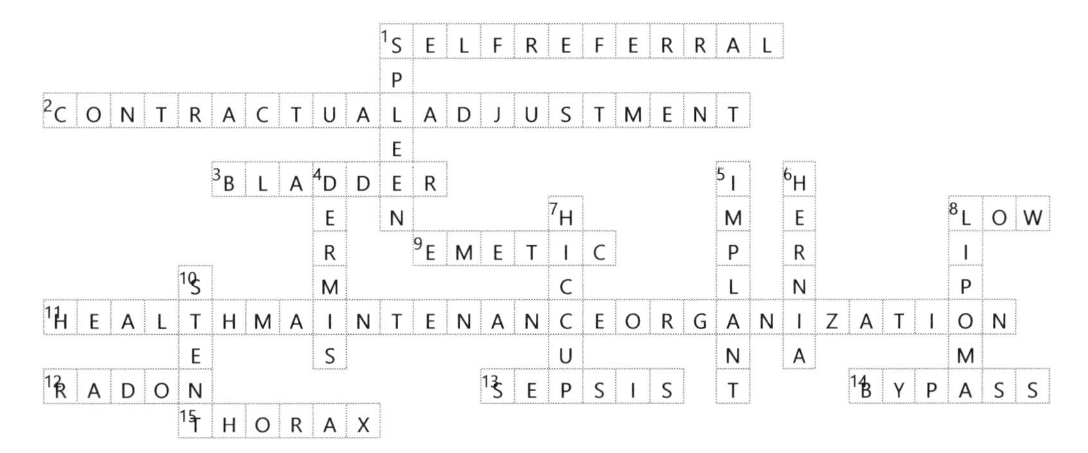

ACROSS

1. When a patient does their own research to find a provider and acts outside of their primary care physician's referral.
2. Refers to a binding agree between a provider, patient, and insurance company wherein the provider agrees to charges that it will write off on behalf of the patient.
3. An organ located in the pelvis whose function is to collect and store urine until it is expelled
8. Density lipoprotein- a type of lipoprotein that is the major carrier of cholesterol in the blood, with high levels associated with narrowing of the arteries and heart disease
9. A substance that causes vomiting
11. Networks of healthcare providers that offer healthcare plans to people for medical services exclusively in their network.
12. A colorless, odorless, tasteless radioactive gas that is produced by materials in soil, rocks, and building materials
13. The infection of a wound or tissue with bacteria, causing the spread of the bacteria into the bloodstream
14. A surgical technique in which the flow of blood or another body fluid is redirected around a blockage
15. The chest

DOWN

1. An organ located in the upper left abdomen behind the ribs that removes and destroys old red blood cells and helps fight infection
4. The inner skin layer
5. An organ, tissue, or device surgically inserted and left in the body
6. The bulging of an organ or tissue through a weakened area in the muscle wall
7. Involuntary sudden contraction of the diaphragm along with the closing of the vocal cords, producing a "hiccup" sound
8. A noncancerous tumor of fatty tissue
10. A device used to hold tissues in place, such as to support a skin graft

A. Contractual Adjustment
B. Spleen
C. Low
D. Bladder
E. Hernia
F. Dermis
G. Emetic
H. Thorax
I. Radon
J. Bypass
K. Sepsis
L. Stent
M. Hiccup
N. Health Maintenance Organization
O. Self Referral
P. Implant
Q. Lipoma

29. Using the Across and Down clues, write the correct words in the numbered grid below.

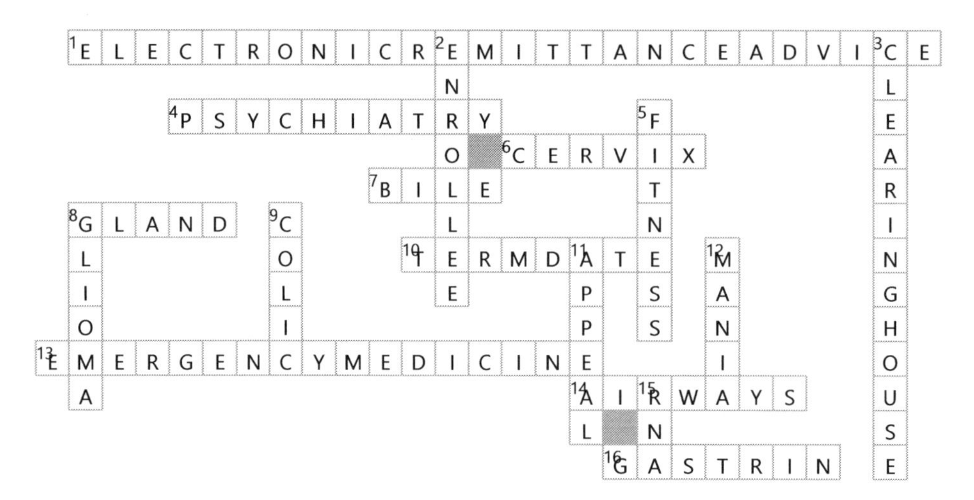

ACROSS

1. The digital version of EOB, which specifies the details of payments made on a claim either by an insurance company or required by the patient.
4. The diagnosis and treatment of mental, emotional and behavioral disorders
6. A small, round organ making up the neck of the uterus and separating it from the vagina
7. A yellow-green liquid produced in the liver whose function is to remove waste from the liver and break down fats as food is digested
8. A group of cells or an organ that produces substances (such as hormones and enzyme) that are used by the body
10. The end date for an insurance policy contract, or the date after which a person no longer receives or is no longer eligible for health insurance with company.
13. the specialty that includes treatment of any symptom, illness or injury requiring urgent evaluation and
14. The passageways that air moves through while traveling in and out of the lungs during breathing
16. A hormone that stimulates the release of gastric acid in the stomach

DOWN

2. A person covered by a health insurance plan.
3. Facilities that review and correct medical claims as necessary before sending them to insurance companies for final processing.
5. A measure of a person's physical strength, flexibility, and endurance
8. A brain tumor arising from cells that support nerve cells
9. Waves of pain in the abdomen that increase in strength, disappear, and return
11. Occurs when a patient or a provider tries to convince an insurance company to pay for healthcare after it has decided not to cover costs for someone on a claim.
12. A mental disorder characterized by extreme excitement, happiness, overactivity, and agitation
15. Ribonucleic acid, which helps to decode and process the information contained in dna

A. RNA
B. Enrollee
C. Airways
D. Bile
E. Gland
F. Mania
G. Glioma
H. Fitness
I. Term Date
J. Gastrin
K. Colic
L. Emergency Medicine
M. Psychiatry
N. Appeal
O. Electronic Remittance Advice
P. Cervix
Q. Clearinghouse

30. Using the Across and Down clues, write the correct words in the numbered grid below.

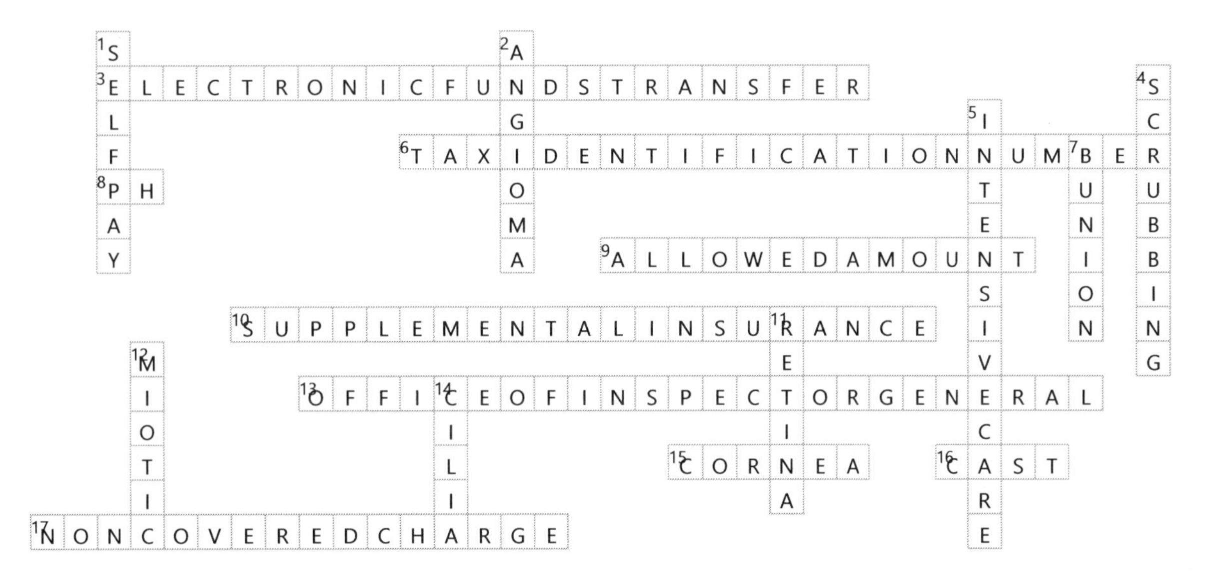

ACROSS

3. A method of transferring money electronically from a patient's bank account to a provider or an insurance carrier.
6. A unique number a patient or a company may have to produce for billing purposes in order to receive healthcare from a provider.
8. A measure of the acidic or basic character of a substance
9. The sum an insurance company will reimburse to cover a healthcare service or procedure.
10. Can be a secondary policy or another insurance company that covers a patient's healthcare costs after receiving coverage from their primary insurance.
13. The organization responsible for establishing guidelines and investigating fraud and misinformation within the healthcare industry.
15. The clear, dome-shaped front portion of the eye's outer covering
16. A hard plaster or fiberglass shell that molds to a body part such as an arm and holds it in place for proper healing
17. Procedures and services not covered by a person's health insurance plan.

DOWN

1. Payment made by the patient for healthcare at the time they receive it at a provider's facilities.
2. A tumor made of blood vessels or lymph vessels that is not cancerous
4. A process by which insurance claims are checked for errors before being sent to an insurance company for final processing.
5. The unit of a hospital reserved for patients that need immediate treatment and close monitoring by healthcare professionals for serious illnesses, conditions, and injuries.
7. A hard, fluid-filled pad along the inside joint of the big toe
11. A membrane lining the inside of the back of the eye that contains light-sensitive nerve cells that convert focused light into nerve impulses, making vision possible
12. A drug that causes the pupil to constrict
14. Tiny, hairlike structures on the outside of some cells, providing mobility

A. Self Pay
B. Allowed Amount
C. Tax Identification Number
D. Scrubbing
E. Electronic Funds Transfer
F. pH
G. Retina
H. Office of Inspector General
I. Miotic
J. Cast
K. Cornea
L. Bunion
M. Angioma
N. Cilia
O. Intensive Care
P. Non Covered Charge
Q. Supplemental Insurance

31. Using the Across and Down clues, write the correct words in the numbered grid below.

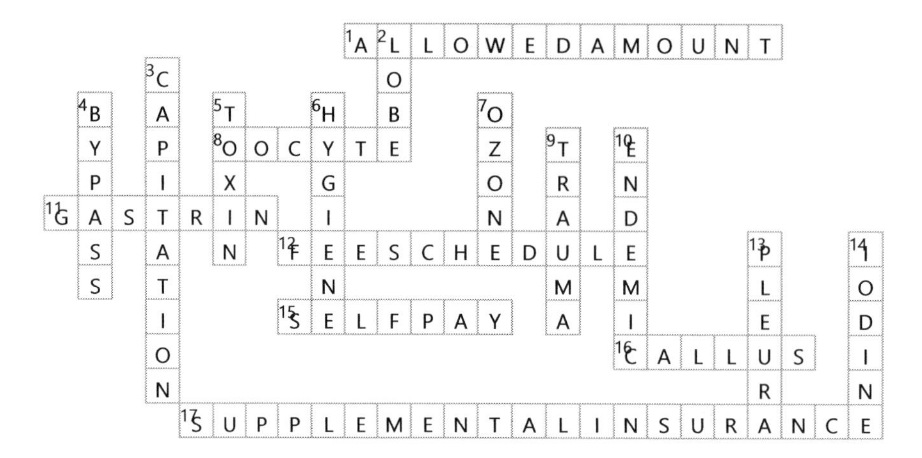

ACROSS

1. The sum an insurance company will reimburse to cover a healthcare service or procedure.
8. An egg cell that has not developed completely
11. A hormone that stimulates the release of gastric acid in the stomach
12. A document that outlines the costs associated for each medical service designated by a CPT code.
15. Payment made by the patient for healthcare at the time they receive it at a provider's facilities.
16. A thickened area of skin due to consistent pressure or friction, or the area around a bone break where new bone is formed
17. Can be a secondary policy or another insurance company that covers a patient's healthcare costs after receiving coverage from their primary insurance.

DOWN

2. A well-defined, separate part of an organ
3. A fixed payment that a patient makes to a health insurance company or provider to recoup costs incurred from various healthcare services.
4. A surgical technique in which the flow of blood or another body fluid is redirected around a blockage
5. A poisonous substance
6. The practice, maintenance, and study of health
7. A poisonous form of oxygen that is present in the earth's upper atmosphere, where it helps to screen the earth from damaging ultraviolet rays
9. Physical injury or emotional shock
10. Describes a disease that is always present in a certain population of people
13. The double- layered membrane that lines the lungs and chest cavity and allows for lung movement during breathing
14. An element for the formation of thyroid hormones

A. Capitation
B. Fee Schedule
C. Self Pay
D. Lobe
E. Callus
F. Allowed Amount
G. Ozone
H. Endemic
I. Toxin
J. Trauma
K. Oocyte
L. Bypass
M. Gastrin
N. Supplemental Insurance
O. Hygiene
P. Pleura
Q. Iodine

32. Using the Across and Down clues, write the correct words in the numbered grid below.

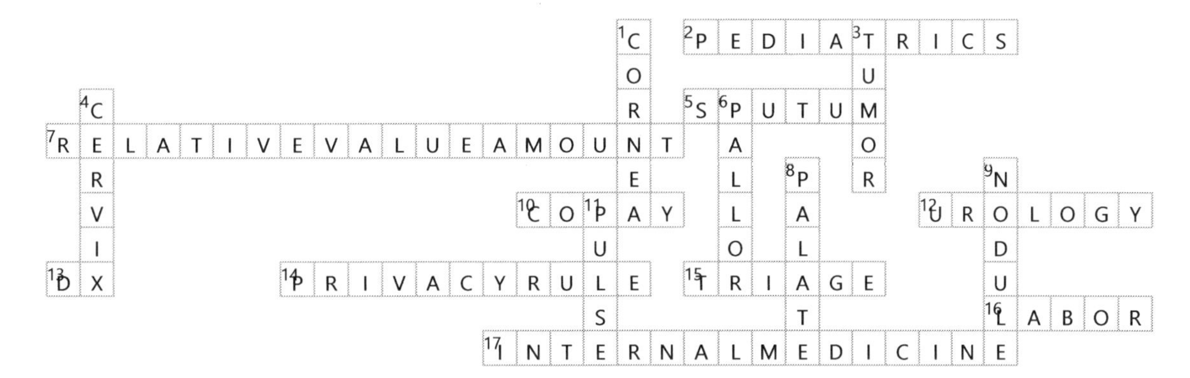

ACROSS

2. The care and treatment of infants, children, and adolescents
5. Mucus and other material produced by the lining of the respiratory tract; also called phlegm
7. The median amount Medicare will repay a provider for certain services and treatments.
10. The amount that must be paid to a provider before they receive any treatment or services.
12. The diagnosis and management, including surgery, of disorders of the urinary tract in both males and females, as well as the male reproductive system
13. The abbreviation for diagnosis codes, also known as ICD -9 codes.
14. Standards for privacy regarding a patient's medical history and all related events, treatments, and data as outlined by HIPAA.
15. A system used to classify sick or injured people according to the severity of their conditions
16. The interval from onset of contractions to birth of a baby
17. the diagnosis and non-surgical treatment of adult health problems

DOWN

1. The clear, dome-shaped front portion of the eye's outer covering
3. An abnormal mass that occurs when cells in a certain area reproduce unchecked
4. A small, round organ making up the neck of the uterus and separating it from the vagina
6. Abnormally pale skin
8. The roof of the mouth
9. A small lump of tissue that is usually abnormal
11. The expansion and contraction of a blood vessel due to the blood pumped through it

A. Triage
B. Pediatrics
C. Cornea
D. Palate
E. Tumor
F. Privacy Rule
G. Co Pay
H. Pulse
I. Dx
J. Pallor
K. Cervix
L. Sputum
M. Internal Medicine
N. Nodule
O. Urology
P. Labor
Q. Relative Value Amount

33. Using the Across and Down clues, write the correct words in the numbered grid below.

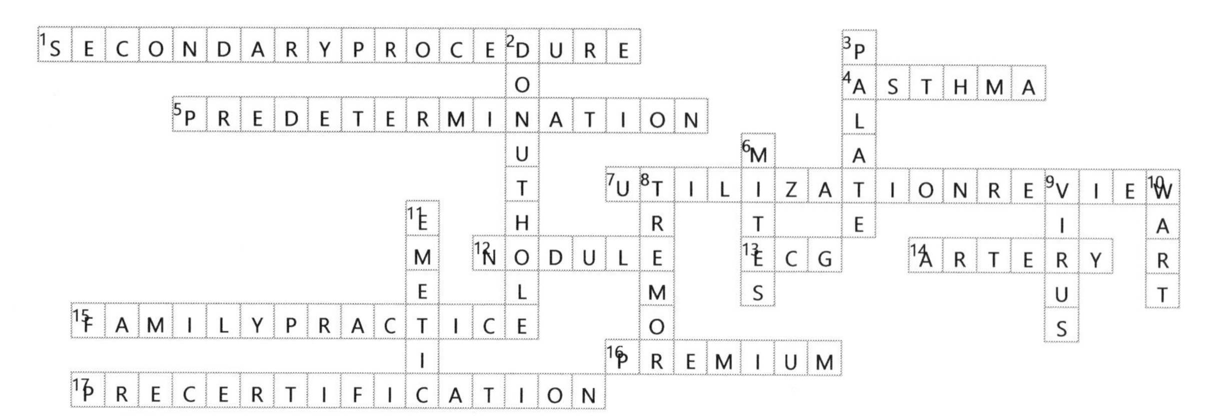

ACROSS

1. This is when provider performs another procedure on a patient covered by a CPT code after first performing a different CPT procedure on them.
4. A disorder characterized by inflamed airways and difficulty breathing
5. A maximum sum as explained in a healthcare plan an insurance company will pay for certain services or treatments.
7. An investigation or audit performed to optimize the number of inpatient and outpatient services a provider performs.
12. A small lump of tissue that is usually abnormal
13. An electrocardiogram, which is a record of the electrical impulses that trigger the heartbeat
14. A large blood vessel that carries blood from the heart to tissues and organs in the body
15. the specialty that provides comprehensive and ongoing medical care to all members of the family unit
16. The sum a person pays to an insurance company on a regular (usually monthly or yearly) basis to receive health insurance.
17. A process similar to preauthorization whereby patients must check with insurance companies to see if a desired healthcare treatment or service is deemed medically necessary

DOWN

2. This term refers to the discrepancy between the limits of healthcare insurance coverage and the Medicare Part D coverage limits for prescription drugs.
3. The roof of the mouth
6. Small eight-legged animals, many of which burrow and feed on blood
8. An involuntary, rhythmic, shaking movement caused by alternating contraction and relaxation of muscles
9. The smallest known disease- causing microorganism
10. A contagious, harmless growth caused by a virus that occurs on the skin or a mucous membrane
11. A substance that causes vomiting

A. Virus
B. Wart
C. Palate
D. Asthma
E. Tremor
F. Emetic
G. Artery
H. Pre Certification
I. Pre determination
J. Secondary Procedure
K. ECG
L. Nodule
M. Family Practice
N. Premium
O. Utilization Review
P. Donut Hole
Q. Mites

34. Using the Across and Down clues, write the correct words in the numbered grid below.

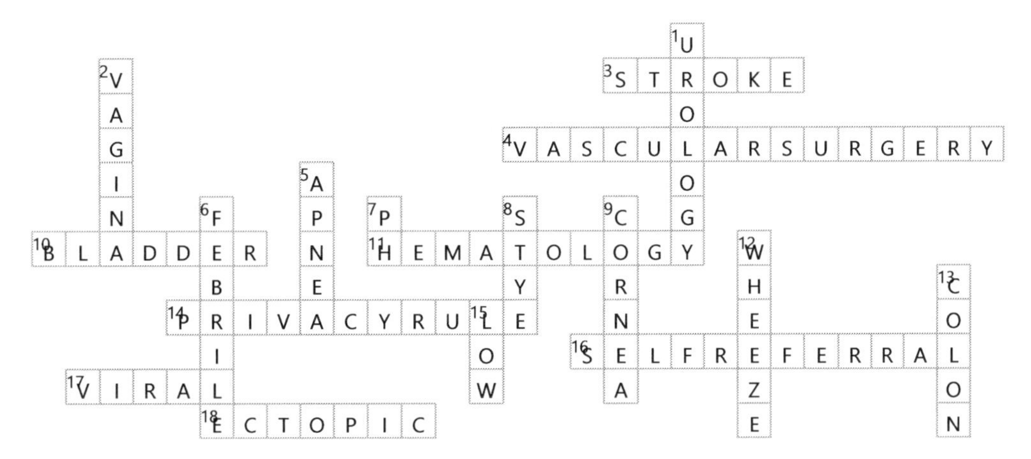

ACROSS

3. Damage to part of the brain because of a lack of blood supply or the rupturing of a blood vessel
4. The diagnosis and treatment of circulatory problems of the extremities, especially the legs
10. An organ located in the pelvis whose function is to collect and store urine until it is expelled
11. Oncology
14. Standards for privacy regarding a patient's medical history and all related events, treatments, and data as outlined by HIPAA.
16. When a patient does their own research to find a provider and acts outside of their primary care physician's referral.
17. A term describing something related to or caused by a virus
18. Occurring at an abnormal position or time

DOWN

1. The diagnosis and management, including surgery, of disorders of the urinary tract in both males and females, as well as the male reproductive system
2. The muscular passage connecting the uterus with the outside genitals
5. A possibly life-threatening condition in which breathing stops, for either a short or long period of time
6. A term used to describe something related to a fever, such as febrile seizures
7. A measure of the acidic or basic character of a substance
8. A pus- filled abscess in the follicle of an eyelash
9. The clear, dome-shaped front portion of the eye's outer covering
12. A high- pitched sound produced during breathing because of narrowing of the airways
13. The main part of the large intestine, between the cecum and the rectum
15. Density lipoprotein- a type of lipoprotein that is the major carrier of cholesterol in the blood, with high levels associated with narrowing of the arteries and heart disease

A. Urology	B. Viral	C. Cornea	D. Stroke
E. Ectopic	F. Colon	G. Hematology	H. Wheeze
I. Privacy Rule	J. Vascular Surgery	K. Vagina	L. Bladder
M. Low	N. pH	O. Febrile	P. Stye
Q. Apnea	R. Self Referral		

35. Using the Across and Down clues, write the correct words in the numbered grid below.

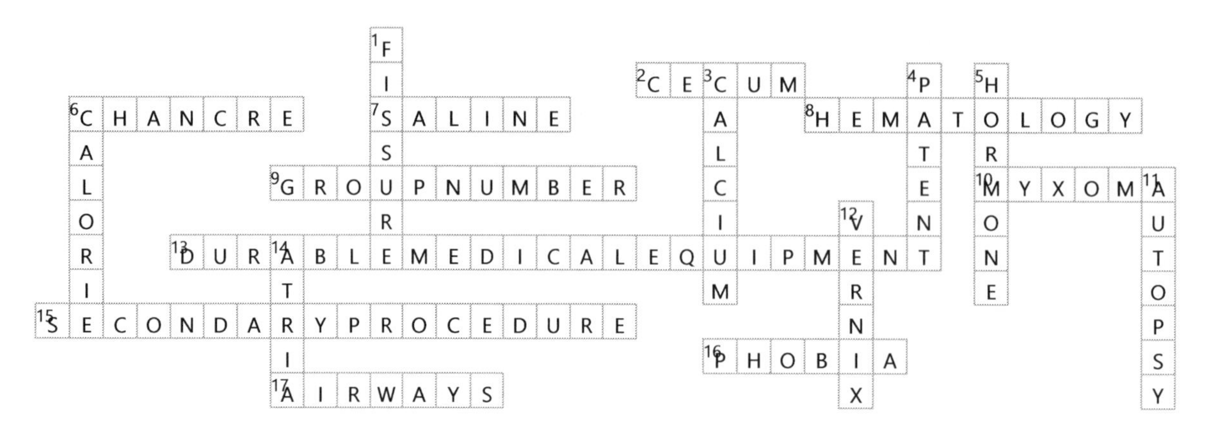

ACROSS

2. The beginning of the large intestine, which is connected to the appendix at its lower end
6. A painless sore that has a thick, rubbery base and a defined edge
7. A salt solution or any substance that contains salt
8. Oncology
9. A number given to a patient by their insurance carrier that identifies the group or plan under which they are covered.
10. A noncancerous tumor made of mucous material and fibrous connective tissue
13. This refers to medical implements that can be reused such as stretchers, wheelchairs, canes, crutches, and bedpans.
15. This is when provider performs another procedure on a patient covered by a CPT code after first performing a different CPT procedure on them.
16. A persisting fear of and desire to avoid something
17. The passageways that air moves through while traveling in and out of the lungs during breathing

DOWN

1. A groove or slit on the body or in an organ
3. A plentiful mineral in the body and the basic component of teeth and bones
4. Not obstructed; open
5. A chemical produced by a gland or tissue that is released into the bloodstream
6. A unit that is used to measure the energy content in food
11. The examination of a body following death, possibly to determine the cause of death or for research
12. The thick, greasy substance that covers the skin of a newborn baby
14. The two upper chambers of the heart

A. Group Number
D. Phobia
G. Calcium
J. Hormone
M. Vernix
P. Cecum

B. Hematology
E. Durable Medical Equipment
H. Calorie
K. Patent
N. Secondary Procedure
Q. Atria

C. Autopsy
F. Airways
I. Myxoma
L. Chancre
O. Saline
R. Fissure

36. Using the Across and Down clues, write the correct words in the numbered grid below.

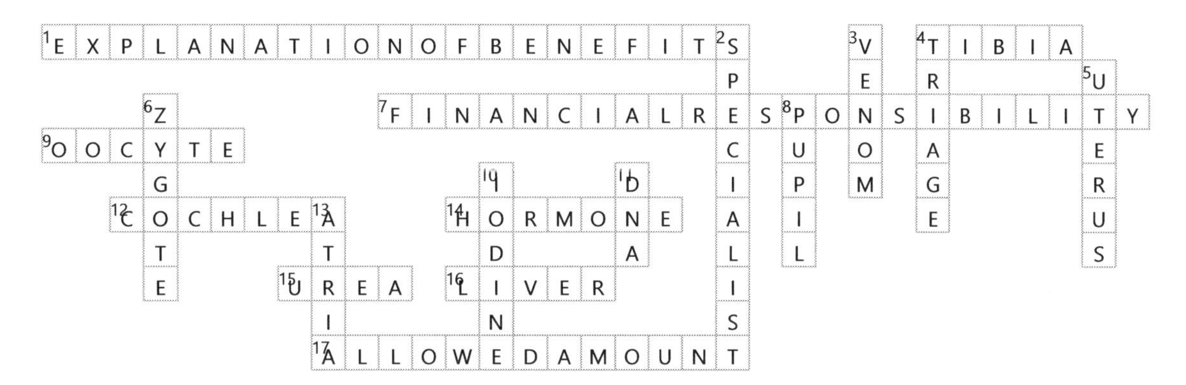

ACROSS

1. A document attached to a processed medical claim wherein the insurance company explains the services they will cover for a patient's healthcare treatments.
4. The thicker of the two long bones in the lower leg; commonly called the shin
7. Whoever owes the healthcare provider money has financial responsibility for the services rendered.
9. An egg cell that has not developed completely
12. A coiled organ in the inner ear that plays a large role in hearing by picking up sound vibrations and transmitting them as electrical signals
14. A chemical produced by a gland or tissue that is released into the bloodstream
15. A waste product of the metabolism of proteins that is formed by the liver and secreted by the kidneys
16. The largest organ in the body, producing many essential chemicals and regulating the levels of most vital substances in the blood
17. The sum an insurance company will reimburse to cover a healthcare service or procedure.

DOWN

2. A physician or medical assistant with expertise in a specific area of medicine.
3. A poisonous substance produced by certain animals
4. A system used to classify sick or injured people according to the severity of their conditions
5. The hollow female reproductive organ in which a fertilized egg is implanted and a fetus develops
6. The cell that results when an egg is fertilized by a sperm
8. The opening at the center of the iris in the eye that constricts (contracts) and dilates (widens) in response to light
10. An element for the formation of thyroid hormones
11. Deoxyribonucleic acid; responsible for passing genetic information in nearly all organisms
13. The two upper chambers of the heart

A. DNA
B. Explanation of Benefits
C. Iodine
D. Venom
E. Liver
F. Uterus
G. Cochlea
H. Urea
I. Triage
J. Hormone
K. Oocyte
L. Financial Responsibility
M. Zygote
N. Pupil
O. Tibia
P. Atria
Q. Specialist
R. Allowed Amount

37. Using the Across and Down clues, write the correct words in the numbered grid below.

```
                   WRITEOFF
                      H
               PULMONARYMEDICINE
        H         E   I       E
        O   C     D   L   P   U
      FISTULA N   I   L GOUT  R
        P   SMEAR A P   A S   O
        I   T R  PLEURA V     N
        C     V     V   APPEAL
SUBSCRIBER  CREDENTIALING
                        E
```

ACROSS

1. Refers to the discrepancy between a provider's fee for healthcare services and the amount that an insurance company is willing to pay for those services that a patient is not responsible for.
3. The diagnosis and treatment of acute and chronic diseases and conditions of the respiratory system, such as bronchitis, asthma, emphysema and occupational lung disease
9. An abnormal passageway from one organ to another or from an organ to the body surface
11. A disorder marked by high levels of uric acid in the blood
12. A sample of cells spread across a glass slide to be examined through a microscope
14. The double- layered membrane that lines the lungs and chest cavity and allows for lung movement during breathing
15. Occurs when a patient or a provider tries to convince an insurance company to pay for healthcare after it has decided not to cover costs for someone on a claim.
16. The individual covered under a group policy. For instance, an employee of a company with a group health policy would be one of many subscribers on that policy.
17. The application process for a provider to coordinate with an insurance company.

DOWN

2. A vibration felt when the hand is placed flat on the chest; caused by abnormal blood flow through the heart as a result of disease
4. A term used to describe something situated on or near the midline of the body or a body structure
5. Another term for a nerve cell
6. This refers to medical care and treatment for persons who are terminally ill.
7. A hard plaster or fiberglass shell that molds to a body part such as an arm and holds it in place for proper healing
8. A thick, yellowish or greenish fluid that contains dead white blood cells, tissues, and bacteria; occurs at the site of a bacterial infection
10. A bundle of fibers that transmit electrical messages between the brain and areas of the body
11. An artificial feeding technique in which liquids are passed into the stomach by way of a tube inserted through the nose
13. A form of phototherapy that combines the use of psoralens and ultraviolet light to treat skin disorders

A. Subscriber	B. Cast	C. Thrill	D. Fistula
E. Medial	F. Pus	G. Nerve	H. PUVA
I. Pleura	J. Credentialing	K. Gout	L. Write Off
M. Smear	N. Neuron	O. Gavage	P. Hospice
Q. Pulmonary Medicine	R. Appeal		

38. Using the Across and Down clues, write the correct words in the numbered grid below.

ACROSS

1. Payment made by the patient for healthcare at the time they receive it at a provider's facilities.
8. Muscle damage resulting from excessive stretching or forceful contraction
9. A term used to describe a child in the womb from fertilization to 8 weeks following fertilization
10. A group of cells or an organ that produces substances (such as hormones and enzyme) that are used by the body
12. This term is used in ICD-9 codes to describe conditions with unspecified diagnoses.
14. A chemical, originating in a cell, that regulates reactions in the body
15. A term describing something related to or caused by a virus
16. Abnormal crackling or bubbling sounds heard in the lungs during breathing
17. The sum an insurance company will reimburse to cover a healthcare service or procedure.

DOWN

2. An area of buildup of fat deposits in an artery, causing narrowing of the artery and possibly heart disease
3. A noncancerous tumor of the uterus made up of smooth muscle and connective tissue
4. A painless sore that has a thick, rubbery base and a defined edge
5. The diagnosis and management, including surgery, of disorders of the urinary tract in both males and females, as well as the male reproductive system
6. A structure that allows fluid flow in only one direction
7. A brown to dark-brown spot on the skin that can be flat or raised
11. The bone located between the hip and the knee
13. One of the two bones that form the hip on either side of the body

A. Embryo	B. Enzyme	C. Fibroid
D. Viral	E. Strain	F. Allowed Amount
G. Valve	H. Ilium	I. Gland
J. Chancre	K. Plaque	L. Rales
M. Mole	N. Urology	O. Not Otherwise Specified
P. Self Pay	Q. Femur	

39. Using the Across and Down clues, write the correct words in the numbered grid below.

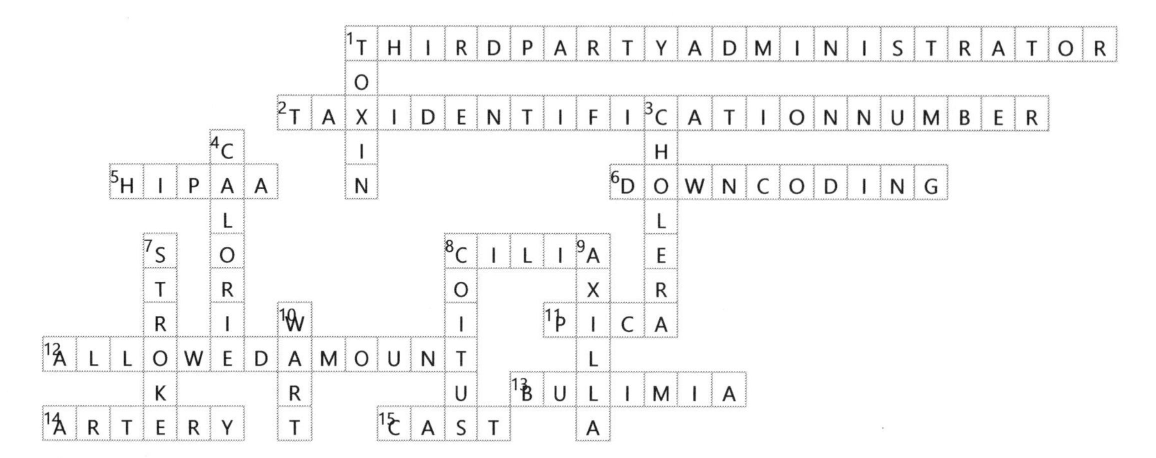

ACROSS

1. The name for the organization or individual that manages healthcare group benefits, claims, and administrative duties on behalf of a group plan or a company with a group plan.
2. A unique number a patient or a company may have to produce for billing purposes in order to receive healthcare from a provider.
5. Law passed in 1996 with an aim to improve the scope of healthcare services and establish regulations for securing healthcare records from unwanted parties.
6. Occurs when an insurance company finds there is insufficient evidence on a claim to prove that a provider performed coded medical services and so they reduce or remove those codes.
8. Tiny, hairlike structures on the outside of some cells, providing mobility
11. A desire to eat materials that are not food
12. The sum an insurance company will reimburse to cover a healthcare service or procedure.
13. A disorder in which a person eats large amounts of food then forces vomiting or uses laxatives to prevent weight gain (called binging and purging)
14. A large blood vessel that carries blood from the heart to tissues and organs in the body
15. A hard plaster or fiberglass shell that molds to a body part such as an arm and holds it in place for proper healing

DOWN

1. A poisonous substance
3. A bacterial infection of the small intestine that causes severe watery diarrhea, dehydration, and possibly death
4. A unit that is used to measure the energy content in food
7. Damage to part of the brain because of a lack of blood supply or the rupturing of a blood vessel
8. Sexual intercourse
9. Medical term for the armpit
10. A contagious, harmless growth caused by a virus that occurs on the skin or a mucous membrane

A. Cilia
B. Cast
C. HIPAA
D. Toxin
E. Artery
F. Bulimia
G. Downcoding
H. Cholera
I. Tax Identification Number
J. Coitus
K. Allowed Amount
L. Wart
M. Pica
N. Stroke
O. Calorie
P. Axilla
Q. Third Party Administrator

40. Using the Across and Down clues, write the correct words in the numbered grid below.

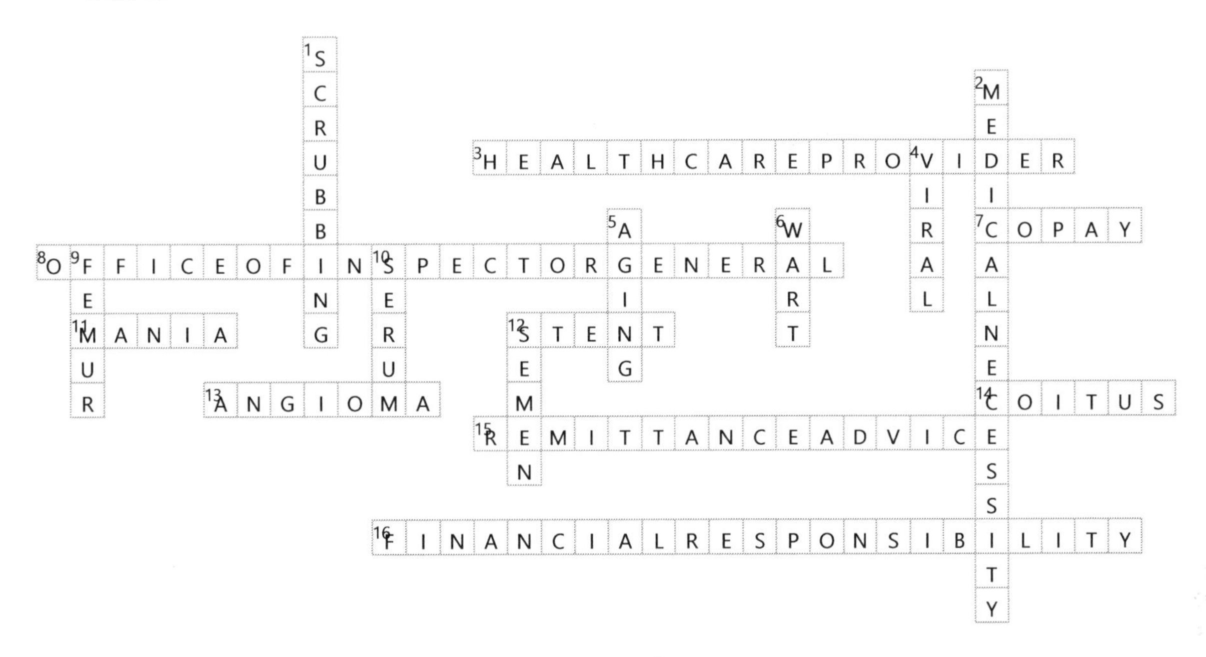

ACROSS

3. These are the entities that offer healthcare services to patients, including hospitals, physicians, and private clinics, hospices, nursing homes, and other healthcare facilities.
7. The amount that must be paid to a provider before they receive any treatment or services.
8. The organization responsible for establishing guidelines and investigating fraud and misinformation within the healthcare industry.
11. A mental disorder characterized by extreme excitement, happiness, overactivity, and agitation
12. A device used to hold tissues in place, such as to support a skin graft
13. A tumor made of blood vessels or lymph vessels that is not cancerous
14. Sexual intercourse
15. The document attached to a processed claim that explains the information regarding coverage and payments on a claim.
16. Whoever owes the healthcare provider money has financial responsibility for the services rendered.

DOWN

1. A process by which insurance claims are checked for errors before being sent to an insurance company for final processing.
2. Refers to healthcare services or treatments that a patient requires to treat a serious medical condition or illness.
4. A term describing something related to or caused by a virus
5. A formal medical billing term that refers to insurance claims that haven't been paid or balances owed by patients overdue by more than 30 days.
6. A contagious, harmless growth caused by a virus that occurs on the skin or a mucous membrane
9. The bone located between the hip and the knee
10. The clear, watery fluid that separates from clotted blood
12. Fluid released during ejaculation that contains sperm along with fluids produced by the prostate gland and the seminal vesicles

A. Viral
B. Femur
C. Remittance Advice
D. Office of Inspector General
E. Serum
F. Coitus
G. Wart
H. Angioma
I. Financial Responsibility
J. Co Pay
K. Aging
L. Semen
M. Medical Necessity
N. Healthcare Provider
O. Mania
P. Scrubbing
Q. Stent

Multiple Choice

A. From the words provided for each clue, provide the letter of the word which best matches the clue.

1. ____ A group of diseases caused by the microorganism rickettsia, spread by the bites of fleas, mites, or ticks
A. Typhus B. Stoma C. Medicaid D. Penis

2. ____ A small, rounded tissue mass
A. Bulimia B. Gastrin C. Ovum D. Node

3. ____ A marking on the skin; can be present at birth (birthmark) or develop later (such as a mole)
A. Tic B. Thrill C. Nevus D. Lipoma

4. ____ the administration of medications as a means to block pain or diminish consciousness for surgery, usually by injection or inhalation
A. Out of Network B. Preferred Provider Organization C. Myxoma D. Anesthesiology

5. ____ Additions to CPT codes that explain alterations and modifications to an otherwise routine treatment, exam, or service.
A. Application Service Provider B. Cilia C. Modifier D. Canal

6. ____ The person who pays for a patient's medical expenses, also known as the guarantor.
A. Preferred Provider Organization B. Mumps C. Responsible Party D. Allergy

7. ____ A disorder in which a person eats large amounts of food then forces vomiting or uses laxatives to prevent weight gain (called binging and purging)
A. Bulimia B. Boil C. Subscriber D. Fetus

8. ____ The process of translating a physician's documentation about a patient's medical condition and health services rendered into medical codes that are then plugged into a claim for processing.
A. Stoma B. Pathology C. Low D. Coding

9. ____ A growth that occurs on mucous membranes such as those in the nose and intestine
A. Mites B. Bunion C. Medigap D. Polyp

10. ____ Healthy tissue that is used to replace diseased or defective tissue
A. Culture B. Graft C. Smear D. Bile

11. ____ The amount a patient is required to pay.
A. Maximum Out of Pocket B. Venom C. Preauthorization D. Supplemental Insurance

12. ____ The lowest section of the small intestine, which attaches to the large intestine
A. Aging B. Ileum C. Stroke D. Shock

13. ____ Refers to the sum shown in the "balance" column of a billing statement that reflects the amount due for services rendered.
A. Credit Balance B. Hepatic C. Medigap D. Stent

14. ____ The practice, maintenance, and study of health
A. Sodium B. Nevus C. Bypass D. Hygiene

15. ____ The claim filed with the secondary insurance company after the primary insurance company pays for their portion of healthcare costs.
A. Patent B. Secondary Insurance Claim C. Canal D. Spasm

16. ____ A term used to describe something that is related to the liver
A. Hepatic B. Provider C. Coding D. Date of Birth

17. ____ A tunnel-like passage
A. Tic B. Canal C. Medigap D. Fraud

18. ____ A structure that allows fluid flow in only one direction
A. Rectum B. Sputum C. Valve D. Fetus

19. ____ This is when a provider recommends another provider to a patient to receive specialized treatment.
A. Referral B. Sodium C. Medicaid D. Capitation

20. ____ The colored part of the eye
A. Iris B. Bladder C. Superbill D. Third Party Administrator

21. ____ An employee in the healthcare system such as a physician's assistant or a nurse practitioner who perform duties in administration, nursing, and other ancillary care.
A. Airways B. Medical Assistant C. Hepatic D. Practice Management Software

22. ____ The drooping of the upper eyelid
A. Demographics B. B cell C. Ptosis D. Otolaryngology

23. ____ The limit per year for coverage under certain available healthcare services for Medicare enrollees.
A. Fitness B. Tar C. TRICARE D. Utilization Limit

24. ____ A group of fats stored in the body and used for energy
A. Lipids B. Preferred Provider Organization C. In Network D. Palate

25. ____ Software used for scheduling, billing, and recordkeeping at a provider's office.
A. Practice Management Software B. Urea C. Downcoding D. Bowel

26. ____ Procedures and services not covered by a person's health insurance plan.
A. Geriatrics B. Tertiary Claim C. Non Covered Charge D. Rectum

27. ____ The specialty of physicians who are trained to examine surgical specimens and biopsies for diagnostic purposes.
A. Hernia B. Pathology C. Modifier D. Ilium

28. ____ A digestive disorder in which nutrients cannot be properly absorbed from food, causing weakness and loss of weight
A. Valve B. Sprue C. Non Covered Charge D. Stent

29. ____ Law passed in 1996 with an aim to improve the scope of healthcare services and establish regulations for securing healthcare records from unwanted parties.
A. Primary Care Physician B. Ovum C. Referral D. HIPAA

30. ____ the care of women during and after pregnancy and childbirth, and the care of the female reproductive system and treatment of associated disorders
A. Gynecology B. Fraud C. Node D. Lesion

31. ____ A surgical technique in which the flow of blood or another body fluid is redirected around a blockage
A. Bypass B. Unbundling C. Referral D. Shunt

32. ____ The clear, dome-shaped front portion of the eye's outer covering
A. Preferred Provider Organization B. Cornea C. Medical Transcription D. Gene

33. ____ The healthcare facility that administered healthcare to an individual. Physicians, clinics, and hospitals are all considered providers.
A. Provider B. Fibroma C. Subscriber D. Fraud

34. ____ A plentiful mineral in the body and the basic component of teeth and bones
A. Third Party Administrator B. Out of Network C. Calcium D. Remittance Advice

35. ____ A sample of cells spread across a glass slide to be examined through a microscope
A. Place of Service Code B. Smear C. Graft D. Splint

36. ____ Referring to 61st through 90th days of inpatient treatment, the law requires that patients pay for a portion of their healthcare during Medicare coinsurance days.
A. Taxonomy Code B. Cecum C. pH D. Medicare Coinsurance Days

37. ____ Can be a secondary policy or another insurance company that covers a patient's healthcare costs after receiving coverage from their primary insurance.
A. Patient Responsibility B. Niacin C. Supplemental Insurance D. Sebum

38. ____ The end date for an insurance policy contract, or the date after which a person no longer receives or is no longer eligible for health insurance with company.
A. Term Date B. Appeal C. Application Service Provider D. Lungs

39. ____ A hospital or an area of a hospital dedicated to treating people who are dying, often of a specific cause
A. Lipids B. Suture C. Hospice D. Otolaryngology

40. ____ A fixed payment that a patient makes to a health insurance company or provider to recoup costs incurred from various healthcare services.
A. Fibroid B. Capitation C. Out of Network D. Croup

41. ____ This term refers to a provider's relationship with a health insurance company.
A. Canal B. Gynecology C. In Network D. Dermis

42. ____ A federal program that allows a person terminated from their employer to retain health insurance they had with that employer.
A. Mumps B. Valve C. COBRA D. Thrush

43. ____ Serves as the guidelines for policies and practices necessary to reduce security risks within the healthcare system.
A. Non Covered Charge B. Security Standard C. Geriatrics D. Bulimia

44. ____ A short tube located at the end of the large intestine, which connects the intestine to the anus
A. Rectum B. Outpatient C. Point of Service Plans D. Referral

45. ____ The structure of bodies; commonly refers to the study of body structure
A. Niacin B. Bursa C. Sebum D. Anatomy

46. ____ The bulging of an organ or tissue through a weakened area in the muscle wall
A. Radius B. Sprue C. Hernia D. Medicaid

47. ____ A reduced flow of blood throughout the body, usually caused by severe bleeding or a weak heart
A. Medical Record Number B. PUVA C. Shock D. Office of Inspector General

48. ____ Responsible for assigning various medical codes to services and healthcare plans described by a physician on a patient's super-bill.
A. Medical Coder B. Bladder C. Endemic D. Hernia

49. ____ The diagnosis and treatment of acute and chronic diseases and conditions of the respiratory system, such as bronchitis, asthma, emphysema and occupational lung disease
A. Orthopaedics B. Pulmonary Medicine C. Geriatrics D. Patient Responsibility

50. ____ A vitamin important in many chemical processes in the body
A. Indemnity B. Airways C. Niacin D. Non Covered Charge

51. ____ The sticky, brown substance in cigarettes that coats the lungs; causes lung and other cancers
A. Medigap B. Graft C. Tar D. Anatomy

52. ____ Ribonucleic acid, which helps to decode and process the information contained in dna
A. Gastrin B. Referral C. Term Date D. RNA

53. ____ The beginning of the large intestine, which is connected to the appendix at its lower end
A. Place of Service Code B. Cholera C. Wart D. Cecum

54. ______ A poisonous substance produced by certain animals
A. Tar B. Larynx C. Artery D. Venom

55. ______ A usually mild and temporary condition common in children in which the walls of the airways become inflamed and narrow, resulting in wheezing and coughing
A. Endemic B. Sclera C. Medical Transcription D. Croup

56. ______ Describes a disorder that continues for a long period of time
A. Chronic B. Lipoma C. Primary Care Physician D. Suture

57. ______ A noncancerous tumor of connective tissue
A. Coitus B. Capitation C. Spine D. Fibroma

58. ______ An organ located in the upper left abdomen behind the ribs that removes and destroys old red blood cells and helps fight infection
A. Signature on File B. Low C. Pulp D. Spleen

59. ______ The document attached to a processed claim that explains the information regarding coverage and payments on a claim.
A. Culture B. Allergy C. Aging D. Remittance Advice

60. ______ The cell that results when an egg is fertilized by a sperm
A. Angioma B. Zygote C. Labia D. Croup

61. ______ The complete set of an organism's genes
A. Demographics B. Genome C. Angioma D. Labia

62. ______ A poisonous form of oxygen that is present in the earth's upper atmosphere, where it helps to screen the earth from damaging ultraviolet rays
A. Polyp B. Ozone C. Orthopaedics D. Corn

63. ______ Refers to providers outside of an established network of providers who contract with an insurance company to offer patients healthcare at a discounted rate.
A. Out of Network B. Allergy C. Financial Responsibility D. Gynecology

64. ______ A bacterial infection of the small intestine that causes severe watery diarrhea, dehydration, and possibly death
A. Atresia B. Orgasm C. Cholera D. Pulmonary Medicine

65. ______ Supplemental health insurance under Medicaid for eligible persons who need help covering co-pays, deductibles, and other large fees.
A. Patent B. Canal C. Medigap D. Urea

66. ______ The organization responsible for establishing guidelines and investigating fraud and misinformation within the healthcare industry.
A. Signature on File B. Cast C. Office of Inspector General D. Remittance Advice

67. ______ An inflamed, raised area of skin that is pus-filled
A. Fee for Service B. Boil C. Place of Service Code D. RNA

68. ______ A measure of the acidic or basic character of a substance
A. pH B. Gavage C. Neonatology D. Non Covered Charge

69. ______ An artificial feeding technique in which liquids are passed into the stomach by way of a tube inserted through the nose
A. Gavage B. Aging C. Tic D. Medical Transcription

70. ______ A negative reaction to a substance that in most people causes no reaction
A. Incremental Nursing Charge B. ECG C. Primary Care Physician D. Allergy

71. ______ Networks of healthcare providers that offer healthcare plans to people for medical services exclusively in their network.
A. Health Maintenance Organization B. Inpatient C. Stroke D. Hernia

72. ____ A candidiasis infection
A. Thrush B. Applied to Deductible C. Health Maintenance Organization D. Ptosis

73. ____ The party paying for an insurance plan who is not the patient. Parents, for example, would be the guarantors for their children's health insurance.
A. Tax Identification Number B. Cardiology C. Guarantor D. Hepatic

74. ____ A digital network that allows healthcare providers to access quality medical billing software and technologies without needing to purchase and maintain it themselves.
A. Application Service Provider B. Medicaid C. Supplemental Insurance D. Gynecology

75. ____ The inner skin layer
A. Dermis B. Larynx C. Pulse D. Contractual Adjustment

76. ____ The technique of creating pictures of structures inside of the body using x-rays, ultrasound waves, or magnetic fields
A. Imaging B. Downcoding C. Remittance Advice D. Boil

77. ____ The artificial growth of cells, tissue, or microorganisms such as bacteria in a laboratory
A. Fee for Service B. Ancillary Services C. Culture D. Unbundling

78. ____ A device used to hold tissues in place, such as to support a skin graft
A. Neonatology B. Stent C. Corn D. In Network

79. ____ One of the two long bones of the forearm
A. Radius B. Atresia C. Sprue D. PUVA

80. ____ Sexual intercourse
A. Medicare Coinsurance Days B. Downcoding C. Cornea D. Coitus

81. ____ A device that is used to immobilize a part of the body
A. Splint B. Penis C. Iris D. Gavage

82. ____ A unique number a patient or a company may have to produce for billing purposes in order to receive healthcare from a provider.
A. Privacy Rule B. HIPAA C. Sebum D. Tax Identification Number

83. ____ The two pairs of skinfolds that protect the opening of the vagina
A. Labia B. Neonatology C. Tertiary Claim D. Medicaid

84. ____ Damage to part of the brain because of a lack of blood supply or the rupturing of a blood vessel
A. Emergency Medicine B. Application Service Provider C. Thrush D. Stroke

85. ____ The external male reproductive organ, which passes urine and semen out of the body
A. Outpatient B. Non Covered Charge C. Group Number D. Penis

86. ____ A document used by healthcare staff and physicians to write down information about a patient receiving care.
A. Canal B. Medical Transcription C. Type of Service D. Superbill

87. ____ Involuntary contraction of genital muscles experienced at the peak of sexual excitement
A. Signature on File B. Hospice C. Niacin D. Orgasm

88. ____ The soft tissue inside of a tooth that contains blood vessels and nerves
A. Pulp B. Fetus C. Cast D. Corn

89. ____ A claim filed by a provider after they have filed claims for primary and secondary health insurance coverage on behalf of a patient.
A. Tertiary Claim B. Venom C. Endemic D. Typhus

90. ____ A group of common infections occurring on the skin, hair, and nails that are caused by a fungus
A. Medicaid B. Tinea C. Culture D. Ancillary Services

91. ____ A poisonous substance
A. Medicaid B. Type of Service C. Toxin D. Niacin

92. ____ Density lipoprotein- a type of lipoprotein that is the major carrier of cholesterol in the blood, with high levels associated with narrowing of the arteries and heart disease
A. Low B. Bulimia C. Typhus D. Preferred Provider Organization

93. ____ A substance that causes vomiting
A. Mites B. Otolaryngology C. Culture D. Emetic

94. ____ Occurs when a patient or a provider tries to convince an insurance company to pay for healthcare after it has decided not to cover costs for someone on a claim.
A. Mites B. Mumps C. Appeal D. Patent

95. ____ An area of inflammation or a group of spots on the skin
A. Suture B. Culture C. Labia D. Rash

96. ____ The individual covered under a group policy. For instance, an employee of a company with a group health policy would be one of many subscribers on that policy.
A. Mumps B. Subscriber C. Point of Service Plans D. Preauthorization

97. ____ The exact date a patient was born.
A. Non Covered Charge B. Unbundling C. Date of Birth D. Supplemental Insurance

98. ____ A white blood cell that makes antibodies to fight infections caused by foreign proteins
A. Tertiary Claim B. B cell C. Medical Coder D. Tar

99. ____ A vibration felt when the hand is placed flat on the chest; caused by abnormal blood flow through the heart as a result of disease
A. Term Date B. Thrill C. Hymen D. Sclera

100. ____ A field on a claim for describing what kind of healthcare services or procedures a provider administered.
A. Gout B. Credit Balance C. Type of Service D. Remittance Advice

B. From the words provided for each clue, provide the letter of the word which best matches the clue.

1. ____ A federal program that allows a person terminated from their employer to retain health insurance they had with that employer.
A. Pica B. COBRA C. Rales D. Workers Compensation

2. ____ the diagnosis and non-surgical treatment of adult health problems
A. Lesion B. Internal Medicine C. Rales D. Pupil

3. ____ A hormone that stimulates the release of gastric acid in the stomach
A. Tinea B. Gastrin C. Endemic D. Coitus

4. ____ A hard, fluid-filled pad along the inside joint of the big toe
A. Primary Care Physician B. Bunion C. ERISA D. Indemnity

5. ____ Referring to 61st through 90th days of inpatient treatment, the law requires that patients pay for a portion of their healthcare during Medicare coinsurance days.
A. Security Standard B. Skilled Nursing Facility C. Hypoxia D. Medicare Coinsurance Days

6. ____ Describes a condition or illness that begins suddenly and is usually short- lasting
A. Clearinghouse B. Acute C. Gavage D. Indemnity

7. ____ The examination of a body following death, possibly to determine the cause of death or for research
A. Financial Responsibility B. Genome C. Autopsy D. Myopia

8. ____ When claim information is sent from a primary insurance carrier to a secondary insurance carrier, or vice versa.
A. Eardrum B. Crossover Claim C. Anus D. Medicare Coinsurance Days

9. ____ Some insurance plans require that a patient receive preauthorization from the insurance company prior to receiving certain medical services.
A. Hypoxia B. Preauthorization C. Spleen D. Cervix

10. ____ The smallest known disease- causing microorganism
A. Bifocal B. Nevus C. Venom D. Virus

11. ____ This is when a provider refuses to accept Medicare payments as a sufficient amount for the services rendered to a patient.
A. Venom B. Utilization Review C. Non participation D. Appeal

12. ____ A colorless, odorless, tasteless radioactive gas that is produced by materials in soil, rocks, and building materials
A. Pulse B. Atrophy C. Gastroenterology D. Radon

13. ____ The care and treatment of infants, children, and adolescents
A. Medicare Coinsurance Days B. Eardrum C. Gland D. Pediatrics

14. ____ Facilities that review and correct medical claims as necessary before sending them to insurance companies for final processing.
A. Skull B. Untimely Submission C. Tendon D. Clearinghouse

15. ____ The federal health insurance program for active and retired service members, their families, and the survivors of service members.
A. Mole B. TRICARE C. Plague D. Node

16. ____ Feeling the need to vomit
A. Acute B. Nausea C. Demographics D. Thrill

17. ____ This refers to medical implements that can be reused such as stretchers, wheelchairs, canes, crutches, and bedpans.
A. Durable Medical Equipment B. Spleen C. Crossover Claim D. Anesthesiology

18. ____ A desire to eat materials that are not food
A. Oxygen B. Labia C. Pica D. Palmetto GBA

19. ____ The abbreviation for diagnosis codes, also known as ICD-9 codes.
A. Dx B. Canal C. Phlegm D. Hormone

20. ____ The main artery in the body, carrying oxygenated blood from the heart to other arteries in the body
A. Pediatrics B. Spine C. Aorta D. Tertiary Claim

21. ____ This refers to the amount a patient owes a provider after an insurance company pays for their portion of the medical expenses.
A. Pleura B. Patient Responsibility C. Thrill D. Orbit

22. ____ An egg cell that has not developed completely
A. Radiology B. Oocyte C. Skilled Nursing Facility D. Chancre

23. ____ A groove or slit on the body or in an organ
A. Unbundling B. Referral C. Radiology D. Fissure

24. ____ Paid by an employer when an employee becomes ill or injured while performing routine job duties.
A. Workers Compensation B. Imaging C. Beneficiary D. Internal Medicine

25. ____ The tough, white coating that covers and protects the inner structures of the eye
A. Tendon B. Sclera C. Imaging D. Capitation

26. ____ A drug that neutralizes stomach acids
A. Antacid B. Cochlea C. Phlegm D. Thorax

27. ____ A lump filled with either fluid or soft material, occurring in any organ or tissue
A. Anemia B. COBRA C. Cyst D. Plague

28. ____ A milky fluid containing white blood cells, proteins, and fats
A. Canal B. Lymph C. Credentialing D. Revenue Code

29. ____ The complete set of an organism's genes
A. Tibia B. Tendon C. Genome D. Emetic

30. ____ The medical term for the voice box, the organ in the throat that produces voice and also prevents food from entering the airway
A. Larynx B. Group Health Plan C. Not Otherwise Specified D. Practice Management Software

31. ____ A thin, oval-shaped membrane that separates the inner ear from the outer ear and is responsible for transmitting sound waves
A. Airways B. Larynx C. Eardrum D. Orbit

32. ____ Small eight-legged animals, many of which burrow and feed on blood
A. Internal Medicine B. Mites C. Maximum Out of Pocket D. Bifocal

33. ____ An involuntary muscle contraction
A. Patient Responsibility B. Spasm C. Venom D. Atrophy

34. ____ Sexual intercourse
A. Coitus B. Bile C. Ulcer D. Hospice

35. ____ An involuntary, rhythmic, shaking movement caused by alternating contraction and relaxation of muscles
A. Tremor B. Pupil C. Gavage D. Beneficiary

36. ____ A lens that corrects both near and distant vision by having two parts with different focusing strengths
A. Cochlea B. Angioma C. Bifocal D. Relative Value Amount

37. ____ A claim filed by a provider after they have filed claims for primary and secondary health insurance coverage on behalf of a patient.
A. Formulary B. Pupil C. Phlegm D. Tertiary Claim

38. ____ A sample of cells spread across a glass slide to be examined through a microscope
A. Renin B. Smear C. Nevus D. Dx

39. ____ Supplemental health insurance under Medicaid for eligible persons who need help covering co-pays, deductibles, and other large fees.
A. Oxygen B. Formulary C. Group Health Plan D. Medigap

40. ____ Any service administered in a hospital or other healthcare facility other than room and board.
A. Bunion B. Credit Balance C. Lesion D. Ancillary Services

41. ____ The name of the group, insurance carrier, or insurance plan that covers a patient.
A. Angioma B. Group Name C. Point of Service Plans D. Scrubbing

42. ______ The end date for an insurance policy contract, or the date after which a person no longer receives or is no longer eligible for health insurance with company.
A. Antacid B. Node C. Myopia D. Term Date

43. ______ A disorder characterized by inflamed airways and difficulty breathing
A. Authorization B. Saline C. Asthma D. Preauthorization

44. ______ Software used for scheduling, billing, and recordkeeping at a provider's office.
A. Cochlea B. Responsible Party C. Practice Management Software D. Anesthesiology

45. ______ A substance that causes vomiting
A. Formulary B. Referral C. Emetic D. Spine

46. ______ Serves as the guidelines for policies and practices necessary to reduce security risks within the healthcare system.
A. Downcoding B. Aorta C. Security Standard D. Co Insurance

47. ______ An involuntary, repetitive movement such as a twitch
A. Ptosis B. Preventive Medicine C. Forceps D. Tic

48. ______ A noncancerous tumor made of mucous material and fibrous connective tissue
A. Medigap B. Renin C. Plastic D. Myxoma

49. ______ A vibration felt when the hand is placed flat on the chest; caused by abnormal blood flow through the heart as a result of disease
A. Cilia B. Ptosis C. Gavage D. Thrill

50. ______ An investigation or audit performed to optimize the number of inpatient and outpatient services a provider performs.
A. Reflex B. Utilization Review C. Secondary Procedure D. Thorax

51. ______ A digestive disorder in which nutrients cannot be properly absorbed from food, causing weakness and loss of weight
A. Medicaid B. Sprue C. Skull D. Cochlea

52. ______ The technique of creating pictures of structures inside of the body using x-rays, ultrasound waves, or magnetic fields
A. Pulse B. Imaging C. Node D. Asthma

53. ______ A coiled organ in the inner ear that plays a large role in hearing by picking up sound vibrations and transmitting them as electrical signals
A. Medicaid B. Cochlea C. Responsible Party D. Emergency Medicine

54. ______ Oncology
A. Hematology B. Cochlea C. Antacid D. Internal Medicine

55. ______ The healthcare facility that administered healthcare to an individual. Physicians, clinics, and hospitals are all considered providers.
A. Venom B. Uvea C. Gastrin D. Provider

56. ______ A parasitic flatworm that can infest humans
A. Labia B. Imaging C. Gastroenterology D. Fluke

57. ______ A surgical technique in which the flow of blood or another body fluid is redirected around a blockage
A. Pupil B. Bypass C. Suture D. Radon

58. ______ A patient's official signature on file for the purpose of billing and claims processing.
A. Signature on File B. Anus C. Emetic D. Point of Service Plans

59. ______ A waste product of the metabolism of proteins that is formed by the liver and secreted by the kidneys
A. Premium B. Hiccup C. Tibia D. Urea

60. ____ Instruments resembling tweezers that are used to handle objects or tissue during surgery
A. Forceps B. Medicaid C. Beneficiary D. Outpatient

61. ____ A structure consisting of the colored area of the eye and the middle layer of the eye that contains blood vessels
A. TRICARE B. Urea C. Emetic D. Uvea

62. ____ Refers to the fraudulent practice of ascribing more than one code to a service or procedure on a superbill or claim form when only one is necessary.
A. Demographics B. DNA C. Primary Care Physician D. Unbundling

63. ____ The medical term for nearsightedness
A. Serum B. Secondary Procedure C. Myopia D. Pediatrics

64. ____ A marking on the skin; can be present at birth (birthmark) or develop later (such as a mole)
A. Acne B. Bile C. Aorta D. Nevus

65. ____ A condition in which the blood does not contain enough hemoglobin, the compound that carries oxygen from the lungs to other parts of the body
A. Plastic B. Rabies C. Appeal D. Anemia

66. ____ Involuntary sudden contraction of the diaphragm along with the closing of the vocal cords, producing a "hiccup" sound
A. Hiccup B. Node C. COBRA D. ERISA

67. ____ Refers to the ratio of payments received relative to the total amount owed to providers.
A. Airways B. Collection Ratio C. Ulcer D. Reflex

68. ____ An artificial feeding technique in which liquids are passed into the stomach by way of a tube inserted through the nose
A. Sprue B. Out of Network C. Gavage D. Lymph

69. ____ An enzyme that plays a role in increasing a low blood pressure
A. Renin B. Goiter C. Coding D. Nerve

70. ____ Refers to the sum shown in the “balance” column of a billing statement that reflects the amount due for services rendered.
A. Durable Medical Equipment B. Credit Balance C. Serum D. Valve

71. ____ A MAC based in Columbia, South Carolina that is also a subsidiary of Blue Cross Blue Shield.
A. Villi B. Atresia C. Palmetto GBA D. Splint

72. ____ The bones that form the framework of the head and enclose and protect the brain and other sensory organs
A. Imaging B. Cervix C. Skull D. Capitation

73. ____ The opening at the center of the iris in the eye that constricts (contracts) and dilates (widens) in response to light
A. Pupil B. Tinea C. Utilization Review D. Skull

74. ____ The practice, maintenance, and study of health
A. ERISA B. Anus C. Assignment of Benefits D. Hygiene

75. ____ A mental disorder characterized by an inability to relate to other people and extreme withdrawal
A. Autism B. Neuron C. Capitation D. Applied to Deductible

76. ____ This term is used in ICD-9 codes to describe conditions with unspecified diagnoses.
A. Credentialing B. Beneficiary C. Pleura D. Not Otherwise Specified

77. ____ A tumor made of blood vessels or lymph vessels that is not cancerous
A. Angioma B. Radiology C. Radon D. Gynecology

78. ____ An agent that is believed to cause several degenerative brain diseases
A. Prion B. Atrophy C. Medigap D. Rabies

79. ______ A viral infection that causes inflammation of salivary glands
A. ERISA B. Medigap C. Mumps D. Responsible Party

80. ______ A skin condition characterized by inflamed, pus-filled areas that occur on the skin's surface, most commonly occurring during adolescence
A. Tic B. Labor C. Acne D. Untimely Submission

81. ______ A plan provided by an employer to provide healthcare options to a large group of employees.
A. Group Health Plan B. Relative Value Amount C. Crossover Claim D. Autopsy

82. ______ The insurance company that covers any remaining expenses after Medicare has paid for a patient's coverage.
A. Medicare Secondary Payer B. Tinea C. Anemia D. Valve

83. ______ A painless sore that has a thick, rubbery base and a defined edge
A. Allergy B. Chancre C. Stoma D. Pica

84. ______ The opening through which feces are passed from the body
A. Anus B. Neuron C. Ancillary Services D. Cilia

85. ______ A term describing something related to or caused by a virus
A. Larynx B. Viral C. Durable Medical Equipment D. Capitation

86. ______ The infection of a wound or tissue with bacteria, causing the spread of the bacteria into the bloodstream
A. Sepsis B. Application Service Provider C. Renin D. Capitation

87. ______ Describes a disorder that continues for a long period of time
A. Hypoxia B. Chronic C. Plastic D. Anus

88. ______ The presence of white blood cells in the urine
A. Larynx B. Pyuria C. Cyst D. Labia

89. ______ The chest
A. Oxygen B. Mites C. Thorax D. Financial Responsibility

90. ______ This act established guidelines and requirements for health and life insurance policies including appeals and disclosure of grievances.
A. Financial Responsibility B. DNA C. Credentialing D. ERISA

91. ______ The specialty that focuses on the health of individuals in order to protect, promote and maintain health and prevent disease, disability and premature death
A. Cervix B. Point of Service Plans C. Preventive Medicine D. Untimely Submission

92. ______ The repair, restoration or improvement of conditions or injuries to the skin and external features resulting from disease, injury or birth defects
A. Plastic B. Boil C. Place of Service Code D. Spleen

93. ______ A document attached to a processed medical claim wherein the insurance company explains the services they will cover for a patient's healthcare treatments.
A. Cast B. Explanation of Benefits C. Pyuria D. Oocyte

94. ______ A surgically formed opening on a body surface
A. Medigap B. Endemic C. Stoma D. Explanation of Benefits

95. ______ A surgical stitch that helps close an incision or wound so that it can heal properly
A. Suture B. Antacid C. Applied to Deductible D. Hematology

96. ______ The interval from onset of contractions to birth of a baby
A. Atresia B. Atrophy C. Labor D. Medicaid

97. ______ The column of bones and cartilage running along the midline of the back that surrounds and protects the spinal cord and supports the head
A. Myopia B. Remittance Advice C. Spine D. Atresia

98. ______ A bundle of fibers that transmit electrical messages between the brain and areas of the body
A. Endemic B. Boil C. Nerve D. Gland

99. ______ Describes a disease that is always present in a certain population of people
A. Credentialing B. Endemic C. Hygiene D. Thrill

100. ______ This term refers to the amount of money a patient owes a provider that goes to paying their yearly deductible.
A. Thorax B. Sclera C. Applied to Deductible D. Airways

C. From the words provided for each clue, provide the letter of the word which best matches the clue.

1. ______ The name of the group, insurance carrier, or insurance plan that covers a patient.
A. Cervix B. Spleen C. Group Name D. Eczema

2. ______ A desire to eat materials that are not food
A. Non participation B. Vernix C. Pica D. Fistula

3. ______ A method of transferring money electronically from a patient's bank account to a provider or an insurance carrier.
A. Autism B. Electronic Funds Transfer C. Group Name D. Scurvy

4. ______ The beginning of the large intestine, which is connected to the appendix at its lower end
A. Coma B. Cecum C. Medial D. Electronic Medical Records

5. ______ The structure of bodies; commonly refers to the study of body structure
A. Miotic B. Anatomy C. Tibia D. Mumps

6. ______ A drug that causes the pupil to constrict
A. Plague B. Miotic C. Larynx D. Pallor

7. ______ Abnormally pale skin
A. Enzyme B. Psychology C. Pallor D. Boil

8. ______ A process by which insurance claims are checked for errors before being sent to an insurance company for final processing.
A. Venom B. Clean Claim C. Podiatry D. Scrubbing

9. ______ A provider within a health insurance company's network that has contracted with the company to provide discounted services to a patient covered under the company's plan.
A. Miotic B. Chronic C. ECG D. Network Provider

10. ______ The interval from onset of contractions to birth of a baby
A. Stye B. Thorax C. Genome D. Labor

11. ______ Another term for a nerve cell
A. Neuron B. Patient Responsibility C. Plastic D. Guarantor

12. ______ Occurring at an abnormal position or time
A. Ocular B. Lipoma C. Miotic D. Ectopic

13. ______ The lowest section of the small intestine, which attaches to the large intestine
A. Ileum B. Polyp C. Trauma D. Group Name

14. ____ Pertaining to the eyes
A. Optic B. Polyp C. Self Referral D. Workers Compensation

15. ____ The fraudulent practice of ascribing a higher ICD-9 code to a healthcare procedure in an attempt to get more money than necessary from the insurance company or patient.
A. Network Provider B. Clone C. Reflex D. Upcoding

16. ____ The group of bones in the lower part of the trunk that support the upper body and protect the abdominal organs
A. Implant B. Pelvis C. Fungus D. Medicaid

17. ____ Refers to healthcare services or treatments that a patient requires to treat a serious medical condition or illness.
A. Radiology B. Medical Necessity C. Allergy D. Ileum

18. ____ A person covered by a health insurance plan.
A. Node B. Imaging C. Enrollee D. Strain

19. ____ Immunology
A. Medigap B. Mites C. Allergy D. Patient Responsibility

20. ____ An involuntary muscle contraction
A. Spasm B. Plastic C. Eczema D. Shock

21. ____ A thick, yellowish or greenish fluid that contains dead white blood cells, tissues, and bacteria; occurs at the site of a bacterial infection
A. Mumps B. Pus C. Rash D. Health Insurance Claim

22. ____ The presence of white blood cells in the urine
A. Thrush B. Genome C. Pyuria D. Aorta

23. ____ A health insurance plan whereby patients can only receive coverage if they see providers who operate in the insurance company's network.
A. Managed Care Plan B. Boil C. Strain D. Specialist

24. ____ The abbreviation for diagnosis codes, also known as ICD-9 codes.
A. Palmetto GBA B. Dx C. Strain D. Self Pay

25. ____ This is when provider performs another procedure on a patient covered by a CPT code after first performing a different CPT procedure on them.
A. Self Referral B. Pallor C. Dyspnea D. Secondary Procedure

26. ____ Refers to a binding agree between a provider, patient, and insurance company wherein the provider agrees to charges that it will write off on behalf of the patient.
A. Self Pay B. Forceps C. Emergency Medicine D. Contractual Adjustment

27. ____ A substance that causes vomiting
A. Plaque B. Callus C. Clone D. Emetic

28. ____ The bone located between the hip and the knee
A. Femur B. Authorization C. Imaging D. Premium

29. ____ Supplemental health insurance under Medicaid for eligible persons who need help covering co-pays, deductibles, and other large fees.
A. Superbill B. Hiccup C. Medigap D. Patient Responsibility

30. ____ The exact date a patient was born.
A. Financial Responsibility B. Strain C. Urea D. Date of Birth

31. ____ The use of radiation, ultrasound, X-rays, computerized tomography, magnetic resonance imaging, mammography, and other imaging technologies to diagnose diseases and internal disorders
A. Geriatrics B. Sprue C. Anatomy D. Radiology

32. ______ Abnormally high levels of waste products such as urea in the blood
A. Autism B. Cervix C. Uremia D. Palmetto GBA

33. ______ A joint federal and state assistance program started in 1965 to provide health insurance to lower-income persons.
A. Workers Compensation B. Premium C. Medicaid D. Medical Necessity

34. ______ This term refers to the amount of money a patient owes a provider that goes to paying their yearly deductible.
A. Superbill B. Medical Necessity C. Reflex D. Applied to Deductible

35. ______ An investigation or audit performed to optimize the number of inpatient and outpatient services a provider performs.
A. ECG B. Utilization Review C. Neurology D. Pupil

36. ______ A physician or medical assistant with expertise in a specific area of medicine.
A. Superbill B. Podiatry C. ERISA D. Specialist

37. ______ The unique number ascribed to an individual to identify them as a beneficiary of Medicare.
A. Gynecology B. Health Insurance Claim C. Skilled Nursing Facility D. Bursa

38. ______ The medical term for nearsightedness
A. Myopia B. Palmetto GBA C. Cervix D. Self Referral

39. ______ A pus- filled abscess in the follicle of an eyelash
A. Tar B. Stye C. Emetic D. Aorta

40. ______ The care and treatment of the foot and ankle
A. Lipoma B. Aplasia C. Tar D. Podiatry

41. ______ An area of buildup of fat deposits in an artery, causing narrowing of the artery and possibly heart disease
A. Unbundling B. Pica C. Plaque D. Splint

42. ______ When a patient does their own research to find a provider and acts outside of their primary care physician's referral.
A. Ocular B. Patient Responsibility C. Taxonomy Code D. Self Referral

43. ______ A noncancerous tumor of fatty tissue
A. ECG B. Lipoma C. Eczema D. Allowed Amount

44. ______ One of two organs that are part of the urinary tract
A. Kidney B. Macula C. Cecum D. Gastroenterology

45. ______ An organ located in the upper left abdomen behind the ribs that removes and destroys old red blood cells and helps fight infection
A. Patient Responsibility B. Spleen C. Utilization Review D. Autism

46. ______ An exact copy of a gene, cell, or organism
A. Ozone B. Scrubbing C. Clone D. Pleura

47. ______ Describes a disorder that continues for a long period of time
A. Chronic B. Health Insurance Claim C. Tic D. Nausea

48. ______ Another term for feces
A. Sperm B. Embryo C. Stool D. Antacid

49. ______ The clear, watery fluid that separates from clotted blood
A. Fee Schedule B. Geriatrics C. Enrollee D. Serum

50. ______ A condition in which the area of the brain involved in maintaining consciousness is somehow affected, resulting in a state of unconsciousness in which the patient does not respond to stimulation
A. Coma B. Node C. Upcoding D. Term Date

51. ____ A type of health insurance plan whereby a patient can receive care with any provider in exchange for higher deductibles and co-pays. Indemnity is also known as fee-for-service insurance.
A. Cecum B. Uterus C. Indemnity D. Scrubbing

52. ____ A candidiasis infection
A. Thrush B. Liver C. Beneficiary D. Psychology

53. ____ The external male reproductive organ, which passes urine and semen out of the body
A. Aplasia B. Polyp C. Penis D. Anatomy

54. ____ A noncancerous tumor of the uterus made up of smooth muscle and connective tissue
A. Fee Schedule B. Skilled Nursing Facility C. Fibroid D. Kidney

55. ____ The complete or partial failure of any organ or tissue to grow
A. Optic B. Neuron C. Specialist D. Aplasia

56. ____ The largest organ in the body, producing many essential chemicals and regulating the levels of most vital substances in the blood
A. Ileum B. Liver C. pH D. Uterus

57. ____ The sticky, brown substance in cigarettes that coats the lungs; causes lung and other cancers
A. Electronic Medical Records B. Shock C. Pelvis D. Tar

58. ____ A thickened area of skin due to consistent pressure or friction, or the area around a bone break where new bone is formed
A. Angioma B. ERISA C. Callus D. Clone

59. ____ The technique of creating pictures of structures inside of the body using x-rays, ultrasound waves, or magnetic fields
A. Scurvy B. Imaging C. Skull D. Aorta

60. ____ The person who receives benefits and
A. Beneficiary B. Group Health Plan C. Vulva D. ECG

61. ____ A MAC based in Columbia, South Carolina that is also a subsidiary of Blue Cross Blue Shield.
A. Palmetto GBA B. Healthcare Reform Act C. Uterus D. Villi

62. ____ Inflammation of the skin, usually causing itchiness and sometimes blisters and scaling
A. Prion B. Eczema C. Imaging D. Liver

63. ____ These are facilities for the severely ill or elderly that provide specialized long-term care for recovering patients.
A. Medical Necessity B. Contractual Adjustment C. Utilization Limit D. Skilled Nursing Facility

64. ____ A measure of the acidic or basic character of a substance
A. Toxin B. pH C. Lungs D. Hematology

65. ____ Whoever owes the healthcare provider money has financial responsibility for the services rendered.
A. Term Date B. Financial Responsibility C. Patient Responsibility D. Security Standard

66. ____ The application process for a provider to coordinate with an insurance company.
A. Hives B. Ectopic C. Credentialing D. Premium

67. ____ This type of care is administered at reduced or zero cost to patients who cannot afford healthcare.
A. Strain B. Iris C. Gland D. Charity Care

68. ____ Payment made by the patient for healthcare at the time they receive it at a provider's facilities.
A. Tibia B. Financial Responsibility C. Toxin D. Self Pay

69. ____ A device that is used to immobilize a part of the body
A. Cervix B. Splint C. Toxin D. Forceps

70. .... An open sore that occurs on the skin or on a mucous membrane because of the destruction of surface tissue
A. Node B. Ulcer C. Urea D. Aplasia

71. .... The area of the retina that allows fine details to be observed at the center of vision
A. Fungus B. Health Insurance Claim C. Pleura D. Macula

72. .... A digestive disorder in which nutrients cannot be properly absorbed from food, causing weakness and loss of weight
A. Sprue B. Gland C. Allowed Amount D. Primary Care Physician

73. .... This is when a provider refuses to accept Medicare payments as a sufficient amount for the services rendered to a patient.
A. Orthopaedics B. Non participation C. Coordination of Benefits D. Serum

74. .... A chemical, originating in a cell, that regulates reactions in the body
A. Enzyme B. Tar C. Vein D. Vernix

75. .... The science of dealing with mental processes and their effects on behavior
A. Pus B. Psychology C. Optic D. Urea

76. .... Describes something related to the eyes
A. Allowed Amount B. Medical Necessity C. Ocular D. Vein

77. .... The male sex cell produced in the testicles
A. Premium B. Medial C. Sperm D. Chronic

78. .... The tiny structures that make up all the tissues of the body and carry out all of its functions
A. Fibroid B. Cell C. Kidney D. Radiology

79. .... Instruments resembling tweezers that are used to handle objects or tissue during surgery
A. Primary Care Physician B. Anesthesiology C. Villi D. Forceps

80. .... A term used to describe a child in the womb from fertilization to 8 weeks following fertilization
A. Group Name B. Myopia C. Embryo D. Podiatry

81. .... Muscle damage resulting from excessive stretching or forceful contraction
A. Autopsy B. Gland C. Strain D. Scrubbing

82. .... An additional dose of a vaccine taken after the first dose to maintain or renew the first one
A. Booster B. Non participation C. Forceps D. Strain

83. .... The basic unit of dna, which is responsible for passing genetic information
A. Gene B. Mites C. Autism D. Appeal

84. .... Digitized medical record for a patient managed by a provider onsite.
A. Anesthesiology B. Enzyme C. Electronic Medical Records D. Term Date

85. .... The hollow female reproductive organ in which a fertilized egg is implanted and a fetus develops
A. Uterus B. Pathology C. Aorta D. Autism

86. .... An involuntary, repetitive movement such as a twitch
A. Iris B. Tic C. Demographics D. Medigap

87. .... The main artery in the body, carrying oxygenated blood from the heart to other arteries in the body
A. Aorta B. Indemnity C. Gene D. Wheeze

88. .... The sum an insurance company will reimburse to cover a healthcare service or procedure.
A. Mumps B. Allowed Amount C. Imaging D. Angioma

89. ____ The name for the organization or individual that manages healthcare group benefits, claims, and administrative duties on behalf of a group plan or a company with a group plan.
A. Third Party Administrator B. Managed Care Plan C. Gland D. Prion

90. ____ A large blood vessel that carries blood from the heart to tissues and organs in the body
A. Plaque B. Skilled Nursing Facility C. Acne D. Artery

91. ____ The term used to refer to an unborn child from 8 weeks after fertilization to birth
A. Sprue B. Dyspnea C. Fetus D. Tar

92. ____ The patient's information required for filing a claim, such as age, sex, address, and family information. An insurance company may deny a claim if it contains inaccurate demographics.
A. Authorization B. Implant C. Demographics D. Reflex

93. ____ A group of cells or an organ that produces substances (such as hormones and enzyme) that are used by the body
A. Self Referral B. Rectum C. Lobe D. Gland

94. ____ Medical billing specialists utilize this unique codeset for identifying a healthcare provider's specialty field.
A. Specialist B. Taxonomy Code C. Authorization D. Splint

95. ____ A poisonous substance produced by certain animals
A. Lipoma B. Liver C. Venom D. Sacrum

96. ____ The bones that form the framework of the head and enclose and protect the brain and other sensory organs
A. Emetic B. Utilization Limit C. Skull D. Wheeze

97. ____ An area of inflammation or a group of spots on the skin
A. Boil B. Forceps C. Group Name D. Rash

98. ____ An electrocardiogram, which is a record of the electrical impulses that trigger the heartbeat
A. ECG B. Lungs C. Spasm D. Serum

99. ____ Density lipoprotein- a type of lipoprotein that is the major carrier of cholesterol in the blood, with high levels associated with narrowing of the arteries and heart disease
A. Autism B. Ozone C. Upcoding D. Low

100. ____ Serves as the guidelines for policies and practices necessary to reduce security risks within the healthcare system.
A. Scurvy B. Security Standard C. Polyp D. Anatomy

D. From the words provided for each clue, provide the letter of the word which best matches the clue.

1. ____ Digitized medical record for a patient managed by a provider onsite.
A. Spine B. Tibia C. Acute D. Electronic Medical Records

2. ____ A surgical technique in which the flow of blood or another body fluid is redirected around a blockage
A. Plasma B. Ileum C. Bypass D. Provider

3. ____ A document used by healthcare staff and physicians to write down information about a patient receiving care.
A. Superbill B. Appeal C. Ilium D. Retina

4. ____ The basic unit of dna, which is responsible for passing genetic information
A. Tinea B. Sputum C. Point of Service Plans D. Gene

5. ____ A digestive disorder in which nutrients cannot be properly absorbed from food, causing weakness and loss of weight
A. DNA B. Sprue C. Non participation D. Allergy

6. ______ The passageways that air moves through while traveling in and out of the lungs during breathing
A. Shock B. Airways C. Fee Schedule D. Ileum

7. ______ An optional health insurance payments plan whereby a person apportions part of their untaxed earnings to an account reserved for healthcare expenses.
A. Non Covered Charge B. Group Number C. Medical Savings Account D. Term Date

8. ______ Describes a condition or illness that begins suddenly and is usually short- lasting
A. Credentialing B. Edema C. Acute D. Apnea

9. ______ Refers to the ratio of payments received relative to the total amount owed to providers.
A. Collection Ratio B. Pallor C. Spleen D. Miotic

10. ______ The person who pays for a patient's medical expenses, also known as the guarantor.
A. Group Health Plan B. COBRA C. Point of Service Plans D. Responsible Party

11. ______ An automatic, involuntary response of the nervous system to a stimulus
A. Reflex B. Suture C. Subscriber D. Provider

12. ______ A thin fold of membrane partly closing the opening of the vagina
A. Vulva B. Smear C. Hymen D. Skilled Nursing Facility

13. ______ A chemical, originating in a cell, that regulates reactions in the body
A. Enzyme B. Calcium C. Non Covered Charge D. Contractual Adjustment

14. ______ A birth defect in which a normal body opening or canal is absent
A. Uterus B. Allergy C. Atresia D. Phlegm

15. ______ The area of the retina that allows fine details to be observed at the center of vision
A. Macula B. Thrill C. Ancillary Services D. Donut Hole

16. ______ The male sex cell produced in the testicles
A. Aorta B. Plasma C. Mumps D. Sperm

17. ______ The lowest section of the small intestine, which attaches to the large intestine
A. Atresia B. Ileum C. Tartar D. Taxonomy Code

18. ______ The person who receives benefits and
A. Vascular Surgery B. Internal Medicine C. Beneficiary D. Authorization

19. ______ Pertaining to the eyes
A. Skilled Nursing Facility B. Responsible Party C. Optic D. Indemnity

20. ______ Networks of healthcare providers that offer healthcare plans to people for medical services exclusively in their network.
A. Tendon B. Health Maintenance Organization C. Medicaid D. Sebum

21. ______ Refers to the discrepancy between a provider's fee for healthcare services and the amount that an insurance company is willing to pay for those services that a patient is not responsible for.
A. Mole B. Write Off C. Nevus D. Untimely Submission

22. ______ A mineral necessary for the formation of important biological substances such as hemoglobin, myoglobin, and certain enzymes
A. Glioma B. Term Date C. Pepsin D. Iron

23. ______ An egg cell that has not developed completely
A. Oocyte B. Preauthorization C. Internal Medicine D. Cervix

24. .... The healthcare facility that administered healthcare to an individual. Physicians, clinics, and hospitals are all considered providers.
A. In Network B. B cell C. Calcium D. Provider

25. .... A substance that causes vomiting
A. Credit Balance B. Thrush C. Semen D. Emetic

26. .... Refers to a medical claim filed with a health insurance company that is free of errors and processed in a timely manner.
A. Tinea B. Forceps C. Colitis D. Clean Claim

27. .... The amount a patient must pay before an insurance carrier starts their healthcare coverage.
A. Boil B. Mumps C. Deductible D. Credit Balance

28. .... A term used to describe something related to a fever, such as febrile seizures
A. Febrile B. Downcoding C. Superbill D. Palsy

29. .... Instruments resembling tweezers that are used to handle objects or tissue during surgery
A. DNA B. Mole C. Pallor D. Forceps

30. .... The smallest known disease- causing microorganism
A. Eardrum B. Thrill C. Virus D. Boil

31. .... A surgical stitch that helps close an incision or wound so that it can heal properly
A. Enzyme B. Femur C. Suture D. Pleura

32. .... Four fused bones that form a triangular shape at the base of the spine (also known as the tailbone)
A. Allowed Amount B. Uterus C. Coccyx D. Macula

33. .... The liquid part of the blood, containing substances such as nutrients, salts, and proteins
A. Appeal B. Plasma C. Ancillary Services D. Lymph

34. .... The muscular passage connecting the uterus with the outside genitals
A. Superbill B. Palsy C. Vagina D. Electronic Medical Records

35. .... A number given to a patient by their insurance carrier that identifies the group or plan under which they are covered.
A. Lipids B. Sperm C. Group Number D. Not Otherwise Specified

36. .... The unit of a hospital reserved for patients that need immediate treatment and close monitoring by healthcare professionals for serious illnesses, conditions, and injuries.
A. Intensive Care B. Spine C. Pathology D. Eardrum

37. .... Medical billing specialists utilize this unique codeset for identifying a healthcare provider's specialty field.
A. Femur B. Uvea C. Maximum Out of Pocket D. Taxonomy Code

38. .... The tiny structures that make up all the tissues of the body and carry out all of its functions
A. Privacy Rule B. Fraud C. Cell D. Deductible

39. .... A bacterial infection of the small intestine that causes severe watery diarrhea, dehydration, and possibly death
A. Enzyme B. Cholera C. Anus D. RNA

40. .... A white blood cell that makes antibodies to fight infections caused by foreign proteins
A. Bursa B. B cell C. Sebum D. Pus

41. .... The outer, visible portion of the female genitals
A. Vulva B. Shock C. Workers Compensation D. Labia

42. .... the diagnosis and non-surgical treatment of adult health problems
A. Provider B. Enzyme C. Medical Savings Account D. Internal Medicine

43. ______ Abnormally pale skin
A. Pallor B. Vernix C. Modifier D. Subscriber

44. ______ The science of dealing with mental processes and their effects on behavior
A. Health Insurance Claim B. Maximum Out of Pocket C. Graft D. Psychology

45. ______ The main artery in the body, carrying oxygenated blood from the heart to other arteries in the body
A. Untimely Submission B. Aorta C. Ileum D. Preauthorization

46. ______ The diagnosis and treatment of mental, emotional and behavioral disorders
A. Group Health Plan B. Secondary Procedure C. Iron D. Psychiatry

47. ______ Tiny, hairlike structures on the outside of some cells, providing mobility
A. Vagina B. Cilia C. Typhus D. Pleura

48. ______ A plan whereby patients with HMO membership may receive care at non-HMO providers in exchange for a referral and paying a higher deductible.
A. Cilia B. Thrush C. Network Provider D. Point of Service Plans

49. ______ A provider within a health insurance company's network that has contracted with the company to provide discounted services to a patient covered under the company's plan.
A. Relative Value Amount B. Group Name C. Network Provider D. Macula

50. ______ Mucus and other material produced by the lining of the respiratory tract; also called phlegm
A. Sputum B. Bypass C. Stent D. Managed Care Plan

51. ______ Healthy tissue that is used to replace diseased or defective tissue
A. Superbill B. Graft C. pH D. Cornea

52. ______ The enzyme found in gastric juice that helps digest protein
A. Preferred Provider Organization B. Sinus C. Vagina D. Pepsin

53. ______ A device used to hold tissues in place, such as to support a skin graft
A. Authorization B. Allergy C. Non Covered Charge D. Stent

54. ______ An abnormality of structure or function in the body
A. Colon B. Donut Hole C. Lesion D. Anus

55. ______ Ribonucleic acid, which helps to decode and process the information contained in dna
A. Thrush B. Lipids C. RNA D. Coccyx

56. ______ Occurs when a person has a stay at a healthcare facility for more than 24 hours.
A. Inpatient B. COBRA C. Point of Service Plans D. Medical Record Number

57. ______ A device that is used to immobilize a part of the body
A. Sinus B. Splint C. Nevus D. Medicare Secondary Payer

58. ______ A formal medical billing term that refers to insurance claims that haven't been paid or balances owed by patients overdue by more than 30 days.
A. Sinus B. Semen C. Referral D. Aging

59. ______ This is when a provider refuses to accept Medicare payments as a sufficient amount for the services rendered to a patient.
A. Reflex B. Non participation C. Lipids D. Network Provider

60. ______ A group of cells or an organ that produces substances (such as hormones and enzyme) that are used by the body
A. Cholera B. Non Covered Charge C. Gland D. Kidney

61. ______ A groove or slit on the body or in an organ
A. Medicare Secondary Payer B. Fissure C. Group Number D. Utilization Limit

62. ______ The digital version of EOB, which specifies the details of payments made on a claim either by an insurance company or required by the patient.
A. Tic B. Suture C. Uterus D. Electronic Remittance Advice

63. ______ Inflammation of the large intestine (the colon), which usually leads to abdominal pain, fever, and diarrhea with blood and mucus
A. Colitis B. Appeal C. Fissure D. Rabies

64. ______ A unique number ascribed to a person's medical record so it can be differentiated from other medical records.
A. Medical Record Number B. Spine C. Primary Care Physician D. Donut Hole

65. ______ One of two organs that are part of the urinary tract
A. Fraud B. Skilled Nursing Facility C. Ileum D. Kidney

66. ______ A fluid-filled sac that cushions and reduces friction in certain parts of the body
A. Optic B. Contractual Adjustment C. Office of Inspector General D. Bursa

67. ______ A membrane lining the inside of the back of the eye that contains light-sensitive nerve cells that convert focused light into nerve impulses, making vision possible
A. Stroke B. Primary Care Physician C. Retina D. Skull

68. ______ One of the two bones that form the hip on either side of the body
A. Lymph B. Ilium C. Bunion D. Medical Billing Specialist

69. ______ A thickened area of skin due to consistent pressure or friction, or the area around a bone break where new bone is formed
A. Thrush B. Electronic Medical Records C. Clean Claim D. Callus

70. ______ This term refers to the discrepancy between the limits of healthcare insurance coverage and the Medicare Part D coverage limits for prescription drugs.
A. Reflex B. Relative Value Amount C. B cell D. Donut Hole

71. ______ A persisting fear of and desire to avoid something
A. Febrile B. Tendon C. Graft D. Phobia

72. ______ A sugar that is the main source of energy for the body
A. Rabies B. Glucose C. Nevus D. Medicare Secondary Payer

73. ______ Mucus and other material produced by the lining of the respiratory tract; also called sputum
A. Phlegm B. Psychiatry C. pH D. Superbill

74. ______ The artificial growth of cells, tissue, or microorganisms such as bacteria in a laboratory
A. Not Otherwise Specified B. Culture C. RNA D. Phobia

75. ______ Deoxyribonucleic acid; responsible for passing genetic information in nearly all organisms
A. Pepsin B. Lipids C. DNA D. Privacy Rule

76. ______ the diagnosis and treatment, including surgery, of diseases and disorders of the musculoskeletal system, including bones, joints, tendons, ligaments, muscles and nerves
A. Callus B. Premium C. Sputum D. Orthopaedics

77. ______ A unique number a patient or a company may have to produce for billing purposes in order to receive healthcare from a provider.
A. Zygote B. Nodule C. Tax Identification Number D. Pelvis

78. .... A type of health insurance plan whereby a patient can receive care with any provider in exchange for higher deductibles and co-pays. Indemnity is also known as fee-for-service insurance.
A. Internal Medicine B. Indemnity C. Gene D. Appeal

79. .... Some insurance plans require that a patient receive preauthorization from the insurance company prior to receiving certain medical services.
A. Cervix B. Internal Medicine C. Fissure D. Preauthorization

80. .... A drug that causes the pupil to constrict
A. Clone B. Untimely Submission C. Anus D. Miotic

81. .... A negative reaction to a substance that in most people causes no reaction
A. Tremor B. Gland C. Allergy D. Subscriber

82. .... A joint federal and state assistance program started in 1965 to provide health insurance to lower-income persons.
A. Forceps B. Medicaid C. Network Provider D. Taxonomy Code

83. .... The individual covered under a group policy. For instance, an employee of a company with a group health policy would be one of many subscribers on that policy.
A. Subscriber B. Thrill C. Acute D. Self Referral

84. .... A thick, yellowish or greenish fluid that contains dead white blood cells, tissues, and bacteria; occurs at the site of a bacterial infection
A. Lesion B. Pelvis C. Pus D. Bunion

85. .... The opening through which feces are passed from the body
A. Labia B. Anus C. Thrill D. Allowed Amount

86. .... The end date for an insurance policy contract, or the date after which a person no longer receives or is no longer eligible for health insurance with company.
A. Palsy B. Term Date C. Donut Hole D. Not Otherwise Specified

87. .... A sample of cells spread across a glass slide to be examined through a microscope
A. Secondary Procedure B. Non Covered Charge C. Smear D. Spine

88. .... Occurs when a patient or a provider tries to convince an insurance company to pay for healthcare after it has decided not to cover costs for someone on a claim.
A. Indemnity B. Appeal C. Vagina D. Autism

89. .... A small lump of tissue that is usually abnormal
A. Oocyte B. Nodule C. Deductible D. Femur

90. .... The limit per year for coverage under certain available healthcare services for Medicare enrollees.
A. Aorta B. Orthopaedics C. Utilization Limit D. Primary Care Physician

91. .... The double- layered membrane that lines the lungs and chest cavity and allows for lung movement during breathing
A. Non participation B. Acute C. Pleura D. Office of Inspector General

92. .... A process similar to preauthorization whereby patients must check with insurance companies to see if a desired healthcare treatment or service is deemed medically necessary
A. Coccyx B. COBRA C. Pre Certification D. Enzyme

93. .... The repair, restoration or improvement of conditions or injuries to the skin and external features resulting from disease, injury or birth defects
A. Gene B. Place of Service Code C. Iron D. Plastic

94. .... The two pairs of skinfolds that protect the opening of the vagina
A. Labia B. Miotic C. Stroke D. Orthopaedics

95. ____ A mineral that plays a role in the body's water balance, heart rhythm, nerve impulses, and muscle contraction
A. Electronic Remittance Advice B. Sodium C. Femur D. Pus

96. ____ A plentiful mineral in the body and the basic component of teeth and bones
A. Calcium B. Clearinghouse C. Shock D. Miotic

97. ____ The insurance company that covers any remaining expenses after Medicare has paid for a patient's coverage.
A. Applied to Deductible B. Medicare Secondary Payer C. Allowed Amount D. Orthopaedics

98. ____ A MAC based in Columbia, South Carolina that is also a subsidiary of Blue Cross Blue Shield.
A. Bifocal B. Palmetto GBA C. Plastic D. Durable Medical Equipment

99. ____ The column of bones and cartilage running along the midline of the back that surrounds and protects the spinal cord and supports the head
A. Spine B. Hematology C. Referral D. Apnea

100. ____ The exact date a patient was born.
A. Date of Birth B. Cilia C. Pre Certification D. Office of Inspector General

A. From the words provided for each clue, provide the letter of the word which best matches the clue.

1. A A group of diseases caused by the microorganism rickettsia, spread by the bites of fleas, mites, or ticks
A. Typhus B. Stoma C. Medicaid D. Penis

2. D A small, rounded tissue mass
A. Bulimia B. Gastrin C. Ovum D. Node

3. C A marking on the skin; can be present at birth (birthmark) or develop later (such as a mole)
A. Tic B. Thrill C. Nevus D. Lipoma

4. D the administration of medications as a means to block pain or diminish consciousness for surgery, usually by injection or inhalation
A. Out of Network B. Preferred Provider Organization C. Myxoma D. Anesthesiology

5. C Additions to CPT codes that explain alterations and modifications to an otherwise routine treatment, exam, or service.
A. Application Service Provider B. Cilia C. Modifier D. Canal

6. C The person who pays for a patient's medical expenses, also known as the guarantor.
A. Preferred Provider Organization B. Mumps C. Responsible Party D. Allergy

7. A A disorder in which a person eats large amounts of food then forces vomiting or uses laxatives to prevent weight gain (called binging and purging)
A. Bulimia B. Boil C. Subscriber D. Fetus

8. D The process of translating a physician's documentation about a patient's medical condition and health services rendered into medical codes that are then plugged into a claim for processing.
A. Stoma B. Pathology C. Low D. Coding

9. D A growth that occurs on mucous membranes such as those in the nose and intestine
A. Mites B. Bunion C. Medigap D. Polyp

10. B Healthy tissue that is used to replace diseased or defective tissue
A. Culture B. Graft C. Smear D. Bile

11. A The amount a patient is required to pay.
A. Maximum Out of Pocket B. Venom C. Preauthorization D. Supplemental Insurance

12. B The lowest section of the small intestine, which attaches to the large intestine
A. Aging B. Ileum C. Stroke D. Shock

13. A Refers to the sum shown in the "balance" column of a billing statement that reflects the amount due for services rendered.
A. Credit Balance B. Hepatic C. Medigap D. Stent

14. D The practice, maintenance, and study of health
A. Sodium B. Nevus C. Bypass D. Hygiene

15. B The claim filed with the secondary insurance company after the primary insurance company pays for their portion of healthcare costs.
A. Patent B. Secondary Insurance Claim C. Canal D. Spasm

16. A A term used to describe something that is related to the liver
A. Hepatic B. Provider C. Coding D. Date of Birth

17. B A tunnel-like passage
A. Tic B. Canal C. Medigap D. Fraud

18. C A structure that allows fluid flow in only one direction
A. Rectum B. Sputum C. Valve D. Fetus

19. A This is when a provider recommends another provider to a patient to receive specialized treatment.
A. Referral B. Sodium C. Medicaid D. Capitation

20. A The colored part of the eye
A. Iris B. Bladder C. Superbill D. Third Party Administrator

21. B An employee in the healthcare system such as a physician's assistant or a nurse practitioner who perform duties in administration, nursing, and other ancillary care.
A. Airways B. Medical Assistant C. Hepatic D. Practice Management Software

22. C The drooping of the upper eyelid
A. Demographics B. B cell C. Ptosis D. Otolaryngology

23. D The limit per year for coverage under certain available healthcare services for Medicare enrollees.
A. Fitness B. Tar C. TRICARE D. Utilization Limit

24. A A group of fats stored in the body and used for energy
A. Lipids B. Preferred Provider Organization C. In Network D. Palate

25. A Software used for scheduling, billing, and recordkeeping at a provider's office.
A. Practice Management Software B. Urea C. Downcoding D. Bowel

26. C Procedures and services not covered by a person's health insurance plan.
A. Geriatrics B. Tertiary Claim C. Non Covered Charge D. Rectum

27. B The specialty of physicians who are trained to examine surgical specimens and biopsies for diagnostic purposes.
A. Hernia B. Pathology C. Modifier D. Ilium

28. B A digestive disorder in which nutrients cannot be properly absorbed from food, causing weakness and loss of weight
A. Valve B. Sprue C. Non Covered Charge D. Stent

29. D Law passed in 1996 with an aim to improve the scope of healthcare services and establish regulations for securing healthcare records from unwanted parties.
A. Primary Care Physician B. Ovum C. Referral D. HIPAA

30. A the care of women during and after pregnancy and childbirth, and the care of the female reproductive system and treatment of associated disorders
A. Gynecology B. Fraud C. Node D. Lesion

31. A A surgical technique in which the flow of blood or another body fluid is redirected around a blockage
A. Bypass B. Unbundling C. Referral D. Shunt

32. B The clear, dome-shaped front portion of the eye's outer covering
A. Preferred Provider Organization B. Cornea C. Medical Transcription D. Gene

33. A The healthcare facility that administered healthcare to an individual. Physicians, clinics, and hospitals are all considered providers.
A. Provider B. Fibroma C. Subscriber D. Fraud

34. C A plentiful mineral in the body and the basic component of teeth and bones
A. Third Party Administrator B. Out of Network C. Calcium D. Remittance Advice

35. B A sample of cells spread across a glass slide to be examined through a microscope
A. Place of Service Code B. Smear C. Graft D. Splint

36. D Referring to 61st through 90th days of inpatient treatment, the law requires that patients pay for a portion of their healthcare during Medicare coinsurance days.
A. Taxonomy Code B. Cecum C. pH D. Medicare Coinsurance Days

37. C Can be a secondary policy or another insurance company that covers a patient's healthcare costs after receiving coverage from their primary insurance.
A. Patient Responsibility B. Niacin C. Supplemental Insurance D. Sebum

38. A The end date for an insurance policy contract, or the date after which a person no longer receives or is no longer eligible for health insurance with company.
A. Term Date B. Appeal C. Application Service Provider D. Lungs

39. C A hospital or an area of a hospital dedicated to treating people who are dying, often of a specific cause
A. Lipids B. Suture C. Hospice D. Otolaryngology

40. B A fixed payment that a patient makes to a health insurance company or provider to recoup costs incurred from various healthcare services.
A. Fibroid B. Capitation C. Out of Network D. Croup

41. C This term refers to a provider's relationship with a health insurance company.
A. Canal B. Gynecology C. In Network D. Dermis

42. C A federal program that allows a person terminated from their employer to retain health insurance they had with that employer.
A. Mumps B. Valve C. COBRA D. Thrush

43. B Serves as the guidelines for policies and practices necessary to reduce security risks within the healthcare system.
A. Non Covered Charge B. Security Standard C. Geriatrics D. Bulimia

44. A A short tube located at the end of the large intestine, which connects the intestine to the anus
A. Rectum B. Outpatient C. Point of Service Plans D. Referral

45. D The structure of bodies; commonly refers to the study of body structure
A. Niacin B. Bursa C. Sebum D. Anatomy

46. C The bulging of an organ or tissue through a weakened area in the muscle wall
A. Radius B. Sprue C. Hernia D. Medicaid

47. C A reduced flow of blood throughout the body, usually caused by severe bleeding or a weak heart
A. Medical Record Number B. PUVA C. Shock D. Office of Inspector General

48. A Responsible for assigning various medical codes to services and healthcare plans described by a physician on a patient's super-bill.
A. Medical Coder B. Bladder C. Endemic D. Hernia

49. B The diagnosis and treatment of acute and chronic diseases and conditions of the respiratory system, such as bronchitis, asthma, emphysema and occupational lung disease
A. Orthopaedics B. Pulmonary Medicine C. Geriatrics D. Patient Responsibility

50. C A vitamin important in many chemical processes in the body
A. Indemnity B. Airways C. Niacin D. Non Covered Charge

51. C The sticky, brown substance in cigarettes that coats the lungs; causes lung and other cancers
A. Medigap B. Graft C. Tar D. Anatomy

52. D Ribonucleic acid, which helps to decode and process the information contained in dna
A. Gastrin B. Referral C. Term Date D. RNA

53. D The beginning of the large intestine, which is connected to the appendix at its lower end
A. Place of Service Code B. Cholera C. Wart D. Cecum

54. D A poisonous substance produced by certain animals
A. Tar B. Larynx C. Artery D. Venom

55. D A usually mild and temporary condition common in children in which the walls of the airways become inflamed and narrow, resulting in wheezing and coughing
A. Endemic B. Sclera C. Medical Transcription D. Croup

56. A Describes a disorder that continues for a long period of time
A. Chronic B. Lipoma C. Primary Care Physician D. Suture

57. D A noncancerous tumor of connective tissue
A. Coitus B. Capitation C. Spine D. Fibroma

58. D An organ located in the upper left abdomen behind the ribs that removes and destroys old red blood cells and helps fight infection
A. Signature on File B. Low C. Pulp D. Spleen

59. D The document attached to a processed claim that explains the information regarding coverage and payments on a claim.
A. Culture B. Allergy C. Aging D. Remittance Advice

60. B The cell that results when an egg is fertilized by a sperm
A. Angioma B. Zygote C. Labia D. Croup

61. B The complete set of an organism's genes
A. Demographics B. Genome C. Angioma D. Labia

62. B A poisonous form of oxygen that is present in the earth's upper atmosphere, where it helps to screen the earth from damaging ultraviolet rays
A. Polyp B. Ozone C. Orthopaedics D. Corn

63. A Refers to providers outside of an established network of providers who contract with an insurance company to offer patients healthcare at a discounted rate.
A. Out of Network B. Allergy C. Financial Responsibility D. Gynecology

64. C A bacterial infection of the small intestine that causes severe watery diarrhea, dehydration, and possibly death
A. Atresia B. Orgasm C. Cholera D. Pulmonary Medicine

65. C Supplemental health insurance under Medicaid for eligible persons who need help covering co-pays, deductibles, and other large fees.
A. Patent B. Canal C. Medigap D. Urea

66. C The organization responsible for establishing guidelines and investigating fraud and misinformation within the healthcare industry.
A. Signature on File B. Cast C. Office of Inspector General D. Remittance Advice

67. B An inflamed, raised area of skin that is pus-filled
A. Fee for Service B. Boil C. Place of Service Code D. RNA

68. A A measure of the acidic or basic character of a substance
A. pH B. Gavage C. Neonatology D. Non Covered Charge

69. A An artificial feeding technique in which liquids are passed into the stomach by way of a tube inserted through the nose
A. Gavage B. Aging C. Tic D. Medical Transcription

70. D A negative reaction to a substance that in most people causes no reaction
A. Incremental Nursing Charge B. ECG C. Primary Care Physician D. Allergy

71. A Networks of healthcare providers that offer healthcare plans to people for medical services exclusively in their network.
A. Health Maintenance Organization B. Inpatient C. Stroke D. Hernia

72. A A candidiasis infection
A. Thrush B. Applied to Deductible C. Health Maintenance Organization D. Ptosis

73. C The party paying for an insurance plan who is not the patient. Parents, for example, would be the guarantors for their children's health insurance.
A. Tax Identification Number B. Cardiology C. Guarantor D. Hepatic

74. A A digital network that allows healthcare providers to access quality medical billing software and technologies without needing to purchase and maintain it themselves.
A. Application Service Provider B. Medicaid C. Supplemental Insurance D. Gynecology

75. A The inner skin layer
A. Dermis B. Larynx C. Pulse D. Contractual Adjustment

76. A The technique of creating pictures of structures inside of the body using x-rays, ultrasound waves, or magnetic fields
A. Imaging B. Downcoding C. Remittance Advice D. Boil

77. C The artificial growth of cells, tissue, or microorganisms such as bacteria in a laboratory
A. Fee for Service B. Ancillary Services C. Culture D. Unbundling

78. B A device used to hold tissues in place, such as to support a skin graft
A. Neonatology B. Stent C. Corn D. In Network

79. A One of the two long bones of the forearm
A. Radius B. Atresia C. Sprue D. PUVA

80. D Sexual intercourse
A. Medicare Coinsurance Days B. Downcoding C. Cornea D. Coitus

81. A A device that is used to immobilize a part of the body
A. Splint B. Penis C. Iris D. Gavage

82. D A unique number a patient or a company may have to produce for billing purposes in order to receive healthcare from a provider.
A. Privacy Rule B. HIPAA C. Sebum D. Tax Identification Number

83. A The two pairs of skinfolds that protect the opening of the vagina
A. Labia B. Neonatology C. Tertiary Claim D. Medicaid

84. D Damage to part of the brain because of a lack of blood supply or the rupturing of a blood vessel
A. Emergency Medicine B. Application Service Provider C. Thrush D. Stroke

85. D The external male reproductive organ, which passes urine and semen out of the body
A. Outpatient B. Non Covered Charge C. Group Number D. Penis

86. D A document used by healthcare staff and physicians to write down information about a patient receiving care.
A. Canal B. Medical Transcription C. Type of Service D. Superbill

87. D Involuntary contraction of genital muscles experienced at the peak of sexual excitement
A. Signature on File B. Hospice C. Niacin D. Orgasm

88. A The soft tissue inside of a tooth that contains blood vessels and nerves
A. Pulp B. Fetus C. Cast D. Corn

89. A A claim filed by a provider after they have filed claims for primary and secondary health insurance coverage on behalf of a patient.
A. Tertiary Claim B. Venom C. Endemic D. Typhus

90. B A group of common infections occurring on the skin, hair, and nails that are caused by a fungus
A. Medicaid B. Tinea C. Culture D. Ancillary Services

91. C A poisonous substance
A. Medicaid B. Type of Service C. Toxin D. Niacin

92. A Density lipoprotein- a type of lipoprotein that is the major carrier of cholesterol in the blood, with high levels associated with narrowing of the arteries and heart disease
A. Low B. Bulimia C. Typhus D. Preferred Provider Organization

93. D A substance that causes vomiting
A. Mites B. Otolaryngology C. Culture D. Emetic

94. C Occurs when a patient or a provider tries to convince an insurance company to pay for healthcare after it has decided not to cover costs for someone on a claim.
A. Mites B. Mumps C. Appeal D. Patent

95. D An area of inflammation or a group of spots on the skin
A. Suture B. Culture C. Labia D. Rash

96. B The individual covered under a group policy. For instance, an employee of a company with a group health policy would be one of many subscribers on that policy.
A. Mumps B. Subscriber C. Point of Service Plans D. Preauthorization

97. C The exact date a patient was born.
A. Non Covered Charge B. Unbundling C. Date of Birth D. Supplemental Insurance

98. B A white blood cell that makes antibodies to fight infections caused by foreign proteins
A. Tertiary Claim B. B cell C. Medical Coder D. Tar

99. B A vibration felt when the hand is placed flat on the chest; caused by abnormal blood flow through the heart as a result of disease
A. Term Date B. Thrill C. Hymen D. Sclera

100. C A field on a claim for describing what kind of healthcare services or procedures a provider administered.
A. Gout B. Credit Balance C. Type of Service D. Remittance Advice

B. From the words provided for each clue, provide the letter of the word which best matches the clue.

1. B A federal program that allows a person terminated from their employer to retain health insurance they had with that employer.
A. Pica B. COBRA C. Rales D. Workers Compensation

2. B the diagnosis and non-surgical treatment of adult health problems
A. Lesion B. Internal Medicine C. Rales D. Pupil

3. B A hormone that stimulates the release of gastric acid in the stomach
A. Tinea B. Gastrin C. Endemic D. Coitus

4. B A hard, fluid-filled pad along the inside joint of the big toe
A. Primary Care Physician B. Bunion C. ERISA D. Indemnity

5. D Referring to 61st through 90th days of inpatient treatment, the law requires that patients pay for a portion of their healthcare during Medicare coinsurance days.
A. Security Standard B. Skilled Nursing Facility C. Hypoxia D. Medicare Coinsurance Days

6. B Describes a condition or illness that begins suddenly and is usually short- lasting
A. Clearinghouse B. Acute C. Gavage D. Indemnity

7. C The examination of a body following death, possibly to determine the cause of death or for research
A. Financial Responsibility B. Genome C. Autopsy D. Myopia

8. B When claim information is sent from a primary insurance carrier to a secondary insurance carrier, or vice versa.
A. Eardrum B. Crossover Claim C. Anus D. Medicare Coinsurance Days

9. B Some insurance plans require that a patient receive preauthorization from the insurance company prior to receiving certain medical services.
A. Hypoxia B. Preauthorization C. Spleen D. Cervix

10. D The smallest known disease- causing microorganism
A. Bifocal B. Nevus C. Venom D. Virus

11. C This is when a provider refuses to accept Medicare payments as a sufficient amount for the services rendered to a patient.
A. Venom B. Utilization Review C. Non participation D. Appeal

12. D A colorless, odorless, tasteless radioactive gas that is produced by materials in soil, rocks, and building materials
A. Pulse B. Atrophy C. Gastroenterology D. Radon

13. D The care and treatment of infants, children, and adolescents
A. Medicare Coinsurance Days B. Eardrum C. Gland D. Pediatrics

14. D Facilities that review and correct medical claims as necessary before sending them to insurance companies for final processing.
A. Skull B. Untimely Submission C. Tendon D. Clearinghouse

15. B The federal health insurance program for active and retired service members, their families, and the survivors of service members.
A. Mole B. TRICARE C. Plague D. Node

16. B Feeling the need to vomit
A. Acute B. Nausea C. Demographics D. Thrill

17. A This refers to medical implements that can be reused such as stretchers, wheelchairs, canes, crutches, and bedpans.
A. Durable Medical Equipment B. Spleen C. Crossover Claim D. Anesthesiology

18. C A desire to eat materials that are not food
A. Oxygen B. Labia C. Pica D. Palmetto GBA

19. A The abbreviation for diagnosis codes, also known as ICD-9 codes.
A. Dx B. Canal C. Phlegm D. Hormone

20. C The main artery in the body, carrying oxygenated blood from the heart to other arteries in the body
A. Pediatrics B. Spine C. Aorta D. Tertiary Claim

21. B This refers to the amount a patient owes a provider after an insurance company pays for their portion of the medical expenses.
A. Pleura B. Patient Responsibility C. Thrill D. Orbit

22. B An egg cell that has not developed completely
A. Radiology B. Oocyte C. Skilled Nursing Facility D. Chancre

23. D A groove or slit on the body or in an organ
A. Unbundling B. Referral C. Radiology D. Fissure

24. A Paid by an employer when an employee becomes ill or injured while performing routine job duties.
A. Workers Compensation B. Imaging C. Beneficiary D. Internal Medicine

25. B The tough, white coating that covers and protects the inner structures of the eye
A. Tendon B. Sclera C. Imaging D. Capitation

26. A A drug that neutralizes stomach acids
A. Antacid B. Cochlea C. Phlegm D. Thorax

27. C A lump filled with either fluid or soft material, occurring in any organ or tissue
A. Anemia B. COBRA C. Cyst D. Plague

28. B A milky fluid containing white blood cells, proteins, and fats
A. Canal B. Lymph C. Credentialing D. Revenue Code

29. C The complete set of an organism's genes
A. Tibia B. Tendon C. Genome D. Emetic

30. A The medical term for the voice box, the organ in the throat that produces voice and also prevents food from entering the airway
A. Larynx B. Group Health Plan C. Not Otherwise Specified D. Practice Management Software

31. C A thin, oval-shaped membrane that separates the inner ear from the outer ear and is responsible for transmitting sound waves
A. Airways B. Larynx C. Eardrum D. Orbit

32. B Small eight-legged animals, many of which burrow and feed on blood
A. Internal Medicine B. Mites C. Maximum Out of Pocket D. Bifocal

33. B An involuntary muscle contraction
A. Patient Responsibility B. Spasm C. Venom D. Atrophy

34. A Sexual intercourse
A. Coitus B. Bile C. Ulcer D. Hospice

35. A An involuntary, rhythmic, shaking movement caused by alternating contraction and relaxation of muscles
A. Tremor B. Pupil C. Gavage D. Beneficiary

36. C A lens that corrects both near and distant vision by having two parts with different focusing strengths
A. Cochlea B. Angioma C. Bifocal D. Relative Value Amount

37. D A claim filed by a provider after they have filed claims for primary and secondary health insurance coverage on behalf of a patient.
A. Formulary B. Pupil C. Phlegm D. Tertiary Claim

38. B A sample of cells spread across a glass slide to be examined through a microscope
A. Renin B. Smear C. Nevus D. Dx

39. D Supplemental health insurance under Medicaid for eligible persons who need help covering co-pays, deductibles, and other large fees.
A. Oxygen B. Formulary C. Group Health Plan D. Medigap

40. D Any service administered in a hospital or other healthcare facility other than room and board.
A. Bunion B. Credit Balance C. Lesion D. Ancillary Services

41. B The name of the group, insurance carrier, or insurance plan that covers a patient.
A. Angioma B. Group Name C. Point of Service Plans D. Scrubbing

42. D The end date for an insurance policy contract, or the date after which a person no longer receives or is no longer eligible for health insurance with company.
A. Antacid B. Node C. Myopia D. Term Date

43. C A disorder characterized by inflamed airways and difficulty breathing
A. Authorization B. Saline C. Asthma D. Preauthorization

44. C Software used for scheduling, billing, and recordkeeping at a provider's office.
A. Cochlea B. Responsible Party C. Practice Management Software D. Anesthesiology

45. C A substance that causes vomiting
A. Formulary B. Referral C. Emetic D. Spine

46. C Serves as the guidelines for policies and practices necessary to reduce security risks within the healthcare system.
A. Downcoding B. Aorta C. Security Standard D. Co Insurance

47. D An involuntary, repetitive movement such as a twitch
A. Ptosis B. Preventive Medicine C. Forceps D. Tic

48. D A noncancerous tumor made of mucous material and fibrous connective tissue
A. Medigap B. Renin C. Plastic D. Myxoma

49. D A vibration felt when the hand is placed flat on the chest; caused by abnormal blood flow through the heart as a result of disease
A. Cilia B. Ptosis C. Gavage D. Thrill

50. B An investigation or audit performed to optimize the number of inpatient and outpatient services a provider performs.
A. Reflex B. Utilization Review C. Secondary Procedure D. Thorax

51. B A digestive disorder in which nutrients cannot be properly absorbed from food, causing weakness and loss of weight
A. Medicaid B. Sprue C. Skull D. Cochlea

52. B The technique of creating pictures of structures inside of the body using x-rays, ultrasound waves, or magnetic fields
A. Pulse B. Imaging C. Node D. Asthma

53. B A coiled organ in the inner ear that plays a large role in hearing by picking up sound vibrations and transmitting them as electrical signals
A. Medicaid B. Cochlea C. Responsible Party D. Emergency Medicine

54. A Oncology
A. Hematology B. Cochlea C. Antacid D. Internal Medicine

55. D The healthcare facility that administered healthcare to an individual. Physicians, clinics, and hospitals are all considered providers.
A. Venom B. Uvea C. Gastrin D. Provider

56. D A parasitic flatworm that can infest humans
A. Labia B. Imaging C. Gastroenterology D. Fluke

57. B A surgical technique in which the flow of blood or another body fluid is redirected around a blockage
A. Pupil B. Bypass C. Suture D. Radon

58. A A patient's official signature on file for the purpose of billing and claims processing.
A. Signature on File B. Anus C. Emetic D. Point of Service Plans

59. D A waste product of the metabolism of proteins that is formed by the liver and secreted by the kidneys
A. Premium B. Hiccup C. Tibia D. Urea

60. A Instruments resembling tweezers that are used to handle objects or tissue during surgery
A. Forceps B. Medicaid C. Beneficiary D. Outpatient

61. D A structure consisting of the colored area of the eye and the middle layer of the eye that contains blood vessels
A. TRICARE B. Urea C. Emetic D. Uvea

62. D Refers to the fraudulent practice of ascribing more than one code to a service or procedure on a superbill or claim form when only one is necessary.
A. Demographics B. DNA C. Primary Care Physician D. Unbundling

63. C The medical term for nearsightedness
A. Serum B. Secondary Procedure C. Myopia D. Pediatrics

64. D A marking on the skin; can be present at birth (birthmark) or develop later (such as a mole)
A. Acne B. Bile C. Aorta D. Nevus

65. D A condition in which the blood does not contain enough hemoglobin, the compound that carries oxygen from the lungs to other parts of the body
A. Plastic B. Rabies C. Appeal D. Anemia

66. A Involuntary sudden contraction of the diaphragm along with the closing of the vocal cords, producing a "hiccup" sound
A. Hiccup B. Node C. COBRA D. ERISA

67. B Refers to the ratio of payments received relative to the total amount owed to providers.
A. Airways B. Collection Ratio C. Ulcer D. Reflex

68. C An artificial feeding technique in which liquids are passed into the stomach by way of a tube inserted through the nose
A. Sprue B. Out of Network C. Gavage D. Lymph

69. A An enzyme that plays a role in increasing a low blood pressure
A. Renin B. Goiter C. Coding D. Nerve

70. B Refers to the sum shown in the “balance” column of a billing statement that reflects the amount due for services rendered.
A. Durable Medical Equipment B. Credit Balance C. Serum D. Valve

71. C A MAC based in Columbia, South Carolina that is also a subsidiary of Blue Cross Blue Shield.
A. Villi B. Atresia C. Palmetto GBA D. Splint

72. C The bones that form the framework of the head and enclose and protect the brain and other sensory organs
A. Imaging B. Cervix C. Skull D. Capitation

73. A The opening at the center of the iris in the eye that constricts (contracts) and dilates (widens) in response to light
A. Pupil B. Tinea C. Utilization Review D. Skull

74. D The practice, maintenance, and study of health
A. ERISA B. Anus C. Assignment of Benefits D. Hygiene

75. A A mental disorder characterized by an inability to relate to other people and extreme withdrawal
A. Autism B. Neuron C. Capitation D. Applied to Deductible

76. D This term is used in ICD-9 codes to describe conditions with unspecified diagnoses.
A. Credentialing B. Beneficiary C. Pleura D. Not Otherwise Specified

77. A A tumor made of blood vessels or lymph vessels that is not cancerous
A. Angioma B. Radiology C. Radon D. Gynecology

78. A An agent that is believed to cause several degenerative brain diseases
A. Prion B. Atrophy C. Medigap D. Rabies

79. C A viral infection that causes inflammation of salivary glands
A. ERISA B. Medigap C. Mumps D. Responsible Party

80. C A skin condition characterized by inflamed, pus-filled areas that occur on the skin's surface, most commonly occurring during adolescence
A. Tic B. Labor C. Acne D. Untimely Submission

81. A A plan provided by an employer to provide healthcare options to a large group of employees.
A. Group Health Plan B. Relative Value Amount C. Crossover Claim D. Autopsy

82. A The insurance company that covers any remaining expenses after Medicare has paid for a patient's coverage.
A. Medicare Secondary Payer B. Tinea C. Anemia D. Valve

83. B A painless sore that has a thick, rubbery base and a defined edge
A. Allergy B. Chancre C. Stoma D. Pica

84. A The opening through which feces are passed from the body
A. Anus B. Neuron C. Ancillary Services D. Cilia

85. B A term describing something related to or caused by a virus
A. Larynx B. Viral C. Durable Medical Equipment D. Capitation

86. A The infection of a wound or tissue with bacteria, causing the spread of the bacteria into the bloodstream
A. Sepsis B. Application Service Provider C. Renin D. Capitation

87. B Describes a disorder that continues for a long period of time
A. Hypoxia B. Chronic C. Plastic D. Anus

88. B The presence of white blood cells in the urine
A. Larynx B. Pyuria C. Cyst D. Labia

89. C The chest
A. Oxygen B. Mites C. Thorax D. Financial Responsibility

90. D This act established guidelines and requirements for health and life insurance policies including appeals and disclosure of grievances.
A. Financial Responsibility B. DNA C. Credentialing D. ERISA

91. C The specialty that focuses on the health of individuals in order to protect, promote and maintain health and prevent disease, disability and premature death
A. Cervix B. Point of Service Plans C. Preventive Medicine D. Untimely Submission

92. A The repair, restoration or improvement of conditions or injuries to the skin and external features resulting from disease, injury or birth defects
A. Plastic B. Boil C. Place of Service Code D. Spleen

93. B A document attached to a processed medical claim wherein the insurance company explains the services they will cover for a patient's healthcare treatments.
A. Cast B. Explanation of Benefits C. Pyuria D. Oocyte

94. C A surgically formed opening on a body surface
A. Medigap B. Endemic C. Stoma D. Explanation of Benefits

95. A A surgical stitch that helps close an incision or wound so that it can heal properly
A. Suture B. Antacid C. Applied to Deductible D. Hematology

96. C The interval from onset of contractions to birth of a baby
A. Atresia B. Atrophy C. Labor D. Medicaid

97. C The column of bones and cartilage running along the midline of the back that surrounds and protects the spinal cord and supports the head
A. Myopia B. Remittance Advice C. Spine D. Atresia

98. C A bundle of fibers that transmit electrical messages between the brain and areas of the body
A. Endemic B. Boil C. Nerve D. Gland

99. B Describes a disease that is always present in a certain population of people
A. Credentialing B. Endemic C. Hygiene D. Thrill

100. C This term refers to the amount of money a patient owes a provider that goes to paying their yearly deductible.
A. Thorax B. Sclera C. Applied to Deductible D. Airways

C. From the words provided for each clue, provide the letter of the word which best matches the clue.

1. C The name of the group, insurance carrier, or insurance plan that covers a patient.
A. Cervix B. Spleen C. Group Name D. Eczema

2. C A desire to eat materials that are not food
A. Non participation B. Vernix C. Pica D. Fistula

3. B A method of transferring money electronically from a patient's bank account to a provider or an insurance carrier.
A. Autism B. Electronic Funds Transfer C. Group Name D. Scurvy

4. B The beginning of the large intestine, which is connected to the appendix at its lower end
A. Coma B. Cecum C. Medial D. Electronic Medical Records

5. B The structure of bodies; commonly refers to the study of body structure
A. Miotic B. Anatomy C. Tibia D. Mumps

6. B A drug that causes the pupil to constrict
A. Plague B. Miotic C. Larynx D. Pallor

7. C Abnormally pale skin
A. Enzyme B. Psychology C. Pallor D. Boil

8. D A process by which insurance claims are checked for errors before being sent to an insurance company for final processing.
A. Venom B. Clean Claim C. Podiatry D. Scrubbing

9. D A provider within a health insurance company's network that has contracted with the company to provide discounted services to a patient covered under the company's plan.
A. Miotic B. Chronic C. ECG D. Network Provider

10. D The interval from onset of contractions to birth of a baby
A. Stye B. Thorax C. Genome D. Labor

11. A Another term for a nerve cell
A. Neuron B. Patient Responsibility C. Plastic D. Guarantor

12. D Occurring at an abnormal position or time
A. Ocular B. Lipoma C. Miotic D. Ectopic

13. A The lowest section of the small intestine, which attaches to the large intestine
A. Ileum B. Polyp C. Trauma D. Group Name

14. A Pertaining to the eyes
A. Optic B. Polyp C. Self Referral D. Workers Compensation

15. D The fraudulent practice of ascribing a higher ICD-9 code to a healthcare procedure in an attempt to get more money than necessary from the insurance company or patient.
A. Network Provider B. Clone C. Reflex D. Upcoding

16. B The group of bones in the lower part of the trunk that support the upper body and protect the abdominal organs
A. Implant B. Pelvis C. Fungus D. Medicaid

17. B Refers to healthcare services or treatments that a patient requires to treat a serious medical condition or illness.
A. Radiology B. Medical Necessity C. Allergy D. Ileum

18. C A person covered by a health insurance plan.
A. Node B. Imaging C. Enrollee D. Strain

19. C Immunology
A. Medigap B. Mites C. Allergy D. Patient Responsibility

20. A An involuntary muscle contraction
A. Spasm B. Plastic C. Eczema D. Shock

21. B A thick, yellowish or greenish fluid that contains dead white blood cells, tissues, and bacteria; occurs at the site of a bacterial infection
A. Mumps B. Pus C. Rash D. Health Insurance Claim

22. C The presence of white blood cells in the urine
A. Thrush B. Genome C. Pyuria D. Aorta

23. A A health insurance plan whereby patients can only receive coverage if they see providers who operate in the insurance company's network.
A. Managed Care Plan B. Boil C. Strain D. Specialist

24. B The abbreviation for diagnosis codes, also known as ICD-9 codes.
A. Palmetto GBA B. Dx C. Strain D. Self Pay

25. D This is when provider performs another procedure on a patient covered by a CPT code after first performing a different CPT procedure on them.
A. Self Referral B. Pallor C. Dyspnea D. Secondary Procedure

26. D Refers to a binding agree between a provider, patient, and insurance company wherein the provider agrees to charges that it will write off on behalf of the patient.
A. Self Pay B. Forceps C. Emergency Medicine D. Contractual Adjustment

27. D A substance that causes vomiting
A. Plaque B. Callus C. Clone D. Emetic

28. A The bone located between the hip and the knee
A. Femur B. Authorization C. Imaging D. Premium

29. C Supplemental health insurance under Medicaid for eligible persons who need help covering co-pays, deductibles, and other large fees.
A. Superbill B. Hiccup C. Medigap D. Patient Responsibility

30. D The exact date a patient was born.
A. Financial Responsibility B. Strain C. Urea D. Date of Birth

31. D The use of radiation, ultrasound, X-rays, computerized tomography, magnetic resonance imaging, mammography, and other imaging technologies to diagnose diseases and internal disorders
A. Geriatrics B. Sprue C. Anatomy D. Radiology

32. C Abnormally high levels of waste products such as urea in the blood
A. Autism B. Cervix C. Uremia D. Palmetto GBA

33. C A joint federal and state assistance program started in 1965 to provide health insurance to lower-income persons.
A. Workers Compensation B. Premium C. Medicaid D. Medical Necessity

34. D This term refers to the amount of money a patient owes a provider that goes to paying their yearly deductible.
A. Superbill B. Medical Necessity C. Reflex D. Applied to Deductible

35. B An investigation or audit performed to optimize the number of inpatient and outpatient services a provider performs.
A. ECG B. Utilization Review C. Neurology D. Pupil

36. D A physician or medical assistant with expertise in a specific area of medicine.
A. Superbill B. Podiatry C. ERISA D. Specialist

37. B The unique number ascribed to an individual to identify them as a beneficiary of Medicare.
A. Gynecology B. Health Insurance Claim C. Skilled Nursing Facility D. Bursa

38. A The medical term for nearsightedness
A. Myopia B. Palmetto GBA C. Cervix D. Self Referral

39. B A pus- filled abscess in the follicle of an eyelash
A. Tar B. Stye C. Emetic D. Aorta

40. D The care and treatment of the foot and ankle
A. Lipoma B. Aplasia C. Tar D. Podiatry

41. C An area of buildup of fat deposits in an artery, causing narrowing of the artery and possibly heart disease
A. Unbundling B. Pica C. Plaque D. Splint

42. D When a patient does their own research to find a provider and acts outside of their primary care physician's referral.
A. Ocular B. Patient Responsibility C. Taxonomy Code D. Self Referral

43. B A noncancerous tumor of fatty tissue
A. ECG B. Lipoma C. Eczema D. Allowed Amount

44. A One of two organs that are part of the urinary tract
A. Kidney B. Macula C. Cecum D. Gastroenterology

45. B An organ located in the upper left abdomen behind the ribs that removes and destroys old red blood cells and helps fight infection
A. Patient Responsibility B. Spleen C. Utilization Review D. Autism

46. C An exact copy of a gene, cell, or organism
A. Ozone B. Scrubbing C. Clone D. Pleura

47. A Describes a disorder that continues for a long period of time
A. Chronic B. Health Insurance Claim C. Tic D. Nausea

48. C Another term for feces
A. Sperm B. Embryo C. Stool D. Antacid

49. D The clear, watery fluid that separates from clotted blood
A. Fee Schedule B. Geriatrics C. Enrollee D. Serum

50. A A condition in which the area of the brain involved in maintaining consciousness is somehow affected, resulting in a state of unconsciousness in which the patient does not respond to stimulation
A. Coma B. Node C. Upcoding D. Term Date

51. C A type of health insurance plan whereby a patient can receive care with any provider in exchange for higher deductibles and co-pays. Indemnity is also known as fee-for-service insurance.
A. Cecum B. Uterus C. Indemnity D. Scrubbing

52. A A candidiasis infection
A. Thrush B. Liver C. Beneficiary D. Psychology

53. C The external male reproductive organ, which passes urine and semen out of the body
A. Aplasia B. Polyp C. Penis D. Anatomy

54. C A noncancerous tumor of the uterus made up of smooth muscle and connective tissue
A. Fee Schedule B. Skilled Nursing Facility C. Fibroid D. Kidney

55. D The complete or partial failure of any organ or tissue to grow
A. Optic B. Neuron C. Specialist D. Aplasia

56. B The largest organ in the body, producing many essential chemicals and regulating the levels of most vital substances in the blood
A. Ileum B. Liver C. pH D. Uterus

57. D The sticky, brown substance in cigarettes that coats the lungs; causes lung and other cancers
A. Electronic Medical Records B. Shock C. Pelvis D. Tar

58. C A thickened area of skin due to consistent pressure or friction, or the area around a bone break where new bone is formed
A. Angioma B. ERISA C. Callus D. Clone

59. B The technique of creating pictures of structures inside of the body using x-rays, ultrasound waves, or magnetic fields
A. Scurvy B. Imaging C. Skull D. Aorta

60. A The person who receives benefits and
A. Beneficiary B. Group Health Plan C. Vulva D. ECG

61. A A MAC based in Columbia, South Carolina that is also a subsidiary of Blue Cross Blue Shield.
A. Palmetto GBA B. Healthcare Reform Act C. Uterus D. Villi

62. B Inflammation of the skin, usually causing itchiness and sometimes blisters and scaling
A. Prion B. Eczema C. Imaging D. Liver

63. D These are facilities for the severely ill or elderly that provide specialized long-term care for recovering patients.
A. Medical Necessity B. Contractual Adjustment C. Utilization Limit D. Skilled Nursing Facility

64. B A measure of the acidic or basic character of a substance
A. Toxin B. pH C. Lungs D. Hematology

65. B Whoever owes the healthcare provider money has financial responsibility for the services rendered.
A. Term Date B. Financial Responsibility C. Patient Responsibility D. Security Standard

66. C The application process for a provider to coordinate with an insurance company.
A. Hives B. Ectopic C. Credentialing D. Premium

67. D This type of care is administered at reduced or zero cost to patients who cannot afford healthcare.
A. Strain B. Iris C. Gland D. Charity Care

68. D Payment made by the patient for healthcare at the time they receive it at a provider's facilities.
A. Tibia B. Financial Responsibility C. Toxin D. Self Pay

69. B A device that is used to immobilize a part of the body
A. Cervix B. Splint C. Toxin D. Forceps

70. B An open sore that occurs on the skin or on a mucous membrane because of the destruction of surface tissue
A. Node B. Ulcer C. Urea D. Aplasia

71. D The area of the retina that allows fine details to be observed at the center of vision
A. Fungus B. Health Insurance Claim C. Pleura D. Macula

72. A A digestive disorder in which nutrients cannot be properly absorbed from food, causing weakness and loss of weight
A. Sprue B. Gland C. Allowed Amount D. Primary Care Physician

73. B This is when a provider refuses to accept Medicare payments as a sufficient amount for the services rendered to a patient.
A. Orthopaedics B. Non participation C. Coordination of Benefits D. Serum

74. A A chemical, originating in a cell, that regulates reactions in the body
A. Enzyme B. Tar C. Vein D. Vernix

75. B The science of dealing with mental processes and their effects on behavior
A. Pus B. Psychology C. Optic D. Urea

76. C Describes something related to the eyes
A. Allowed Amount B. Medical Necessity C. Ocular D. Vein

77. C The male sex cell produced in the testicles
A. Premium B. Medial C. Sperm D. Chronic

78. B The tiny structures that make up all the tissues of the body and carry out all of its functions
A. Fibroid B. Cell C. Kidney D. Radiology

79. D Instruments resembling tweezers that are used to handle objects or tissue during surgery
A. Primary Care Physician B. Anesthesiology C. Villi D. Forceps

80. C A term used to describe a child in the womb from fertilization to 8 weeks following fertilization
A. Group Name B. Myopia C. Embryo D. Podiatry

81. C Muscle damage resulting from excessive stretching or forceful contraction
A. Autopsy B. Gland C. Strain D. Scrubbing

82. A An additional dose of a vaccine taken after the first dose to maintain or renew the first one
A. Booster B. Non participation C. Forceps D. Strain

83. A The basic unit of dna, which is responsible for passing genetic information
A. Gene B. Mites C. Autism D. Appeal

84. C Digitized medical record for a patient managed by a provider onsite.
A. Anesthesiology B. Enzyme C. Electronic Medical Records D. Term Date

85. A The hollow female reproductive organ in which a fertilized egg is implanted and a fetus develops
A. Uterus B. Pathology C. Aorta D. Autism

86. B An involuntary, repetitive movement such as a twitch
A. Iris B. Tic C. Demographics D. Medigap

87. A The main artery in the body, carrying oxygenated blood from the heart to other arteries in the body
A. Aorta B. Indemnity C. Gene D. Wheeze

88. B The sum an insurance company will reimburse to cover a healthcare service or procedure.
A. Mumps B. Allowed Amount C. Imaging D. Angioma

89. A The name for the organization or individual that manages healthcare group benefits, claims, and administrative duties on behalf of a group plan or a company with a group plan.
A. Third Party Administrator B. Managed Care Plan C. Gland D. Prion

90. D A large blood vessel that carries blood from the heart to tissues and organs in the body
A. Plaque B. Skilled Nursing Facility C. Acne D. Artery

91. C The term used to refer to an unborn child from 8 weeks after fertilization to birth
A. Sprue B. Dyspnea C. Fetus D. Tar

92. C The patient's information required for filing a claim, such as age, sex, address, and family information. An insurance company may deny a claim if it contains inaccurate demographics.
A. Authorization B. Implant C. Demographics D. Reflex

93. D A group of cells or an organ that produces substances (such as hormones and enzyme) that are used by the body
A. Self Referral B. Rectum C. Lobe D. Gland

94. B Medical billing specialists utilize this unique codeset for identifying a healthcare provider's specialty field.
A. Specialist B. Taxonomy Code C. Authorization D. Splint

95. C A poisonous substance produced by certain animals
A. Lipoma B. Liver C. Venom D. Sacrum

96. C The bones that form the framework of the head and enclose and protect the brain and other sensory organs
A. Emetic B. Utilization Limit C. Skull D. Wheeze

97. D An area of inflammation or a group of spots on the skin
A. Boil B. Forceps C. Group Name D. Rash

98. A An electrocardiogram, which is a record of the electrical impulses that trigger the heartbeat
A. ECG B. Lungs C. Spasm D. Serum

99. D Density lipoprotein- a type of lipoprotein that is the major carrier of cholesterol in the blood, with high levels associated with narrowing of the arteries and heart disease
A. Autism B. Ozone C. Upcoding D. Low

100. B Serves as the guidelines for policies and practices necessary to reduce security risks within the healthcare system.
A. Scurvy B. Security Standard C. Polyp D. Anatomy

D. From the words provided for each clue, provide the letter of the word which best matches the clue.

1. D Digitized medical record for a patient managed by a provider onsite.
A. Spine B. Tibia C. Acute D. Electronic Medical Records

2. C A surgical technique in which the flow of blood or another body fluid is redirected around a blockage
A. Plasma B. Ileum C. Bypass D. Provider

3. A A document used by healthcare staff and physicians to write down information about a patient receiving care.
A. Superbill B. Appeal C. Ilium D. Retina

4. D The basic unit of dna, which is responsible for passing genetic information
A. Tinea B. Sputum C. Point of Service Plans D. Gene

5. B A digestive disorder in which nutrients cannot be properly absorbed from food, causing weakness and loss of weight
A. DNA B. Sprue C. Non participation D. Allergy

6. B The passageways that air moves through while traveling in and out of the lungs during breathing
A. Shock B. Airways C. Fee Schedule D. Ileum

7. C An optional health insurance payments plan whereby a person apportions part of their untaxed earnings to an account reserved for healthcare expenses.
A. Non Covered Charge B. Group Number C. Medical Savings Account D. Term Date

8. C Describes a condition or illness that begins suddenly and is usually short- lasting
A. Credentialing B. Edema C. Acute D. Apnea

9. A Refers to the ratio of payments received relative to the total amount owed to providers.
A. Collection Ratio B. Pallor C. Spleen D. Miotic

10. D The person who pays for a patient's medical expenses, also known as the guarantor.
A. Group Health Plan B. COBRA C. Point of Service Plans D. Responsible Party

11. A An automatic, involuntary response of the nervous system to a stimulus
A. Reflex B. Suture C. Subscriber D. Provider

12. C A thin fold of membrane partly closing the opening of the vagina
A. Vulva B. Smear C. Hymen D. Skilled Nursing Facility

13. A A chemical, originating in a cell, that regulates reactions in the body
A. Enzyme B. Calcium C. Non Covered Charge D. Contractual Adjustment

14. C A birth defect in which a normal body opening or canal is absent
A. Uterus B. Allergy C. Atresia D. Phlegm

15. A The area of the retina that allows fine details to be observed at the center of vision
A. Macula B. Thrill C. Ancillary Services D. Donut Hole

16. D The male sex cell produced in the testicles
A. Aorta B. Plasma C. Mumps D. Sperm

17. B The lowest section of the small intestine, which attaches to the large intestine
A. Atresia B. Ileum C. Tartar D. Taxonomy Code

18. C The person who receives benefits and
A. Vascular Surgery B. Internal Medicine C. Beneficiary D. Authorization

19. C Pertaining to the eyes
A. Skilled Nursing Facility B. Responsible Party C. Optic D. Indemnity

20. B Networks of healthcare providers that offer healthcare plans to people for medical services exclusively in their network.
A. Tendon B. Health Maintenance Organization C. Medicaid D. Sebum

21. B Refers to the discrepancy between a provider's fee for healthcare services and the amount that an insurance company is willing to pay for those services that a patient is not responsible for.
A. Mole B. Write Off C. Nevus D. Untimely Submission

22. D A mineral necessary for the formation of important biological substances such as hemoglobin, myoglobin, and certain enzymes
A. Glioma B. Term Date C. Pepsin D. Iron

23. A An egg cell that has not developed completely
A. Oocyte B. Preauthorization C. Internal Medicine D. Cervix

24. D The healthcare facility that administered healthcare to an individual. Physicians, clinics, and hospitals are all considered providers.
A. In Network B. B cell C. Calcium D. Provider

25. D A substance that causes vomiting
A. Credit Balance B. Thrush C. Semen D. Emetic

26. D Refers to a medical claim filed with a health insurance company that is free of errors and processed in a timely manner.
A. Tinea B. Forceps C. Colitis D. Clean Claim

27. C The amount a patient must pay before an insurance carrier starts their healthcare coverage.
A. Boil B. Mumps C. Deductible D. Credit Balance

28. A A term used to describe something related to a fever, such as febrile seizures
A. Febrile B. Downcoding C. Superbill D. Palsy

29. D Instruments resembling tweezers that are used to handle objects or tissue during surgery
A. DNA B. Mole C. Pallor D. Forceps

30. C The smallest known disease- causing microorganism
A. Eardrum B. Thrill C. Virus D. Boil

31. C A surgical stitch that helps close an incision or wound so that it can heal properly
A. Enzyme B. Femur C. Suture D. Pleura

32. C Four fused bones that form a triangular shape at the base of the spine (also known as the tailbone)
A. Allowed Amount B. Uterus C. Coccyx D. Macula

33. B The liquid part of the blood, containing substances such as nutrients, salts, and proteins
A. Appeal B. Plasma C. Ancillary Services D. Lymph

34. C The muscular passage connecting the uterus with the outside genitals
A. Superbill B. Palsy C. Vagina D. Electronic Medical Records

35. C A number given to a patient by their insurance carrier that identifies the group or plan under which they are covered.
A. Lipids B. Sperm C. Group Number D. Not Otherwise Specified

36. A The unit of a hospital reserved for patients that need immediate treatment and close monitoring by healthcare professionals for serious illnesses, conditions, and injuries.
A. Intensive Care B. Spine C. Pathology D. Eardrum

37. D Medical billing specialists utilize this unique codeset for identifying a healthcare provider's specialty field.
A. Femur B. Uvea C. Maximum Out of Pocket D. Taxonomy Code

38. C The tiny structures that make up all the tissues of the body and carry out all of its functions
A. Privacy Rule B. Fraud C. Cell D. Deductible

39. B A bacterial infection of the small intestine that causes severe watery diarrhea, dehydration, and possibly death
A. Enzyme B. Cholera C. Anus D. RNA

40. B A white blood cell that makes antibodies to fight infections caused by foreign proteins
A. Bursa B. B cell C. Sebum D. Pus

41. A The outer, visible portion of the female genitals
A. Vulva B. Shock C. Workers Compensation D. Labia

42. D the diagnosis and non-surgical treatment of adult health problems
A. Provider B. Enzyme C. Medical Savings Account D. Internal Medicine

43. A Abnormally pale skin
A. Pallor B. Vernix C. Modifier D. Subscriber

44. D The science of dealing with mental processes and their effects on behavior
A. Health Insurance Claim B. Maximum Out of Pocket C. Graft D. Psychology

45. B The main artery in the body, carrying oxygenated blood from the heart to other arteries in the body
A. Untimely Submission B. Aorta C. Ileum D. Preauthorization

46. D The diagnosis and treatment of mental, emotional and behavioral disorders
A. Group Health Plan B. Secondary Procedure C. Iron D. Psychiatry

47. B Tiny, hairlike structures on the outside of some cells, providing mobility
A. Vagina B. Cilia C. Typhus D. Pleura

48. D A plan whereby patients with HMO membership may receive care at non-HMO providers in exchange for a referral and paying a higher deductible.
A. Cilia B. Thrush C. Network Provider D. Point of Service Plans

49. C A provider within a health insurance company's network that has contracted with the company to provide discounted services to a patient covered under the company's plan.
A. Relative Value Amount B. Group Name C. Network Provider D. Macula

50. A Mucus and other material produced by the lining of the respiratory tract; also called phlegm
A. Sputum B. Bypass C. Stent D. Managed Care Plan

51. B Healthy tissue that is used to replace diseased or defective tissue
A. Superbill B. Graft C. pH D. Cornea

52. D The enzyme found in gastric juice that helps digest protein
A. Preferred Provider Organization B. Sinus C. Vagina D. Pepsin

53. D A device used to hold tissues in place, such as to support a skin graft
A. Authorization B. Allergy C. Non Covered Charge D. Stent

54. C An abnormality of structure or function in the body
A. Colon B. Donut Hole C. Lesion D. Anus

55. C Ribonucleic acid, which helps to decode and process the information contained in dna
A. Thrush B. Lipids C. RNA D. Coccyx

56. A Occurs when a person has a stay at a healthcare facility for more than 24 hours.
A. Inpatient B. COBRA C. Point of Service Plans D. Medical Record Number

57. B A device that is used to immobilize a part of the body
A. Sinus B. Splint C. Nevus D. Medicare Secondary Payer

58. D A formal medical billing term that refers to insurance claims that haven't been paid or balances owed by patients overdue by more than 30 days.
A. Sinus B. Semen C. Referral D. Aging

59. B This is when a provider refuses to accept Medicare payments as a sufficient amount for the services rendered to a patient.
A. Reflex B. Non participation C. Lipids D. Network Provider

60. C A group of cells or an organ that produces substances (such as hormones and enzyme) that are used by the body
A. Cholera B. Non Covered Charge C. Gland D. Kidney

61. B A groove or slit on the body or in an organ
A. Medicare Secondary Payer B. Fissure C. Group Number D. Utilization Limit

62. D The digital version of EOB, which specifies the details of payments made on a claim either by an insurance company or required by the patient.
A. Tic B. Suture C. Uterus D. Electronic Remittance Advice

63. A Inflammation of the large intestine (the colon), which usually leads to abdominal pain, fever, and diarrhea with blood and mucus
A. Colitis B. Appeal C. Fissure D. Rabies

64. A A unique number ascribed to a person's medical record so it can be differentiated from other medical records.
A. Medical Record Number B. Spine C. Primary Care Physician D. Donut Hole

65. D One of two organs that are part of the urinary tract
A. Fraud B. Skilled Nursing Facility C. Ileum D. Kidney

66. D A fluid-filled sac that cushions and reduces friction in certain parts of the body
A. Optic B. Contractual Adjustment C. Office of Inspector General D. Bursa

67. C A membrane lining the inside of the back of the eye that contains light-sensitive nerve cells that convert focused light into nerve impulses, making vision possible
A. Stroke B. Primary Care Physician C. Retina D. Skull

68. B One of the two bones that form the hip on either side of the body
A. Lymph B. Ilium C. Bunion D. Medical Billing Specialist

69. D A thickened area of skin due to consistent pressure or friction, or the area around a bone break where new bone is formed
A. Thrush B. Electronic Medical Records C. Clean Claim D. Callus

70. D This term refers to the discrepancy between the limits of healthcare insurance coverage and the Medicare Part D coverage limits for prescription drugs.
A. Reflex B. Relative Value Amount C. B cell D. Donut Hole

71. D A persisting fear of and desire to avoid something
A. Febrile B. Tendon C. Graft D. Phobia

72. B A sugar that is the main source of energy for the body
A. Rabies B. Glucose C. Nevus D. Medicare Secondary Payer

73. A Mucus and other material produced by the lining of the respiratory tract; also called sputum
A. Phlegm B. Psychiatry C. pH D. Superbill

74. B The artificial growth of cells, tissue, or microorganisms such as bacteria in a laboratory
A. Not Otherwise Specified B. Culture C. RNA D. Phobia

75. C Deoxyribonucleic acid; responsible for passing genetic information in nearly all organisms
A. Pepsin B. Lipids C. DNA D. Privacy Rule

76. D the diagnosis and treatment, including surgery, of diseases and disorders of the musculoskeletal system, including bones, joints, tendons, ligaments, muscles and nerves
A. Callus B. Premium C. Sputum D. Orthopaedics

77. C A unique number a patient or a company may have to produce for billing purposes in order to receive healthcare from a provider.
A. Zygote B. Nodule C. Tax Identification Number D. Pelvis

78. B A type of health insurance plan whereby a patient can receive care with any provider in exchange for higher deductibles and co-pays. Indemnity is also known as fee-for-service insurance.
A. Internal Medicine B. Indemnity C. Gene D. Appeal

79. D Some insurance plans require that a patient receive preauthorization from the insurance company prior to receiving certain medical services.
A. Cervix B. Internal Medicine C. Fissure D. Preauthorization

80. D A drug that causes the pupil to constrict
A. Clone B. Untimely Submission C. Anus D. Miotic

81. C A negative reaction to a substance that in most people causes no reaction
A. Tremor B. Gland C. Allergy D. Subscriber

82. B A joint federal and state assistance program started in 1965 to provide health insurance to lower-income persons.
A. Forceps B. Medicaid C. Network Provider D. Taxonomy Code

83. A The individual covered under a group policy. For instance, an employee of a company with a group health policy would be one of many subscribers on that policy.
A. Subscriber B. Thrill C. Acute D. Self Referral

84. C A thick, yellowish or greenish fluid that contains dead white blood cells, tissues, and bacteria; occurs at the site of a bacterial infection
A. Lesion B. Pelvis C. Pus D. Bunion

85. B The opening through which feces are passed from the body
A. Labia B. Anus C. Thrill D. Allowed Amount

86. B The end date for an insurance policy contract, or the date after which a person no longer receives or is no longer eligible for health insurance with company.
A. Palsy B. Term Date C. Donut Hole D. Not Otherwise Specified

87. C A sample of cells spread across a glass slide to be examined through a microscope
A. Secondary Procedure B. Non Covered Charge C. Smear D. Spine

88. B Occurs when a patient or a provider tries to convince an insurance company to pay for healthcare after it has decided not to cover costs for someone on a claim.
A. Indemnity B. Appeal C. Vagina D. Autism

89. B A small lump of tissue that is usually abnormal
A. Oocyte B. Nodule C. Deductible D. Femur

90. C The limit per year for coverage under certain available healthcare services for Medicare enrollees.
A. Aorta B. Orthopaedics C. Utilization Limit D. Primary Care Physician

91. C The double- layered membrane that lines the lungs and chest cavity and allows for lung movement during breathing
A. Non participation B. Acute C. Pleura D. Office of Inspector General

92. C A process similar to preauthorization whereby patients must check with insurance companies to see if a desired healthcare treatment or service is deemed medically necessary
A. Coccyx B. COBRA C. Pre Certification D. Enzyme

93. D The repair, restoration or improvement of conditions or injuries to the skin and external features resulting from disease, injury or birth defects
A. Gene B. Place of Service Code C. Iron D. Plastic

94. A The two pairs of skinfolds that protect the opening of the vagina
A. Labia B. Miotic C. Stroke D. Orthopaedics

95. B A mineral that plays a role in the body's water balance, heart rhythm, nerve impulses, and muscle contraction
A. Electronic Remittance Advice B. Sodium C. Femur D. Pus

96. A A plentiful mineral in the body and the basic component of teeth and bones
A. Calcium B. Clearinghouse C. Shock D. Miotic

97. B The insurance company that covers any remaining expenses after Medicare has paid for a patient's coverage.
A. Applied to Deductible B. Medicare Secondary Payer C. Allowed Amount D. Orthopaedics

98. B A MAC based in Columbia, South Carolina that is also a subsidiary of Blue Cross Blue Shield.
A. Bifocal B. Palmetto GBA C. Plastic D. Durable Medical Equipment

99. A The column of bones and cartilage running along the midline of the back that surrounds and protects the spinal cord and supports the head
A. Spine B. Hematology C. Referral D. Apnea

100. A The exact date a patient was born.
A. Date of Birth B. Cilia C. Pre Certification D. Office of Inspector General

Matching

A. Provide the word that best matches each clue.

1. ______________ An enzyme that plays a role in increasing a low blood pressure
2. ______________ A physician or medical assistant with expertise in a specific area of medicine.
3. ______________ A method of transferring money electronically from a patient's bank account to a provider or an insurance carrier.
4. ______________ The tiny structures that make up all the tissues of the body and carry out all of its functions
5. ______________ Occurs when a person has a stay at a healthcare facility for more than 24 hours.
6. ______________ A contagious, harmless growth caused by a virus that occurs on the skin or a mucous membrane
7. ______________ A slippery fluid produced by mucous membranes that lubricates and protects the internal surfaces of the body
8. ______________ A structure consisting of the colored area of the eye and the middle layer of the eye that contains blood vessels
9. ______________ Software used for scheduling, billing, and recordkeeping at a provider's office.
10. ______________ Responsible for assigning various medical codes to services and healthcare plans described by a physician on a patient's super-bill.
11. ______________ The structure of bodies; commonly refers to the study of body structure
12. ______________ An involuntary, rhythmic, shaking movement caused by alternating contraction and relaxation of muscles
13. ______________ The liquid part of the blood, containing substances such as nutrients, salts, and proteins
14. ______________ Not obstructed; open
15. ______________ Waves of pain in the abdomen that increase in strength, disappear, and return
16. ______________ The enzyme found in gastric juice that helps digest protein
17. ______________ An organ located in the pelvis whose function is to collect and store urine until it is expelled

18. ______________________ A device used to hold tissues in place, such as to support a skin graft

19. ______________________ A structure that allows fluid flow in only one direction

20. ______________________ The unit of a hospital reserved for patients that need immediate treatment and close monitoring by healthcare professionals for serious illnesses, conditions, and injuries.

21. ______________________ The main artery in the body, carrying oxygenated blood from the heart to other arteries in the body

22. ______________________ A poisonous substance

23. ______________________ A medical condition a patient had before receiving coverage from an insurance company.

24. ______________________ An infectious viral disease primarily affecting animals; can be transmitted to humans through an infected animal's bite

25. ______________________ Abnormally high levels of waste products such as urea in the blood

A. Plasma
B. Intensive Care
C. Renin
D. Valve
E. Rabies
F. Pepsin
G. Specialist
H. Inpatient
I. Anatomy
J. Cell
K. Uvea
L. Mucus
M. Wart
N. Aorta
O. Pre existing Condition
P. Stent
Q. Colic
R. Uremia
S. Tremor
T. Bladder
U. Patent
V. Electronic Funds Transfer
W. Practice Management Software
X. Medical Coder
Y. Toxin

B. Provide the word that best matches each clue.

1. ______________________ A patient’s official signature on file for the purpose of billing and claims processing.

2. ______________________ The care and treatment of the foot and ankle

3. ______________________ The insurance company that covers any remaining expenses after Medicare has paid for a patient’s coverage.

4. ______________________ A characteristic sound of blood flowing irregularly through the heart

5. ______________ the control of pain or discomfort through medication, stress reduction, relaxation, exercise, massage, heat, cold, or providing a comfortable environment

6. ______________ A raised, firm, thick scar that forms as a result of a defect in the natural healing process

7. ______________ A noncancerous tumor of the uterus made up of smooth muscle and connective tissue

8. ______________ A birth defect in which a normal body opening or canal is absent

9. ______________ A bacterial infection of the small intestine that causes severe watery diarrhea, dehydration, and possibly death

10. ______________ The roof of the mouth

11. ______________ One of two organs that are part of the urinary tract

12. ______________ A desire to eat materials that are not food

13. ______________ A unique number a patient or a company may have to produce for billing purposes in order to receive healthcare from a provider.

14. ______________ A negative reaction to a substance that in most people causes no reaction

15. ______________ An abnormal mass that occurs when cells in a certain area reproduce unchecked

16. ______________ The complete set of an organism's genes

17. ______________ A table or list provided by an insurance carrier that explains what prescription drugs are covered under their health plans.

18. ______________ A physician or medical assistant with expertise in a specific area of medicine.

19. ______________ A well-defined, separate part of an organ

20. ______________ Any service administered in a hospital or other healthcare facility other than room and board.

21. ______________ Small eight-legged animals, many of which burrow and feed on blood

22. ______________ Intestine

23. ______________ These are facilities for the severely ill or elderly that provide specialized long-term care for recovering patients.

24. ______________ Serves as the guidelines for policies and practices necessary to reduce security risks within the healthcare system.

25. ______________________ Another term for feces

A. Signature on File
B. Mites
C. Fibroid
D. Kidney
E. Security Standard
F. Lobe
G. Formulary
H. Pain Management
I. Tumor
J. Palate
K. Atresia
L. Stool
M. Podiatry
N. Genome
O. Bowel
P. Medicare Secondary Payer
Q. Ancillary Services
R. Cholera
S. Skilled Nursing Facility
T. Pica
U. Keloid
V. Specialist
W. Murmur
X. Tax Identification Number
Y. Allergy

C. Provide the word that best matches each clue.

1. ______________________ A pus- filled abscess in the follicle of an eyelash

2. ______________________ Involuntary sudden contraction of the diaphragm along with the closing of the vocal cords, producing a "hiccup" sound

3. ______________________ A reduced level of oxygen in tissues

4. ______________________ An artificial feeding technique in which liquids are passed into the stomach by way of a tube inserted through the nose

5. ______________________ Strong connective tissue cords that attach muscle to bone or muscle to muscle

6. ______________________ The fraudulent practice of ascribing a higher ICD-9 code to a healthcare procedure in an attempt to get more money than necessary from the insurance company or patient.

7. ______________________ A document attached to a processed medical claim wherein the insurance company explains the services they will cover for a patient's healthcare treatments.

8. ______________________ A brain tumor arising from cells that support nerve cells

9. ______________________ A fixed payment that a patient makes to a health insurance company or provider to recoup costs incurred from various healthcare services.

10. ______________________ The lowest section of the small intestine, which attaches to the large intestine

11. ______________________ The median amount Medicare will repay a provider for certain services and treatments.

12. ______________________ The name for the organization or individual that manages healthcare group benefits, claims, and administrative duties on behalf of a group plan or a company with a group plan.

13. ______________________ A marking on the skin; can be present at birth (birthmark) or develop later (such as a mole)

14. ______________________ The individual covered under a group policy. For instance, an employee of a company with a group health policy would be one of many subscribers on that policy.

15. ______________________ A birth defect in which a normal body opening or canal is absent

16. ______________________ Describes a disorder that continues for a long period of time

17. ______________________ This term refers to the amount of money a patient owes a provider that goes to paying their yearly deductible.

18. ______________________ A thin, oval-shaped membrane that separates the inner ear from the outer ear and is responsible for transmitting sound waves

19. ______________________ The tiny structures that make up all the tissues of the body and carry out all of its functions

20. ______________________ The federal health insurance program for active and retired service members, their families, and the survivors of service members.

21. ______________________ These are the entities that offer healthcare services to patients, including hospitals, physicians, and private clinics, hospices, nursing homes, and other healthcare facilities.

22. ______________________ A milky fluid containing white blood cells, proteins, and fats

23. ______________________ The specialty of physicians who are trained to examine surgical specimens and biopsies for diagnostic purposes.

24. ______________________ The smallest known disease- causing microorganism

25. ______________________ An accumulation of pus in a body tissue, usually caused by a bacterial infection

A. Explanation of Benefits
B. Third Party Administrator
C. Subscriber
D. Eardrum
E. Nevus
F. Stye
G. Hiccup
H. Healthcare Provider
I. Hypoxia
J. Ileum
K. Applied to Deductible
L. Upcoding
M. Abscess
N. Cell
O. Chronic
P. Relative Value Amount
Q. Lymph
R. Pathology
S. Virus
T. TRICARE
U. Capitation
V. Gavage
W. Glioma
X. Tendon
Y. Atresia

D. Provide the word that best matches each clue.

1. ______ This refers to the amount a patient owes a provider after an insurance company pays for their portion of the medical expenses.

2. ______ The limit per year for coverage under certain available healthcare services for Medicare enrollees.

3. ______ A raised, firm, thick scar that forms as a result of a defect in the natural healing process

4. ______ A term used to describe something related to a fever, such as febrile seizures

5. ______ The process of translating a physician's documentation about a patient's medical condition and health services rendered into medical codes that are then plugged into a claim for processing.

6. ______ A marking on the skin; can be present at birth (birthmark) or develop later (such as a mole)

7. ______ The major healthcare legislation passed in 2010 designed to make healthcare accessible and less expensive for more Americans.

8. ______ A salt solution or any substance that contains salt

9. ______ An organ located in the pelvis whose function is to collect and store urine until it is expelled

10. ______ Procedures and services not covered by a person's health insurance plan.

11. ______ An additional dose of a vaccine taken after the first dose to maintain or renew the first one

12. ______ Describes a disorder that continues for a long period of time

13. ______ The infection of a wound or tissue with bacteria, causing the spread of the bacteria into the bloodstream

14. ______ the control of pain or discomfort through medication, stress reduction, relaxation, exercise, massage, heat, cold, or providing a comfortable environment

15. ______ The name for Medicare representatives who process Medicare claims.

16. ______ The physician who provides the basic healthcare services for a patient and recommends additional care for more serious treatments as necessary.

17. ______ A document that outlines the costs associated for each medical service designated by a CPT code.

18. ______________________ Refers to the sum shown in the "balance" column of a billing statement that reflects the amount due for services rendered.

19. ______________________ A digital network that allows healthcare providers to access quality medical billing software and technologies without needing to purchase and maintain it themselves.

20. ______________________ Damage to part of the brain because of a lack of blood supply or the rupturing of a blood vessel

21. ______________________ the specialty that includes treatment of any symptom, illness or injury requiring urgent evaluation and

22. ______________________ Can be a secondary policy or another insurance company that covers a patient's healthcare costs after receiving coverage from their primary insurance.

23. ______________________ A noncancerous tumor of fatty tissue

24. ______________________ The patient's information required for filing a claim, such as age, sex, address, and family information. An insurance company may deny a claim if it contains inaccurate demographics.

25. ______________________ The double- layered membrane that lines the lungs and chest cavity and allows for lung movement during breathing

A. Fiscal Intermediary
B. Lipoma
C. Healthcare Reform Act
D. Chronic
E. Application Service Provider
F. Primary Care Physician
G. Supplemental Insurance
H. Sepsis
I. Nevus
J. Pain Management
K. Emergency Medicine
L. Febrile
M. Utilization Limit
N. Credit Balance
O. Saline
P. Demographics
Q. Fee Schedule
R. Booster
S. Stroke
T. Coding
U. Patient Responsibility
V. Keloid
W. Bladder
X. Non Covered Charge
Y. Pleura

E. Provide the word that best matches each clue.

1. ______________________ A contagious, harmless growth caused by a virus that occurs on the skin or a mucous membrane

2. ______________________ An inflamed, raised area of skin that is pus-filled

3. ______________________ One of two organs that are part of the urinary tract

4. ______________________ The chest

5. ______________________ Small, eight- legged animals that can attach to humans and animals and feed on blood

6. ______ Refers to providers outside of an established network of providers who contract with an insurance company to offer patients healthcare at a discounted rate.

7. ______ Occurs when a person has a stay at a healthcare facility for more than 24 hours.

8. ______ A group of diseases caused by the microorganism rickettsia, spread by the bites of fleas, mites, or ticks

9. ______ Loss of sensation or ability to move

10. ______ An exact copy of a gene, cell, or organism

11. ______ A poisonous substance

12. ______ The column of bones and cartilage running along the midline of the back that surrounds and protects the spinal cord and supports the head

13. ______ the diagnosis and treatment, including surgery, of diseases and disorders of the eye, such as cataracts and glaucoma

14. ______ Refers to insurance payments made directly to a healthcare provider for medical services received by the patient.

15. ______ Referring to 61st through 90th days of inpatient treatment, the law requires that patients pay for a portion of their healthcare during Medicare coinsurance days.

16. ______ A white blood cell that makes antibodies to fight infections caused by foreign proteins

17. ______ The medical term for nearsightedness

18. ______ A structure that allows fluid flow in only one direction

19. ______ Refers to healthcare services or treatments that a patient requires to treat a serious medical condition or illness.

20. ______ A gas that is colorless, odorless, and tasteless

21. ______ Responsible for using information regarding services and treatments performed by a healthcare provider to complete a claim for filing with an insurance company.

22. ______ The sticky, brown substance in cigarettes that coats the lungs; causes lung and other cancers

23. ______ Feeling the need to vomit

24. ______________________ Refers to a binding agree between a provider, patient, and insurance company wherein the provider agrees to charges that it will write off on behalf of the patient.

25. ______________________ Abnormally pale skin

A. Thorax	B. Pallor	C. Typhus
D. B cell	E. Palsy	F. Myopia
G. Clone	H. Wart	I. Medicare Coinsurance Days
J. Tar	K. Ticks	L. Ophthalmology
M. Spine	N. Contractual Adjustment	O. Out of Network
P. Nausea	Q. Medical Necessity	R. Inpatient
S. Oxygen	T. Valve	U. Toxin
V. Boil	W. Medical Billing Specialist	X. Kidney
Y. Assignment of Benefits		

F. Provide the word that best matches each clue.

1. ______________________ The unit of a hospital reserved for patients that need immediate treatment and close monitoring by healthcare professionals for serious illnesses, conditions, and injuries.

2. ______________________ A drug that neutralizes stomach acids

3. ______________________ The care and treatment of the foot and ankle

4. ______________________ Feeling the need to vomit

5. ______________________ A noncancerous tumor made of mucous material and fibrous connective tissue

6. ______________________ An agent that is believed to cause several degenerative brain diseases

7. ______________________ An accumulation of pus in a body tissue, usually caused by a bacterial infection

8. ______________________ A unique number ascribed to a person’s medical record so it can be differentiated from other medical records.

9. ______________________ A measure of a person's physical strength, flexibility, and endurance

10. ______________________ The digital version of EOB, which specifies the details of payments made on a claim either by an insurance company or required by the patient.

11. ______________________ A contagious, harmless growth caused by a virus that occurs on the skin or a mucous membrane

12. ______________________ Serves as the guidelines for policies and practices necessary to reduce security risks within the healthcare system.

13. ______ Fluid released during ejaculation that contains sperm along with fluids produced by the prostate gland and the seminal vesicles

14. ______ Describes a condition or illness that begins suddenly and is usually short- lasting

15. ______ A thin fold of membrane partly closing the opening of the vagina

16. ______ The common term for urticaria, an itchy, inflamed rash that results from an allergic reaction

17. ______ The presence of white blood cells in the urine

18. ______ A noncancerous tumor of connective tissue

19. ______ the diagnosis and non-surgical treatment of adult health problems

20. ______ An area of inflammation or a group of spots on the skin

21. ______ The triangular bone located at the bottom of the spine that is connected to the tailbone, the hipbones near the sacroilial joints, and the rest of the spine

22. ______ A unit that is used to measure the energy content in food

23. ______ A disorder marked by high levels of uric acid in the blood

24. ______ This refers to a type of health insurance wherein the provider is paid for every service they perform.

25. ______ A noncancerous tumor of the uterus made up of smooth muscle and connective tissue

A. Hymen
B. Fee for Service
C. Abscess
D. Electronic Remittance Advice
E. Security Standard
F. Hives
G. Prion
H. Podiatry
I. Wart
J. Fitness
K. Fibroma
L. Antacid
M. Acute
N. Fibroid
O. Calorie
P. Pyuria
Q. Nausea
R. Gout
S. Medical Record Number
T. Internal Medicine
U. Sacrum
V. Rash
W. Intensive Care
X. Myxoma
Y. Semen

G. Provide the word that best matches each clue.

1. ______ The hard deposit formed on teeth when mineral salts in saliva combine with plaque

2. ______ A bacterial infection of the small intestine that causes severe watery diarrhea, dehydration, and possibly death

3. ____________ A two-digit code used on claims to explain what type of provider performed healthcare services on a patient.

4. ____________ A mental disorder characterized by extreme excitement, happiness, overactivity, and agitation

5. ____________ The median amount Medicare will repay a provider for certain services and treatments.

6. ____________ An automatic, involuntary response of the nervous system to a stimulus

7. ____________ A cavity within bone or a channel that contains blood

8. ____________ the care of women during and after pregnancy and childbirth, and the care of the female reproductive system and treatment of associated disorders

9. ____________ A digital network that allows healthcare providers to access quality medical billing software and technologies without needing to purchase and maintain it themselves.

10. ____________ Whoever owes the healthcare provider money has financial responsibility for the services rendered.

11. ____________ A group of diseases caused by the microorganism rickettsia, spread by the bites of fleas, mites, or ticks

12. ____________ The person who receives benefits and

13. ____________ An additional dose of a vaccine taken after the first dose to maintain or renew the first one

14. ____________ Medical billing specialists utilize this unique codeset for identifying a healthcare provider's specialty field.

15. ____________ A type of health insurance plan whereby a patient can receive care with any provider in exchange for higher deductibles and co-pays. Indemnity is also known as fee-for-service insurance.

16. ____________ Supplemental health insurance under Medicaid for eligible persons who need help covering co-pays, deductibles, and other large fees.

17. ____________ The process of converting dictated or handwritten instructions, observations, and documentation into digital text formats.

18. ____________ This type of care is administered at reduced or zero cost to patients who cannot afford healthcare.

19. ____________ The enzyme found in gastric juice that helps digest protein

20. ______________________ The medical term for the voice box, the organ in the throat that produces voice and also prevents food from entering the airway

21. ______________________ An area of buildup of fat deposits in an artery, causing narrowing of the artery and possibly heart disease

22. ______________________ This is when a provider refuses to accept Medicare payments as a sufficient amount for the services rendered to a patient.

23. ______________________ Describes a condition or illness that begins suddenly and is usually short- lasting

24. ______________________ A fluid-filled sac that cushions and reduces friction in certain parts of the body

25. ______________________ A physician or medical assistant with expertise in a specific area of medicine.

A. Financial Responsibility	B. Medical Transcription	C. Reflex
D. Acute	E. Charity Care	F. Specialist
G. Plaque	H. Bursa	I. Sinus
J. Tartar	K. Gynecology	L. Cholera
M. Medigap	N. Taxonomy Code	O. Booster
P. Place of Service Code	Q. Relative Value Amount	R. Indemnity
S. Pepsin	T. Application Service Provider	U. Non participation
V. Beneficiary	W. Larynx	X. Typhus
Y. Mania		

H. Provide the word that best matches each clue.

1. ______________________ These are the entities that offer healthcare services to patients, including hospitals, physicians, and private clinics, hospices, nursing homes, and other healthcare facilities.

2. ______________________ A joint federal and state assistance program started in 1965 to provide health insurance to lower-income persons.

3. ______________________ A reduced level of oxygen in tissues

4. ______________________ A unique number ascribed to a person's medical record so it can be differentiated from other medical records.

5. ______________________ A disorder characterized by inflamed airways and difficulty breathing

6. ______________________ The complete set of an organism's genes

7. ______________________ The specialty that focuses on the health of individuals in order to protect, promote and maintain health and prevent disease, disability and premature death

8. ______ The federal health insurance program for active and retired service members, their families, and the survivors of service members.

9. ______ This refers to medical care and treatment for persons who are terminally ill.

10. ______ The care and treatment of infants, children, and adolescents

11. ______ Muscle damage resulting from excessive stretching or forceful contraction

12. ______ The median amount Medicare will repay a provider for certain services and treatments.

13. ______ An element for the formation of thyroid hormones

14. ______ The drooping of the upper eyelid

15. ______ Tiny, hairlike structures on the outside of some cells, providing mobility

16. ______ A membrane lining the inside of the back of the eye that contains light-sensitive nerve cells that convert focused light into nerve impulses, making vision possible

17. ______ A contagious, harmless growth caused by a virus that occurs on the skin or a mucous membrane

18. ______ A reduced flow of blood throughout the body, usually caused by severe bleeding or a weak heart

19. ______ the diagnosis and treatment of disorders of the heart and major blood vessels

20. ______ A gas that is colorless, odorless, and tasteless

21. ______ An optional health insurance payments plan whereby a person apportions part of their untaxed earnings to an account reserved for healthcare expenses.

22. ______ A type of health insurance plan whereby a patient can receive care with any provider in exchange for higher deductibles and co-pays. Indemnity is also known as fee-for-service insurance.

23. ______ The tearing or stretching of the ligaments in a joint, characterized by pain, swelling, and an inability to move the joint

24. ______ Refers to healthcare services or treatments that a patient requires to treat a serious medical condition or illness.

25. ______________________ The digital version of EOB, which specifies the details of payments made on a claim either by an insurance company or required by the patient.

A. Cilia
B. Genome
C. Preventive Medicine
D. Cardiology
E. Asthma
F. TRICARE
G. Electronic Remittance Advice
H. Hospice
I. Iodine
J. Strain
K. Hypoxia
L. Ptosis
M. Retina
N. Medical Necessity
O. Medicaid
P. Indemnity
Q. Medical Record Number
R. Sprain
S. Wart
T. Pediatrics
U. Oxygen
V. Medical Savings Account
W. Healthcare Provider
X. Shock
Y. Relative Value Amount

I. Provide the word that best matches each clue.

1. ______________________ These are facilities for the severely ill or elderly that provide specialized long-term care for recovering patients.

2. ______________________ A thin fold of membrane partly closing the opening of the vagina

3. ______________________ Networks of healthcare providers that offer healthcare plans to people for medical services exclusively in their network.

4. ______________________ Ribonucleic acid, which helps to decode and process the information contained in dna

5. ______________________ The cell that results when an egg is fertilized by a sperm

6. ______________________ The abbreviation for diagnosis codes, also known as ICD-9 codes.

7. ______________________ the care of women during and after pregnancy and childbirth, and the care of the female reproductive system and treatment of associated disorders

8. ______________________ The claim filed with the secondary insurance company after the primary insurance company pays for their portion of healthcare costs.

9. ______________________ Refers to the ratio of payments received relative to the total amount owed to providers.

10. ______________________ A hard plaster or fiberglass shell that molds to a body part such as an arm and holds it in place for proper healing

11. ______________________ The digital version of EOB, which specifies the details of payments made on a claim either by an insurance company or required by the patient.

12. ______ This term refers to the discrepancy between the limits of healthcare insurance coverage and the Medicare Part D coverage limits for prescription drugs.

13. ______ The specialty of physicians who are trained to examine surgical specimens and biopsies for diagnostic purposes.

14. ______ A noncancerous tumor of fatty tissue

15. ______ Refers to when a patient's health insurance plan requires them to get permission from their insurance providers before receiving certain healthcare services.

16. ______ The sum a person pays to an insurance company on a regular (usually monthly or yearly) basis to receive health insurance.

17. ______ The passageways that air moves through while traveling in and out of the lungs during breathing

18. ______ A measure of the acidic or basic character of a substance

19. ______ A physician or medical assistant with expertise in a specific area of medicine.

20. ______ The federal health insurance program for active and retired service members, their families, and the survivors of service members.

21. ______ Describes a disease that is always present in a certain population of people

22. ______ This type of care is administered at reduced or zero cost to patients who cannot afford healthcare.

23. ______ the treatment of diseases and internal disorders of the elderly

24. ______ A skin condition characterized by inflamed, pus-filled areas that occur on the skin's surface, most commonly occurring during adolescence

25. ______ A "warning" signal that comes before a migraine headache or an epileptic seizure, which might include emotions or sensations of movement or discomfort

A. Premium
B. Acne
C. Pathology
D. Secondary Insurance Claim
E. Aura
F. Skilled Nursing Facility
G. RNA
H. Specialist
I. TRICARE
J. Authorization
K. Cast
L. Health Maintenance Organization
M. Dx
N. Endemic

O. Donut Hole
P. Geriatrics
Q. Hymen
R. Charity Care
S. Zygote
T. Airways
U. Gynecology
V. pH
W. Electronic Remittance Advice
X. Collection Ratio
Y. Lipoma

J. Provide the word that best matches each clue.

1. ____________ A thickened callus on the foot that is caused by an improperly fitting shoe

2. ____________ Density lipoprotein- a type of lipoprotein that is the major carrier of cholesterol in the blood, with high levels associated with narrowing of the arteries and heart disease

3. ____________ This type of care is administered at reduced or zero cost to patients who cannot afford healthcare.

4. ____________ A disease caused by a lack of vitamin c, characterized by weakness, bleeding and pain in joints and muscles, bleeding gums, and abnormal bone and tooth growth

5. ____________ An artificially constructed or an abnormal passage connecting two usually separate structures in the body

6. ____________ A drug that causes the pupil to constrict

7. ____________ A digital network that allows healthcare providers to access quality medical billing software and technologies without needing to purchase and maintain it themselves.

8. ____________ A maximum sum as explained in a healthcare plan an insurance company will pay for certain services or treatments.

9. ____________ A unique number a patient or a company may have to produce for billing purposes in order to receive healthcare from a provider.

10. ____________ The external male reproductive organ, which passes urine and semen out of the body

11. ____________ Pertaining to the eyes

12. ____________ A negative reaction to a substance that in most people causes no reaction

13. ____________ A structure consisting of the colored area of the eye and the middle layer of the eye that contains blood vessels

14. ____________ A blood vessel that carries blood toward the heart

15. ______________________ A colorless, odorless, tasteless radioactive gas that is produced by materials in soil, rocks, and building materials

16. ______________________ A field on a claim for describing what kind of healthcare services or procedures a provider administered.

17. ______________________ The tiny structures that make up all the tissues of the body and carry out all of its functions

18. ______________________ the care of women during and after pregnancy and childbirth, and the care of the female reproductive system and treatment of associated disorders

19. ______________________ The fraudulent practice of ascribing a higher ICD-9 code to a healthcare procedure in an attempt to get more money than necessary from the insurance company or patient.

20. ______________________ This is when a provider refuses to accept Medicare payments as a sufficient amount for the services rendered to a patient.

21. ______________________ A pus- filled abscess in the follicle of an eyelash

22. ______________________ An abnormality of structure or function in the body

23. ______________________ A tumor made of blood vessels or lymph vessels that is not cancerous

24. ______________________ An organ, tissue, or device surgically inserted and left in the body

25. ______________________ the medical and surgical care for diseases of the ears, nose and throat (ENT)

A. Optic
B. Allergy
C. Pre determination
D. Shunt
E. Otolaryngology
F. Low
G. Non participation
H. Penis
I. Upcoding
J. Implant
K. Angioma
L. Stye
M. Vein
N. Miotic
O. Type of Service
P. Uvea
Q. Tax Identification Number
R. Scurvy
S. Lesion
T. Cell
U. Gynecology
V. Radon
W. Corn
X. Application Service Provider
Y. Charity Care

K. Provide the word that best matches each clue.

1. ______________________ A painless sore that has a thick, rubbery base and a defined edge

2. ______________________ A noncancerous tumor made of mucous material and fibrous connective tissue

3. ______________________ Muscle damage resulting from excessive stretching or forceful contraction

4. ______ The chest

5. ______ A condition in which the area of the brain involved in maintaining consciousness is somehow affected, resulting in a state of unconsciousness in which the patient does not respond to stimulation

6. ______ Digitized medical record for a patient managed by a provider onsite.

7. ______ The fraudulent practice of ascribing a higher ICD-9 code to a healthcare procedure in an attempt to get more money than necessary from the insurance company or patient.

8. ______ A milky fluid containing white blood cells, proteins, and fats

9. ______ An optional health insurance payments plan whereby a person apportions part of their untaxed earnings to an account reserved for healthcare expenses.

10. ______ A provider within a health insurance company's network that has contracted with the company to provide discounted services to a patient covered under the company's plan.

11. ______ A measure of a person's physical strength, flexibility, and endurance

12. ______ Refers to when a patient's health insurance plan requires them to get permission from their insurance providers before receiving certain healthcare services.

13. ______ Abnormal crackling or bubbling sounds heard in the lungs during breathing

14. ______ A patient's official signature on file for the purpose of billing and claims processing.

15. ______ The inner skin layer

16. ______ Payment made by the patient for healthcare at the time they receive it at a provider's facilities.

17. ______ An organ located in the pelvis whose function is to collect and store urine until it is expelled

18. ______ A plan whereby patients with HMO membership may receive care at non-HMO providers in exchange for a referral and paying a higher deductible.

19. ______ The colored part of the eye

20. ______ A drug that neutralizes stomach acids

21. ____________ A process similar to preauthorization whereby patients must check with insurance companies to see if a desired healthcare treatment or service is deemed medically necessary

22. ____________ An enzyme that plays a role in increasing a low blood pressure

23. ____________ Referring to 61st through 90th days of inpatient treatment, the law requires that patients pay for a portion of their healthcare during Medicare coinsurance days.

24. ____________ An electrocardiogram, which is a record of the electrical impulses that trigger the heartbeat

25. ____________ These are facilities for the severely ill or elderly that provide specialized long-term care for recovering patients.

A. Electronic Medical Records
B. Medicare Coinsurance Days
C. Skilled Nursing Facility
D. Self Pay
E. Myxoma
F. Upcoding
G. Thorax
H. Chancre
I. Iris
J. Antacid
K. Point of Service Plans
L. Fitness
M. Rales
N. Strain
O. Lymph
P. Pre Certification
Q. Dermis
R. Medical Savings Account
S. Coma
T. Bladder
U. Signature on File
V. Renin
W. ECG
X. Network Provider
Y. Authorization

L. Provide the word that best matches each clue.

1. ____________ A document attached to a processed medical claim wherein the insurance company explains the services they will cover for a patient's healthcare treatments.

2. ____________ An involuntary, repetitive movement such as a twitch

3. ____________ An organism that is dependent on another organism for nourishment

4. ____________ A lens that corrects both near and distant vision by having two parts with different focusing strengths

5. ____________ the diagnosis and medical treatment of the nervous system and brain, including conditions such as strokes and seizures

6. ____________ This refers to a type of health insurance wherein the provider is paid for every service they perform.

7. ____________ An artificially constructed or an abnormal passage connecting two usually separate structures in the body

8. ____________ Deoxyribonucleic acid; responsible for passing genetic information in nearly all organisms

9. ______________ The specialty that focuses on the health of individuals in order to protect, promote and maintain health and prevent disease, disability and premature death

10. ______________ A term describing something related to or caused by a virus

11. ______________ One of the two long bones of the forearm

12. ______________ the treatment of diseases and internal disorders of the elderly

13. ______________ the specialty that provides comprehensive and ongoing medical care to all members of the family unit

14. ______________ The basic unit of dna, which is responsible for passing genetic information

15. ______________ These are the entities that offer healthcare services to patients, including hospitals, physicians, and private clinics, hospices, nursing homes, and other healthcare facilities.

16. ______________ A hospital or an area of a hospital dedicated to treating people who are dying, often of a specific cause

17. ______________ This is when provider performs another procedure on a patient covered by a CPT code after first performing a different CPT procedure on them.

18. ______________ A vitamin important in many chemical processes in the body

19. ______________ A gas that is colorless, odorless, and tasteless

20. ______________ The application process for a provider to coordinate with an insurance company.

21. ______________ An organ located in the upper left abdomen behind the ribs that removes and destroys old red blood cells and helps fight infection

22. ______________ A term used to describe a child in the womb from fertilization to 8 weeks following fertilization

23. ______________ A noncancerous tumor of fatty tissue

24. ______________ A claim filed by a provider after they have filed claims for primary and secondary health insurance coverage on behalf of a patient.

25. ______________ A desire to eat materials that are not food

A. Family Practice
B. Gene
C. Fee for Service
D. Lipoma
E. Spleen
F. DNA
G. Bifocal
H. Niacin
I. Embryo
J. Shunt
K. Hospice
L. Secondary Procedure
M. Preventive Medicine
N. Oxygen
O. Credentialing
P. Explanation of Benefits
Q. Tertiary Claim
R. Fungus

S. Healthcare Provider
T. Pica
U. Viral
V. Tic
W. Neurology
X. Geriatrics
Y. Radius

M. Provide the word that best matches each clue.

1. ______________ A desire to eat materials that are not food
2. ______________ This term refers to a provider's relationship with a health insurance company.
3. ______________ Involuntary contraction of genital muscles experienced at the peak of sexual excitement
4. ______________ An open sore that occurs on the skin or on a mucous membrane because of the destruction of surface tissue
5. ______________ The oily, lubricating substance that is secreted by glands in the skin
6. ______________ A drug that causes the pupil to constrict
7. ______________ Waves of pain in the abdomen that increase in strength, disappear, and return
8. ______________ The muscular passage connecting the uterus with the outside genitals
9. ______________ A poisonous substance
10. ______________ A measure of a person's physical strength, flexibility, and endurance
11. ______________ A reduced level of oxygen in tissues
12. ______________ The chest
13. ______________ The limit per year for coverage under certain available healthcare services for Medicare enrollees.
14. ______________ An automatic, involuntary response of the nervous system to a stimulus
15. ______________ Strong connective tissue cords that attach muscle to bone or muscle to muscle
16. ______________ The colored part of the eye
17. ______________ A MAC based in Columbia, South Carolina that is also a subsidiary of Blue Cross Blue Shield.
18. ______________ A digital network that allows healthcare providers to access quality medical billing software and technologies without needing to purchase and maintain it themselves.

19. ______________ A disorder in which a person eats large amounts of food then forces vomiting or uses laxatives to prevent weight gain (called binging and purging)

20. ______________ Describes something related to the eyes

21. ______________ Medical billing specialists utilize this unique codeset for identifying a healthcare provider's specialty field.

22. ______________ The tearing or stretching of the ligaments in a joint, characterized by pain, swelling, and an inability to move the joint

23. ______________ An involuntary muscle contraction

24. ______________ A colorless, odorless, tasteless radioactive gas that is produced by materials in soil, rocks, and building materials

25. ______________ The thick, greasy substance that covers the skin of a newborn baby

A. Palmetto GBA
B. Orgasm
C. Radon
D. Thorax
E. Taxonomy Code
F. Vernix
G. Spasm
H. Hypoxia
I. Sebum
J. Bulimia
K. Miotic
L. Pica
M. Iris
N. Application Service Provider
O. Tendon
P. Sprain
Q. In Network
R. Ocular
S. Fitness
T. Reflex
U. Vagina
V. Colic
W. Ulcer
X. Toxin
Y. Utilization Limit

N. Provide the word that best matches each clue.

1. ______________ A surgical stitch that helps close an incision or wound so that it can heal properly

2. ______________ A thickened area of skin due to consistent pressure or friction, or the area around a bone break where new bone is formed

3. ______________ The outer, visible portion of the female genitals

4. ______________ This term refers to the discrepancy between the limits of healthcare insurance coverage and the Medicare Part D coverage limits for prescription drugs.

5. ______________ This refers to medical implements that can be reused such as stretchers, wheelchairs, canes, crutches, and bedpans.

6. ______________ A term describing something related to or caused by a virus

7. ______________ The document attached to a processed claim that explains the information regarding coverage and payments on a claim.

8. ______________________ A disorder characterized by inflamed airways and difficulty breathing

9. ______________________ A plan provided by an employer to provide healthcare options to a large group of employees.

10. ______________________ When a patient does their own research to find a provider and acts outside of their primary care physician's referral.

11. ______________________ This is when a provider recommends another provider to a patient to receive specialized treatment.

12. ______________________ A mineral necessary for the formation of important biological substances such as hemoglobin, myoglobin, and certain enzymes

13. ______________________ An employee in the healthcare system such as a physician's assistant or a nurse practitioner who perform duties in administration, nursing, and other ancillary care.

14. ______________________ A membrane lining the inside of the back of the eye that contains light-sensitive nerve cells that convert focused light into nerve impulses, making vision possible

15. ______________________ An involuntary, repetitive movement such as a twitch

16. ______________________ An area of buildup of fat deposits in an artery, causing narrowing of the artery and possibly heart disease

17. ______________________ Mucus and other material produced by the lining of the respiratory tract; also called sputum

18. ______________________ A salt solution or any substance that contains salt

19. ______________________ Responsible for assigning various medical codes to services and healthcare plans described by a physician on a patient's super-bill.

20. ______________________ The external male reproductive organ, which passes urine and semen out of the body

21. ______________________ the medical and surgical care for diseases of the ears, nose and throat (ENT)

22. ______________________ A plan similar to an HMO whereby a patient can receive healthcare from providers within an established network set up by an insurance company.

23. ______________________ The socket in the skull that contains the eyeball, along with its blood vessels, nerves, and muscles

24. ______________________ Excess fluid in the abdominal cavity, which leads to swelling

25. ______________________ The sum a person pays to an insurance company on a regular (usually monthly or yearly) basis to receive health insurance.

A. Phlegm
B. Referral
C. Callus
D. Durable Medical Equipment
E. Penis
F. Medical Coder
G. Donut Hole
H. Viral
I. Preferred Provider Organization
J. Self Referral
K. Asthma
L. Orbit
M. Group Health Plan
N. Vulva
O. Suture
P. Premium
Q. Iron
R. Remittance Advice
S. Retina
T. Ascites
U. Tic
V. Plaque
W. Medical Assistant
X. Saline
Y. Otolaryngology

O. Provide the word that best matches each clue.

1. ______________________ Describes a condition or illness that begins suddenly and is usually short-lasting

2. ______________________ Loss of sensation or ability to move

3. ______________________ The individual covered under a group policy. For instance, an employee of a company with a group health policy would be one of many subscribers on that policy.

4. ______________________ A surgically formed opening on a body surface

5. ______________________ A digestive disorder in which nutrients cannot be properly absorbed from food, causing weakness and loss of weight

6. ______________________ This refers to a type of health insurance wherein the provider is paid for every service they perform.

7. ______________________ A condition in which the blood does not contain enough hemoglobin, the compound that carries oxygen from the lungs to other parts of the body

8. ______________________ The major healthcare legislation passed in 2010 designed to make healthcare accessible and less expensive for more Americans.

9. ______________________ Describes a disorder that continues for a long period of time

10. ______________________ the specialized care and treatment of a newborn up to six weeks of age

11. ______________ The unit of a hospital reserved for patients that need immediate treatment and close monitoring by healthcare professionals for serious illnesses, conditions, and injuries.

12. ______________ A high- pitched sound produced during breathing because of narrowing of the airways

13. ______________ The name for the organization or individual that manages healthcare group benefits, claims, and administrative duties on behalf of a group plan or a company with a group plan.

14. ______________ Physical injury or emotional shock

15. ______________ A table or list provided by an insurance carrier that explains what prescription drugs are covered under their health plans.

16. ______________ A persisting fear of and desire to avoid something

17. ______________ Occurs when a patient is covered by more than one insurance plan.

18. ______________ Refers to insurance payments made directly to a healthcare provider for medical services received by the patient.

19. ______________ The insurance company that covers any remaining expenses after Medicare has paid for a patient's coverage.

20. ______________ The physician who provides the basic healthcare services for a patient and recommends additional care for more serious treatments as necessary.

21. ______________ A field on a claim for describing what kind of healthcare services or procedures a provider administered.

22. ______________ The interval from onset of contractions to birth of a baby

23. ______________ A viral infection that causes inflammation of salivary glands

24. ______________ A drug that causes the pupil to constrict

25. ______________ Refers to the fraudulent practice of ascribing more than one code to a service or procedure on a superbill or claim form when only one is necessary.

A. Subscriber
B. Assignment of Benefits
C. Primary Care Physician
D. Anemia
E. Third Party Administrator
F. Unbundling
G. Acute
H. Medicare Secondary Payer
I. Intensive Care
J. Neonatology
K. Wheeze
L. Mumps
M. Coordination of Benefits
N. Type of Service
O. Palsy
P. Fee for Service
Q. Labor
R. Miotic
S. Healthcare Reform Act
T. Formulary
U. Sprue
V. Stoma
W. Phobia
X. Chronic
Y. Trauma

P. Provide the word that best matches each clue.

1. ______________ Refers to the sum shown in the "balance" column of a billing statement that reflects the amount due for services rendered.

2. ______________ The sum an insurance company will reimburse to cover a healthcare service or procedure.

3. ______________ Describes a condition or illness that begins suddenly and is usually short- lasting

4. ______________ Describes a disease that is always present in a certain population of people

5. ______________ Networks of healthcare providers that offer healthcare plans to people for medical services exclusively in their network.

6. ______________ A joint federal and state assistance program started in 1965 to provide health insurance to lower-income persons.

7. ______________ Describes a disorder that continues for a long period of time

8. ______________ The socket in the skull that contains the eyeball, along with its blood vessels, nerves, and muscles

9. ______________ A group of cells or an organ that produces substances (such as hormones and enzyme) that are used by the body

10. ______________ A three-digit code used on medical bills that explains the kind of facility in which a patient received treatment.

11. ______________ A noncancerous tumor made of mucous material and fibrous connective tissue

12. ______________ A form of phototherapy that combines the use of psoralens and ultraviolet light to treat skin disorders

13. ______________ A salt solution or any substance that contains salt

14. ______________ An infectious viral disease primarily affecting animals; can be transmitted to humans through an infected animal's bite

15. ______________ Occurs when an insurance company finds there is insufficient evidence on a claim to prove that a provider performed coded medical services and so they reduce or remove those codes.

16. ______________ Refers to healthcare services or treatments that a patient requires to treat a serious medical condition or illness.

17. ______________________ A government insurance program started in 1965 to provide healthcare coverage for persons over 65 and eligible people with disabilities.

18. ______________________ Can be a secondary policy or another insurance company that covers a patient's healthcare costs after receiving coverage from their primary insurance.

19. ______________________ Describes something related to the eyes

20. ______________________ A mineral necessary for the formation of important biological substances such as hemoglobin, myoglobin, and certain enzymes

21. ______________________ A bacterial infection of the small intestine that causes severe watery diarrhea, dehydration, and possibly death

22. ______________________ Medical term for the armpit

23. ______________________ The two pairs of skinfolds that protect the opening of the vagina

24. ______________________ An unaware clenching or grinding of the teeth, usually during sleep

25. ______________________ The process of converting dictated or handwritten instructions, observations, and documentation into digital text formats.

A. Orbit
B. Iron
C. PUVA
D. Health Maintenance Organization
E. Gland
F. Bruxism
G. Ocular
H. Rabies
I. Downcoding
J. Allowed Amount
K. Axilla
L. Medical Necessity
M. Supplemental Insurance
N. Credit Balance
O. Medicare
P. Medical Transcription
Q. Revenue Code
R. Labia
S. Myxoma
T. Endemic
U. Saline
V. Chronic
W. Acute
X. Medicaid
Y. Cholera

A. Provide the word that best matches each clue.

1. RENIN	An enzyme that plays a role in increasing a low blood pressure
2. SPECIALIST	A physician or medical assistant with expertise in a specific area of medicine.
3. ELECTRONIC FUNDS TRANSFER	A method of transferring money electronically from a patient's bank account to a provider or an insurance carrier.
4. CELL	The tiny structures that make up all the tissues of the body and carry out all of its functions
5. INPATIENT	Occurs when a person has a stay at a healthcare facility for more than 24 hours.
6. WART	A contagious, harmless growth caused by a virus that occurs on the skin or a mucous membrane
7. MUCUS	A slippery fluid produced by mucous membranes that lubricates and protects the internal surfaces of the body
8. UVEA	A structure consisting of the colored area of the eye and the middle layer of the eye that contains blood vessels
9. PRACTICE MANAGEMENT SOFTWARE	Software used for scheduling, billing, and recordkeeping at a provider's office.
10. MEDICAL CODER	Responsible for assigning various medical codes to services and healthcare plans described by a physician on a patient's super-bill.
11. ANATOMY	The structure of bodies; commonly refers to the study of body structure
12. TREMOR	An involuntary, rhythmic, shaking movement caused by alternating contraction and relaxation of muscles
13. PLASMA	The liquid part of the blood, containing substances such as nutrients, salts, and proteins
14. PATENT	Not obstructed; open
15. COLIC	Waves of pain in the abdomen that increase in strength, disappear, and return
16. PEPSIN	The enzyme found in gastric juice that helps digest protein
17. BLADDER	An organ located in the pelvis whose function is to collect and store urine until it is expelled

18. STENT — A device used to hold tissues in place, such as to support a skin graft

19. VALVE — A structure that allows fluid flow in only one direction

20. INTENSIVE CARE — The unit of a hospital reserved for patients that need immediate treatment and close monitoring by healthcare professionals for serious illnesses, conditions, and injuries.

21. AORTA — The main artery in the body, carrying oxygenated blood from the heart to other arteries in the body

22. TOXIN — A poisonous substance

23. PRE EXISTING CONDITION — A medical condition a patient had before receiving coverage from an insurance company.

24. RABIES — An infectious viral disease primarily affecting animals; can be transmitted to humans through an infected animal's bite

25. UREMIA — Abnormally high levels of waste products such as urea in the blood

A. Plasma
B. Intensive Care
C. Renin
D. Valve
E. Rabies
F. Pepsin
G. Specialist
H. Inpatient
I. Anatomy
J. Cell
K. Uvea
L. Mucus
M. Wart
N. Aorta
O. Pre existing Condition
P. Stent
Q. Colic
R. Uremia
S. Tremor
T. Bladder
U. Patent
V. Electronic Funds Transfer
W. Practice Management Software
X. Medical Coder
Y. Toxin

B. Provide the word that best matches each clue.

1. SIGNATURE ON FILE — A patient's official signature on file for the purpose of billing and claims processing.

2. PODIATRY — The care and treatment of the foot and ankle

3. MEDICARE SECONDARY PAYER — The insurance company that covers any remaining expenses after Medicare has paid for a patient's coverage.

4. MURMUR — A characteristic sound of blood flowing irregularly through the heart

5. PAIN MANAGEMENT — the control of pain or discomfort through medication, stress reduction, relaxation, exercise, massage, heat, cold, or providing a comfortable environment

6. KELOID — A raised, firm, thick scar that forms as a result of a defect in the natural healing process

7. FIBROID — A noncancerous tumor of the uterus made up of smooth muscle and connective tissue

8. ATRESIA — A birth defect in which a normal body opening or canal is absent

9. CHOLERA — A bacterial infection of the small intestine that causes severe watery diarrhea, dehydration, and possibly death

10. PALATE — The roof of the mouth

11. KIDNEY — One of two organs that are part of the urinary tract

12. PICA — A desire to eat materials that are not food

13. TAX IDENTIFICATION NUMBER — A unique number a patient or a company may have to produce for billing purposes in order to receive healthcare from a provider.

14. ALLERGY — A negative reaction to a substance that in most people causes no reaction

15. TUMOR — An abnormal mass that occurs when cells in a certain area reproduce unchecked

16. GENOME — The complete set of an organism's genes

17. FORMULARY — A table or list provided by an insurance carrier that explains what prescription drugs are covered under their health plans.

18. SPECIALIST — A physician or medical assistant with expertise in a specific area of medicine.

19. LOBE — A well-defined, separate part of an organ

20. ANCILLARY SERVICES — Any service administered in a hospital or other healthcare facility other than room and board.

21. MITES — Small eight-legged animals, many of which burrow and feed on blood

22. BOWEL — Intestine

23. SKILLED NURSING FACILITY — These are facilities for the severely ill or elderly that provide specialized long-term care for recovering patients.

24. SECURITY STANDARD — Serves as the guidelines for policies and practices necessary to reduce security risks within the healthcare system.

25. STOOL — Another term for feces

A. Signature on File
B. Mites
C. Fibroid
D. Kidney
E. Security Standard
F. Lobe
G. Formulary
H. Pain Management
I. Tumor
J. Palate
K. Atresia
L. Stool
M. Podiatry
N. Genome
O. Bowel
P. Medicare Secondary Payer
Q. Ancillary Services
R. Cholera
S. Skilled Nursing Facility
T. Pica
U. Keloid
V. Specialist
W. Murmur
X. Tax Identification Number
Y. Allergy

C. Provide the word that best matches each clue.

1. STYE — A pus- filled abscess in the follicle of an eyelash

2. HICCUP — Involuntary sudden contraction of the diaphragm along with the closing of the vocal cords, producing a "hiccup" sound

3. HYPOXIA — A reduced level of oxygen in tissues

4. GAVAGE — An artificial feeding technique in which liquids are passed into the stomach by way of a tube inserted through the nose

5. TENDON — Strong connective tissue cords that attach muscle to bone or muscle to muscle

6. UPCODING — The fraudulent practice of ascribing a higher ICD-9 code to a healthcare procedure in an attempt to get more money than necessary from the insurance company or patient.

7. EXPLANATION OF BENEFITS — A document attached to a processed medical claim wherein the insurance company explains the services they will cover for a patient's healthcare treatments.

8. GLIOMA — A brain tumor arising from cells that support nerve cells

9. CAPITATION — A fixed payment that a patient makes to a health insurance company or provider to recoup costs incurred from various healthcare services.

10. ILEUM — The lowest section of the small intestine, which attaches to the large intestine

11. RELATIVE VALUE AMOUNT — The median amount Medicare will repay a provider for certain services and treatments.

12. THIRD PARTY ADMINISTRATOR — The name for the organization or individual that manages healthcare group benefits, claims, and administrative duties on behalf of a group plan or a company with a group plan.

13. NEVUS — A marking on the skin; can be present at birth (birthmark) or develop later (such as a mole)

14. SUBSCRIBER — The individual covered under a group policy. For instance, an employee of a company with a group health policy would be one of many subscribers on that policy.

15. ATRESIA — A birth defect in which a normal body opening or canal is absent

16. CHRONIC — Describes a disorder that continues for a long period of time

17. APPLIED TO DEDUCTIBLE — This term refers to the amount of money a patient owes a provider that goes to paying their yearly deductible.

18. EARDRUM — A thin, oval-shaped membrane that separates the inner ear from the outer ear and is responsible for transmitting sound waves

19. CELL — The tiny structures that make up all the tissues of the body and carry out all of its functions

20. TRICARE — The federal health insurance program for active and retired service members, their families, and the survivors of service members.

21. HEALTHCARE PROVIDER — These are the entities that offer healthcare services to patients, including hospitals, physicians, and private clinics, hospices, nursing homes, and other healthcare facilities.

22. LYMPH — A milky fluid containing white blood cells, proteins, and fats

23. PATHOLOGY — The specialty of physicians who are trained to examine surgical specimens and biopsies for diagnostic purposes.

24. VIRUS — The smallest known disease- causing microorganism

25. ABSCESS — An accumulation of pus in a body tissue, usually caused by a bacterial infection

A. Explanation of Benefits	B. Third Party Administrator	C. Subscriber
D. Eardrum	E. Nevus	F. Stye
G. Hiccup	H. Healthcare Provider	I. Hypoxia
J. Ileum	K. Applied to Deductible	L. Upcoding
M. Abscess	N. Cell	O. Chronic
P. Relative Value Amount	Q. Lymph	R. Pathology
S. Virus	T. TRICARE	U. Capitation
V. Gavage	W. Glioma	X. Tendon
Y. Atresia		

D. Provide the word that best matches each clue.

1. PATIENT RESPONSIBILITY — This refers to the amount a patient owes a provider after an insurance company pays for their portion of the medical expenses.

2. UTILIZATION LIMIT — The limit per year for coverage under certain available healthcare services for Medicare enrollees.

3. KELOID — A raised, firm, thick scar that forms as a result of a defect in the natural healing process

4. FEBRILE — A term used to describe something related to a fever, such as febrile seizures

5. CODING — The process of translating a physician's documentation about a patient's medical condition and health services rendered into medical codes that are then plugged into a claim for processing.

6. NEVUS — A marking on the skin; can be present at birth (birthmark) or develop later (such as a mole)

7. HEALTHCARE REFORM ACT — The major healthcare legislation passed in 2010 designed to make healthcare accessible and less expensive for more Americans.

8. SALINE — A salt solution or any substance that contains salt

9. BLADDER — An organ located in the pelvis whose function is to collect and store urine until it is expelled

10. NON COVERED CHARGE — Procedures and services not covered by a person's health insurance plan.

11. BOOSTER — An additional dose of a vaccine taken after the first dose to maintain or renew the first one

12. CHRONIC — Describes a disorder that continues for a long period of time

13. SEPSIS — The infection of a wound or tissue with bacteria, causing the spread of the bacteria into the bloodstream

14. PAIN MANAGEMENT — the control of pain or discomfort through medication, stress reduction, relaxation, exercise, massage, heat, cold, or providing a comfortable environment

15. FISCAL INTERMEDIARY — The name for Medicare representatives who process Medicare claims.

16. PRIMARY CARE PHYSICIAN — The physician who provides the basic healthcare services for a patient and recommends additional care for more serious treatments as necessary.

17. FEE SCHEDULE — A document that outlines the costs associated for each medical service designated by a CPT code.

18. CREDIT BALANCE — Refers to the sum shown in the "balance" column of a billing statement that reflects the amount due for services rendered.

19. APPLICATION SERVICE PROVIDER — A digital network that allows healthcare providers to access quality medical billing software and technologies without needing to purchase and maintain it themselves.

20. STROKE — Damage to part of the brain because of a lack of blood supply or the rupturing of a blood vessel

21. EMERGENCY MEDICINE — the specialty that includes treatment of any symptom, illness or injury requiring urgent evaluation and

22. SUPPLEMENTAL INSURANCE — Can be a secondary policy or another insurance company that covers a patient's healthcare costs after receiving coverage from their primary insurance.

23. LIPOMA — A noncancerous tumor of fatty tissue

24. DEMOGRAPHICS — The patient's information required for filing a claim, such as age, sex, address, and family information. An insurance company may deny a claim if it contains inaccurate demographics.

25. PLEURA — The double- layered membrane that lines the lungs and chest cavity and allows for lung movement during breathing

A. Fiscal Intermediary
B. Lipoma
C. Healthcare Reform Act
D. Chronic
E. Application Service Provider
F. Primary Care Physician
G. Supplemental Insurance
H. Sepsis
I. Nevus
J. Pain Management
K. Emergency Medicine
L. Febrile
M. Utilization Limit
N. Credit Balance
O. Saline
P. Demographics
Q. Fee Schedule
R. Booster
S. Stroke
T. Coding
U. Patient Responsibility
V. Keloid
W. Bladder
X. Non Covered Charge
Y. Pleura

E. Provide the word that best matches each clue.

1. WART — A contagious, harmless growth caused by a virus that occurs on the skin or a mucous membrane

2. BOIL — An inflamed, raised area of skin that is pus-filled

3. KIDNEY — One of two organs that are part of the urinary tract

4. THORAX — The chest

5. TICKS — Small, eight- legged animals that can attach to humans and animals and feed on blood

6. OUT OF NETWORK — Refers to providers outside of an established network of providers who contract with an insurance company to offer patients healthcare at a discounted rate.

7. INPATIENT — Occurs when a person has a stay at a healthcare facility for more than 24 hours.

8. TYPHUS — A group of diseases caused by the microorganism rickettsia, spread by the bites of fleas, mites, or ticks

9. PALSY — Loss of sensation or ability to move

10. CLONE — An exact copy of a gene, cell, or organism

11. TOXIN — A poisonous substance

12. SPINE — The column of bones and cartilage running along the midline of the back that surrounds and protects the spinal cord and supports the head

13. OPHTHALMOLOGY — the diagnosis and treatment, including surgery, of diseases and disorders of the eye, such as cataracts and glaucoma

14. ASSIGNMENT OF BENEFITS — Refers to insurance payments made directly to a healthcare provider for medical services received by the patient.

15. MEDICARE COINSURANCE DAYS — Referring to 61st through 90th days of inpatient treatment, the law requires that patients pay for a portion of their healthcare during Medicare coinsurance days.

16. B CELL — A white blood cell that makes antibodies to fight infections caused by foreign proteins

17. MYOPIA — The medical term for nearsightedness

18. VALVE — A structure that allows fluid flow in only one direction

19. MEDICAL NECESSITY — Refers to healthcare services or treatments that a patient requires to treat a serious medical condition or illness.

20. OXYGEN — A gas that is colorless, odorless, and tasteless

21. MEDICAL BILLING SPECIALIST — Responsible for using information regarding services and treatments performed by a healthcare provider to complete a claim for filing with an insurance company.

22. TAR — The sticky, brown substance in cigarettes that coats the lungs; causes lung and other cancers

23. NAUSEA — Feeling the need to vomit

24. CONTRACTUAL ADJUSTMENT — Refers to a binding agree between a provider, patient, and insurance company wherein the provider agrees to charges that it will write off on behalf of the patient.

25. PALLOR — Abnormally pale skin

A. Thorax
B. Pallor
C. Typhus
D. B cell
E. Palsy
F. Myopia
G. Clone
H. Wart
I. Medicare Coinsurance Days
J. Tar
K. Ticks
L. Ophthalmology
M. Spine
N. Contractual Adjustment
O. Out of Network
P. Nausea
Q. Medical Necessity
R. Inpatient
S. Oxygen
T. Valve
U. Toxin
V. Boil
W. Medical Billing Specialist
X. Kidney
Y. Assignment of Benefits

F. Provide the word that best matches each clue.

1. INTENSIVE CARE — The unit of a hospital reserved for patients that need immediate treatment and close monitoring by healthcare professionals for serious illnesses, conditions, and injuries.

2. ANTACID — A drug that neutralizes stomach acids

3. PODIATRY — The care and treatment of the foot and ankle

4. NAUSEA — Feeling the need to vomit

5. MYXOMA — A noncancerous tumor made of mucous material and fibrous connective tissue

6. PRION — An agent that is believed to cause several degenerative brain diseases

7. ABSCESS — An accumulation of pus in a body tissue, usually caused by a bacterial infection

8. MEDICAL RECORD NUMBER — A unique number ascribed to a person's medical record so it can be differentiated from other medical records.

9. FITNESS — A measure of a person's physical strength, flexibility, and endurance

10. ELECTRONIC REMITTANCE ADVICE — The digital version of EOB, which specifies the details of payments made on a claim either by an insurance company or required by the patient.

11. WART — A contagious, harmless growth caused by a virus that occurs on the skin or a mucous membrane

12. SECURITY STANDARD — Serves as the guidelines for policies and practices necessary to reduce security risks within the healthcare system.

13. SEMEN — Fluid released during ejaculation that contains sperm along with fluids produced by the prostate gland and the seminal vesicles

14. ACUTE — Describes a condition or illness that begins suddenly and is usually short- lasting

15. HYMEN — A thin fold of membrane partly closing the opening of the vagina

16. HIVES — The common term for urticaria, an itchy, inflamed rash that results from an allergic reaction

17. PYURIA — The presence of white blood cells in the urine

18. FIBROMA — A noncancerous tumor of connective tissue

19. INTERNAL MEDICINE — the diagnosis and non-surgical treatment of adult health problems

20. RASH — An area of inflammation or a group of spots on the skin

21. SACRUM — The triangular bone located at the bottom of the spine that is connected to the tailbone, the hipbones near the sacroilial joints, and the rest of the spine

22. CALORIE — A unit that is used to measure the energy content in food

23. GOUT — A disorder marked by high levels of uric acid in the blood

24. FEE FOR SERVICE — This refers to a type of health insurance wherein the provider is paid for every service they perform.

25. FIBROID — A noncancerous tumor of the uterus made up of smooth muscle and connective tissue

A. Hymen
B. Fee for Service
C. Abscess
D. Electronic Remittance Advice
E. Security Standard
F. Hives
G. Prion
H. Podiatry
I. Wart
J. Fitness
K. Fibroma
L. Antacid
M. Acute
N. Fibroid
O. Calorie
P. Pyuria
Q. Nausea
R. Gout
S. Medical Record Number
T. Internal Medicine
U. Sacrum
V. Rash
W. Intensive Care
X. Myxoma
Y. Semen

G. Provide the word that best matches each clue.

1. TARTAR — The hard deposit formed on teeth when mineral salts in saliva combine with plaque

2. CHOLERA — A bacterial infection of the small intestine that causes severe watery diarrhea, dehydration, and possibly death

3. PLACE OF SERVICE CODE — A two-digit code used on claims to explain what type of provider performed healthcare services on a patient.

4. MANIA — A mental disorder characterized by extreme excitement, happiness, overactivity, and agitation

5. RELATIVE VALUE AMOUNT — The median amount Medicare will repay a provider for certain services and treatments.

6. REFLEX — An automatic, involuntary response of the nervous system to a stimulus

7. SINUS — A cavity within bone or a channel that contains blood

8. GYNECOLOGY — the care of women during and after pregnancy and childbirth, and the care of the female reproductive system and treatment of associated disorders

9. APPLICATION SERVICE PROVIDER — A digital network that allows healthcare providers to access quality medical billing software and technologies without needing to purchase and maintain it themselves.

10. FINANCIAL RESPONSIBILITY — Whoever owes the healthcare provider money has financial responsibility for the services rendered.

11. TYPHUS — A group of diseases caused by the microorganism rickettsia, spread by the bites of fleas, mites, or ticks

12. BENEFICIARY — The person who receives benefits and

13. BOOSTER — An additional dose of a vaccine taken after the first dose to maintain or renew the first one

14. TAXONOMY CODE — Medical billing specialists utilize this unique codeset for identifying a healthcare provider's specialty field.

15. INDEMNITY — A type of health insurance plan whereby a patient can receive care with any provider in exchange for higher deductibles and co-pays. Indemnity is also known as fee-for-service insurance.

16. MEDIGAP — Supplemental health insurance under Medicaid for eligible persons who need help covering co-pays, deductibles, and other large fees.

17. MEDICAL TRANSCRIPTION — The process of converting dictated or handwritten instructions, observations, and documentation into digital text formats.

18. CHARITY CARE — This type of care is administered at reduced or zero cost to patients who cannot afford healthcare.

19. PEPSIN — The enzyme found in gastric juice that helps digest protein

20. LARYNX — The medical term for the voice box, the organ in the throat that produces voice and also prevents food from entering the airway

21. PLAQUE — An area of buildup of fat deposits in an artery, causing narrowing of the artery and possibly heart disease

22. NON PARTICIPATION — This is when a provider refuses to accept Medicare payments as a sufficient amount for the services rendered to a patient.

23. ACUTE — Describes a condition or illness that begins suddenly and is usually short- lasting

24. BURSA — A fluid-filled sac that cushions and reduces friction in certain parts of the body

25. SPECIALIST — A physician or medical assistant with expertise in a specific area of medicine.

A. Financial Responsibility
B. Medical Transcription
C. Reflex
D. Acute
E. Charity Care
F. Specialist
G. Plaque
H. Bursa
I. Sinus
J. Tartar
K. Gynecology
L. Cholera
M. Medigap
N. Taxonomy Code
O. Booster
P. Place of Service Code
Q. Relative Value Amount
R. Indemnity
S. Pepsin
T. Application Service Provider
U. Non participation
V. Beneficiary
W. Larynx
X. Typhus
Y. Mania

H. Provide the word that best matches each clue.

1. HEALTHCARE PROVIDER — These are the entities that offer healthcare services to patients, including hospitals, physicians, and private clinics, hospices, nursing homes, and other healthcare facilities.

2. MEDICAID — A joint federal and state assistance program started in 1965 to provide health insurance to lower-income persons.

3. HYPOXIA — A reduced level of oxygen in tissues

4. MEDICAL RECORD NUMBER — A unique number ascribed to a person's medical record so it can be differentiated from other medical records.

5. ASTHMA — A disorder characterized by inflamed airways and difficulty breathing

6. GENOME — The complete set of an organism's genes

7. PREVENTIVE MEDICINE — The specialty that focuses on the health of individuals in order to protect, promote and maintain health and prevent disease, disability and premature death

8. TRICARE — The federal health insurance program for active and retired service members, their families, and the survivors of service members.

9. HOSPICE — This refers to medical care and treatment for persons who are terminally ill.

10. PEDIATRICS — The care and treatment of infants, children, and adolescents

11. STRAIN — Muscle damage resulting from excessive stretching or forceful contraction

12. RELATIVE VALUE AMOUNT — The median amount Medicare will repay a provider for certain services and treatments.

13. IODINE — An element for the formation of thyroid hormones

14. PTOSIS — The drooping of the upper eyelid

15. CILIA — Tiny, hairlike structures on the outside of some cells, providing mobility

16. RETINA — A membrane lining the inside of the back of the eye that contains light-sensitive nerve cells that convert focused light into nerve impulses, making vision possible

17. WART — A contagious, harmless growth caused by a virus that occurs on the skin or a mucous membrane

18. SHOCK — A reduced flow of blood throughout the body, usually caused by severe bleeding or a weak heart

19. CARDIOLOGY — the diagnosis and treatment of disorders of the heart and major blood vessels

20. OXYGEN — A gas that is colorless, odorless, and tasteless

21. MEDICAL SAVINGS ACCOUNT — An optional health insurance payments plan whereby a person apportions part of their untaxed earnings to an account reserved for healthcare expenses.

22. INDEMNITY — A type of health insurance plan whereby a patient can receive care with any provider in exchange for higher deductibles and co-pays. Indemnity is also known as fee-for-service insurance.

23. SPRAIN — The tearing or stretching of the ligaments in a joint, characterized by pain, swelling, and an inability to move the joint

24. MEDICAL NECESSITY — Refers to healthcare services or treatments that a patient requires to treat a serious medical condition or illness.

25. ELECTRONIC REMITTANCE ADVICE — The digital version of EOB, which specifies the details of payments made on a claim either by an insurance company or required by the patient.

A. Cilia
B. Genome
C. Preventive Medicine
D. Cardiology
E. Asthma
F. TRICARE
G. Electronic Remittance Advice
H. Hospice
I. Iodine
J. Strain
K. Hypoxia
L. Ptosis
M. Retina
N. Medical Necessity
O. Medicaid
P. Indemnity
Q. Medical Record Number
R. Sprain
S. Wart
T. Pediatrics
U. Oxygen
V. Medical Savings Account
W. Healthcare Provider
X. Shock
Y. Relative Value Amount

I. Provide the word that best matches each clue.

1. SKILLED NURSING FACILITY — These are facilities for the severely ill or elderly that provide specialized long-term care for recovering patients.

2. HYMEN — A thin fold of membrane partly closing the opening of the vagina

3. HEALTH MAINTENANCE ORGANIZATION — Networks of healthcare providers that offer healthcare plans to people for medical services exclusively in their network.

4. RNA — Ribonucleic acid, which helps to decode and process the information contained in dna

5. ZYGOTE — The cell that results when an egg is fertilized by a sperm

6. DX — The abbreviation for diagnosis codes, also known as ICD-9 codes.

7. GYNECOLOGY — the care of women during and after pregnancy and childbirth, and the care of the female reproductive system and treatment of associated disorders

8. SECONDARY INSURANCE CLAIM — The claim filed with the secondary insurance company after the primary insurance company pays for their portion of healthcare costs.

9. COLLECTION RATIO — Refers to the ratio of payments received relative to the total amount owed to providers.

10. CAST — A hard plaster or fiberglass shell that molds to a body part such as an arm and holds it in place for proper healing

11. ELECTRONIC REMITTANCE ADVICE — The digital version of EOB, which specifies the details of payments made on a claim either by an insurance company or required by the patient.

12. DONUT HOLE — This term refers to the discrepancy between the limits of healthcare insurance coverage and the Medicare Part D coverage limits for prescription drugs.

13. PATHOLOGY — The specialty of physicians who are trained to examine surgical specimens and biopsies for diagnostic purposes.

14. LIPOMA — A noncancerous tumor of fatty tissue

15. AUTHORIZATION — Refers to when a patient's health insurance plan requires them to get permission from their insurance providers before receiving certain healthcare services.

16. PREMIUM — The sum a person pays to an insurance company on a regular (usually monthly or yearly) basis to receive health insurance.

17. AIRWAYS — The passageways that air moves through while traveling in and out of the lungs during breathing

18. PH — A measure of the acidic or basic character of a substance

19. SPECIALIST — A physician or medical assistant with expertise in a specific area of medicine.

20. TRICARE — The federal health insurance program for active and retired service members, their families, and the survivors of service members.

21. ENDEMIC — Describes a disease that is always present in a certain population of people

22. CHARITY CARE — This type of care is administered at reduced or zero cost to patients who cannot afford healthcare.

23. GERIATRICS — the treatment of diseases and internal disorders of the elderly

24. ACNE — A skin condition characterized by inflamed, pus-filled areas that occur on the skin's surface, most commonly occurring during adolescence

25. AURA — A "warning" signal that comes before a migraine headache or an epileptic seizure, which might include emotions or sensations of movement or discomfort

A. Premium
B. Acne
C. Pathology
D. Secondary Insurance Claim
E. Aura
F. Skilled Nursing Facility
G. RNA
H. Specialist
I. TRICARE
J. Authorization
K. Cast
L. Health Maintenance Organization
M. Dx
N. Endemic

O. Donut Hole
P. Geriatrics
Q. Hymen
R. Charity Care
S. Zygote
T. Airways
U. Gynecology
V. pH
W. Electronic Remittance Advice
X. Collection Ratio
Y. Lipoma

J. Provide the word that best matches each clue.

1. CORN — A thickened callus on the foot that is caused by an improperly fitting shoe

2. LOW — Density lipoprotein- a type of lipoprotein that is the major carrier of cholesterol in the blood, with high levels associated with narrowing of the arteries and heart disease

3. CHARITY CARE — This type of care is administered at reduced or zero cost to patients who cannot afford healthcare.

4. SCURVY — A disease caused by a lack of vitamin c, characterized by weakness, bleeding and pain in joints and muscles, bleeding gums, and abnormal bone and tooth growth

5. SHUNT — An artificially constructed or an abnormal passage connecting two usually separate structures in the body

6. MIOTIC — A drug that causes the pupil to constrict

7. APPLICATION SERVICE PROVIDER — A digital network that allows healthcare providers to access quality medical billing software and technologies without needing to purchase and maintain it themselves.

8. PRE DETERMINATION — A maximum sum as explained in a healthcare plan an insurance company will pay for certain services or treatments.

9. TAX IDENTIFICATION NUMBER — A unique number a patient or a company may have to produce for billing purposes in order to receive healthcare from a provider.

10. PENIS — The external male reproductive organ, which passes urine and semen out of the body

11. OPTIC — Pertaining to the eyes

12. ALLERGY — A negative reaction to a substance that in most people causes no reaction

13. UVEA — A structure consisting of the colored area of the eye and the middle layer of the eye that contains blood vessels

14. VEIN — A blood vessel that carries blood toward the heart

15. RADON — A colorless, odorless, tasteless radioactive gas that is produced by materials in soil, rocks, and building materials

16. TYPE OF SERVICE — A field on a claim for describing what kind of healthcare services or procedures a provider administered.

17. CELL — The tiny structures that make up all the tissues of the body and carry out all of its functions

18. GYNECOLOGY — the care of women during and after pregnancy and childbirth, and the care of the female reproductive system and treatment of associated disorders

19. UPCODING — The fraudulent practice of ascribing a higher ICD-9 code to a healthcare procedure in an attempt to get more money than necessary from the insurance company or patient.

20. NON PARTICIPATION — This is when a provider refuses to accept Medicare payments as a sufficient amount for the services rendered to a patient.

21. STYE — A pus- filled abscess in the follicle of an eyelash

22. LESION — An abnormality of structure or function in the body

23. ANGIOMA — A tumor made of blood vessels or lymph vessels that is not cancerous

24. IMPLANT — An organ, tissue, or device surgically inserted and left in the body

25. OTOLARYNGOLOGY — the medical and surgical care for diseases of the ears, nose and throat (ENT)

A. Optic
B. Allergy
C. Pre determination
D. Shunt
E. Otolaryngology
F. Low
G. Non participation
H. Penis
I. Upcoding
J. Implant
K. Angioma
L. Stye
M. Vein
N. Miotic
O. Type of Service
P. Uvea
Q. Tax Identification Number
R. Scurvy
S. Lesion
T. Cell
U. Gynecology
V. Radon
W. Corn
X. Application Service Provider
Y. Charity Care

K. Provide the word that best matches each clue.

1. CHANCRE — A painless sore that has a thick, rubbery base and a defined edge

2. MYXOMA — A noncancerous tumor made of mucous material and fibrous connective tissue

3. STRAIN — Muscle damage resulting from excessive stretching or forceful contraction

4. THORAX — The chest

5. COMA — A condition in which the area of the brain involved in maintaining consciousness is somehow affected, resulting in a state of unconsciousness in which the patient does not respond to stimulation

6. ELECTRONIC MEDICAL RECORDS — Digitized medical record for a patient managed by a provider onsite.

7. UPCODING — The fraudulent practice of ascribing a higher ICD-9 code to a healthcare procedure in an attempt to get more money than necessary from the insurance company or patient.

8. LYMPH — A milky fluid containing white blood cells, proteins, and fats

9. MEDICAL SAVINGS ACCOUNT — An optional health insurance payments plan whereby a person apportions part of their untaxed earnings to an account reserved for healthcare expenses.

10. NETWORK PROVIDER — A provider within a health insurance company's network that has contracted with the company to provide discounted services to a patient covered under the company's plan.

11. FITNESS — A measure of a person's physical strength, flexibility, and endurance

12. AUTHORIZATION — Refers to when a patient's health insurance plan requires them to get permission from their insurance providers before receiving certain healthcare services.

13. RALES — Abnormal crackling or bubbling sounds heard in the lungs during breathing

14. SIGNATURE ON FILE — A patient's official signature on file for the purpose of billing and claims processing.

15. DERMIS — The inner skin layer

16. SELF PAY — Payment made by the patient for healthcare at the time they receive it at a provider's facilities.

17. BLADDER — An organ located in the pelvis whose function is to collect and store urine until it is expelled

18. POINT OF SERVICE PLANS — A plan whereby patients with HMO membership may receive care at non-HMO providers in exchange for a referral and paying a higher deductible.

19. IRIS — The colored part of the eye

20. ANTACID — A drug that neutralizes stomach acids

21. PRE CERTIFICATION — A process similar to preauthorization whereby patients must check with insurance companies to see if a desired healthcare treatment or service is deemed medically necessary

22. RENIN — An enzyme that plays a role in increasing a low blood pressure

23. MEDICARE COINSURANCE DAYS — Referring to 61st through 90th days of inpatient treatment, the law requires that patients pay for a portion of their healthcare during Medicare coinsurance days.

24. ECG — An electrocardiogram, which is a record of the electrical impulses that trigger the heartbeat

25. SKILLED NURSING FACILITY — These are facilities for the severely ill or elderly that provide specialized long-term care for recovering patients.

A. Electronic Medical Records
B. Medicare Coinsurance Days
C. Skilled Nursing Facility
D. Self Pay
E. Myxoma
F. Upcoding
G. Thorax
H. Chancre
I. Iris
J. Antacid
K. Point of Service Plans
L. Fitness
M. Rales
N. Strain
O. Lymph
P. Pre Certification
Q. Dermis
R. Medical Savings Account
S. Coma
T. Bladder
U. Signature on File
V. Renin
W. ECG
X. Network Provider
Y. Authorization

L. Provide the word that best matches each clue.

1. EXPLANATION OF BENEFITS — A document attached to a processed medical claim wherein the insurance company explains the services they will cover for a patient's healthcare treatments.

2. TIC — An involuntary, repetitive movement such as a twitch

3. FUNGUS — An organism that is dependent on another organism for nourishment

4. BIFOCAL — A lens that corrects both near and distant vision by having two parts with different focusing strengths

5. NEUROLOGY — the diagnosis and medical treatment of the nervous system and brain, including conditions such as strokes and seizures

6. FEE FOR SERVICE — This refers to a type of health insurance wherein the provider is paid for every service they perform.

7. SHUNT — An artificially constructed or an abnormal passage connecting two usually separate structures in the body

8. DNA — Deoxyribonucleic acid; responsible for passing genetic information in nearly all organisms

9. PREVENTIVE MEDICINE — The specialty that focuses on the health of individuals in order to protect, promote and maintain health and prevent disease, disability and premature death

10. VIRAL — A term describing something related to or caused by a virus

11. RADIUS — One of the two long bones of the forearm

12. GERIATRICS — the treatment of diseases and internal disorders of the elderly

13. FAMILY PRACTICE — the specialty that provides comprehensive and ongoing medical care to all members of the family unit

14. GENE — The basic unit of dna, which is responsible for passing genetic information

15. HEALTHCARE PROVIDER — These are the entities that offer healthcare services to patients, including hospitals, physicians, and private clinics, hospices, nursing homes, and other healthcare facilities.

16. HOSPICE — A hospital or an area of a hospital dedicated to treating people who are dying, often of a specific cause

17. SECONDARY PROCEDURE — This is when provider performs another procedure on a patient covered by a CPT code after first performing a different CPT procedure on them.

18. NIACIN — A vitamin important in many chemical processes in the body

19. OXYGEN — A gas that is colorless, odorless, and tasteless

20. CREDENTIALING — The application process for a provider to coordinate with an insurance company.

21. SPLEEN — An organ located in the upper left abdomen behind the ribs that removes and destroys old red blood cells and helps fight infection

22. EMBRYO — A term used to describe a child in the womb from fertilization to 8 weeks following fertilization

23. LIPOMA — A noncancerous tumor of fatty tissue

24. TERTIARY CLAIM — A claim filed by a provider after they have filed claims for primary and secondary health insurance coverage on behalf of a patient.

25. PICA — A desire to eat materials that are not food

A. Family Practice
B. Gene
C. Fee for Service
D. Lipoma
E. Spleen
F. DNA
G. Bifocal
H. Niacin
I. Embryo
J. Shunt
K. Hospice
L. Secondary Procedure
M. Preventive Medicine
N. Oxygen
O. Credentialing
P. Explanation of Benefits
Q. Tertiary Claim
R. Fungus

S. Healthcare Provider
T. Pica
U. Viral
V. Tic
W. Neurology
X. Geriatrics
Y. Radius

M. Provide the word that best matches each clue.

1. PICA — A desire to eat materials that are not food

2. IN NETWORK — This term refers to a provider's relationship with a health insurance company.

3. ORGASM — Involuntary contraction of genital muscles experienced at the peak of sexual excitement

4. ULCER — An open sore that occurs on the skin or on a mucous membrane because of the destruction of surface tissue

5. SEBUM — The oily, lubricating substance that is secreted by glands in the skin

6. MIOTIC — A drug that causes the pupil to constrict

7. COLIC — Waves of pain in the abdomen that increase in strength, disappear, and return

8. VAGINA — The muscular passage connecting the uterus with the outside genitals

9. TOXIN — A poisonous substance

10. FITNESS — A measure of a person's physical strength, flexibility, and endurance

11. HYPOXIA — A reduced level of oxygen in tissues

12. THORAX — The chest

13. UTILIZATION LIMIT — The limit per year for coverage under certain available healthcare services for Medicare enrollees.

14. REFLEX — An automatic, involuntary response of the nervous system to a stimulus

15. TENDON — Strong connective tissue cords that attach muscle to bone or muscle to muscle

16. IRIS — The colored part of the eye

17. PALMETTO GBA — A MAC based in Columbia, South Carolina that is also a subsidiary of Blue Cross Blue Shield.

18. APPLICATION SERVICE PROVIDER — A digital network that allows healthcare providers to access quality medical billing software and technologies without needing to purchase and maintain it themselves.

19. BULIMIA — A disorder in which a person eats large amounts of food then forces vomiting or uses laxatives to prevent weight gain (called binging and purging)

20. OCULAR — Describes something related to the eyes

21. TAXONOMY CODE — Medical billing specialists utilize this unique codeset for identifying a healthcare provider's specialty field.

22. SPRAIN — The tearing or stretching of the ligaments in a joint, characterized by pain, swelling, and an inability to move the joint

23. SPASM — An involuntary muscle contraction

24. RADON — A colorless, odorless, tasteless radioactive gas that is produced by materials in soil, rocks, and building materials

25. VERNIX — The thick, greasy substance that covers the skin of a newborn baby

A. Palmetto GBA
B. Orgasm
C. Radon
D. Thorax
E. Taxonomy Code
F. Vernix
G. Spasm
H. Hypoxia
I. Sebum
J. Bulimia
K. Miotic
L. Pica
M. Iris
N. Application Service Provider
O. Tendon
P. Sprain
Q. In Network
R. Ocular
S. Fitness
T. Reflex
U. Vagina
V. Colic
W. Ulcer
X. Toxin
Y. Utilization Limit

N. Provide the word that best matches each clue.

1. SUTURE — A surgical stitch that helps close an incision or wound so that it can heal properly

2. CALLUS — A thickened area of skin due to consistent pressure or friction, or the area around a bone break where new bone is formed

3. VULVA — The outer, visible portion of the female genitals

4. DONUT HOLE — This term refers to the discrepancy between the limits of healthcare insurance coverage and the Medicare Part D coverage limits for prescription drugs.

5. DURABLE MEDICAL EQUIPMENT — This refers to medical implements that can be reused such as stretchers, wheelchairs, canes, crutches, and bedpans.

6. VIRAL — A term describing something related to or caused by a virus

7. REMITTANCE ADVICE — The document attached to a processed claim that explains the information regarding coverage and payments on a claim.

8. ASTHMA — A disorder characterized by inflamed airways and difficulty breathing

9. GROUP HEALTH PLAN — A plan provided by an employer to provide healthcare options to a large group of employees.

10. SELF REFERRAL — When a patient does their own research to find a provider and acts outside of their primary care physician's referral.

11. REFERRAL — This is when a provider recommends another provider to a patient to receive specialized treatment.

12. IRON — A mineral necessary for the formation of important biological substances such as hemoglobin, myoglobin, and certain enzymes

13. MEDICAL ASSISTANT — An employee in the healthcare system such as a physician's assistant or a nurse practitioner who perform duties in administration, nursing, and other ancillary care.

14. RETINA — A membrane lining the inside of the back of the eye that contains light-sensitive nerve cells that convert focused light into nerve impulses, making vision possible

15. TIC — An involuntary, repetitive movement such as a twitch

16. PLAQUE — An area of buildup of fat deposits in an artery, causing narrowing of the artery and possibly heart disease

17. PHLEGM — Mucus and other material produced by the lining of the respiratory tract; also called sputum

18. SALINE — A salt solution or any substance that contains salt

19. MEDICAL CODER — Responsible for assigning various medical codes to services and healthcare plans described by a physician on a patient's super-bill.

20. PENIS — The external male reproductive organ, which passes urine and semen out of the body

21. OTOLARYNGOLOGY — the medical and surgical care for diseases of the ears, nose and throat (ENT)

22. PREFERRED PROVIDER ORGANIZATION — A plan similar to an HMO whereby a patient can receive healthcare from providers within an established network set up by an insurance company.

23. ORBIT — The socket in the skull that contains the eyeball, along with its blood vessels, nerves, and muscles

24. ASCITES — Excess fluid in the abdominal cavity, which leads to swelling

25. PREMIUM — The sum a person pays to an insurance company on a regular (usually monthly or yearly) basis to receive health insurance.

A. Phlegm
B. Referral
C. Callus
D. Durable Medical Equipment
E. Penis
F. Medical Coder
G. Donut Hole
H. Viral
I. Preferred Provider Organization
J. Self Referral
K. Asthma
L. Orbit
M. Group Health Plan
N. Vulva
O. Suture
P. Premium
Q. Iron
R. Remittance Advice
S. Retina
T. Ascites
U. Tic
V. Plaque
W. Medical Assistant
X. Saline
Y. Otolaryngology

O. Provide the word that best matches each clue.

1. ACUTE — Describes a condition or illness that begins suddenly and is usually short-lasting

2. PALSY — Loss of sensation or ability to move

3. SUBSCRIBER — The individual covered under a group policy. For instance, an employee of a company with a group health policy would be one of many subscribers on that policy.

4. STOMA — A surgically formed opening on a body surface

5. SPRUE — A digestive disorder in which nutrients cannot be properly absorbed from food, causing weakness and loss of weight

6. FEE FOR SERVICE — This refers to a type of health insurance wherein the provider is paid for every service they perform.

7. ANEMIA — A condition in which the blood does not contain enough hemoglobin, the compound that carries oxygen from the lungs to other parts of the body

8. HEALTHCARE REFORM ACT — The major healthcare legislation passed in 2010 designed to make healthcare accessible and less expensive for more Americans.

9. CHRONIC — Describes a disorder that continues for a long period of time

10. NEONATOLOGY — the specialized care and treatment of a newborn up to six weeks of age

11. INTENSIVE CARE — The unit of a hospital reserved for patients that need immediate treatment and close monitoring by healthcare professionals for serious illnesses, conditions, and injuries.

12. WHEEZE — A high- pitched sound produced during breathing because of narrowing of the airways

13. THIRD PARTY ADMINISTRATOR — The name for the organization or individual that manages healthcare group benefits, claims, and administrative duties on behalf of a group plan or a company with a group plan.

14. TRAUMA — Physical injury or emotional shock

15. FORMULARY — A table or list provided by an insurance carrier that explains what prescription drugs are covered under their health plans.

16. PHOBIA — A persisting fear of and desire to avoid something

17. COORDINATION OF BENEFITS — Occurs when a patient is covered by more than one insurance plan.

18. ASSIGNMENT OF BENEFITS — Refers to insurance payments made directly to a healthcare provider for medical services received by the patient.

19. MEDICARE SECONDARY PAYER — The insurance company that covers any remaining expenses after Medicare has paid for a patient's coverage.

20. PRIMARY CARE PHYSICIAN — The physician who provides the basic healthcare services for a patient and recommends additional care for more serious treatments as necessary.

21. TYPE OF SERVICE — A field on a claim for describing what kind of healthcare services or procedures a provider administered.

22. LABOR — The interval from onset of contractions to birth of a baby

23. MUMPS — A viral infection that causes inflammation of salivary glands

24. MIOTIC — A drug that causes the pupil to constrict

25. UNBUNDLING — Refers to the fraudulent practice of ascribing more than one code to a service or procedure on a superbill or claim form when only one is necessary.

A. Subscriber
B. Assignment of Benefits
C. Primary Care Physician
D. Anemia
E. Third Party Administrator
F. Unbundling
G. Acute
H. Medicare Secondary Payer
I. Intensive Care
J. Neonatology
K. Wheeze
L. Mumps
M. Coordination of Benefits
N. Type of Service
O. Palsy
P. Fee for Service
Q. Labor
R. Miotic
S. Healthcare Reform Act
T. Formulary
U. Sprue
V. Stoma
W. Phobia
X. Chronic
Y. Trauma

P. Provide the word that best matches each clue.

	Answer	Clue
1.	CREDIT BALANCE	Refers to the sum shown in the "balance" column of a billing statement that reflects the amount due for services rendered.
2.	ALLOWED AMOUNT	The sum an insurance company will reimburse to cover a healthcare service or procedure.
3.	ACUTE	Describes a condition or illness that begins suddenly and is usually short- lasting
4.	ENDEMIC	Describes a disease that is always present in a certain population of people
5.	HEALTH MAINTENANCE ORGANIZATION	Networks of healthcare providers that offer healthcare plans to people for medical services exclusively in their network.
6.	MEDICAID	A joint federal and state assistance program started in 1965 to provide health insurance to lower-income persons.
7.	CHRONIC	Describes a disorder that continues for a long period of time
8.	ORBIT	The socket in the skull that contains the eyeball, along with its blood vessels, nerves, and muscles
9.	GLAND	A group of cells or an organ that produces substances (such as hormones and enzyme) that are used by the body
10.	REVENUE CODE	A three-digit code used on medical bills that explains the kind of facility in which a patient received treatment.
11.	MYXOMA	A noncancerous tumor made of mucous material and fibrous connective tissue
12.	PUVA	A form of phototherapy that combines the use of psoralens and ultraviolet light to treat skin disorders
13.	SALINE	A salt solution or any substance that contains salt
14.	RABIES	An infectious viral disease primarily affecting animals; can be transmitted to humans through an infected animal's bite
15.	DOWNCODING	Occurs when an insurance company finds there is insufficient evidence on a claim to prove that a provider performed coded medical services and so they reduce or remove those codes.
16.	MEDICAL NECESSITY	Refers to healthcare services or treatments that a patient requires to treat a serious medical condition or illness.

17. MEDICARE

A government insurance program started in 1965 to provide healthcare coverage for persons over 65 and eligible people with disabilities.

18. SUPPLEMENTAL INSURANCE

Can be a secondary policy or another insurance company that covers a patient's healthcare costs after receiving coverage from their primary insurance.

19. OCULAR

Describes something related to the eyes

20. IRON

A mineral necessary for the formation of important biological substances such as hemoglobin, myoglobin, and certain enzymes

21. CHOLERA

A bacterial infection of the small intestine that causes severe watery diarrhea, dehydration, and possibly death

22. AXILLA

Medical term for the armpit

23. LABIA

The two pairs of skinfolds that protect the opening of the vagina

24. BRUXISM

An unaware clenching or grinding of the teeth, usually during sleep

25. MEDICAL TRANSCRIPTION

The process of converting dictated or handwritten instructions, observations, and documentation into digital text formats.

A. Orbit
B. Iron
C. PUVA
D. Health Maintenance Organization
E. Gland
F. Bruxism
G. Ocular
H. Rabies
I. Downcoding
J. Allowed Amount
K. Axilla
L. Medical Necessity
M. Supplemental Insurance
N. Credit Balance
O. Medicare
P. Medical Transcription
Q. Revenue Code
R. Labia
S. Myxoma
T. Endemic
U. Saline
V. Chronic
W. Acute
X. Medicaid
Y. Cholera

Word Search

A. Find the hidden words. The words have been placed horizontally, vertically, or diagonally. When you locate a word, draw an ellipse around it.

N	C	G	L	I	V	C	O	D	E	S	B	W	A	T	S	K	T	W	D	I	W	U
L	Y	Q	B	X	L	Y	G	V	A	I	V	S	M	B	N	V	P	K	O	B	S	M
O	P	U	G	Q	G	M	N	H	L	C	O	C	C	Y	X	G	A	T	V	T	B	I
Q	R	H	F	N	T	A	H	H	L	Q	X	X	H	T	U	U	C	Z	K	B	H	R
V	R	T	I	A	A	P	R	S	O	F	T	P	T	G	U	X	U	N	Z	V	O	N
Z	Z	J	P	F	L	O	M	G	W	R	V	O	J	A	B	Z	W	P	L	E	S	K
P	O	L	E	D	L	A	Y	W	E	E	N	D	E	M	I	C	A	P	A	P	A	M
U	R	V	I	E	E	C	M	D	D	L	B	I	J	J	T	F	V	B	E	B	U	U
C	E	S	X	K	R	O	E	L	A	F	P	A	P	F	C	V	U	O	G	H	T	P
A	G	P	H	C	G	F	H	D	M	N	B	T	U	K	U	D	V	V	N	F	O	L
M	I	L	W	H	Y	H	E	T	O	X	W	R	N	G	Y	O	P	E	Y	N	P	A
A	X	I	U	R	X	W	T	W	U	M	J	Y	A	K	L	U	J	O	P	H	S	Q
G	K	N	Z	T	C	C	O	I	N	S	U	R	A	N	C	E	N	F	J	T	Y	U
X	P	T	N	F	F	V	Q	U	T	Y	T	O	P	G	E	N	E	L	D	K	U	E
U	T	M	K	T	U	T	I	L	I	Z	A	T	I	O	N	L	I	M	I	T	W	J
Y	E	X	P	L	A	N	A	T	I	O	N	O	F	B	E	N	E	F	I	T	S	H

1. Immunology
2. A device that is used to immobilize a part of the body
3. The percentage of coverage that a patient is responsible for paying after an insurance company pays the portion agreed upon in a health plan.
4. The examination of a body following death, possibly to determine the cause of death or for research
5. A document attached to a processed medical claim wherein the insurance company explains the services they will cover for a patient's healthcare treatments.
6. Four fused bones that form a triangular shape at the base of the spine (also known as the tailbone)
7. Describes a disease that is always present in a certain population of people
8. A codeset under ICD-9-CM used to organize healthcare services rendered for reasons other than illness or injury.
9. The sum an insurance company will reimburse to cover a healthcare service or procedure.
10. An area of buildup of fat deposits in an artery, causing narrowing of the artery and possibly heart disease
11. The limit per year for coverage under certain available healthcare services for Medicare enrollees.
12. The care and treatment of the foot and ankle
13. The basic unit of dna, which is responsible for passing genetic information

A. Allergy
B. Utilization Limit
C. Splint
D. V Codes
E. Explanation of Benefits
F. Plaque
G. Endemic
H. Autopsy
I. Co Insurance
J. Coccyx
K. Podiatry
L. Allowed Amount
M. Gene

B. Find the hidden words. The words have been placed horizontally, vertically, or diagonally. When you locate a word, draw an ellipse around it.

Y	O	N	H	V	G	M	N	C	V	H	Z	E	U	O	V	A	L	V	B	S	U	G
O	Y	I	U	S	Y	A	B	F	O	X	G	G	M	O	D	I	F	I	E	R	C	A
M	C	M	B	B	I	I	D	U	Q	Y	X	P	T	K	N	W	O	D	I	Y	I	L
N	M	T	P	P	R	E	A	U	T	H	O	R	I	Z	A	T	I	O	N	B	T	L
B	K	G	N	H	T	N	I	J	A	R	M	Y	L	D	R	V	U	J	H	Q	R	E
R	J	D	Y	D	D	P	Z	H	L	G	O	C	K	K	L	Q	V	F	B	E	W	R
R	E	L	A	T	I	V	E	V	A	L	U	E	A	M	O	U	N	T	X	R	K	G
N	F	V	Q	Y	G	U	D	J	S	X	A	O	R	T	A	S	T	E	N	T	K	Y
J	Q	J	S	J	S	G	G	K	J	T	H	K	E	N	C	O	N	G	U	L	L	O
P	Y	U	I	J	F	M	L	S	E	S	R	N	A	H	E	W	J	A	V	E	R	C
K	R	E	T	I	N	A	C	T	C	Z	E	L	O	G	T	S	R	S	O	W	Y	Y
L	Y	U	A	L	Y	A	O	O	G	I	A	U	Z	R	C	U	J	T	X	J	G	S
F	S	Q	U	B	O	L	D	M	M	G	C	P	M	U	W	V	T	R	B	C	M	T
E	K	K	U	W	Q	Q	I	A	A	N	J	T	W	W	J	L	I	I	E	H	Q	X
G	P	Y	S	Y	T	N	N	A	C	V	J	S	H	L	E	V	V	N	X	T	E	L
N	Y	D	M	F	S	D	G	I	O	Q	L	L	F	F	O	M	S	W	C	C	Q	Y

1. The main artery in the body, carrying oxygenated blood from the heart to other arteries in the body
2. The process of translating a physician's documentation about a patient's medical condition and health services rendered into medical codes that are then plugged into a claim for processing.
3. Additions to CPT codes that explain alterations and modifications to an otherwise routine treatment, exam, or service.
4. A negative reaction to a substance that in most people causes no reaction
5. A lump filled with either fluid or soft material, occurring in any organ or tissue
6. The median amount Medicare will repay a provider for certain services and treatments.
7. A device used to hold tissues in place, such as to support a skin graft
8. An electrocardiogram, which is a record of the electrical impulses that trigger the heartbeat
9. Some insurance plans require that a patient receive preauthorization from the insurance company prior to receiving certain medical services.
10. A hormone that stimulates the release of gastric acid in the stomach
11. A surgically formed opening on a body surface
12. A membrane lining the inside of the back of the eye that contains light-sensitive nerve cells that convert focused light into nerve impulses, making vision possible

A. Retina
B. Preauthorization
C. Gastrin
D. Aorta
E. Cyst
F. Stent
G. ECG
H. Coding
I. Stoma
J. Modifier
K. Relative Value Amount
L. Allergy

C. Find the hidden words. The words have been placed horizontally, vertically, or diagonally. When you locate a word, draw an ellipse around it.

R	A	R	B	P	O	L	E	Q	N	H	C	A	N	A	L	O	L	L	S	R	U	F
S	A	E	K	R	T	O	E	X	H	C	F	Q	I	N	D	B	R	C	V	O	G	D
T	L	V	Q	H	O	Y	S	A	J	X	Z	T	M	E	X	R	M	D	C	R	Y	K
A	M	E	C	T	L	M	F	O	H	K	F	W	J	U	Q	E	L	R	T	C	S	B
X	L	N	Y	N	A	V	P	A	H	J	S	S	R	R	Q	X	O	K	W	E	T	U
O	B	U	R	D	R	C	A	K	L	Q	C	E	A	O	P	C	I	M	A	S	B	R
N	J	E	G	A	Y	W	T	R	B	M	A	D	N	N	V	P	T	I	H	Z	U	S
O	Z	C	R	Q	N	C	H	Y	Q	B	P	N	C	U	L	T	U	R	E	W	R	A
M	A	O	R	H	G	J	O	G	R	X	I	V	P	F	D	V	D	H	B	Z	F	A
Y	O	D	O	V	O	W	L	V	S	Q	T	H	U	J	U	J	A	Q	D	T	F	M
C	A	E	A	A	L	U	O	W	S	D	A	P	S	Y	V	M	Y	C	V	Y	R	P
O	Q	W	X	B	O	M	G	R	T	Z	T	V	I	B	Z	A	S	L	H	H	S	M
D	Y	J	H	B	G	Y	Y	L	O	E	I	L	Y	W	B	I	H	P	U	I	R	F
E	T	U	F	R	Y	S	U	A	M	F	O	S	S	W	D	E	E	R	O	U	Q	W
P	K	O	R	L	T	Q	N	V	A	Y	N	M	S	H	Q	I	E	G	N	N	M	V
G	A	N	E	S	T	H	E	S	I	O	L	O	G	Y	O	H	T	V	G	S	I	H

1. A surgically formed opening on a body surface
2. Medical billing specialists utilize this unique codeset for identifying a healthcare provider's specialty field.
3. A three-digit code used on medical bills that explains the kind of facility in which a patient received treatment.
4. The artificial growth of cells, tissue, or microorganisms such as bacteria in a laboratory
5. A document that summarizes the services, treatments, payments, and charges that a patient received on a given day.
6. A thick, yellowish or greenish fluid that contains dead white blood cells, tissues, and bacteria; occurs at the site of a bacterial infection
7. A tunnel-like passage
8. Another term for a nerve cell
9. A fixed payment that a patient makes to a health insurance company or provider to recoup costs incurred from various healthcare services.
10. the administration of medications as a means to block pain or diminish consciousness for surgery, usually by injection or inhalation
11. A fluid-filled sac that cushions and reduces friction in certain parts of the body
12. the medical and surgical care for diseases of the ears, nose and throat (ENT)
13. The specialty of physicians who are trained to examine surgical specimens and biopsies for diagnostic purposes.

A. Pathology
B. Pus
C. Anesthesiology
D. Neuron
E. Revenue Code
F. Taxonomy Code
G. Canal
H. Bursa
I. Capitation
J. Stoma
K. Day Sheet
L. Culture
M. Otolaryngology

D. Find the hidden words. The words have been placed horizontally, vertically, or diagonally. When you locate a word, draw an ellipse around it.

U	F	M	O	Z	X	T	H	R	C	I	M	A	E	Z	B	S	A	L	F	U	X	D
A	I	V	Q	B	D	S	L	S	L	I	T	U	P	L	Y	S	J	X	B	P	L	E
Z	U	C	O	F	D	F	H	C	M	W	C	V	F	L	E	C	T	O	P	I	C	F
E	H	R	E	Y	Q	Q	B	R	L	K	P	E	I	U	H	B	S	P	I	N	E	H
T	I	R	W	I	A	N	M	X	P	F	L	A	S	I	W	W	M	Z	S	O	C	G
X	Q	V	O	X	C	Q	E	P	I	Y	F	U	S	T	O	K	P	W	D	T	F	U
F	E	E	F	O	R	S	E	R	V	I	C	E	U	P	G	J	L	E	T	V	P	T
X	I	P	B	S	Z	B	W	S	W	H	L	X	R	E	W	L	I	P	O	M	A	E
I	N	H	G	H	F	N	C	H	C	K	V	L	E	D	I	A	Q	G	J	J	E	R
H	N	B	G	A	V	A	G	E	H	A	G	F	G	I	T	X	V	O	I	L	F	U
W	E	O	U	T	O	F	N	E	T	W	O	R	K	A	X	S	Z	D	E	Z	F	S
S	T	H	V	A	F	G	G	R	A	F	L	M	Y	T	H	U	Q	V	B	H	Z	B
Y	W	U	F	O	M	N	C	K	G	L	D	R	D	R	F	T	J	Y	O	U	L	U
A	O	Y	P	R	S	R	K	B	J	E	O	B	W	I	R	U	D	C	A	L	M	V
H	R	D	W	T	A	F	X	N	H	H	O	I	B	C	A	R	P	M	Y	C	J	B
N	K	B	L	A	S	F	R	J	H	A	A	C	J	S	M	E	C	Z	E	Q	E	Y

1. A noncancerous tumor of fatty tissue
2. The care and treatment of infants, children, and adolescents
3. An artificial feeding technique in which liquids are passed into the stomach by way of a tube inserted through the nose
4. A groove or slit on the body or in an organ
5. A surgical stitch that helps close an incision or wound so that it can heal properly
6. The column of bones and cartilage running along the midline of the back that surrounds and protects the spinal cord and supports the head
7. This refers to a type of health insurance wherein the provider is paid for every service they perform.
8. This term refers to a provider's relationship with a health insurance company.
9. A structure consisting of the colored area of the eye and the middle layer of the eye that contains blood vessels
10. Occurring at an abnormal position or time
11. The hollow female reproductive organ in which a fertilized egg is implanted and a fetus develops
12. The main artery in the body, carrying oxygenated blood from the heart to other arteries in the body
13. Refers to providers outside of an established network of providers who contract with an insurance company to offer patients healthcare at a discounted rate.

A. Uterus
B. Gavage
C. Fee for Service
D. Ectopic
E. Aorta
F. Uvea
G. Fissure
H. Spine
I. Out of Network
J. Suture
K. In Network
L. Lipoma
M. Pediatrics

E. Find the hidden words. The words have been placed horizontally, vertically, or diagonally. When you locate a word, draw an ellipse around it.

J	V	E	C	U	V	V	N	A	G	E	E	A	R	K	Z	T	V	L	Q	J	V	P
N	B	R	U	X	I	S	M	H	E	E	W	Z	B	L	W	U	E	Z	F	H	J	Y
R	W	K	E	J	A	V	V	C	R	R	C	D	F	I	F	O	P	O	G	O	R	R
V	Q	R	Z	N	Z	V	I	K	W	E	R	F	P	U	E	P	G	E	M	S	O	E
R	L	B	M	U	W	B	E	N	E	F	I	C	I	A	R	Y	V	D	Q	P	G	C
O	L	Z	R	D	A	F	K	Q	J	L	F	M	L	G	A	X	N	L	D	I	Q	T
I	K	B	R	Z	J	O	E	F	R	E	D	S	R	E	C	H	F	F	X	C	R	U
D	K	V	O	C	J	E	A	V	M	X	X	J	K	Z	A	C	A	X	E	E	J	M
H	S	T	M	B	F	Y	G	N	V	H	Y	H	U	R	S	O	P	T	T	A	G	M
W	Y	H	U	J	T	R	I	I	S	S	Q	I	G	C	T	L	W	X	I	F	X	R
I	Q	P	W	W	M	A	C	U	L	A	J	P	T	W	R	I	F	T	C	Q	Z	U
K	I	L	A	Y	K	T	J	W	Q	O	U	A	E	A	W	C	Y	T	K	J	W	I
X	W	G	L	O	W	C	L	K	Q	W	Z	A	C	O	B	T	W	V	S	U	K	X
H	M	X	Z	T	Y	I	C	F	S	T	R	A	I	N	S	A	T	R	I	A	G	E
T	M	J	U	Q	X	O	B	I	O	N	U	W	J	T	B	M	A	I	E	B	N	V
C	J	L	X	C	I	U	J	F	X	W	G	Q	E	H	D	Y	H	T	B	J	U	S

1. The person who receives benefits and
2. An automatic, involuntary response of the nervous system to a stimulus
3. A hard plaster or fiberglass shell that molds to a body part such as an arm and holds it in place for proper healing
4. Small, eight- legged animals that can attach to humans and animals and feed on blood
5. A short tube located at the end of the large intestine, which connects the intestine to the anus
6. Muscle damage resulting from excessive stretching or forceful contraction
7. Density lipoprotein- a type of lipoprotein that is the major carrier of cholesterol in the blood, with high levels associated with narrowing of the arteries and heart disease
8. An unaware clenching or grinding of the teeth, usually during sleep
9. Law passed in 1996 with an aim to improve the scope of healthcare services and establish regulations for securing healthcare records from unwanted parties.
10. Waves of pain in the abdomen that increase in strength, disappear, and return
11. A system used to classify sick or injured people according to the severity of their conditions
12. The area of the retina that allows fine details to be observed at the center of vision
13. This refers to medical care and treatment for persons who are terminally ill.

A. Low
B. Macula
C. Colic
D. Triage
E. Ticks
F. Bruxism
G. Beneficiary
H. HIPAA
I. Hospice
J. Rectum
K. Strain
L. Cast
M. Reflex

F. Find the hidden words. The words have been placed horizontally, vertically, or diagonally. When you locate a word, draw an ellipse around it.

B	Q	R	A	W	V	B	A	R	T	E	R	Y	W	N	Z	C	F	Q	H	K	F	A
M	T	E	O	F	H	W	A	D	D	X	F	X	J	X	H	O	L	M	F	I	Q	K
H	D	S	C	L	Y	H	I	S	J	W	A	A	X	W	X	P	Y	U	O	A	N	D
M	O	P	V	A	M	X	Z	T	P	D	N	Q	R	U	D	A	Y	T	R	U	S	K
H	W	O	Q	X	Y	N	D	Y	D	D	A	J	Z	L	C	Y	H	Y	C	I	W	U
J	N	N	U	F	L	I	E	E	V	T	F	F	W	Y	C	C	F	K	E	S	W	G
N	C	S	I	W	J	T	Z	G	S	D	B	N	K	V	U	C	Y	L	P	Y	F	W
H	O	I	T	D	T	D	N	A	P	Y	E	N	R	O	L	L	E	E	S	X	G	B
G	D	B	W	F	R	O	C	C	R	I	M	N	L	L	M	C	A	T	G	P	U	K
B	I	L	V	D	R	H	F	W	A	O	M	K	P	X	M	N	E	C	Z	E	M	A
X	N	E	Z	H	W	V	V	T	I	R	U	M	X	N	T	K	F	T	J	N	N	D
M	G	P	F	G	D	E	Y	M	N	R	N	Q	Y	X	P	Y	Y	O	C	I	T	X
K	Y	A	Q	J	B	Q	U	U	L	M	J	S	A	B	T	Z	H	R	W	S	C	X
J	E	R	G	B	V	P	P	U	V	A	H	O	V	V	C	A	L	C	F	W	W	F
M	K	T	P	R	E	E	X	I	S	T	I	N	G	C	O	N	D	I	T	I	O	N
E	A	Y	F	E	X	X	V	W	Z	Q	X	G	Q	A	B	U	K	H	F	B	M	G

1. The external male reproductive organ, which passes urine and semen out of the body
2. A person covered by a health insurance plan.
3. The amount that must be paid to a provider before they receive any treatment or services.
4. Deoxyribonucleic acid; responsible for passing genetic information in nearly all organisms
5. A large blood vessel that carries blood from the heart to tissues and organs in the body
6. A form of phototherapy that combines the use of psoralens and ultraviolet light to treat skin disorders
7. The person who pays for a patient's medical expenses, also known as the guarantor.
8. Inflammation of the skin, usually causing itchiness and sometimes blisters and scaling
9. Occurs when an insurance company finds there is insufficient evidence on a claim to prove that a provider performed coded medical services and so they reduce or remove those codes.
10. A pus- filled abscess in the follicle of an eyelash
11. A medical condition a patient had before receiving coverage from an insurance company.
12. Instruments resembling tweezers that are used to handle objects or tissue during surgery
13. The tearing or stretching of the ligaments in a joint, characterized by pain, swelling, and an inability to move the joint

A. DNA
B. Downcoding
C. Stye
D. Responsible Party
E. Forceps
F. PUVA
G. Artery
H. Eczema
I. Sprain
J. Enrollee
K. Penis
L. Pre existing Condition
M. Co Pay

G. Find the hidden words. The words have been placed horizontally, vertically, or diagonally. When you locate a word, draw an ellipse around it.

Q	R	G	C	S	P	Y	F	E	T	U	S	O	D	L	G	O	I	T	E	R	L	J
R	T	J	A	N	O	D	E	Y	C	D	Y	T	M	L	O	F	Y	W	J	L	B	C
K	L	O	P	A	K	X	Y	K	O	X	F	I	U	X	H	W	U	R	E	A	F	A
L	W	Z	I	H	S	W	I	D	G	H	B	R	M	K	S	J	J	D	W	E	R	S
X	L	P	T	Y	U	V	Z	K	E	Y	Q	W	P	D	R	A	M	Z	K	E	J	T
O	D	L	A	K	T	D	V	G	Z	V	N	W	S	E	A	D	F	H	Z	X	F	F
L	T	E	T	L	D	D	X	E	Q	K	Y	A	K	F	K	Y	Z	N	Q	N	I	N
S	V	U	I	Y	P	Z	O	Q	C	S	P	R	A	I	N	L	W	A	M	S	T	N
B	E	R	O	S	Q	C	R	A	L	E	S	A	F	C	S	X	F	O	P	D	N	X
F	M	A	N	M	S	U	H	C	H	W	T	W	N	C	F	O	X	O	S	S	E	I
T	G	X	N	N	H	P	C	A	J	L	Z	M	F	G	J	N	T	X	F	Z	S	X
V	W	G	M	D	X	D	A	R	V	X	V	D	Y	P	Y	E	N	R	Z	G	S	N
H	X	A	W	Y	F	J	U	V	N	L	Y	M	P	H	I	W	K	A	H	A	E	S
Z	A	R	Q	B	R	C	I	U	O	O	K	N	A	R	I	P	I	M	H	Z	Y	Q
X	A	K	M	H	N	O	R	E	I	Z	A	G	W	R	V	I	T	Q	L	U	F	K
Z	I	F	C	L	Z	N	X	S	A	J	T	Q	R	E	V	U	F	X	K	B	O	A

1. Enlargement of the thyroid gland, which produces a swelling on the neck
2. A viral infection that causes inflammation of salivary glands
3. Abnormal crackling or bubbling sounds heard in the lungs during breathing
4. A hard plaster or fiberglass shell that molds to a body part such as an arm and holds it in place for proper healing
5. A fixed payment that a patient makes to a health insurance company or provider to recoup costs incurred from various healthcare services.
6. A measure of a person's physical strength, flexibility, and endurance
7. The tearing or stretching of the ligaments in a joint, characterized by pain, swelling, and an inability to move the joint
8. The abbreviation for diagnosis codes, also known as ICD-9 codes.
9. A small, rounded tissue mass
10. A waste product of the metabolism of proteins that is formed by the liver and secreted by the kidneys
11. The double- layered membrane that lines the lungs and chest cavity and allows for lung movement during breathing
12. A milky fluid containing white blood cells, proteins, and fats
13. The term used to refer to an unborn child from 8 weeks after fertilization to birth

A. Fetus
B. Mumps
C. Goiter
D. Sprain
E. Node
F. Fitness
G. Cast
H. Urea
I. Capitation
J. Lymph
K. Rales
L. Pleura
M. Dx

H. Find the hidden words. The words have been placed horizontally, vertically, or diagonally. When you locate a word, draw an ellipse around it.

K	M	X	M	E	D	I	C	A	L	T	R	A	N	S	C	R	I	P	T	I	O	N
M	D	N	I	N	V	B	S	P	K	E	C	L	C	R	Q	L	G	Z	L	W	C	B
E	E	Y	V	F	W	O	V	J	L	H	U	Q	N	M	K	K	K	N	A	O	B	A
G	Z	T	J	D	G	I	T	Q	H	A	N	J	W	I	Z	O	N	I	B	Y	X	G
Z	X	H	U	O	F	L	G	B	W	P	M	I	B	A	X	E	F	M	I	C	Q	B
S	D	G	H	G	Q	D	K	V	X	L	E	P	E	U	G	C	L	O	A	O	A	M
P	K	T	R	E	M	O	R	O	E	A	I	W	L	U	J	B	S	G	H	V	N	V
Q	A	C	O	I	T	U	S	N	X	Q	C	W	G	Z	F	H	T	T	W	F	Q	C
T	X	I	L	E	U	M	N	Q	P	U	D	T	S	C	I	Y	Y	U	S	Q	L	V
Y	H	J	H	K	L	L	B	Q	Y	E	Q	J	L	G	B	L	E	L	R	U	R	V
Q	D	S	R	G	J	C	X	X	P	D	J	F	U	D	E	I	L	N	Y	F	Q	C
H	V	W	R	Y	U	H	L	R	N	D	X	Y	V	S	R	F	P	C	Y	I	N	O
N	M	N	O	K	O	H	X	Z	X	T	O	B	I	S	E	R	U	M	I	W	A	D
H	O	C	L	E	A	N	C	L	A	I	M	U	M	F	B	A	M	H	Y	L	C	E
W	K	Z	N	O	N	P	A	R	T	I	C	I	P	A	T	I	O	N	X	C	U	S
J	J	C	O	G	A	N	S	P	K	I	X	N	J	J	P	V	J	N	B	H	K	N

1. An involuntary, rhythmic, shaking movement caused by alternating contraction and relaxation of muscles
2. The lowest section of the small intestine, which attaches to the large intestine
3. The clear, watery fluid that separates from clotted blood
4. The process of converting dictated or handwritten instructions, observations, and documentation into digital text formats.
5. A codeset under ICD-9-CM used to organize healthcare services rendered for reasons other than illness or injury.
6. This is when a provider refuses to accept Medicare payments as a sufficient amount for the services rendered to a patient.
7. The two pairs of skinfolds that protect the opening of the vagina
8. A pus- filled abscess in the follicle of an eyelash
9. Refers to a medical claim filed with a health insurance company that is free of errors and processed in a timely manner.
10. An inflamed, raised area of skin that is pus-filled
11. A constituent of plants that cannot be digested, which helps maintain healthy functioning of the bowels
12. Sexual intercourse
13. An area of buildup of fat deposits in an artery, causing narrowing of the artery and possibly heart disease

A. Serum
B. Boil
C. Coitus
D. Tremor
E. Non participation
F. V Codes
G. Ileum
H. Plaque
I. Medical Transcription
J. Labia
K. Fiber
L. Clean Claim
M. Stye

I. Find the hidden words. The words have been placed horizontally, vertically, or diagonally. When you locate a word, draw an ellipse around it.

C	C	P	W	P	U	C	M	T	Q	Y	O	Y	M	X	S	B	I	U	Y	N	M	P
D	K	L	B	L	T	H	P	Q	K	B	M	Z	W	A	L	Y	Q	E	T	P	C	R
S	Z	Z	L	E	X	C	R	C	B	S	M	A	N	I	A	P	D	U	X	X	Y	S
D	U	B	V	U	X	O	C	G	W	C	Z	Q	X	H	R	A	Q	F	Y	K	Y	L
K	M	Q	V	R	V	R	S	A	L	I	N	E	P	M	O	S	S	Y	R	B	Z	C
S	M	J	R	A	A	N	U	U	L	C	E	R	E	O	L	S	V	E	N	O	M	C
X	M	G	U	V	L	K	B	X	W	N	Y	N	I	R	E	G	F	K	O	O	Y	K
X	R	V	O	E	V	H	O	D	F	K	Z	I	P	D	O	V	R	E	Q	A	V	O
A	P	K	V	F	E	L	O	T	A	X	E	M	P	P	Z	G	F	U	J	S	I	N
N	P	R	E	V	E	N	T	I	V	E	M	E	D	I	C	I	N	E	A	C	O	A
R	J	T	J	Y	Y	P	J	Q	F	E	J	B	D	P	L	K	C	D	C	O	R	Z
W	K	Z	V	Q	C	F	M	B	K	T	E	T	E	Z	Q	Z	F	X	F	Y	B	T
C	V	S	G	D	W	D	K	W	Z	M	R	N	J	J	D	H	M	D	D	E	I	T
Q	X	J	K	L	T	D	X	E	I	A	D	H	D	C	K	Z	J	J	Q	N	T	T
S	B	R	E	L	A	T	I	V	E	V	A	L	U	E	A	M	O	U	N	T	R	Q
H	W	Y	L	C	V	P	I	F	V	X	S	L	K	H	Y	V	D	R	K	B	G	A

1. The double- layered membrane that lines the lungs and chest cavity and allows for lung movement during breathing
2. An open sore that occurs on the skin or on a mucous membrane because of the destruction of surface tissue
3. The median amount Medicare will repay a provider for certain services and treatments.
4. The socket in the skull that contains the eyeball, along with its blood vessels, nerves, and muscles
5. A thickened callus on the foot that is caused by an improperly fitting shoe
6. The specialty that focuses on the health of individuals in order to protect, promote and maintain health and prevent disease, disability and premature death
7. A surgical technique in which the flow of blood or another body fluid is redirected around a blockage
8. A salt solution or any substance that contains salt
9. A structure that allows fluid flow in only one direction
10. A mental disorder characterized by extreme excitement, happiness, overactivity, and agitation
11. A poisonous substance produced by certain animals

A. Pleura
B. Valve
C. Bypass
D. Orbit
E. Venom
F. Preventive Medicine
G. Mania
H. Ulcer
I. Corn
J. Relative Value Amount
K. Saline

J. Find the hidden words. The words have been placed horizontally, vertically, or diagonally. When you locate a word, draw an ellipse around it.

X	M	U	U	N	F	X	F	H	T	V	M	G	Z	S	G	F	O	Z	X	G	N	H
X	Y	J	P	Y	U	N	T	I	M	E	L	Y	S	U	B	M	I	S	S	I	O	N
O	K	H	O	A	V	A	Z	H	A	B	C	I	P	P	Z	Q	Y	B	Z	C	W	M
W	C	I	T	K	F	W	V	E	Q	P	A	L	A	T	E	Y	Q	X	M	G	L	L
Y	T	Z	E	M	W	P	Q	N	E	U	R	O	L	O	G	Y	X	H	H	A	I	Q
V	S	X	K	M	S	A	N	U	S	B	Q	A	S	T	H	M	A	U	K	F	X	M
J	Z	R	N	K	M	P	A	I	X	H	K	G	I	T	D	M	X	P	U	V	A	D
Y	Z	B	U	T	J	I	Z	O	Z	O	K	F	N	R	G	U	X	S	O	S	Q	N
U	P	A	G	Y	Y	D	W	V	E	K	C	L	P	G	B	R	L	C	P	T	F	R
J	J	I	W	V	O	L	G	C	N	S	G	D	A	K	Q	P	D	R	K	A	O	U
L	F	S	T	O	M	A	C	S	R	O	M	Y	T	Y	P	H	S	U	O	I	H	V
M	Y	D	L	H	E	K	M	I	O	T	I	C	I	K	M	W	K	B	U	D	E	Y
B	Q	Y	H	L	B	Y	U	M	L	G	Q	T	E	K	X	P	U	B	V	S	T	K
L	R	L	M	R	C	W	D	K	L	Y	I	I	N	P	K	N	L	I	W	I	R	G
X	F	W	S	L	X	V	N	U	E	N	V	Q	T	E	A	S	L	N	T	H	Q	D
H	C	E	R	V	I	X	E	P	E	X	N	V	E	X	A	J	W	G	A	G	E	L

1. The opening through which feces are passed from the body
2. A surgically formed opening on a body surface
3. A process by which insurance claims are checked for errors before being sent to an insurance company for final processing.
4. the diagnosis and medical treatment of the nervous system and brain, including conditions such as strokes and seizures
5. Occurs when a person has a stay at a healthcare facility for more than 24 hours.
6. A drug that causes the pupil to constrict
7. A measure of the acidic or basic character of a substance
8. The bones that form the framework of the head and enclose and protect the brain and other sensory organs
9. A disorder characterized by inflamed airways and difficulty breathing
10. A person covered by a health insurance plan.
11. The roof of the mouth
12. Claims have a specific timeframe in which they can be sent off to an insurance company for processing.
13. A small, round organ making up the neck of the uterus and separating it from the vagina

A. Palate
B. Stoma
C. Enrollee
D. Untimely Submission
E. Anus
F. Miotic
G. Skull
H. Asthma
I. Neurology
J. Scrubbing
K. Inpatient
L. pH
M. Cervix

K. Find the hidden words. The words have been placed horizontally, vertically, or diagonally. When you locate a word, draw an ellipse around it.

W	E	O	Z	A	O	V	P	B	Q	P	H	E	M	I	W	R	G	G	E	K	B	I
I	J	C	Y	S	T	W	O	O	C	Y	T	E	A	H	Z	U	E	S	P	A	S	M
Y	M	O	M	S	D	O	F	I	P	P	L	P	N	N	H	Y	N	Z	P	E	R	P
H	E	M	A	T	O	L	O	G	Y	T	B	U	I	K	O	W	E	T	C	S	P	B
K	D	D	A	V	M	E	I	M	Y	Q	I	P	A	Z	L	U	C	E	A	K	I	H
J	Q	M	I	T	M	S	H	P	R	A	O	F	U	X	A	J	O	R	F	J	D	S
Y	S	N	L	V	F	R	C	M	V	Y	D	T	N	V	U	U	R	T	K	F	K	P
X	V	K	N	C	E	A	C	U	T	E	I	P	B	Q	L	S	N	I	T	P	P	L
G	L	X	M	P	U	Y	V	H	Q	Q	N	A	U	X	J	W	E	A	W	F	L	E
M	V	Y	H	O	S	K	Q	I	V	E	E	T	N	Z	I	X	A	R	F	R	L	E
I	A	G	I	N	G	X	I	E	P	G	P	Q	D	F	U	N	F	Y	U	S	E	N
U	G	G	H	T	Q	Y	W	E	B	Z	M	D	L	Q	N	Q	H	C	C	R	S	R
O	Y	X	G	W	P	J	R	J	Y	W	K	N	I	C	K	N	S	L	B	D	I	P
T	L	T	G	F	D	D	Z	C	O	M	K	N	N	D	E	W	I	A	Z	K	O	E
H	G	N	G	E	O	Y	A	G	A	X	F	Z	G	C	Y	D	F	I	R	B	N	T
M	J	P	U	L	M	X	K	Y	N	E	S	Q	Y	I	N	X	M	M	B	Q	E	C

1. An egg cell that has not developed completely
2. An abnormality of structure or function in the body
3. An element for the formation of thyroid hormones
4. A lump filled with either fluid or soft material, occurring in any organ or tissue
5. A formal medical billing term that refers to insurance claims that haven't been paid or balances owed by patients overdue by more than 30 days.
6. An organ located in the upper left abdomen behind the ribs that removes and destroys old red blood cells and helps fight infection
7. An involuntary muscle contraction
8. Describes a condition or illness that begins suddenly and is usually short- lasting
9. A claim filed by a provider after they have filed claims for primary and secondary health insurance coverage on behalf of a patient.
10. Refers to the fraudulent practice of ascribing more than one code to a service or procedure on a superbill or claim form when only one is necessary.
11. A mental disorder characterized by extreme excitement, happiness, overactivity, and agitation
12. The clear, dome-shaped front portion of the eye's outer covering
13. Oncology

A. Lesion
B. Unbundling
C. Mania
D. Cornea
E. Spleen
F. Hematology
G. Aging
H. Cyst
I. Acute
J. Iodine
K. Oocyte
L. Tertiary Claim
M. Spasm

L. Find the hidden words. The words have been placed horizontally, vertically, or diagonally. When you locate a word, draw an ellipse around it.

D	S	B	Q	G	T	R	I	C	A	R	E	L	L	F	B	Q	R	X	R	S	X	Q
O	S	U	M	E	D	I	C	A	L	T	R	A	N	S	C	R	I	P	T	I	O	N
N	S	R	O	B	S	V	G	U	A	R	A	N	T	O	R	F	P	A	T	K	F	S
U	P	L	O	J	P	R	E	V	E	N	T	I	V	E	M	E	D	I	C	I	N	E
T	R	N	E	F	B	L	F	W	W	N	U	Z	G	L	W	E	S	I	Z	Q	B	Z
H	G	L	R	P	L	A	S	T	I	C	K	R	U	W	Y	B	M	D	J	F	D	O
O	P	R	F	J	O	F	V	I	M	K	Q	U	I	O	A	Z	G	M	X	H	R	H
L	S	N	Q	T	P	K	A	Y	O	L	I	V	W	F	T	P	D	R	T	H	W	E
E	X	B	B	E	T	P	J	F	D	V	Y	U	A	M	Y	X	O	M	A	F	B	O
V	W	B	A	D	I	L	Y	E	I	X	X	B	U	Y	D	V	K	W	P	S	Q	L
N	J	R	L	E	C	B	K	F	F	E	Z	Q	I	Q	U	Q	X	T	B	R	I	J
R	G	A	Z	M	H	R	F	K	I	K	C	F	H	P	P	B	L	F	Q	Y	A	S
Z	X	G	T	A	E	D	N	Y	E	R	V	X	K	G	U	T	Y	P	H	U	S	G
J	R	E	J	F	V	E	M	E	R	G	E	N	C	Y	M	E	D	I	C	I	N	E
U	X	K	A	A	E	P	L	O	L	S	H	Q	R	J	T	G	C	O	S	M	T	H
T	H	I	R	D	P	A	R	T	Y	A	D	M	I	N	I	S	T	R	A	T	O	R

1. Abnormal buildup of fluid in the body, which may cause visible swelling
2. The federal health insurance program for active and retired service members, their families, and the survivors of service members.
3. The party paying for an insurance plan who is not the patient. Parents, for example, would be the guarantors for their children's health insurance.
4. Pertaining to the eyes
5. The repair, restoration or improvement of conditions or injuries to the skin and external features resulting from disease, injury or birth defects
6. This term refers to the discrepancy between the limits of healthcare insurance coverage and the Medicare Part D coverage limits for prescription drugs.
7. The name for the organization or individual that manages healthcare group benefits, claims, and administrative duties on behalf of a group plan or a company with a group plan.
8. Additions to CPT codes that explain alterations and modifications to an otherwise routine treatment, exam, or service.
9. The process of converting dictated or handwritten instructions, observations, and documentation into digital text formats.
10. A group of diseases caused by the microorganism rickettsia, spread by the bites of fleas, mites, or ticks
11. A noncancerous tumor made of mucous material and fibrous connective tissue
12. the specialty that includes treatment of any symptom, illness or injury requiring urgent evaluation and
13. The specialty that focuses on the health of individuals in order to protect, promote and maintain health and prevent disease, disability and premature death

A. Preventive Medicine
B. Typhus
C. Optic
D. Donut Hole
E. Guarantor
F. Emergency Medicine
G. Third Party Administrator
H. Edema
I. Modifier
J. TRICARE
K. Medical Transcription
L. Myxoma
M. Plastic

M. Find the hidden words. The words have been placed horizontally, vertically, or diagonally. When you locate a word, draw an ellipse around it.

I	S	K	I	L	L	E	D	N	U	R	S	I	N	G	F	A	C	I	L	I	T	Y
X	I	V	V	C	N	L	P	V	X	F	Z	W	T	D	Y	X	B	I	M	D	J	F
D	Q	C	W	P	L	B	V	N	J	B	Q	C	C	R	J	U	U	M	J	A	Z	D
B	R	E	S	P	O	N	S	I	B	L	E	P	A	R	T	Y	L	A	L	T	M	J
O	X	M	Z	P	U	Z	P	X	C	U	S	S	Y	M	C	J	I	G	U	I	N	D
O	J	T	R	L	P	D	D	C	K	G	C	R	W	Q	N	S	M	I	Y	C	F	S
S	J	L	T	Z	H	Z	Q	V	W	E	Y	P	I	D	F	I	I	N	A	D	V	N
T	A	Q	W	N	N	A	D	W	B	R	L	T	D	H	P	P	A	G	E	S	Q	T
E	N	O	T	O	T	H	E	R	W	I	S	E	S	P	E	C	I	F	I	E	D	J
R	M	Y	I	G	E	U	T	N	Q	A	I	M	C	H	O	L	E	R	A	P	D	P
C	A	P	I	T	A	T	I	O	N	T	E	C	N	X	B	I	F	O	C	A	L	G
Y	E	D	P	K	C	U	I	T	O	R	B	B	E	N	E	F	I	C	I	A	R	Y
P	K	J	L	A	C	I	P	J	S	I	H	Q	F	S	Y	E	Z	R	K	N	Q	U
J	V	F	J	I	X	D	J	M	Z	C	Z	P	S	C	F	S	O	R	N	A	B	T
X	O	N	R	O	Y	W	L	Y	V	S	Q	J	B	L	V	A	O	G	R	T	K	L
A	G	I	R	P	N	O	N	P	A	R	T	I	C	I	P	A	T	I	O	N	Z	W

1. the treatment of diseases and internal disorders of the elderly
2. A fixed payment that a patient makes to a health insurance company or provider to recoup costs incurred from various healthcare services.
3. A bacterial infection of the small intestine that causes severe watery diarrhea, dehydration, and possibly death
4. The person who pays for a patient's medical expenses, also known as the guarantor.
5. This is when a provider refuses to accept Medicare payments as a sufficient amount for the services rendered to a patient.
6. This term is used in ICD-9 codes to describe conditions with unspecified diagnoses.
7. Ribonucleic acid, which helps to decode and process the information contained in dna
8. The person who receives benefits and
9. The technique of creating pictures of structures inside of the body using x-rays, ultrasound waves, or magnetic fields
10. A lens that corrects both near and distant vision by having two parts with different focusing strengths
11. These are facilities for the severely ill or elderly that provide specialized long-term care for recovering patients.
12. An additional dose of a vaccine taken after the first dose to maintain or renew the first one
13. A disorder in which a person eats large amounts of food then forces vomiting or uses laxatives to prevent weight gain (called binging and purging)

A. Beneficiary
B. Bulimia
C. Capitation
D. Booster
E. Not Otherwise Specified
F. Cholera
G. Geriatrics
H. Responsible Party
I. Imaging
J. Bifocal
K. RNA
L. Skilled Nursing Facility
M. Non participation

N. Find the hidden words. The words have been placed horizontally, vertically, or diagonally. When you locate a word, draw an ellipse around it.

Y	H	D	I	T	S	G	W	D	Q	L	I	M	M	F	N	V	Q	Y	E	X	B	R
B	O	W	E	L	L	X	I	J	L	N	L	G	J	D	X	C	I	W	P	A	O	N
A	H	S	O	D	K	P	F	G	Y	G	I	M	K	O	R	O	T	L	C	U	G	V
O	V	U	M	F	A	J	H	S	Q	U	U	T	D	N	C	C	Q	W	F	Z	I	P
Q	M	J	Y	H	V	S	B	L	F	A	M	V	R	U	U	H	D	W	U	U	T	S
I	A	X	K	W	N	P	V	C	Q	B	B	N	C	T	L	L	C	C	Z	S	W	Z
A	N	Y	C	H	A	R	I	T	Y	C	A	R	E	H	T	E	Y	C	R	U	D	Q
G	A	R	T	E	R	Y	V	B	M	H	A	O	S	O	U	A	B	N	K	R	Z	P
K	J	D	N	T	P	B	W	B	Y	T	R	U	B	L	R	Z	I	E	T	M	F	V
U	Z	P	F	B	N	K	Y	F	L	I	A	X	O	E	E	P	Y	E	A	N	O	K
D	U	R	A	B	L	E	M	E	D	I	C	A	L	E	Q	U	I	P	M	E	N	T
U	D	S	P	F	N	T	S	I	R	E	U	T	P	J	O	C	H	S	C	Q	Y	V
M	K	R	X	N	J	K	Z	S	Z	Q	L	A	W	W	Q	Y	V	A	Q	G	X	U
E	G	E	Y	F	K	W	I	L	X	L	Y	R	I	Y	I	S	N	I	A	C	I	N
Z	J	H	I	Z	E	D	H	P	N	R	R	W	C	A	S	T	Y	R	F	L	S	P
E	A	C	J	N	S	Z	B	B	U	N	I	O	N	E	O	R	N	A	G	I	N	G

1. A hard, fluid-filled pad along the inside joint of the big toe
2. This refers to medical implements that can be reused such as stretchers, wheelchairs, canes, crutches, and bedpans.
3. A formal medical billing term that refers to insurance claims that haven't been paid or balances owed by patients overdue by more than 30 days.
4. A large blood vessel that carries blood from the heart to tissues and organs in the body
5. The artificial growth of cells, tissue, or microorganisms such as bacteria in a laboratory
6. Another term for an egg cell
7. One of the two bones that form the hip on either side of the body
8. This term refers to the discrepancy between the limits of healthcare insurance coverage and the Medicare Part D coverage limits for prescription drugs.
9. A coiled organ in the inner ear that plays a large role in hearing by picking up sound vibrations and transmitting them as electrical signals
10. A lump filled with either fluid or soft material, occurring in any organ or tissue
11. This type of care is administered at reduced or zero cost to patients who cannot afford healthcare.
12. A vitamin important in many chemical processes in the body
13. Intestine

A. Bunion
B. Bowel
C. Niacin
D. Aging
E. Charity Care
F. Culture
G. Ovum
H. Artery
I. Cochlea
J. Durable Medical Equipment
K. Ilium
L. Donut Hole
M. Cyst

O. Find the hidden words. The words have been placed horizontally, vertically, or diagonally. When you locate a word, draw an ellipse around it.

A	H	Y	O	V	Z	D	W	I	S	S	F	L	J	X	T	E	M	B	R	Y	O	A
Z	C	N	P	J	F	H	G	P	Q	K	S	H	N	I	D	Z	J	B	S	U	K	W
F	H	W	C	R	O	U	P	H	M	I	H	X	Y	S	E	V	G	B	F	L	E	X
R	C	Q	H	G	I	T	O	U	J	O	U	F	C	T	H	F	Z	P	C	W	F	T
C	T	Z	I	R	M	P	B	M	D	R	N	V	M	R	C	O	L	I	C	J	Q	D
C	Q	X	O	H	M	C	T	R	V	W	T	P	G	O	L	C	O	Y	D	P	I	R
Z	O	W	E	M	I	F	W	J	Q	Y	O	W	N	K	M	Z	Q	M	Q	Q	G	Q
V	B	I	F	O	C	A	L	P	Z	V	B	B	D	E	X	I	U	H	M	D	B	A
S	E	C	O	N	D	A	R	Y	I	N	S	U	R	A	N	C	E	C	L	A	I	M
K	S	T	O	O	L	U	D	W	W	I	F	Y	B	J	X	P	P	H	Q	Y	S	L
I	T	H	E	M	E	D	I	C	A	L	N	E	C	E	S	S	I	T	Y	R	G	E
T	M	H	D	G	K	K	K	Z	G	S	O	M	T	J	I	Q	Q	X	L	D	B	L
N	P	S	V	P	A	U	I	S	F	C	D	X	S	C	V	X	V	U	Z	N	O	E
Q	B	Y	M	Y	B	A	D	Q	H	F	E	D	S	G	W	P	H	R	J	P	W	C
G	A	P	P	B	H	M	S	V	D	M	Q	G	X	N	U	J	R	Z	U	F	E	B
Y	W	T	A	P	R	E	A	U	T	H	O	R	I	Z	A	T	I	O	N	W	L	Z

1. Waves of pain in the abdomen that increase in strength, disappear, and return
2. A lens that corrects both near and distant vision by having two parts with different focusing strengths
3. Another term for feces
4. A term used to describe a child in the womb from fertilization to 8 weeks following fertilization
5. An artificially constructed or an abnormal passage connecting two usually separate structures in the body
6. Damage to part of the brain because of a lack of blood supply or the rupturing of a blood vessel
7. Intestine
8. A small, rounded tissue mass
9. The claim filed with the secondary insurance company after the primary insurance company pays for their portion of healthcare costs.
10. Refers to healthcare services or treatments that a patient requires to treat a serious medical condition or illness.
11. Some insurance plans require that a patient receive preauthorization from the insurance company prior to receiving certain medical services.
12. A usually mild and temporary condition common in children in which the walls of the airways become inflamed and narrow, resulting in wheezing and coughing

A. Medical Necessity
B. Node
C. Stool
D. Croup
E. Shunt
F. Embryo
G. Bifocal
H. Colic
I. Bowel
J. Preauthorization
K. Secondary Insurance Claim
L. Stroke

P. Find the hidden words. The words have been placed horizontally, vertically, or diagonally. When you locate a word, draw an ellipse around it.

I	N	C	Q	X	C	J	B	I	X	X	T	N	K	V	D	T	N	L	I	J	U	Y
A	V	I	R	A	L	J	V	X	E	B	S	C	A	N	C	E	R	V	A	L	N	K
H	A	W	S	E	O	M	M	M	T	G	G	U	G	U	D	G	P	N	Q	N	C	P
C	G	B	A	M	A	N	I	A	E	F	A	P	B	W	H	A	A	N	D	X	O	U
G	P	U	S	W	I	M	G	D	P	D	X	G	P	P	L	X	X	W	S	X	M	P
R	U	A	T	I	M	V	A	S	C	U	L	A	R	S	U	R	G	E	R	Y	A	W
K	S	X	H	Y	G	T	S	R	F	M	I	T	T	E	C	V	C	M	B	H	T	Z
M	K	J	M	C	E	T	Y	P	E	O	F	S	E	R	V	I	C	E	V	F	I	C
G	L	K	A	M	B	J	E	I	J	F	P	K	C	A	A	C	E	E	R	P	C	M
E	Y	B	S	X	Y	M	V	E	N	O	M	O	D	T	P	P	X	M	X	J	C	H
I	S	B	M	Y	E	S	C	E	O	J	I	F	Y	R	L	M	F	D	V	Y	H	K
R	O	D	X	Q	E	T	H	D	N	T	A	W	V	O	A	Y	O	P	O	A	S	G
Z	O	I	O	E	J	F	C	S	I	C	L	U	X	P	S	R	E	X	P	H	M	Z
Y	U	A	B	Q	H	I	C	O	Q	N	G	X	B	H	I	K	C	G	O	T	E	G
Y	Q	P	U	L	H	G	Z	E	U	R	A	G	A	Y	A	H	E	N	G	Y	A	W
A	C	O	P	L	A	C	E	O	F	S	E	R	V	I	C	E	C	O	D	E	R	C

1. A two-digit code used on claims to explain what type of provider performed healthcare services on a patient.
2. A sample of cells spread across a glass slide to be examined through a microscope
3. A group of diseases in which cells grow unrestrained in an organ or tissue in the body
4. The diagnosis and treatment of circulatory problems of the extremities, especially the legs
5. A thick, yellowish or greenish fluid that contains dead white blood cells, tissues, and bacteria; occurs at the site of a bacterial infection
6. A condition in which the area of the brain involved in maintaining consciousness is somehow affected, resulting in a state of unconsciousness in which the patient does not respond to stimulation
7. A poisonous substance produced by certain animals
8. A mental disorder characterized by extreme excitement, happiness, overactivity, and agitation
9. A field on a claim for describing what kind of healthcare services or procedures a provider administered.
10. The complete or partial failure of any organ or tissue to grow
11. A disorder characterized by inflamed airways and difficulty breathing
12. A term describing something related to or caused by a virus
13. The shrinkage or near disappearance of a tissue or organ

A. Place of Service Code
B. Type of Service
C. Vascular Surgery
D. Venom
E. Atrophy
F. Smear
G. Pus
H. Mania
I. Coma
J. Viral
K. Aplasia
L. Asthma
M. Cancer

Q. Find the hidden words. The words have been placed horizontally, vertically, or diagonally. When you locate a word, draw an ellipse around it.

V	E	I	N	U	V	N	T	M	O	X	J	W	A	A	H	F	G	Q	I	B	J	Y
U	Z	N	Z	W	T	F	T	A	X	O	N	O	M	Y	C	O	D	E	P	Z	Q	W
F	W	C	N	Z	P	U	M	M	Q	W	I	E	F	A	Z	Z	H	Q	Q	V	R	E
U	D	H	W	R	Z	G	Y	X	S	A	U	E	F	S	G	A	O	O	X	H	X	R
J	T	W	U	F	H	J	Z	A	O	V	U	L	C	E	R	S	I	J	R	T	C	N
F	R	Z	S	H	O	C	K	P	E	E	K	V	U	H	A	P	B	H	U	W	X	M
Y	C	U	F	A	Q	O	T	Z	G	R	M	W	I	O	G	L	A	R	Q	X	C	E
I	A	Z	F	I	S	T	U	L	A	N	Y	H	T	Y	S	N	I	A	C	I	N	U
T	A	X	I	D	E	N	T	I	F	I	C	A	T	I	O	N	N	U	M	B	E	R
V	H	L	X	T	R	I	I	E	B	X	A	K	W	E	E	J	X	Z	L	I	Q	G
C	O	G	Z	K	T	T	U	F	C	C	J	V	U	G	M	Q	L	K	V	P	D	S
N	R	P	N	F	A	E	Q	C	E	Y	V	K	H	M	R	P	M	N	Z	X	N	C
B	M	R	E	N	I	N	R	P	L	B	X	S	C	U	R	V	Y	S	T	L	P	Q
T	O	N	O	P	Q	L	E	T	L	P	D	D	E	O	K	N	U	U	B	Z	W	V
S	N	P	Q	L	Y	X	E	C	L	X	Q	I	F	R	T	Y	C	Y	A	J	G	H
M	E	D	I	C	A	R	E	S	E	C	O	N	D	A	R	Y	P	A	Y	E	R	K

1. A disease caused by a lack of vitamin c, characterized by weakness, bleeding and pain in joints and muscles, bleeding gums, and abnormal bone and tooth growth
2. A chemical produced by a gland or tissue that is released into the bloodstream
3. A white blood cell that makes antibodies to fight infections caused by foreign proteins
4. An open sore that occurs on the skin or on a mucous membrane because of the destruction of surface tissue
5. An abnormal passageway from one organ to another or from an organ to the body surface
6. A unique number a patient or a company may have to produce for billing purposes in order to receive healthcare from a provider.
7. Medical billing specialists utilize this unique codeset for identifying a healthcare provider's specialty field.
8. The thick, greasy substance that covers the skin of a newborn baby
9. A reduced flow of blood throughout the body, usually caused by severe bleeding or a weak heart
10. An enzyme that plays a role in increasing a low blood pressure
11. The insurance company that covers any remaining expenses after Medicare has paid for a patient's coverage.
12. A blood vessel that carries blood toward the heart
13. A vitamin important in many chemical processes in the body

A. B cell
B. Hormone
C. Shock
D. Fistula
E. Ulcer
F. Renin
G. Tax Identification Number
H. Vernix
I. Niacin
J. Scurvy
K. Vein
L. Medicare Secondary Payer
M. Taxonomy Code

R. Find the hidden words. The words have been placed horizontally, vertically, or diagonally. When you locate a word, draw an ellipse around it.

Y	W	D	E	N	D	X	S	M	S	U	A	X	X	D	S	O	S	Z	Q	E	F	M
V	I	T	T	W	S	C	Z	M	P	L	F	R	O	V	S	C	C	R	Z	O	F	E
P	K	Q	W	A	Y	G	M	K	P	D	E	M	B	U	L	L	U	T	G	F	P	N
O	G	F	P	S	G	O	X	V	H	Q	Q	A	I	F	Y	E	R	D	X	W	T	V
P	N	C	Z	E	M	B	R	Y	O	H	A	F	N	B	S	A	V	H	X	T	J	P
H	Q	J	E	A	D	U	J	J	Q	C	Z	N	E	D	U	R	Y	V	W	I	A	W
T	K	L	T	A	D	G	H	A	S	A	A	W	N	K	T	I	P	T	X	H	S	K
H	S	P	L	E	E	N	S	N	V	T	C	U	B	K	U	N	A	H	M	W	C	A
A	Z	U	W	C	S	E	Z	E	B	J	X	W	Q	G	R	G	T	O	H	Y	I	S
L	L	T	I	N	D	R	B	M	G	U	K	Z	C	F	E	H	H	R	E	C	T	I
M	B	H	E	D	G	N	V	I	Y	I	R	O	J	O	J	O	O	A	P	N	E	B
O	P	V	K	J	I	B	Z	A	S	I	Y	O	C	R	T	U	L	X	A	C	S	U
L	Z	B	W	P	M	C	R	F	P	V	A	W	P	I	N	S	O	R	T	W	G	J
O	J	H	V	S	Z	A	H	L	V	I	Y	T	G	P	O	E	G	A	I	T	K	N
G	M	Y	P	F	L	U	K	E	M	D	E	T	M	A	D	D	Y	S	C	Z	L	R
Y	V	I	J	U	Y	G	B	W	H	A	H	J	H	W	O	L	H	H	V	X	A	K

1. A condition in which the blood does not contain enough hemoglobin, the compound that carries oxygen from the lungs to other parts of the body
2. Excess fluid in the abdominal cavity, which leads to swelling
3. A surgical stitch that helps close an incision or wound so that it can heal properly
4. The specialty of physicians who are trained to examine surgical specimens and biopsies for diagnostic purposes.
5. A term used to describe something that is related to the liver
6. A term used to describe a child in the womb from fertilization to 8 weeks following fertilization
7. A parasitic flatworm that can infest humans
8. The chest
9. A disease caused by a lack of vitamin c, characterized by weakness, bleeding and pain in joints and muscles, bleeding gums, and abnormal bone and tooth growth
10. Facilities that review and correct medical claims as necessary before sending them to insurance companies for final processing.
11. the diagnosis and treatment, including surgery, of diseases and disorders of the eye, such as cataracts and glaucoma
12. An organ located in the upper left abdomen behind the ribs that removes and destroys old red blood cells and helps fight infection
13. An area of inflammation or a group of spots on the skin

A. Spleen
B. Hepatic
C. Embryo
D. Suture
E. Ascites
F. Scurvy
G. Fluke
H. Clearinghouse
I. Rash
J. Ophthalmology
K. Pathology
L. Anemia
M. Thorax

S. Find the hidden words. The words have been placed horizontally, vertically, or diagonally. When you locate a word, draw an ellipse around it.

C	O	I	N	S	U	R	A	N	C	E	H	T	X	D	Q	Z	N	Z	D	H	V	W
M	A	X	I	M	U	M	O	U	T	O	F	P	O	C	K	E	T	G	X	Y	F	T
V	E	L	P	Q	O	F	U	X	X	X	P	W	I	B	L	H	O	P	M	R	P	H
P	R	E	E	X	I	S	T	I	N	G	C	O	N	D	I	T	I	O	N	H	R	N
X	D	T	W	L	M	B	Y	Q	F	N	A	T	O	U	Q	E	S	J	T	B	O	P
K	H	Y	A	U	L	Y	J	I	T	C	N	X	Y	S	M	V	T	I	V	Y	V	G
J	I	I	R	M	H	X	N	X	K	U	I	O	F	I	X	M	W	U	R	A	I	C
P	S	H	T	U	M	K	M	W	P	B	E	J	Y	M	B	Y	C	I	B	Y	D	Q
M	P	O	L	R	T	A	R	T	A	R	M	Y	Z	A	U	Z	R	A	G	Q	E	A
C	A	H	T	M	J	Y	W	Y	V	L	H	L	T	G	B	V	H	Q	C	O	R	S
L	S	U	X	U	E	F	M	R	D	J	N	Q	N	I	E	P	V	N	I	W	U	P
E	M	R	S	R	J	E	A	U	A	H	Z	T	W	N	D	V	A	L	V	E	N	L
J	O	E	L	U	T	W	X	U	B	G	P	J	H	G	H	G	R	Q	G	T	Z	E
N	L	M	K	F	G	W	J	E	F	S	J	M	J	D	E	P	E	A	T	M	Y	E
Z	C	I	M	U	U	T	M	T	P	I	N	D	E	Z	X	E	G	O	X	M	T	N
O	J	A	W	C	A	D	P	R	E	C	E	R	T	I	F	I	C	A	T	I	O	N

1. The percentage of coverage that a patient is responsible for paying after an insurance company pays the portion agreed upon in a health plan.
2. A characteristic sound of blood flowing irregularly through the heart
3. The hard deposit formed on teeth when mineral salts in saliva combine with plaque
4. A contagious, harmless growth caused by a virus that occurs on the skin or a mucous membrane
5. The healthcare facility that administered healthcare to an individual. Physicians, clinics, and hospitals are all considered providers.
6. A process similar to preauthorization whereby patients must check with insurance companies to see if a desired healthcare treatment or service is deemed medically necessary
7. A medical condition a patient had before receiving coverage from an insurance company.
8. An involuntary muscle contraction
9. The technique of creating pictures of structures inside of the body using x-rays, ultrasound waves, or magnetic fields
10. An organ located in the upper left abdomen behind the ribs that removes and destroys old red blood cells and helps fight infection
11. A structure that allows fluid flow in only one direction
12. Abnormally high levels of waste products such as urea in the blood
13. The amount a patient is required to pay.

A. Provider
B. Tartar
C. Valve
D. Wart
E. Maximum Out of Pocket
F. Uremia
G. Co Insurance
H. Pre Certification
I. Murmur
J. Spleen
K. Spasm
L. Imaging
M. Pre existing Condition

T. Find the hidden words. The words have been placed horizontally, vertically, or diagonally. When you locate a word, draw an ellipse around it.

D	Q	N	Q	M	G	A	N	I	Y	K	L	C	X	K	Q	J	W	J	F	D	H	L
Y	M	W	Z	F	K	T	P	R	U	P	J	D	C	S	A	W	D	M	P	G	V	C
U	P	I	Y	A	Z	T	U	A	V	F	O	D	Q	G	V	C	P	I	S	R	N	N
H	N	Q	W	G	O	U	T	M	C	R	R	E	C	J	B	K	W	M	T	P	Y	S
D	U	R	A	B	L	E	M	E	D	I	C	A	L	E	Q	U	I	P	M	E	N	T
Z	P	N	X	N	P	J	Q	I	J	Z	V	X	T	E	N	D	O	N	D	L	H	O
R	E	L	A	T	I	V	E	V	A	L	U	E	A	M	O	U	N	T	N	B	B	O
L	J	D	H	C	S	J	E	B	M	T	L	P	V	Y	Q	P	W	T	E	T	R	L
Y	Z	A	J	O	B	A	B	M	W	U	V	H	S	G	Z	O	Y	U	U	J	V	B
K	M	S	R	C	U	H	G	J	W	B	A	V	U	U	J	L	T	D	R	E	J	U
I	B	T	R	C	N	K	H	Q	K	Y	B	M	U	N	V	Y	U	M	O	C	P	L
H	C	H	K	Y	I	S	P	N	Y	G	R	C	K	O	O	P	B	P	N	E	L	H
D	Q	M	C	X	O	V	G	I	E	X	B	O	Z	A	H	H	D	R	X	G	J	Q
L	E	A	M	A	N	Z	I	O	N	X	S	X	Q	J	F	A	B	S	C	E	S	S
Y	C	O	R	N	E	A	Z	J	L	W	B	N	S	L	K	G	R	U	C	L	W	E
J	U	U	V	Z	D	C	W	X	T	R	Z	J	Q	J	R	C	I	D	I	L	K	H

1. This refers to medical implements that can be reused such as stretchers, wheelchairs, canes, crutches, and bedpans.
2. A disorder marked by high levels of uric acid in the blood
3. Another term for a nerve cell
4. Four fused bones that form a triangular shape at the base of the spine (also known as the tailbone)
5. The median amount Medicare will repay a provider for certain services and treatments.
6. The outer, visible portion of the female genitals
7. An accumulation of pus in a body tissue, usually caused by a bacterial infection
8. The clear, dome-shaped front portion of the eye's outer covering
9. Another term for feces
10. A growth that occurs on mucous membranes such as those in the nose and intestine
11. A disorder characterized by inflamed airways and difficulty breathing
12. A hard, fluid-filled pad along the inside joint of the big toe
13. Strong connective tissue cords that attach muscle to bone or muscle to muscle

A. Cornea
B. Abscess
C. Bunion
D. Vulva
E. Coccyx
F. Durable Medical Equipment
G. Relative Value Amount
H. Gout
I. Asthma
J. Tendon
K. Neuron
L. Polyp
M. Stool

A. Find the hidden words. The words have been placed horizontally, vertically, or diagonally. When you locate a word, draw an ellipse around it.

N	C	G	L	I	V	C	O	D	E	S	B	W	A	T	S	K	T	W	D	I	W	U
L	Y	Q	B	X	L	Y	G	V	A	I	V	S	M	B	N	V	P	K	O	B	S	M
O	P	U	G	Q	G	M	N	H	L	C	O	C	C	Y	X	G	A	T	V	T	B	I
Q	R	H	F	N	T	A	H	H	L	Q	X	X	H	T	U	U	C	Z	K	B	H	R
V	R	T	I	A	A	P	R	S	O	F	T	P	T	G	U	X	U	N	Z	V	O	N
Z	Z	J	P	F	L	O	M	G	W	R	V	O	J	A	B	Z	W	P	L	E	S	K
P	O	L	E	D	L	A	Y	W	E	E	N	D	E	M	I	C	A	P	A	P	A	M
U	R	V	I	E	E	C	M	D	D	L	B	I	J	J	T	F	V	B	E	B	U	U
C	E	S	X	K	R	O	E	L	A	F	P	A	P	F	C	V	U	O	G	H	T	P
A	G	P	H	C	G	F	H	D	M	N	B	T	U	K	U	D	V	V	N	F	O	L
M	I	L	W	H	Y	H	E	T	O	X	W	R	N	G	Y	O	P	E	Y	N	P	A
A	X	I	U	R	X	W	T	W	U	M	J	Y	A	K	L	U	J	O	P	H	S	Q
G	K	N	Z	T	C	C	O	I	N	S	U	R	A	N	C	E	N	F	J	T	Y	U
X	P	T	N	F	F	V	Q	U	T	Y	T	O	P	G	E	N	E	L	D	K	U	E
U	T	M	K	T	U	T	I	L	I	Z	A	T	I	O	N	L	I	M	I	T	W	J
Y	E	X	P	L	A	N	A	T	I	O	N	O	F	B	E	N	E	F	I	T	S	H

1. Immunology
2. A device that is used to immobilize a part of the body
3. The percentage of coverage that a patient is responsible for paying after an insurance company pays the portion agreed upon in a health plan.
4. The examination of a body following death, possibly to determine the cause of death or for research
5. A document attached to a processed medical claim wherein the insurance company explains the services they will cover for a patient's healthcare treatments.
6. Four fused bones that form a triangular shape at the base of the spine (also known as the tailbone)
7. Describes a disease that is always present in a certain population of people
8. A codeset under ICD-9-CM used to organize healthcare services rendered for reasons other than illness or injury.
9. The sum an insurance company will reimburse to cover a healthcare service or procedure.
10. An area of buildup of fat deposits in an artery, causing narrowing of the artery and possibly heart disease
11. The limit per year for coverage under certain available healthcare services for Medicare enrollees.
12. The care and treatment of the foot and ankle
13. The basic unit of dna, which is responsible for passing genetic information

A. Allergy
B. Utilization Limit
C. Splint
D. V Codes
E. Explanation of Benefits
F. Plaque
G. Endemic
H. Autopsy
I. Co Insurance
J. Coccyx
K. Podiatry
L. Allowed Amount
M. Gene

B. Find the hidden words. The words have been placed horizontally, vertically, or diagonally. When you locate a word, draw an ellipse around it.

Y	O	N	H	V	G	M	N	C	V	H	Z	E	U	O	V	A	L	V	B	S	U	G
O	Y	I	U	S	Y	A	B	F	O	X	G	G	M	O	D	I	F	I	E	R	C	A
M	C	M	B	B	I	I	D	U	Q	Y	X	P	T	K	N	W	O	D	I	Y	I	L
N	M	T	P	P	R	E	A	U	T	H	O	R	I	Z	A	T	I	O	N	B	T	L
B	K	G	N	H	T	N	I	J	A	R	M	Y	L	D	R	V	U	J	H	Q	R	E
R	J	D	Y	D	D	P	Z	H	L	G	O	C	K	K	L	Q	V	F	B	E	W	R
R	E	L	A	T	I	V	E	V	A	L	U	E	A	M	O	U	N	T	X	R	K	G
N	F	V	Q	Y	G	U	D	J	S	X	A	O	R	T	A	S	T	E	N	T	K	Y
J	Q	J	S	J	S	G	G	K	J	T	H	K	E	N	C	O	N	G	U	L	L	O
P	Y	U	I	J	F	M	L	S	E	S	R	N	A	H	E	W	J	A	V	E	R	C
K	R	E	T	I	N	A	C	T	C	Z	E	L	O	G	T	S	R	S	O	W	Y	Y
L	Y	U	A	L	Y	A	O	O	G	I	A	U	Z	R	C	U	J	T	X	J	G	S
F	S	Q	U	B	O	L	D	M	M	G	C	P	M	U	W	V	T	R	B	C	M	T
E	K	K	U	W	Q	Q	I	A	A	N	J	T	W	W	J	L	I	I	E	H	Q	X
G	P	Y	S	Y	T	N	N	A	C	V	J	S	H	L	E	V	V	N	X	T	E	L
N	Y	D	M	F	S	D	G	I	O	Q	L	L	F	F	O	M	S	W	C	C	Q	Y

1. The main artery in the body, carrying oxygenated blood from the heart to other arteries in the body
2. The process of translating a physician's documentation about a patient's medical condition and health services rendered into medical codes that are then plugged into a claim for processing.
3. Additions to CPT codes that explain alterations and modifications to an otherwise routine treatment, exam, or service.
4. A negative reaction to a substance that in most people causes no reaction
5. A lump filled with either fluid or soft material, occurring in any organ or tissue
6. The median amount Medicare will repay a provider for certain services and treatments.
7. A device used to hold tissues in place, such as to support a skin graft
8. An electrocardiogram, which is a record of the electrical impulses that trigger the heartbeat
9. Some insurance plans require that a patient receive preauthorization from the insurance company prior to receiving certain medical services.
10. A hormone that stimulates the release of gastric acid in the stomach
11. A surgically formed opening on a body surface
12. A membrane lining the inside of the back of the eye that contains light-sensitive nerve cells that convert focused light into nerve impulses, making vision possible

A. Retina
B. Preauthorization
C. Gastrin
D. Aorta
E. Cyst
F. Stent
G. ECG
H. Coding
I. Stoma
J. Modifier
K. Relative Value Amount
L. Allergy

C. Find the hidden words. The words have been placed horizontally, vertically, or diagonally. When you locate a word, draw an ellipse around it.

R	A	R	B	P	O	L	E	Q	N	H	C	A	N	A	L	O	L	L	S	R	U	F
S	A	E	K	R	T	O	E	X	H	C	F	Q	I	N	D	B	R	C	V	O	G	D
T	L	V	Q	H	O	Y	S	A	J	X	Z	T	M	E	X	R	M	D	C	R	Y	K
A	M	E	C	T	L	M	F	O	H	K	F	W	J	U	Q	E	L	R	T	C	S	B
X	L	N	Y	N	A	V	P	A	H	J	S	S	R	R	Q	X	O	K	W	E	T	U
O	B	U	R	D	R	C	A	K	L	Q	C	E	A	O	P	C	I	M	A	S	B	R
N	J	E	G	A	Y	W	T	R	B	M	A	D	N	N	V	P	T	I	H	Z	U	S
O	Z	C	R	Q	N	C	H	Y	Q	B	P	N	C	U	L	T	U	R	E	W	R	A
M	A	O	R	H	G	J	O	G	R	X	I	V	P	F	D	V	D	H	B	Z	F	A
Y	O	D	O	V	O	W	L	V	S	Q	T	H	U	J	U	J	A	Q	D	T	F	M
C	A	E	A	A	L	U	O	W	S	D	A	P	S	Y	V	M	Y	C	V	Y	R	P
O	Q	W	X	B	O	M	G	R	T	Z	T	V	I	B	Z	A	S	L	H	H	S	M
D	Y	J	H	B	G	Y	Y	L	O	E	I	L	Y	W	B	I	H	P	U	I	R	F
E	T	U	F	R	Y	S	U	A	M	F	O	S	S	W	D	E	E	R	O	U	Q	W
P	K	O	R	L	T	Q	N	V	A	Y	N	M	S	H	Q	I	E	G	N	N	M	V
G	A	N	E	S	T	H	E	S	I	O	L	O	G	Y	O	H	T	V	G	S	I	H

1. A surgically formed opening on a body surface
2. Medical billing specialists utilize this unique codeset for identifying a healthcare provider's specialty field.
3. A three-digit code used on medical bills that explains the kind of facility in which a patient received treatment.
4. The artificial growth of cells, tissue, or microorganisms such as bacteria in a laboratory
5. A document that summarizes the services, treatments, payments, and charges that a patient received on a given day.
6. A thick, yellowish or greenish fluid that contains dead white blood cells, tissues, and bacteria; occurs at the site of a bacterial infection
7. A tunnel-like passage
8. Another term for a nerve cell
9. A fixed payment that a patient makes to a health insurance company or provider to recoup costs incurred from various healthcare services.
10. the administration of medications as a means to block pain or diminish consciousness for surgery, usually by injection or inhalation
11. A fluid-filled sac that cushions and reduces friction in certain parts of the body
12. the medical and surgical care for diseases of the ears, nose and throat (ENT)
13. The specialty of physicians who are trained to examine surgical specimens and biopsies for diagnostic purposes.

A. Pathology
B. Pus
C. Anesthesiology
D. Neuron
E. Revenue Code
F. Taxonomy Code
G. Canal
H. Bursa
I. Capitation
J. Stoma
K. Day Sheet
L. Culture
M. Otolaryngology

D. Find the hidden words. The words have been placed horizontally, vertically, or diagonally. When you locate a word, draw an ellipse around it.

U	F	M	O	Z	X	T	H	R	C	I	M	A	E	Z	B	S	A	L	F	U	X	D
A	I	V	Q	B	D	S	L	S	L	I	T	U	P	L	Y	S	J	X	B	P	L	E
Z	U	C	O	F	D	F	H	C	M	W	C	V	F	L	E	C	T	O	P	I	C	F
E	H	R	E	Y	Q	Q	B	R	L	K	P	E	I	U	H	B	S	P	I	N	E	H
T	I	R	W	I	A	N	M	X	P	F	L	A	S	I	W	W	M	Z	S	O	C	G
X	Q	V	O	X	C	Q	E	P	I	Y	F	U	S	T	O	K	P	W	D	T	F	U
F	E	E	F	O	R	S	E	R	V	I	C	E	U	P	G	J	L	E	T	V	P	T
X	I	P	B	S	Z	B	W	S	W	H	L	X	R	E	W	L	I	P	O	M	A	E
I	N	H	G	H	F	N	C	H	C	K	V	L	E	D	I	A	Q	G	J	J	E	R
H	N	B	G	A	V	A	G	E	H	A	G	F	G	I	T	X	V	O	I	L	F	U
W	E	O	U	T	O	F	N	E	T	W	O	R	K	A	X	S	Z	D	E	Z	F	S
S	T	H	V	A	F	G	G	R	A	F	L	M	Y	T	H	U	Q	V	B	H	Z	B
Y	W	U	F	O	M	N	C	K	G	L	D	R	D	R	F	T	J	Y	O	U	L	U
A	O	Y	P	R	S	R	K	B	J	E	O	B	W	I	R	U	D	C	A	L	M	V
H	R	D	W	T	A	F	X	N	H	H	O	I	B	C	A	R	P	M	Y	C	J	B
N	K	B	L	A	S	F	R	J	H	A	A	C	J	S	M	E	C	Z	E	Q	E	Y

1. A noncancerous tumor of fatty tissue
2. The care and treatment of infants, children, and adolescents
3. An artificial feeding technique in which liquids are passed into the stomach by way of a tube inserted through the nose
4. A groove or slit on the body or in an organ
5. A surgical stitch that helps close an incision or wound so that it can heal properly
6. The column of bones and cartilage running along the midline of the back that surrounds and protects the spinal cord and supports the head
7. This refers to a type of health insurance wherein the provider is paid for every service they perform.
8. This term refers to a provider's relationship with a health insurance company.
9. A structure consisting of the colored area of the eye and the middle layer of the eye that contains blood vessels
10. Occurring at an abnormal position or time
11. The hollow female reproductive organ in which a fertilized egg is implanted and a fetus develops
12. The main artery in the body, carrying oxygenated blood from the heart to other arteries in the body
13. Refers to providers outside of an established network of providers who contract with an insurance company to offer patients healthcare at a discounted rate.

A. Uterus
B. Gavage
C. Fee for Service
D. Ectopic
E. Aorta
F. Uvea
G. Fissure
H. Spine
I. Out of Network
J. Suture
K. In Network
L. Lipoma
M. Pediatrics

E. Find the hidden words. The words have been placed horizontally, vertically, or diagonally. When you locate a word, draw an ellipse around it.

J	V	E	C	U	V	V	N	A	G	E	E	A	R	K	Z	T	V	L	Q	J	V	P
N	B	R	U	X	I	S	M	H	E	E	W	Z	B	L	W	U	E	Z	F	H	J	Y
R	W	K	E	J	A	V	V	C	R	R	C	D	F	I	F	O	P	O	G	O	R	R
V	Q	R	Z	N	Z	V	I	K	W	E	R	F	P	U	E	P	G	E	M	S	O	E
R	L	B	M	U	W	B	E	N	E	F	I	C	I	A	R	Y	V	D	Q	P	G	C
O	L	Z	R	D	A	F	K	Q	J	L	F	M	L	G	A	X	N	L	D	I	Q	T
I	K	B	R	Z	J	O	E	F	R	E	D	S	R	E	C	H	F	F	X	C	R	U
D	K	V	O	C	J	E	A	V	M	X	X	J	K	Z	A	C	A	X	E	E	J	M
H	S	T	M	B	F	Y	G	N	V	H	Y	H	U	R	S	O	P	T	T	A	G	M
W	Y	H	U	J	T	R	I	I	S	S	Q	I	G	C	T	L	W	X	I	F	X	R
I	Q	P	W	W	M	A	C	U	L	A	J	P	T	W	R	I	F	T	C	Q	Z	U
K	I	L	A	Y	K	T	J	W	Q	O	U	A	E	A	W	C	Y	T	K	J	W	I
X	W	G	L	O	W	C	L	K	Q	W	Z	A	C	O	B	T	W	V	S	U	K	X
H	M	X	Z	T	Y	I	C	F	S	T	R	A	I	N	S	A	T	R	I	A	G	E
T	M	J	U	Q	X	O	B	I	O	N	U	W	J	T	B	M	A	I	E	B	N	V
C	J	L	X	C	I	U	J	F	X	W	G	Q	E	H	D	Y	H	T	B	J	U	S

1. The person who receives benefits and
2. An automatic, involuntary response of the nervous system to a stimulus
3. A hard plaster or fiberglass shell that molds to a body part such as an arm and holds it in place for proper healing
4. Small, eight- legged animals that can attach to humans and animals and feed on blood
5. A short tube located at the end of the large intestine, which connects the intestine to the anus
6. Muscle damage resulting from excessive stretching or forceful contraction
7. Density lipoprotein- a type of lipoprotein that is the major carrier of cholesterol in the blood, with high levels associated with narrowing of the arteries and heart disease
8. An unaware clenching or grinding of the teeth, usually during sleep
9. Law passed in 1996 with an aim to improve the scope of healthcare services and establish regulations for securing healthcare records from unwanted parties.
10. Waves of pain in the abdomen that increase in strength, disappear, and return
11. A system used to classify sick or injured people according to the severity of their conditions
12. The area of the retina that allows fine details to be observed at the center of vision
13. This refers to medical care and treatment for persons who are terminally ill.

A. Low
B. Macula
C. Colic
D. Triage
E. Ticks
F. Bruxism
G. Beneficiary
H. HIPAA
I. Hospice
J. Rectum
K. Strain
L. Cast
M. Reflex

F. Find the hidden words. The words have been placed horizontally, vertically, or diagonally. When you locate a word, draw an ellipse around it.

B	Q	R	A	W	V	B	A	R	T	E	R	Y	W	N	Z	C	F	Q	H	K	F	A
M	T	E	O	F	H	W	A	D	D	X	F	X	J	X	H	O	L	M	F	I	Q	K
H	D	S	C	L	Y	H	I	S	J	W	A	A	X	W	X	P	Y	U	O	A	N	D
M	O	P	V	A	M	X	Z	T	P	D	N	Q	R	U	D	A	Y	T	R	U	S	K
H	W	O	Q	X	Y	N	D	Y	D	D	A	J	Z	L	C	Y	H	Y	C	I	W	U
J	N	N	U	F	L	I	E	E	V	T	F	F	W	Y	C	C	F	K	E	S	W	G
N	C	S	I	W	J	T	Z	G	S	D	B	N	K	V	U	C	Y	L	P	Y	F	W
H	O	I	T	D	T	D	N	A	P	Y	E	N	R	O	L	L	E	E	S	X	G	B
G	D	B	W	F	R	O	C	C	R	I	M	N	L	L	M	C	A	T	G	P	U	K
B	I	L	V	D	R	H	F	W	A	O	M	K	P	X	M	N	E	C	Z	E	M	A
X	N	E	Z	H	W	V	V	T	I	R	U	M	X	N	T	K	F	T	J	N	N	D
M	G	P	F	G	D	E	Y	M	N	R	N	Q	Y	X	P	Y	Y	O	C	I	T	X
K	Y	A	Q	J	B	Q	U	U	L	M	J	S	A	B	T	Z	H	R	W	S	C	X
J	E	R	G	B	V	P	P	U	V	A	H	O	V	V	C	A	L	C	F	W	W	F
M	K	T	P	R	E	E	X	I	S	T	I	N	G	C	O	N	D	I	T	I	O	N
E	A	Y	F	E	X	X	V	W	Z	Q	X	G	Q	A	B	U	K	H	F	B	M	G

1. The external male reproductive organ, which passes urine and semen out of the body
2. A person covered by a health insurance plan.
3. The amount that must be paid to a provider before they receive any treatment or services.
4. Deoxyribonucleic acid; responsible for passing genetic information in nearly all organisms
5. A large blood vessel that carries blood from the heart to tissues and organs in the body
6. A form of phototherapy that combines the use of psoralens and ultraviolet light to treat skin disorders
7. The person who pays for a patient's medical expenses, also known as the guarantor.
8. Inflammation of the skin, usually causing itchiness and sometimes blisters and scaling
9. Occurs when an insurance company finds there is insufficient evidence on a claim to prove that a provider performed coded medical services and so they reduce or remove those codes.
10. A pus- filled abscess in the follicle of an eyelash
11. A medical condition a patient had before receiving coverage from an insurance company.
12. Instruments resembling tweezers that are used to handle objects or tissue during surgery
13. The tearing or stretching of the ligaments in a joint, characterized by pain, swelling, and an inability to move the joint

A. DNA
B. Downcoding
C. Stye
D. Responsible Party
E. Forceps
F. PUVA
G. Artery
H. Eczema
I. Sprain
J. Enrollee
K. Penis
L. Pre existing Condition
M. Co Pay

G. Find the hidden words. The words have been placed horizontally, vertically, or diagonally. When you locate a word, draw an ellipse around it.

Q	R	G	C	S	P	Y	F	E	T	U	S	O	D	L	G	O	I	T	E	R	L	J
R	T	J	A	N	O	D	E	Y	C	D	Y	T	M	L	O	F	Y	W	J	L	B	C
K	L	O	P	A	K	X	Y	K	O	X	F	I	U	X	H	W	U	R	E	A	F	A
L	W	Z	I	H	S	W	I	D	G	H	B	R	M	K	S	J	J	D	W	E	R	S
X	L	P	T	Y	U	V	Z	K	E	Y	Q	W	P	D	R	A	M	Z	K	E	J	T
O	D	L	A	K	T	D	V	G	Z	V	N	W	S	E	A	D	F	H	Z	X	F	F
L	T	E	T	L	D	D	X	E	Q	K	Y	A	K	F	K	Y	Z	N	Q	N	I	N
S	V	U	I	Y	P	Z	O	Q	C	S	P	R	A	I	N	L	W	A	M	S	T	N
B	E	R	O	S	Q	C	R	A	L	E	S	A	F	C	S	X	F	O	P	D	N	X
F	M	A	N	M	S	U	H	C	H	W	T	W	N	C	F	O	X	O	S	S	E	I
T	G	X	N	N	H	P	C	A	J	L	Z	M	F	G	J	N	T	X	F	Z	S	X
V	W	G	M	D	X	D	A	R	V	X	V	D	Y	P	Y	E	N	R	Z	G	S	N
H	X	A	W	Y	F	J	U	V	N	L	Y	M	P	H	I	W	K	A	H	A	E	S
Z	A	R	Q	B	R	C	I	U	O	O	K	N	A	R	I	P	I	M	H	Z	Y	Q
X	A	K	M	H	N	O	R	E	I	Z	A	G	W	R	V	I	T	Q	L	U	F	K
Z	I	F	C	L	Z	N	X	S	A	J	T	Q	R	E	V	U	F	X	K	B	O	A

1. Enlargement of the thyroid gland, which produces a swelling on the neck
2. A viral infection that causes inflammation of salivary glands
3. Abnormal crackling or bubbling sounds heard in the lungs during breathing
4. A hard plaster or fiberglass shell that molds to a body part such as an arm and holds it in place for proper healing
5. A fixed payment that a patient makes to a health insurance company or provider to recoup costs incurred from various healthcare services.
6. A measure of a person's physical strength, flexibility, and endurance
7. The tearing or stretching of the ligaments in a joint, characterized by pain, swelling, and an inability to move the joint
8. The abbreviation for diagnosis codes, also known as ICD-9 codes.
9. A small, rounded tissue mass
10. A waste product of the metabolism of proteins that is formed by the liver and secreted by the kidneys
11. The double- layered membrane that lines the lungs and chest cavity and allows for lung movement during breathing
12. A milky fluid containing white blood cells, proteins, and fats
13. The term used to refer to an unborn child from 8 weeks after fertilization to birth

A. Fetus
B. Mumps
C. Goiter
D. Sprain
E. Node
F. Fitness
G. Cast
H. Urea
I. Capitation
J. Lymph
K. Rales
L. Pleura
M. Dx

H. Find the hidden words. The words have been placed horizontally, vertically, or diagonally. When you locate a word, draw an ellipse around it.

K	M	X	M	E	D	I	C	A	L	T	R	A	N	S	C	R	I	P	T	I	O	N
M	D	N	I	N	V	B	S	P	K	E	C	L	C	R	Q	L	G	Z	L	W	C	B
E	E	Y	V	F	W	O	V	J	L	H	U	Q	N	M	K	K	K	N	A	O	B	A
G	Z	T	J	D	G	I	T	Q	H	A	N	J	W	I	Z	O	N	I	B	Y	X	G
Z	X	H	U	O	F	L	G	B	W	P	M	I	B	A	X	E	F	M	I	C	Q	B
S	D	G	H	G	Q	D	K	V	X	L	E	P	E	U	G	C	L	O	A	O	A	M
P	K	T	R	E	M	O	R	O	E	A	I	W	L	U	J	B	S	G	H	V	N	V
Q	A	C	O	I	T	U	S	N	X	Q	C	W	G	Z	F	H	T	T	W	F	Q	C
T	X	I	L	E	U	M	N	Q	P	U	D	T	S	C	I	Y	Y	U	S	Q	L	V
Y	H	J	H	K	L	L	B	Q	Y	E	Q	J	L	G	B	L	E	L	R	U	R	V
Q	D	S	R	G	J	C	X	X	P	D	J	F	U	D	E	I	L	N	Y	F	Q	C
H	V	W	R	Y	U	H	L	R	N	D	X	Y	V	S	R	F	P	C	Y	I	N	O
N	M	N	O	K	O	H	X	Z	X	T	O	B	I	S	E	R	U	M	I	W	A	D
H	O	C	L	E	A	N	C	L	A	I	M	U	M	F	B	A	M	H	Y	L	C	E
W	K	Z	N	O	N	P	A	R	T	I	C	I	P	A	T	I	O	N	X	C	U	S
J	J	C	O	G	A	N	S	P	K	I	X	N	J	J	P	V	J	N	B	H	K	N

1. An involuntary, rhythmic, shaking movement caused by alternating contraction and relaxation of muscles
2. The lowest section of the small intestine, which attaches to the large intestine
3. The clear, watery fluid that separates from clotted blood
4. The process of converting dictated or handwritten instructions, observations, and documentation into digital text formats.
5. A codeset under ICD-9-CM used to organize healthcare services rendered for reasons other than illness or injury.
6. This is when a provider refuses to accept Medicare payments as a sufficient amount for the services rendered to a patient.
7. The two pairs of skinfolds that protect the opening of the vagina
8. A pus- filled abscess in the follicle of an eyelash
9. Refers to a medical claim filed with a health insurance company that is free of errors and processed in a timely manner.
10. An inflamed, raised area of skin that is pus-filled
11. A constituent of plants that cannot be digested, which helps maintain healthy functioning of the bowels
12. Sexual intercourse
13. An area of buildup of fat deposits in an artery, causing narrowing of the artery and possibly heart disease

A. Serum
B. Boil
C. Coitus
D. Tremor
E. Non participation
F. V Codes
G. Ileum
H. Plaque
I. Medical Transcription
J. Labia
K. Fiber
L. Clean Claim
M. Stye

I. Find the hidden words. The words have been placed horizontally, vertically, or diagonally. When you locate a word, draw an ellipse around it.

C	C	P	W	P	U	C	M	T	Q	Y	O	Y	M	X	S	B	I	U	Y	N	M	P
D	K	L	B	L	T	H	P	Q	K	B	M	Z	W	A	L	Y	Q	E	T	P	C	R
S	Z	Z	L	E	X	C	R	C	B	S	M	A	N	I	A	P	D	U	X	X	Y	S
D	U	B	V	U	X	O	C	G	W	C	Z	Q	X	H	R	A	Q	F	Y	K	Y	L
K	M	Q	V	R	V	R	S	A	L	I	N	E	P	M	O	S	S	Y	R	B	Z	C
S	M	J	R	A	A	N	U	U	L	C	E	R	E	O	L	S	V	E	N	O	M	C
X	M	G	U	V	L	K	B	X	W	N	Y	N	I	R	E	G	F	K	O	O	Y	K
X	R	V	O	E	V	H	O	D	F	K	Z	I	P	D	O	V	R	E	Q	A	V	O
A	P	K	V	F	E	L	O	T	A	X	E	M	P	P	Z	G	F	U	J	S	I	N
N	P	R	E	V	E	N	T	I	V	E	M	E	D	I	C	I	N	E	A	C	O	A
R	J	T	J	Y	Y	P	J	Q	F	E	J	B	D	P	L	K	C	D	C	O	R	Z
W	K	Z	V	Q	C	F	M	B	K	T	E	T	E	Z	Q	Z	F	X	F	Y	B	T
C	V	S	G	D	W	D	K	W	Z	M	R	N	J	J	D	H	M	D	D	E	I	T
Q	X	J	K	L	T	D	X	E	I	A	D	H	D	C	K	Z	J	J	Q	N	T	T
S	B	R	E	L	A	T	I	V	E	V	A	L	U	E	A	M	O	U	N	T	R	Q
H	W	Y	L	C	V	P	I	F	V	X	S	L	K	H	Y	V	D	R	K	B	G	A

1. The double- layered membrane that lines the lungs and chest cavity and allows for lung movement during breathing
2. An open sore that occurs on the skin or on a mucous membrane because of the destruction of surface tissue
3. The median amount Medicare will repay a provider for certain services and treatments.
4. The socket in the skull that contains the eyeball, along with its blood vessels, nerves, and muscles
5. A thickened callus on the foot that is caused by an improperly fitting shoe
6. The specialty that focuses on the health of individuals in order to protect, promote and maintain health and prevent disease, disability and premature death
7. A surgical technique in which the flow of blood or another body fluid is redirected around a blockage
8. A salt solution or any substance that contains salt
9. A structure that allows fluid flow in only one direction
10. A mental disorder characterized by extreme excitement, happiness, overactivity, and agitation
11. A poisonous substance produced by certain animals

A. Pleura
B. Valve
C. Bypass
D. Orbit
E. Venom
F. Preventive Medicine
G. Mania
H. Ulcer
I. Corn
J. Relative Value Amount
K. Saline

J. Find the hidden words. The words have been placed horizontally, vertically, or diagonally. When you locate a word, draw an ellipse around it.

X	M	U	U	N	F	X	F	H	T	V	M	G	Z	S	G	F	O	Z	X	G	N	H
X	Y	J	P	Y	U	N	T	I	M	E	L	Y	S	U	B	M	I	S	S	I	O	N
O	K	H	O	A	V	A	Z	H	A	B	C	I	P	P	Z	Q	Y	B	Z	C	W	M
W	C	I	T	K	F	W	V	E	Q	P	A	L	A	T	E	Y	Q	X	M	G	L	L
Y	T	Z	E	M	W	P	Q	N	E	U	R	O	L	O	G	Y	X	H	H	A	I	Q
V	S	X	K	M	S	A	N	U	S	B	Q	A	S	T	H	M	A	U	K	F	X	M
J	Z	R	N	K	M	P	A	I	X	H	K	G	I	T	D	M	X	P	U	V	A	D
Y	Z	B	U	T	J	I	Z	O	Z	O	K	F	N	R	G	U	X	S	O	S	Q	N
U	P	A	G	Y	Y	D	W	V	E	K	C	L	P	G	B	R	L	C	P	T	F	R
J	J	I	W	V	O	L	G	C	N	S	G	D	A	K	Q	P	D	R	K	A	O	U
L	F	S	T	O	M	A	C	S	R	O	M	Y	T	Y	P	H	S	U	O	I	H	V
M	Y	D	L	H	E	K	M	I	O	T	I	C	I	K	M	W	K	B	U	D	E	Y
B	Q	Y	H	L	B	Y	U	M	L	G	Q	T	E	K	X	P	U	B	V	S	T	K
L	R	L	M	R	C	W	D	K	L	Y	I	I	N	P	K	N	L	I	W	I	R	G
X	F	W	S	L	X	V	N	U	E	N	V	Q	T	E	A	S	L	N	T	H	Q	D
H	C	E	R	V	I	X	E	P	E	X	N	V	E	X	A	J	W	G	A	G	E	L

1. The opening through which feces are passed from the body
2. A surgically formed opening on a body surface
3. A process by which insurance claims are checked for errors before being sent to an insurance company for final processing.
4. the diagnosis and medical treatment of the nervous system and brain, including conditions such as strokes and seizures
5. Occurs when a person has a stay at a healthcare facility for more than 24 hours.
6. A drug that causes the pupil to constrict
7. A measure of the acidic or basic character of a substance
8. The bones that form the framework of the head and enclose and protect the brain and other sensory organs
9. A disorder characterized by inflamed airways and difficulty breathing
10. A person covered by a health insurance plan.
11. The roof of the mouth
12. Claims have a specific timeframe in which they can be sent off to an insurance company for processing.
13. A small, round organ making up the neck of the uterus and separating it from the vagina

A. Palate
B. Stoma
C. Enrollee
D. Untimely Submission
E. Anus
F. Miotic
G. Skull
H. Asthma
I. Neurology
J. Scrubbing
K. Inpatient
L. pH
M. Cervix

K. Find the hidden words. The words have been placed horizontally, vertically, or diagonally. When you locate a word, draw an ellipse around it.

W	E	O	Z	A	O	V	P	B	Q	P	H	E	M	I	W	R	G	G	E	K	B	I
I	J	C	Y	S	T	W	O	O	C	Y	T	E	A	H	Z	U	E	S	P	A	S	M
Y	M	O	M	S	D	O	F	I	P	P	L	P	N	N	H	Y	N	Z	P	E	R	P
H	E	M	A	T	O	L	O	G	Y	T	B	U	I	K	O	W	E	T	C	S	P	B
K	D	D	A	V	M	E	I	M	Y	Q	I	P	A	Z	L	U	C	E	A	K	I	H
J	Q	M	I	T	M	S	H	P	R	A	O	F	U	X	A	J	O	R	F	J	D	S
Y	S	N	L	V	F	R	C	M	V	Y	D	T	N	V	U	U	R	T	K	F	K	P
X	V	K	N	C	E	A	C	U	T	E	I	P	B	Q	L	S	N	I	T	P	P	L
G	L	X	M	P	U	Y	V	H	Q	Q	N	A	U	X	J	W	E	A	W	F	L	E
M	V	Y	H	O	S	K	Q	I	V	E	E	T	N	Z	I	X	A	R	F	R	L	E
I	A	G	I	N	G	X	I	E	P	G	P	Q	D	F	U	N	F	Y	U	S	E	N
U	G	G	H	T	Q	Y	W	E	B	Z	M	D	L	Q	N	Q	H	C	C	R	S	R
O	Y	X	G	W	P	J	R	J	Y	W	K	N	I	C	K	N	S	L	B	D	I	P
T	L	T	G	F	D	D	Z	C	O	M	K	N	N	D	E	W	I	A	Z	K	O	E
H	G	N	G	E	O	Y	A	G	A	X	F	Z	G	C	Y	D	F	I	R	B	N	T
M	J	P	U	L	M	X	K	Y	N	E	S	Q	Y	I	N	X	M	M	B	Q	E	C

1. An egg cell that has not developed completely
2. An abnormality of structure or function in the body
3. An element for the formation of thyroid hormones
4. A lump filled with either fluid or soft material, occurring in any organ or tissue
5. A formal medical billing term that refers to insurance claims that haven't been paid or balances owed by patients overdue by more than 30 days.
6. An organ located in the upper left abdomen behind the ribs that removes and destroys old red blood cells and helps fight infection
7. An involuntary muscle contraction
8. Describes a condition or illness that begins suddenly and is usually short- lasting
9. A claim filed by a provider after they have filed claims for primary and secondary health insurance coverage on behalf of a patient.
10. Refers to the fraudulent practice of ascribing more than one code to a service or procedure on a superbill or claim form when only one is necessary.
11. A mental disorder characterized by extreme excitement, happiness, overactivity, and agitation
12. The clear, dome-shaped front portion of the eye's outer covering
13. Oncology

A. Lesion
B. Unbundling
C. Mania
D. Cornea
E. Spleen
F. Hematology
G. Aging
H. Cyst
I. Acute
J. Iodine
K. Oocyte
L. Tertiary Claim
M. Spasm

L. Find the hidden words. The words have been placed horizontally, vertically, or diagonally. When you locate a word, draw an ellipse around it.

D	S	B	Q	G	T	R	I	C	A	R	E	L	L	F	B	Q	R	X	R	S	X	Q
O	S	U	M	E	D	I	C	A	L	T	R	A	N	S	C	R	I	P	T	I	O	N
N	S	R	O	B	S	V	G	U	A	R	A	N	T	O	R	F	P	A	T	K	F	S
U	P	L	O	J	P	R	E	V	E	N	T	I	V	E	M	E	D	I	C	I	N	E
T	R	N	E	F	B	L	F	W	W	N	U	Z	G	L	W	E	S	I	Z	Q	B	Z
H	G	L	R	P	L	A	S	T	I	C	K	R	U	W	Y	B	M	D	J	F	D	O
O	P	R	F	J	O	F	V	I	M	K	Q	U	I	O	A	Z	G	M	X	H	R	H
L	S	N	Q	T	P	K	A	Y	O	L	I	V	W	F	T	P	D	R	T	H	W	E
E	X	B	B	E	T	P	J	F	D	V	Y	U	A	M	Y	X	O	M	A	F	B	O
V	W	B	A	D	I	L	Y	E	I	X	X	B	U	Y	D	V	K	W	P	S	Q	L
N	J	R	L	E	C	B	K	F	F	E	Z	Q	I	Q	U	Q	X	T	B	R	I	J
R	G	A	Z	M	H	R	F	K	I	K	C	F	H	P	P	B	L	F	Q	Y	A	S
Z	X	G	T	A	E	D	N	Y	E	R	V	X	K	G	U	T	Y	P	H	U	S	G
J	R	E	J	F	V	E	M	E	R	G	E	N	C	Y	M	E	D	I	C	I	N	E
U	X	K	A	A	E	P	L	O	L	S	H	Q	R	J	T	G	C	O	S	M	T	H
T	H	I	R	D	P	A	R	T	Y	A	D	M	I	N	I	S	T	R	A	T	O	R

1. Abnormal buildup of fluid in the body, which may cause visible swelling
2. The federal health insurance program for active and retired service members, their families, and the survivors of service members.
3. The party paying for an insurance plan who is not the patient. Parents, for example, would be the guarantors for their children's health insurance.
4. Pertaining to the eyes
5. The repair, restoration or improvement of conditions or injuries to the skin and external features resulting from disease, injury or birth defects
6. This term refers to the discrepancy between the limits of healthcare insurance coverage and the Medicare Part D coverage limits for prescription drugs.
7. The name for the organization or individual that manages healthcare group benefits, claims, and administrative duties on behalf of a group plan or a company with a group plan.
8. Additions to CPT codes that explain alterations and modifications to an otherwise routine treatment, exam, or service.
9. The process of converting dictated or handwritten instructions, observations, and documentation into digital text formats.
10. A group of diseases caused by the microorganism rickettsia, spread by the bites of fleas, mites, or ticks
11. A noncancerous tumor made of mucous material and fibrous connective tissue
12. the specialty that includes treatment of any symptom, illness or injury requiring urgent evaluation and
13. The specialty that focuses on the health of individuals in order to protect, promote and maintain health and prevent disease, disability and premature death

A. Preventive Medicine
B. Typhus
C. Optic
D. Donut Hole
E. Guarantor
F. Emergency Medicine
G. Third Party Administrator
H. Edema
I. Modifier
J. TRICARE
K. Medical Transcription
L. Myxoma
M. Plastic

M. Find the hidden words. The words have been placed horizontally, vertically, or diagonally. When you locate a word, draw an ellipse around it.

I	S	K	I	L	L	E	D	N	U	R	S	I	N	G	F	A	C	I	L	I	T	Y
X	I	V	V	C	N	L	P	V	X	F	Z	W	T	D	Y	X	B	I	M	D	J	F
D	Q	C	W	P	L	B	V	N	J	B	Q	C	C	R	J	U	U	M	J	A	Z	D
B	R	E	S	P	O	N	S	I	B	L	E	P	A	R	T	Y	L	A	L	T	M	J
O	X	M	Z	P	U	Z	P	X	C	U	S	S	Y	M	C	J	I	G	U	I	N	D
O	J	T	R	L	P	D	D	C	K	G	C	R	W	Q	N	S	M	I	Y	C	F	S
S	J	L	T	Z	H	Z	Q	V	W	E	Y	P	I	D	F	I	I	N	A	D	V	N
T	A	Q	W	N	N	A	D	W	B	R	L	T	D	H	P	P	A	G	E	S	Q	T
E	N	O	T	O	T	H	E	R	W	I	S	E	S	P	E	C	I	F	I	E	D	J
R	M	Y	I	G	E	U	T	N	Q	A	I	M	C	H	O	L	E	R	A	P	D	P
C	A	P	I	T	A	T	I	O	N	T	E	C	N	X	B	I	F	O	C	A	L	G
Y	E	D	P	K	C	U	I	T	O	R	B	B	E	N	E	F	I	C	I	A	R	Y
P	K	J	L	A	C	I	P	J	S	I	H	Q	F	S	Y	E	Z	R	K	N	Q	U
J	V	F	J	I	X	D	J	M	Z	C	Z	P	S	C	F	S	O	R	N	A	B	T
X	O	N	R	O	Y	W	L	Y	V	S	Q	J	B	L	V	A	O	G	R	T	K	L
A	G	I	R	P	N	O	N	P	A	R	T	I	C	I	P	A	T	I	O	N	Z	W

1. the treatment of diseases and internal disorders of the elderly
2. A fixed payment that a patient makes to a health insurance company or provider to recoup costs incurred from various healthcare services.
3. A bacterial infection of the small intestine that causes severe watery diarrhea, dehydration, and possibly death
4. The person who pays for a patient's medical expenses, also known as the guarantor.
5. This is when a provider refuses to accept Medicare payments as a sufficient amount for the services rendered to a patient.
6. This term is used in ICD-9 codes to describe conditions with unspecified diagnoses.
7. Ribonucleic acid, which helps to decode and process the information contained in dna
8. The person who receives benefits and
9. The technique of creating pictures of structures inside of the body using x-rays, ultrasound waves, or magnetic fields
10. A lens that corrects both near and distant vision by having two parts with different focusing strengths
11. These are facilities for the severely ill or elderly that provide specialized long-term care for recovering patients.
12. An additional dose of a vaccine taken after the first dose to maintain or renew the first one
13. A disorder in which a person eats large amounts of food then forces vomiting or uses laxatives to prevent weight gain (called binging and purging)

A. Beneficiary
B. Bulimia
C. Capitation
D. Booster
E. Not Otherwise Specified
F. Cholera
G. Geriatrics
H. Responsible Party
I. Imaging
J. Bifocal
K. RNA
L. Skilled Nursing Facility
M. Non participation

N. Find the hidden words. The words have been placed horizontally, vertically, or diagonally. When you locate a word, draw an ellipse around it.

Y	H	D	I	T	S	G	W	D	Q	L	I	M	M	F	N	V	Q	Y	E	X	B	R
B	O	W	E	L	L	X	I	J	L	N	L	G	J	D	X	C	I	W	P	A	O	N
A	H	S	O	D	K	P	F	G	Y	G	I	M	K	O	R	O	T	L	C	U	G	V
O	V	U	M	F	A	J	H	S	Q	U	U	T	D	N	C	C	Q	W	F	Z	I	P
Q	M	J	Y	H	V	S	B	L	F	A	M	V	R	U	U	H	D	W	U	U	T	S
I	A	X	K	W	N	P	V	C	Q	B	B	N	C	T	L	L	C	C	Z	S	W	Z
A	N	Y	C	H	A	R	I	T	Y	C	A	R	E	H	T	E	Y	C	R	U	D	Q
G	A	R	T	E	R	Y	V	B	M	H	A	O	S	O	U	A	B	N	K	R	Z	P
K	J	D	N	T	P	B	W	B	Y	T	R	U	B	L	R	Z	I	E	T	M	F	V
U	Z	P	F	B	N	K	Y	F	L	I	A	X	O	E	E	P	Y	E	A	N	O	K
D	U	R	A	B	L	E	M	E	D	I	C	A	L	E	Q	U	I	P	M	E	N	T
U	D	S	P	F	N	T	S	I	R	E	U	T	P	J	O	C	H	S	C	Q	Y	V
M	K	R	X	N	J	K	Z	S	Z	Q	L	A	W	W	Q	Y	V	A	Q	G	X	U
E	G	E	Y	F	K	W	I	L	X	L	Y	R	I	Y	I	S	N	I	A	C	I	N
Z	J	H	I	Z	E	D	H	P	N	R	R	W	C	A	S	T	Y	R	F	L	S	P
E	A	C	J	N	S	Z	B	B	U	N	I	O	N	E	O	R	N	A	G	I	N	G

1. A hard, fluid-filled pad along the inside joint of the big toe
2. This refers to medical implements that can be reused such as stretchers, wheelchairs, canes, crutches, and bedpans.
3. A formal medical billing term that refers to insurance claims that haven't been paid or balances owed by patients overdue by more than 30 days.
4. A large blood vessel that carries blood from the heart to tissues and organs in the body
5. The artificial growth of cells, tissue, or microorganisms such as bacteria in a laboratory
6. Another term for an egg cell
7. One of the two bones that form the hip on either side of the body
8. This term refers to the discrepancy between the limits of healthcare insurance coverage and the Medicare Part D coverage limits for prescription drugs.
9. A coiled organ in the inner ear that plays a large role in hearing by picking up sound vibrations and transmitting them as electrical signals
10. A lump filled with either fluid or soft material, occurring in any organ or tissue
11. This type of care is administered at reduced or zero cost to patients who cannot afford healthcare.
12. A vitamin important in many chemical processes in the body
13. Intestine

A. Bunion
B. Bowel
C. Niacin
D. Aging
E. Charity Care
F. Culture
G. Ovum
H. Artery
I. Cochlea
J. Durable Medical Equipment
K. Ilium
L. Donut Hole
M. Cyst

O. Find the hidden words. The words have been placed horizontally, vertically, or diagonally. When you locate a word, draw an ellipse around it.

A	H	Y	O	V	Z	D	W	I	S	S	F	L	J	X	T	E	M	B	R	Y	O	A
Z	C	N	P	J	F	H	G	P	Q	K	S	H	N	I	D	Z	J	B	S	U	K	W
F	H	W	C	R	O	U	P	H	M	I	H	X	Y	S	E	V	G	B	F	L	E	X
R	C	Q	H	G	I	T	O	U	J	O	U	F	C	T	H	F	Z	P	C	W	F	T
C	T	Z	I	R	M	P	B	M	D	R	N	V	M	R	C	O	L	I	C	J	Q	D
C	Q	X	O	H	M	C	T	R	V	W	T	P	G	O	L	C	O	Y	D	P	I	R
Z	O	W	E	M	I	F	W	J	Q	Y	O	W	N	K	M	Z	Q	M	Q	Q	G	Q
V	B	I	F	O	C	A	L	P	Z	V	B	B	D	E	X	I	U	H	M	D	B	A
S	E	C	O	N	D	A	R	Y	I	N	S	U	R	A	N	C	E	C	L	A	I	M
K	S	T	O	O	L	U	D	W	W	I	F	Y	B	J	X	P	P	H	Q	Y	S	L
I	T	H	E	M	E	D	I	C	A	L	N	E	C	E	S	S	I	T	Y	R	G	E
T	M	H	D	G	K	K	K	Z	G	S	O	M	T	J	I	Q	Q	X	L	D	B	L
N	P	S	V	P	A	U	I	S	F	C	D	X	S	C	V	X	V	U	Z	N	O	E
Q	B	Y	M	Y	B	A	D	Q	H	F	E	D	S	G	W	P	H	R	J	P	W	C
G	A	P	P	B	H	M	S	V	D	M	Q	G	X	N	U	J	R	Z	U	F	E	B
Y	W	T	A	P	R	E	A	U	T	H	O	R	I	Z	A	T	I	O	N	W	L	Z

1. Waves of pain in the abdomen that increase in strength, disappear, and return
2. A lens that corrects both near and distant vision by having two parts with different focusing strengths
3. Another term for feces
4. A term used to describe a child in the womb from fertilization to 8 weeks following fertilization
5. An artificially constructed or an abnormal passage connecting two usually separate structures in the body
6. Damage to part of the brain because of a lack of blood supply or the rupturing of a blood vessel
7. Intestine
8. A small, rounded tissue mass
9. The claim filed with the secondary insurance company after the primary insurance company pays for their portion of healthcare costs.
10. Refers to healthcare services or treatments that a patient requires to treat a serious medical condition or illness.
11. Some insurance plans require that a patient receive preauthorization from the insurance company prior to receiving certain medical services.
12. A usually mild and temporary condition common in children in which the walls of the airways become inflamed and narrow, resulting in wheezing and coughing

A. Medical Necessity
B. Node
C. Stool
D. Croup
E. Shunt
F. Embryo
G. Bifocal
H. Colic
I. Bowel
J. Preauthorization
K. Secondary Insurance Claim
L. Stroke

P. Find the hidden words. The words have been placed horizontally, vertically, or diagonally. When you locate a word, draw an ellipse around it.

I	N	C	Q	X	C	J	B	I	X	X	T	N	K	V	D	T	N	L	I	J	U	Y
A	V	I	R	A	L	J	V	X	E	B	S	C	A	N	C	E	R	V	A	L	N	K
H	A	W	S	E	O	M	M	M	T	G	G	U	G	U	D	G	P	N	Q	N	C	P
C	G	B	A	M	A	N	I	A	E	F	A	P	B	W	H	A	A	N	D	X	O	U
G	P	U	S	W	I	M	G	D	P	D	X	G	P	P	L	X	X	W	S	X	M	P
R	U	A	T	I	M	V	A	S	C	U	L	A	R	S	U	R	G	E	R	Y	A	W
K	S	X	H	Y	G	T	S	R	F	M	I	T	T	E	C	V	C	M	B	H	T	Z
M	K	J	M	C	E	T	Y	P	E	O	F	S	E	R	V	I	C	E	V	F	I	C
G	L	K	A	M	B	J	E	I	J	F	P	K	C	A	A	C	E	E	R	P	C	M
E	Y	B	S	X	Y	M	V	E	N	O	M	O	D	T	P	P	X	M	X	J	C	H
I	S	B	M	Y	E	S	C	E	O	J	I	F	Y	R	L	M	F	D	V	Y	H	K
R	O	D	X	Q	E	T	H	D	N	T	A	W	V	O	A	Y	O	P	O	A	S	G
Z	O	I	O	E	J	F	C	S	I	C	L	U	X	P	S	R	E	X	P	H	M	Z
Y	U	A	B	Q	H	I	C	O	Q	N	G	X	B	H	I	K	C	G	O	T	E	G
Y	Q	P	U	L	H	G	Z	E	U	R	A	G	A	Y	A	H	E	N	G	Y	A	W
A	C	O	P	L	A	C	E	O	F	S	E	R	V	I	C	E	C	O	D	E	R	C

1. A two-digit code used on claims to explain what type of provider performed healthcare services on a patient.
2. A sample of cells spread across a glass slide to be examined through a microscope
3. A group of diseases in which cells grow unrestrained in an organ or tissue in the body
4. The diagnosis and treatment of circulatory problems of the extremities, especially the legs
5. A thick, yellowish or greenish fluid that contains dead white blood cells, tissues, and bacteria; occurs at the site of a bacterial infection
6. A condition in which the area of the brain involved in maintaining consciousness is somehow affected, resulting in a state of unconsciousness in which the patient does not respond to stimulation
7. A poisonous substance produced by certain animals
8. A mental disorder characterized by extreme excitement, happiness, overactivity, and agitation
9. A field on a claim for describing what kind of healthcare services or procedures a provider administered.
10. The complete or partial failure of any organ or tissue to grow
11. A disorder characterized by inflamed airways and difficulty breathing
12. A term describing something related to or caused by a virus
13. The shrinkage or near disappearance of a tissue or organ

A. Place of Service Code
B. Type of Service
C. Vascular Surgery
D. Venom
E. Atrophy
F. Smear
G. Pus
H. Mania
I. Coma
J. Viral
K. Aplasia
L. Asthma
M. Cancer

Q. Find the hidden words. The words have been placed horizontally, vertically, or diagonally. When you locate a word, draw an ellipse around it.

V	E	I	N	U	V	N	T	M	O	X	J	W	A	A	H	F	G	Q	I	B	J	Y
U	Z	N	Z	W	T	F	T	A	X	O	N	O	M	Y	C	O	D	E	P	Z	Q	W
F	W	C	N	Z	P	U	M	M	Q	W	I	E	F	A	Z	Z	H	Q	Q	V	R	E
U	D	H	W	R	Z	G	Y	X	S	A	U	E	F	S	G	A	O	O	X	H	X	R
J	T	W	U	F	H	J	Z	A	O	V	U	L	C	E	R	S	I	J	R	T	C	N
F	R	Z	S	H	O	C	K	P	E	E	K	V	U	H	A	P	B	H	U	W	X	M
Y	C	U	F	A	Q	O	T	Z	G	R	M	W	I	O	G	L	A	R	Q	X	C	E
I	A	Z	F	I	S	T	U	L	A	N	Y	H	T	Y	S	N	I	A	C	I	N	U
T	A	X	I	D	E	N	T	I	F	I	C	A	T	I	O	N	N	U	M	B	E	R
V	H	L	X	T	R	I	I	E	B	X	A	K	W	E	E	J	X	Z	L	I	Q	G
C	O	G	Z	K	T	T	U	F	C	C	J	V	U	G	M	Q	L	K	V	P	D	S
N	R	P	N	F	A	E	Q	C	E	Y	V	K	H	M	R	P	M	N	Z	X	N	C
B	M	R	E	N	I	N	R	P	L	B	X	S	C	U	R	V	Y	S	T	L	P	Q
T	O	N	O	P	Q	L	E	T	U	P	D	D	E	O	K	N	U	U	B	Z	W	V
S	N	P	Q	L	Y	X	E	C	L	X	Q	I	F	R	T	Y	C	Y	A	J	G	H
M	E	D	I	C	A	R	E	S	E	C	O	N	D	A	R	Y	P	A	Y	E	R	K

1. A disease caused by a lack of vitamin c, characterized by weakness, bleeding and pain in joints and muscles, bleeding gums, and abnormal bone and tooth growth
2. A chemical produced by a gland or tissue that is released into the bloodstream
3. A white blood cell that makes antibodies to fight infections caused by foreign proteins
4. An open sore that occurs on the skin or on a mucous membrane because of the destruction of surface tissue
5. An abnormal passageway from one organ to another or from an organ to the body surface
6. A unique number a patient or a company may have to produce for billing purposes in order to receive healthcare from a provider.
7. Medical billing specialists utilize this unique codeset for identifying a healthcare provider's specialty field.
8. The thick, greasy substance that covers the skin of a newborn baby
9. A reduced flow of blood throughout the body, usually caused by severe bleeding or a weak heart
10. An enzyme that plays a role in increasing a low blood pressure
11. The insurance company that covers any remaining expenses after Medicare has paid for a patient's coverage.
12. A blood vessel that carries blood toward the heart
13. A vitamin important in many chemical processes in the body

A. B cell
B. Hormone
C. Shock
D. Fistula
E. Ulcer
F. Renin
G. Tax Identification Number
H. Vernix
I. Niacin
J. Scurvy
K. Vein
L. Medicare Secondary Payer
M. Taxonomy Code

R. Find the hidden words. The words have been placed horizontally, vertically, or diagonally. When you locate a word, draw an ellipse around it.

Y	W	D	E	N	D	X	S	M	S	U	A	X	X	D	S	O	S	Z	Q	E	F	M
V	I	T	T	W	S	C	Z	M	P	L	F	R	O	V	S	C	C	R	Z	O	F	E
P	K	Q	W	A	Y	G	M	K	P	D	E	M	B	U	L	L	U	T	G	F	P	N
O	G	F	P	S	G	O	X	V	H	Q	Q	A	I	F	Y	E	R	D	X	W	T	V
P	N	C	Z	E	M	B	R	Y	O	H	A	F	N	B	S	A	V	H	X	T	J	P
H	Q	J	E	A	D	U	J	J	Q	C	Z	N	E	D	U	R	Y	V	W	I	A	W
T	K	L	T	A	D	G	H	A	S	A	A	W	N	K	T	I	P	T	X	H	S	K
H	S	P	L	E	E	N	S	N	V	T	C	U	B	K	U	N	A	H	M	W	C	A
A	Z	U	W	C	S	E	Z	E	B	J	X	W	Q	G	R	G	T	O	H	Y	I	S
L	L	T	I	N	D	R	B	M	G	U	K	Z	C	F	E	H	H	R	E	C	T	I
M	B	H	E	D	G	N	V	I	Y	I	R	O	J	O	J	O	O	A	P	N	E	B
O	P	V	K	J	I	B	Z	A	S	I	Y	O	C	R	T	U	L	X	A	C	S	U
L	Z	B	W	P	M	C	R	F	P	V	A	W	P	I	N	S	O	R	T	W	G	J
O	J	H	V	S	Z	A	H	L	V	I	Y	T	G	P	O	E	G	A	I	T	K	N
G	M	Y	P	F	L	U	K	E	M	D	E	T	M	A	D	D	Y	S	C	Z	L	R
Y	V	I	J	U	Y	G	B	W	H	A	H	J	H	W	O	L	H	H	V	X	A	K

1. A condition in which the blood does not contain enough hemoglobin, the compound that carries oxygen from the lungs to other parts of the body
2. Excess fluid in the abdominal cavity, which leads to swelling
3. A surgical stitch that helps close an incision or wound so that it can heal properly
4. The specialty of physicians who are trained to examine surgical specimens and biopsies for diagnostic purposes.
5. A term used to describe something that is related to the liver
6. A term used to describe a child in the womb from fertilization to 8 weeks following fertilization
7. A parasitic flatworm that can infest humans
8. The chest
9. A disease caused by a lack of vitamin c, characterized by weakness, bleeding and pain in joints and muscles, bleeding gums, and abnormal bone and tooth growth
10. Facilities that review and correct medical claims as necessary before sending them to insurance companies for final processing.
11. the diagnosis and treatment, including surgery, of diseases and disorders of the eye, such as cataracts and glaucoma
12. An organ located in the upper left abdomen behind the ribs that removes and destroys old red blood cells and helps fight infection
13. An area of inflammation or a group of spots on the skin

A. Spleen
B. Hepatic
C. Embryo
D. Suture
E. Ascites
F. Scurvy
G. Fluke
H. Clearinghouse
I. Rash
J. Ophthalmology
K. Pathology
L. Anemia
M. Thorax

S. Find the hidden words. The words have been placed horizontally, vertically, or diagonally. When you locate a word, draw an ellipse around it.

C	O	I	N	S	U	R	A	N	C	E	H	T	X	D	Q	Z	N	Z	D	H	V	W
M	A	X	I	M	U	M	O	U	T	O	F	P	O	C	K	E	T	G	X	Y	F	T
V	E	L	P	Q	O	F	U	X	X	X	P	W	I	B	L	H	O	P	M	R	P	H
P	R	E	E	X	I	S	T	I	N	G	C	O	N	D	I	T	I	O	N	H	R	N
X	D	T	W	L	M	B	Y	Q	F	N	A	T	O	U	Q	E	S	J	T	B	O	P
K	H	Y	A	U	L	Y	J	I	T	C	N	X	Y	S	M	V	T	I	V	Y	V	G
J	I	I	R	M	H	X	N	X	K	U	I	O	F	I	X	M	W	U	R	A	I	C
P	S	H	T	U	M	K	M	W	P	B	E	J	Y	M	B	Y	C	I	B	Y	D	Q
M	P	O	L	R	T	A	R	T	A	R	M	Y	Z	A	U	Z	R	A	G	Q	E	A
C	A	H	T	M	J	Y	W	Y	V	L	H	L	T	G	B	V	H	Q	C	O	R	S
L	S	U	X	U	E	F	M	R	D	J	N	Q	N	I	E	P	V	N	I	W	U	P
E	M	R	S	R	J	E	A	U	A	H	Z	T	W	N	D	V	A	L	V	E	N	L
J	O	E	L	U	T	W	X	U	B	G	P	J	H	G	H	G	R	Q	G	T	Z	E
N	L	M	K	F	G	W	J	E	F	S	J	M	J	D	E	P	E	A	T	M	Y	E
Z	C	I	M	U	U	T	M	T	P	I	N	D	E	Z	X	E	G	O	X	M	T	N
O	J	A	W	C	A	D	P	R	E	C	E	R	T	I	F	I	C	A	T	I	O	N

1. The percentage of coverage that a patient is responsible for paying after an insurance company pays the portion agreed upon in a health plan.
2. A characteristic sound of blood flowing irregularly through the heart
3. The hard deposit formed on teeth when mineral salts in saliva combine with plaque
4. A contagious, harmless growth caused by a virus that occurs on the skin or a mucous membrane
5. The healthcare facility that administered healthcare to an individual. Physicians, clinics, and hospitals are all considered providers.
6. A process similar to preauthorization whereby patients must check with insurance companies to see if a desired healthcare treatment or service is deemed medically necessary
7. A medical condition a patient had before receiving coverage from an insurance company.
8. An involuntary muscle contraction
9. The technique of creating pictures of structures inside of the body using x-rays, ultrasound waves, or magnetic fields
10. An organ located in the upper left abdomen behind the ribs that removes and destroys old red blood cells and helps fight infection
11. A structure that allows fluid flow in only one direction
12. Abnormally high levels of waste products such as urea in the blood
13. The amount a patient is required to pay.

A. Provider
B. Tartar
C. Valve
D. Wart
E. Maximum Out of Pocket
F. Uremia
G. Co Insurance
H. Pre Certification
I. Murmur
J. Spleen
K. Spasm
L. Imaging
M. Pre existing Condition

T. Find the hidden words. The words have been placed horizontally, vertically, or diagonally. When you locate a word, draw an ellipse around it.

D	Q	N	Q	M	G	A	N	I	Y	K	L	C	X	K	Q	J	W	J	F	D	H	L
Y	M	W	Z	F	K	T	P	R	U	P	J	D	C	S	A	W	D	M	P	G	V	C
U	P	I	Y	A	Z	T	U	A	V	F	O	D	Q	G	V	C	P	I	S	R	N	N
H	N	Q	W	G	O	U	T	M	C	R	R	E	C	J	B	K	W	M	T	P	Y	S
D	U	R	A	B	L	E	M	E	D	I	C	A	L	E	Q	U	I	P	M	E	N	T
Z	P	N	X	N	P	J	Q	I	J	Z	V	X	T	E	N	D	O	N	D	L	H	O
R	E	L	A	T	I	V	E	V	A	L	U	E	A	M	O	U	N	T	N	B	B	O
L	J	D	H	C	S	J	E	B	M	T	L	P	V	Y	Q	P	W	T	E	T	R	L
Y	Z	A	J	O	B	A	B	M	W	U	V	H	S	G	Z	O	Y	U	U	J	V	B
K	M	S	R	C	U	H	G	J	W	B	A	V	U	U	J	L	T	D	R	E	J	U
I	B	T	R	C	N	K	H	Q	K	Y	B	M	U	N	V	Y	U	M	O	C	P	L
H	C	H	K	Y	I	S	P	N	Y	G	R	C	K	O	O	P	B	P	N	E	L	H
D	Q	M	C	X	O	V	G	I	E	X	B	O	Z	A	H	H	D	R	X	G	J	Q
L	E	A	M	A	N	Z	I	O	N	X	S	X	Q	J	F	A	B	S	C	E	S	S
Y	C	O	R	N	E	A	Z	J	L	W	B	N	S	L	K	G	R	U	C	L	W	E
J	U	U	V	Z	D	C	W	X	T	R	Z	J	Q	J	R	C	I	D	I	L	K	H

1. This refers to medical implements that can be reused such as stretchers, wheelchairs, canes, crutches, and bedpans.
2. A disorder marked by high levels of uric acid in the blood
3. Another term for a nerve cell
4. Four fused bones that form a triangular shape at the base of the spine (also known as the tailbone)
5. The median amount Medicare will repay a provider for certain services and treatments.
6. The outer, visible portion of the female genitals
7. An accumulation of pus in a body tissue, usually caused by a bacterial infection
8. The clear, dome-shaped front portion of the eye's outer covering
9. Another term for feces
10. A growth that occurs on mucous membranes such as those in the nose and intestine
11. A disorder characterized by inflamed airways and difficulty breathing
12. A hard, fluid-filled pad along the inside joint of the big toe
13. Strong connective tissue cords that attach muscle to bone or muscle to muscle

A. Cornea
B. Abscess
C. Bunion
D. Vulva
E. Coccyx
F. Durable Medical Equipment
G. Relative Value Amount
H. Gout
I. Asthma
J. Tendon
K. Neuron
L. Polyp
M. Stool

Made in the USA
San Bernardino, CA
03 February 2019